PRIVACY AND SOLITUDE IN THE MIDDLE AGES

For Tony, Eleanor and Richard

Privacy and Solitude in the Middle Ages

Diana Webb

hambledon continuum

Hambledon Continuum is an imprint of Continuum Books

Continuum UK
The Tower Building
11 York Road
London SE1 7NX

Continuum US
80 Maiden Lane
Suite 704
New York, NY 10038

www.continuumbooks.com

First published 2007

British Library Cataloguing-in-Publication Data
A catalogue record for this book is available from the British Library.

ISBN 1 852 854790

Typeset by Free Range Book Design & Production Ltd
Printed and bound by MPG Books Ltd, Cornwall

Contents

Introduction

This book is a personal and very incomplete exploration of the medieval quest for space and time apart, in both secular and religious environments. The idea for it arose from a combination of individual temperament and professional interests. My starting-point in some ways resembles that of the American sociologist Barrington Moore, who in 1984 justified devoting a book to the subject of privacy:[1]

> Two considerations led to the choice of privacy as a topic for research. I have always had an unusual fondness for privacy, especially the privacy necessary for intellectual work. Hence I wanted to see how other cultures treated this problem and if they were even aware of it.

He explained that he proposed to discuss privacy

> both in the sense of refusing access to other persons in specified situations, and as private rights against holders of authority or other members of the same society. Personal privacy and private rights are linked by the notion of intrusion. Social rules protect what is private from intrusion and interference by other people.

As this last sentence hints, there was a touch of polemic in Moore's agenda, further revealed in his comment that 'injustices and intrusions are not necessarily easier to bear because they come with a socialist label'. He was also more interested in law and legal custom than I am in the present book. His 'privacy' often comes close to 'private life', a more inclusive concept but also in significant respects a different one. In any society which recognizes a distinction between the public and the private spheres, a great deal may fall on the private side of the dividing line. A family may run a farm or a 'private' business; they may exercise close control of family members (for example determining their marriages); their life may be highly communal within the shared living space. All is technically and legally 'private', but it has nothing to do with an individual's aspirations to self-determination or to 'privacy' within the household. It is privacy in this narrower sense with which I am concerned, rather than the legal and economic characteristics of 'private life'. I am interested first in what medieval people regarded as reason or justification for retreating, permanently or temporarily, from the wider society, and secondly in their awareness of their dwelling spaces.

Moore's 'other societies' included ancient Athens, China and Israel; he also included a survey of 'anthropological perspectives' on more recent non-European societies. He did not consider the European middle ages. The society (or, more properly, societies) of that lengthy and rather approximately defined period are often assumed to have had little idea of what we call privacy. Certainly, the word was unknown; indeed, it has sometimes been taken to be peculiar to the modern English language, reflecting the unusual attachment of the Anglophone peoples to the thing that it describes. 'Solitude', by contrast, was a word well known at least to those literate in Latin, and vernacular equivalents were beginning to infiltrate the European languages by the later middle ages. By about 1300, it was even possible, although very occasionally, to describe an individual as 'solitary' by disposition. This did not necessarily imply approval, and the solitary individual is not entirely above suspicion even now.

In a book originally entitled *The School of Genius* but significantly republished as *Solitude*, the psychiatrist Anthony Storr rejected what he saw as the tyranny of a Freudian model of social integration:

> Current wisdom, especially that propagated by the various schools of psycho-analysis, assumes that man is a social being who needs the companionship and affection of other human beings from cradle to grave. It is widely believed that interpersonal relationships of an intimate kind are the chief, it not the only, source of human happiness.[2]

This view in fact had an ancient and respectable pedigree. Medieval monastic superiors may not have been primarily concerned with the earthly happiness of their charges, but the more cultivated of them would have been acquainted with both biblical and classical authorities that insisted on man's unavoidably social nature and its binding consequences. A favourite quotation came from Ecclesiastes 4:10: 'Woe to him who is alone, for there is none to pick him up if he should fall.' Metaphorically intended to warn against moral dangers, these words expressed a more general attitude to the perils of isolation, both practical and moral. Seneca was among the classical authors who argued that association with others imposed a salutary moral discipline on the individual which should not be evaded, while Cicero believed that society was not simply useful and necessary, because by themselves human beings were unable to supply their practical needs, but indispensable to their happiness.

Storr drew attention to numerous highly creative individuals in the history of European culture who abstained from the formation of close personal relationships (or proved unable to forge them). Admittedly, not all of these people could be described as happy, but others seem to have found satisfaction and fulfilment enough. Edward Gibbon was one whose 'chief source of self-esteem and of pleasure was his work'. He had numerous friends and was certainly not unsociable, but when the time came he, like the others on Storr's list, would have sought out 'the privacy necessary for intellectual work', in Barrington Moore's formula. There may well have been men of similar temperament among the luminaries of medieval monastic culture, happy to be absolved from family or civic responsibilities and to take advantage of one of the few environments, in the earlier middle ages at least, which were conducive to study. We shall see that literate pursuits played an important part, both inside and outside the cloister, in shaping medieval privacy.

The popular picture of the middle ages is of an intensely communal society in which all accepted the obligations of fellowship. The lord dining in his great hall surrounded by his retainers corresponded in secular life to the monk surrounded by his fellows whether praying, eating, sleeping, or walking in the cloister. The 'solitude' to which the monk or nun was permanently committed was understood by the wider society as a licensed exception to the rules which governed the lives of most men and women, even indeed as a superior and more arduous option; yet the life of a convent had features in common with that of a great household. The society that centred on the great hall, like that of the monastery, made little allowance for individual privacy.

One difference was that the monk's lack of privacy rested on a theoretical foundation. It was not just a corollary of the prohibition of private property that he should have nowhere to store it; the lack of space and time to himself also signified his total submission of his will to the direction of his superiors. Privacy depends to a high degree on the power to choose with whom one associates and when, and the monk (in theory) had no such choice. The servant or retainer in a great household had little more. The urban or rural poor may not have been consciously enacting a social or religious ideal, but they had no way of avoiding the close proximity of kin and neighbours; their conceptions of sociability were shaped by inescapable reality. Constant company was the general rule.

Social historians and archaeologists have, however, recently pointed to the evidence for a different picture, especially in the later medieval centuries. There was surely never a time when individuals, families or groups did not sometimes claim the right to withdraw from public scrutiny into a space of their own. That right, and indeed the power so to withdraw, was not equally or universally available; it could be affected by numerous variables, including affluence and social or political position. Partly for these reasons, the inclination to seek privacy (or even to think of it) was doubtless less common than it is in many modern western societies, but it was clearly far from unknown. In both lay and monastic life a greater degree of privacy was accorded to persons of senior status, sometimes simply in recognition of their superior dignity, sometimes, in the case of monastic, royal or seigneurial officials, in recognition of their need of somewhere to work and store records or provisions. With the passage of time the generality of monks and nuns showed a desire to withdraw, if they could, into their own space with company of their own choosing. The deracinated individualism of the modern west and its extreme occupational specialisation were still far away, but growing numbers of people were acquiring an education and pursuing literate occupations which required some time and space apart. It has become fashionable recently to investigate the medieval antecedents of such features of modern society as scientific and commercial mentalities; perhaps the same can be done for the ancestry of our attitudes to privacy.

It would be absurd to deny that the multiple transformations which have overtaken western society since the eighteenth century have played a crucial role in the history of privacy, but some of the key processes have older origins. Wherever one looks, between the twelfth century and the twentieth, it is possible to identify groups of people who were achieving some degree of wealth, education and importance without belonging either to the higher ranks of the landed aristocracy or to the clergy. Their story constitutes a series of chapters in the history of lay literacy, an important ingredient in the development of privacy and not unconnected with affluence, which has undoubtedly been another. Some historians, in focusing on the growth of individualism, would draw attention to the Protestant Reformation or the invention of the printing press, judging that increasing opportunities for personal intellectual development and the exercise of private judgement have been vital to the formation of modernity. Medievalists for their part might lay stress on the social and economic changes which saw the late medieval merchant and taxpayer become more and more visible alongside the landlord, and also on pre-Reformation religious change and the growth of the reading public which nurtured the early printing presses.

The desire to read was stimulated as much by religious devotion as by any single cause. That is one reason that individuals both formally and informally vowed to religion play a large part in this book. The monk or nun was son or daughter, brother or sister, nephew, niece or cousin of laymen, often laymen of the rank and wealth to enjoy the best available education and domestic amenities. The poet Petrarch in the fourteenth century composed a treatise on the solitary life which is largely secular in content; his brother became a Carthusian monk but Petrarch did not lose contact with him. Late medieval monasteries were often open to the incursions of the laity, sometimes, although not always or necessarily, to their detriment. The appearance of private rooms and comforts within the late medieval monastery and nunnery may or may not have signified decadence, but it certainly meant that the cloister was not isolated from the forces which were increasingly shaping the secular world that the kin of the monk or nun inhabited. Social history arguably needs to look at laity and religious professionals side by side, remembering also the large numbers of men and women in later medieval society who were leading religious lives of an informal kind in ordinary domestic surroundings.

Lay or clerical, the medieval intellectual drove a wedge into a social structure based on rank and wealth; his claims to consideration (like that of the priest or monk) were based on neither.[3] Intellectuals have to live, however, in the sense of requiring food and shelter. Historically they have tended to be recruited in large numbers from the ranks of the moderately affluent. Edward Gibbon believed that 'Few works of merit or importance have been executed either in a garret or a palace' and regarded his own modest inheritance as a vital precondition of his achievements.[4] His ideas of moderate wealth may have exceeded those of the middle-class intellectual of today, but the principle was sound. The growth of the middling sector of society is a cardinal fact of later medieval history, for such people were able to evade some of the constraints that weighed upon both the rich and the poor around them. By the fifteenth century they were inhabiting a more comfortable, diversified and private world, documented in the plans of late medieval dwelling houses and in inventories of their furniture and fittings. Their circumstances were propitious to the development of privacy for, whether they were Italian or Netherlandish citizens or English gentry, they were at somewhat greater liberty than the prince or great lord to use their space as they pleased.

It has been true at all periods and in most societies that the rich possess more space than the poor. From the earliest times, in medieval as in ancient society, the great man had apartments to which he retired with selected companions. The more complex and extensive his living accommodation, the more finely graded its several parts were likely to be; it was an attribute of status to be able to decree who went where and to invite one's intimates into the inner sanctum. Such a man's womenfolk were frequently secluded from the public gaze, to a greater or lesser degree, and on suitable occasions he would withdraw to share their seclusion. Affluence and power made privacy theoretically possible inasmuch as they supplied its material prerequisites, but they also imposed conflicting demands. A prince might possess any amount of dwelling space but his freedom to choose how to use it or who shared it with him were limited by his circumstances. If he over-indulged his personal preferences and allowed favourites to monopolize him, he would court trouble. There was considerable pressure on a lord to live a great deal in public, aggravated to the extent that he also wielded 'public' powers, for example of jurisdiction. In England, these would often be exercised in his own 'hall' rather than in a purpose-built 'court'; his dwelling was, in part, a public place. He was likely to be constantly accompanied, waking or sleeping, by servants, bodyguards, courtiers, clients, petitioners and miscellaneous hangers-on. To some degree this remains true even today. A mere nobody will put the toothpaste on his own toothbrush and may be completely alone in a big house while he is doing so; the heir to a throne is differently situated.

The cast list of medieval 'private life' therefore included a lot of walk-on parts. In G. K. Chesterton's story *The Invisible Man* a postman commits a murder but several reliable witnesses are prepared to state that 'nobody' entered the building while they were on watch. Father Brown offers the analogy of the lady in a country house who, asked if anyone is staying with her, 'doesn't answer, "Yes: the butler, the three footmen, the parlour-maid, and so on", though the parlour-maid may be in the room or the butler behind her chair'. Pre-modern society abounded in these invisible men. They were important to their masters and mistresses not as individuals but as essential functionaries and collectively as an attribute of status; therefore they may not have intruded on 'privacy' as then understood. The fact that so many individuals in a vastly more populous western world now live entirely alone and that the well-off may unthinkingly spend lengthy periods without servants, without company and even without having a conversation would surely impress a time-traveller from the middle ages very forcibly. In *That Hideous Strength*, one of the fantasy novels of C.S. Lewis, the magician Merlin returns to assist in the dénouement and takes a bath, only to express his surprise at both the splendour of the bathroom fittings and the total absence of attendants.

Friendship too has changed its shape and meaning. In modern circumstances the individual chooses his or her own friends, but this has not always been the case. Like its ancient forerunner, medieval friendship often resembled a more or less formal alliance, contracted for the sake of good neighbourly relations, business or political advantage, or the security of oneself and one's family. That such alliances should often be sealed by marriages to which the couple involved consented only in the most formal sense underlines the difference. Obligations entered into by past generations and other members of a family might be binding on the individual. The 'friendships' mentioned in the Norse sagas sometimes sound more like a state of armed truce. To deny access to one's house to a man who was supposed to be a 'friend' in this sense, or to refuse to come out of one's house to greet him, risked worse consequences than hurt feelings or resentment. Not to have free choice of one's friends or one's company might now seem to us quite incompatible with any notion of privacy. The religious and academic environments offered slightly different possibilities of emotional bonds based on shared goals and compatible personalities.[5]

If the rich lived under certain constraints, the poor hardly enjoyed total liberty. The totally indigent person about whom nobody cares may have all the time and space in the world, but this cannot sensibly be equated with privacy as usually understood. Some medieval hermits (and also perhaps pilgrims and vagabonds) may have been trying to obtain personal liberty at the price of material privation, but the ordinary poor man was handicapped by a shortage of space and in some respects was probably hardly less subject than his lord to the expectation of availability and openness to neighbours and kin. The constant company of the same people may well have weighed heavily on sensitive individuals in small communities. Perhaps such people welcomed the incidental opportunities for solitude and introspection which accompanied occupations such as herding. Yet while genuine solitude, sitting by the edge of the pasture or walking or riding to town on an errand, might be conducive to quiet reflection, it could also bring with it dangers, from robbers, wild beasts, falls or other injuries, with no one near to help.

Sociability has generally been believed – and not only by Cicero – to be both natural and necessary to man. Without constant association and systematic communication with his fellow men, *homo sapiens*, a rather puny creature, could never have survived surrounded by animals that were stronger, faster and better armed than himself; still less could he have become the formidable predator and innovator that he has proved to be. Sociability was the medium for both the development and the employment of the intelligence that was mankind's only real weapon. Genuine solitude, to early man, was not merely dangerous but unproductive, and for much of human history it has been shunned by most and sought by few. Even today solitude may be very differently evaluated by northern and southern Europeans. It is certainly unlikely that it is as much esteemed in Naples as in Norwich.[6]

Possibly there were oddly constituted individuals in the small societies of the Palaeolithic who found the constant company of their fellows oppressive and wanted to be alone. Such a disposition has often been regarded as abnormal, but it has also been associated with unusual gifts, including spiritual or creative genius. From very early times, becoming a religious specialist has been a possible route to respect, influence and even power in society, independent (at least to some extent) of wealth, military muscle and lineage, the more usual qualifications. Withdrawal into solitude (not necessarily permanent), precisely because it is not the normal condition of the majority, leads to the attainment of special insights or to a state of purity which qualifies one for this status. Solitude may be sought in the natural environment (desert, forest, island hillside or cave) or special accommodation may be provided for it. Ethnographers have observed a common tendency in 'small-scale societies around the world' for seekers after 'contemplative solitude' to build themselves 'cramped stone structures'.[7] A monk who spent lengthy periods in a cell so small that he could not stretch his feet out was in his own mind seeking to do penance for his sins, but he may also have been unconsciously obeying a more ancient and general imperative, the belief that physical discomfort and constriction aid enlightenment.

Professional exponents of religious solitude were a familiar and integral feature of western Christian society from the late Roman period onwards. For centuries they included a large proportion of the 'intellectuals' of their times. The appearance of increasing numbers of 'intellectuals' outside the cloister and even outside the clergy, it has already been suggested, marked a late medieval social change. Just as they gradually secularized the content of study, so these people appropriated and adapted the right to seclusion which in the earlier middle ages had been enjoyed by few who were not monks. In the workaday world today, because certain occupations acknowledged to be of value to society in general require more than normal concentration, the practitioners of them are accorded the time and space they need to do a good job. This may have applied to the truly expert maker of stone hand-axes; in the course of time it extended to the 'artist' as well as to the scholar and religious specialist.

To medieval moralists, professionally conscious of the depravity of the human will, it was a dangerous business to withdraw from the scrutiny of one's fellows. Who could tell what mischief might be hatched, what vices indulged, in solitude? There had to be powerful justification for secluding oneself. Some Romans greeted monastic withdrawal with suspicion and criticism precisely because of this unnatural rejection of civic and familial duty. In societies which adopted Protestantism its validity was again rejected in favour of the superior claims of family and civic involvement. In the medieval interval, monasticism came to be accepted as a form of communal organization, but for an individual to try to retreat into genuine solitude and thus avoid supervisory discipline was often regarded as highly problematic. An important aspect of monastic community was collective security against unseen threats, for solitude was invisibly inhabited by demons as well as by God.

In fact, even the most lauded solitary often had a disciple or servant 'living in' and could not have managed otherwise. The real problem that he or she faced was making proper use of the time and *otium* (only loosely translatable as 'leisure') which constituted both the privilege and the challenge of the religious life. Monastic *otium* signified the monk's exemption, individually and collectively, from the practical demands that were made of the knight, the merchant or the peasant in the everyday world. It was the early medieval equivalent of philosophic withdrawal and prompted some profound reflections on the meaning, justification and value of 'solitude'. That it was not 'leisure' as now understood is suggested by the monastic *horarium*, which laid down, in principle, where the monk was to be and what he should be doing at every moment of the day or night. It is not the least interesting feature of Petrarch's fourteenth-century treatment of the solitary life that he takes a very positive view of the freedom to determine one's own timetable.[8]

The monk inhabited a space, or set of spaces, that were developed to house the particular life he was supposed to lead.[9] Outside the cloister, private diversions or quiet mental concentration had to be accommodated within the architectural framework of the ordinary dwelling place. Some needed time and space in which to write letters, cast up accounts or (on a somewhat different plane) study a textbook. This was 'leisure' only insofar as the individual was for the moment not physically on the road or in the marketplace, the schools or the law courts; it was functionally useful, serving the purposes of business rather than representing a withdrawal from it. The lay person or secular clerk experienced intervals in the pursuit of worldly business, but this leisure was not always totally at his free disposal. Shortage of space or other material amenities and also social pressures and demands might dictate how it was spent. By the fifteenth century, such activities as reading, playing chess and performing or listening to music in the home were all being undertaken by substantially increased numbers of people. For the devout, private prayer was another option. Sometimes, although not always, these were solitary activities; inasmuch as they demanded peace and concentration, or inasmuch as those concerned happened to desire privacy, they affected the use that individuals, couples, families or small groups of friends made of their domestic living space.

Solitude and privacy are not identical, although in the experience of many people they overlap, sometimes to a very considerable extent. 'Solitude' (in both singular and plural) may describe places; it may also be used negatively. The lonely, the ostracized or the imprisoned endure solitude (or isolation), not privacy. Privacy implies the right to keep oneself to oneself in company of one's own choosing; choice is integral to it. It is not necessarily individual; couples, families and other small groups enjoy privacy together. To choose no company at all and opt for solitude from time to time may be accepted as a mere extension of the right to privacy, but it is less common as a more or less permanent way of life.

The history of the two words is also revealing of profound changes over time. In classical Latin *solitudo* denoted a place or condition, most often in a negative sense: it tended to imply the antithesis of civilization. A British freedom-fighter imagined by Tacitus offers a sardonic comment on Roman imperialism: *ubi solitudinem faciunt, pacem appellant*, 'Where they create desolation, they call it peace'.[10] In classical usage the related adjective *solitarius*, like the simpler *solus*, was often used pejoratively to mean 'lonely' or 'isolated'; Cicero declares 'Nature loves nothing solitary'.[11] Modern European languages which descend from Latin use derivatives of 'solus' (*seul*, *solo*, *solitario*) to mean both 'lonely' and 'solitary'; the German *einsam* is not dissimilar. The distinct word 'lonely' appeared in the English language only in the early seventeenth century, and for another two centuries after that it was often barely distinguishable in meaning from 'solitary'. We would not now think that a solitary individual, or one who happens to be alone, is necessarily lonely, or indeed that only people who are alone feel lonely.

To medieval Christians *solitudo* might mean 'the desert', but it was viewed with favour as a place of peace and refuge. It was the place or condition occupied by monks, and an exponent of the religious life might correspondingly be called a *solitarius*. 'Solitude' in the sense familiar to us – the state of being alone, temporarily or permanently – was uncommon in French or English, although not unknown, before the seventeenth century.[12] When Andrew Marvell (an accomplished classicist) declared in 'The Garden' that 'Society were all but rude / to this delicious solitude', he was not merely using a word that had 'arrived' but revealing how its meaning had changed; the wit depends on the reader's knowing the traditional connotations of society (good) and solitude (bad).

There was no classical or medieval Latin word exactly equivalent to 'privacy'. *Privatio* meant 'a taking away' (as in 'deprivation') and the adjective *privatus* correspondingly denoted something 'withdrawn', that is from the public sphere. Medieval writers knew *privatus*, as they knew its opposite *publicus*, while the neuter form *privatum* could be used to designate 'the private sphere' or one's private affairs. The view that the English word 'privacy' has no exact equivalent in other modern languages has already been mentioned; the irony that a word with somewhat negative etymological connotations should now bear such a positive meaning has not passed unnoticed.[13] European languages much more closely related to Latin have not formed a similar noun from *privatus* but convey the concept by different means, often using words which have alternative and less positive meanings.[14] The comparison with French is particularly interesting in view of its intimate historical relationship with English. In modern French, it has been said, the noun *privauté* 'has preserved a pejorative nuance' (not unlike the English 'secrecy'), while its other sense, of something 'secret', known in the thirteenth century, has largely disappeared from modern French.[15] By contrast, the related adjective *privé* is unexceptionable and used in similar ways to its English equivalent.

Even in English, 'privacy' was a relative latecomer. The *Oxford English Dictionary* lists an isolated example of 'privace' in the mid-fifteenth century but nothing thereafter before Shakespeare and the early seventeenth. The not dissimilar 'privity' occurs already in the early thirteenth century and the adjective and adverb 'privy' and 'privily' were used quite commonly in the fourteenth by Chaucer, Langland and others. Often, however, their meaning was closer to 'secret', 'secrecy' or 'secretly' than to the modern 'private' or 'privacy'. A variety of words could be used to convey something like the modern sense of privacy or 'the private', but the context must always be evaluated. Readers of modern English versions of classical or medieval texts need to be on their guard when they come across the word 'privacy', for it is highly unlikely to be a literal translation of the original.

The starting-point for this book was found in texts, and also certain buildings, which were familiar to me and prompted my curiosity. It would have been quite impossible to trawl the literature and hagiography or the art, architecture and archaeological discoveries of the whole of medieval Europe in search of everything that might shed light on collective and individual attitudes to solitude and privacy. Certainly there is an immense amount written about both monastic and domestic architecture which I have not been able to read or to refer to. Visits to actual buildings are obviously invaluable, especially for those who (like myself) possess only a limited power to visualize three-dimensional human realities on the basis of building contracts, plans and descriptions, but medieval domestic buildings that have survived unaltered are rare. It is nonetheless possible to get glimpses of the past here and there, and a wide variety of building types in addition to the dwellings of the laity, for example hospitals and monastic guesthouses, can be used to shed light on the ways in which space was used and shared.

My chief emphasis is on texts, and I have drawn on a very miscellaneous selection from the Roman period onwards, wherever possible citing and quoting translations. Much, from the Desert Fathers to the Norse sagas, has been made available in English in recent years. Unless otherwise stated, classical texts and their translations are cited by book and chapter from the Loeb editions; where no credit is given for a translation from a medieval text, it is my own. My endnotes mostly do no more than indicate the sources of quotations and ideas, but I hope they will enable the interested reader to find out more. I do not attempt to provide guidance to the huge literature on all the topics which I have touched on. If I point out that, besides architecture both ecclesiastical and secular, these include monasticism, women, literacy, and gardening, I hope the point will be taken.

I must admit to many limitations of which I have become more and more conscious in the course of my work. I would like to have explored regional or 'national' differences between European cultures much further than I have. As for wider comparative dimensions, I am neither anthropologist nor psychologist. It would surely come as no surprise to specialists in those fields to be told that medieval society fostered and even institutionalized forms of detachment from everyday life which were believed to benefit society at large by keeping open channels of communication with the supernatural, or that there were individuals who sought seclusion for the satisfaction of their own inclinations. This is, as I have said, a personal exploration of a subject which even under my uneven scrutiny has continually displayed fresh facets. Perhaps there are readers who have not previously thought about medieval society in this particular light and may be inspired to find substantiating or conflicting evidence in their own areas of interest or expertise. The audiences for three talks which I gave while preparing this book, in Hampstead, Bristol and St Albans, did just that, and I owe them a special debt of gratitude. Another is owed to my late employers, King's College London, who awarded me sabbatical leave in 2004–5, during which the book was largely finished.

1

Withdrawing from the World

Late in the year 416 the Gallo-Roman Rutilius Claudius Namatianus returned to his native land by sea from Italy. He commemorated the journey in a poem, *De reditu suo*, presumably begun after his homecoming but apparently never finished.[1] Rutilius had held office in the court of the Emperor Honorius and had been prefect of the city of Rome in 412. He had inherited the ideal of public service and was unquestioningly devoted to Rome (sacked only a few years previously by the Goths) as both city and emblem of all that was civilized. Accordingly he pointed the finger at those who, he believed, threatened a culture and system of values which were beyond criticism and of eternal validity.

On the journey, his party encountered a grasping Jewish innkeeper whom he described as an 'anti-social creature' (*animal dissociale*) who rejected 'human foodstuffs'. He also attacked the Jewish beliefs in circumcision and the Sabbath, which would stretch the credulity even of children. Christians, or at least certain Christians, were however a bigger menace, guilty of strange misanthropic behaviour. The ship passed near the island of Caprera, which was full of men who called themselves by a Greek name, *monachos* (from *monos*, 'alone') 'because they wish to live alone, without witness'. Rutilius believed that these individuals had turned their backs on the pleasures of life in the hope of avoiding its pains, instead of accepting that fortune brought both good and bad: 'Who would voluntarily be wretched in order to avoid wretchedness?' He speculated that they might be victims of 'black bile', to which Homer attributed Bellerophon's melancholy.[2]

Later, the ship came within sight of the island of Gorgon, between Corsica and Pisa. Its cliffs were 'a monument to disaster'. A well-born young Roman, significantly designated a 'citizen' (*civis*), had recently consigned himself to 'a living death' there, 'impelled by the furies' and rejecting the claims of office and marriage. Rutilius had called the denizens of Caprera 'fugitives from the light' (*lucifugi*); this young man too had 'credulously' exiled himself to 'a foul hiding-place' (*turpis latebra*). In defiance of Roman notions of religious decorum he believed that heavenly things were compatible with bodily filth (*illuvies*). 'Is not this school of thought worse than the potions of Circe? Then bodies were changed, now it is minds.'[3]

By this date Rutilius might well have known upper-class Christians, at Rome and in Gaul, who did not feel compelled to reject civilized sociability. Those who so scandalised him were extremists; they were among the first western devotees of a way of life that had been pioneered in the previous century in the deserts of fourth-century Egypt and Syria. What Rutilius saw and deplored was the rejection of a whole cultural environment. He was by no means the first to do so. Half a century earlier, the Emperor Julian had observed: 'There are some who leave the cities in order to take refuge in the deserts, although by his very nature man is a social and a civilized animal. But the perverse spirits to whom they have given themselves up impel them to this misanthropic way of life.'[4]

The personal friendships of cultivated Romans could and did fall victim to the onset of religious conviction. The Gaulish poet Ausonius, who died in the closing years of the fourth century, was a middle-aged professor of rhetoric at Bordeaux when he became tutor to the imperial prince Gratian, the son of Valentinian. During Gratian's reign as emperor, Ausonius was consul (in 379) and several of his relatives were appointed to high office. His pupil Paulinus, another Gaul, was made governor of Campania and consul at a younger age than his master. Both later returned to their homeland, but their association was rudely interrupted when Paulinus decided that he must as a Christian retire from the world. He first vanished into Spain (the native land of his wife Therasia) and for some time letters from Ausonius failed to reach him. Early in 395, now ordained priest, he retired with Therasia to Nola in Campania. He became the guardian of the shrine of St Felix, whom he had apparently adopted as his patron during his previous sojourn in Campania as governor, and here he ended his days, now a bishop, in 431.

Before Paulinus' departure for Italy he and Ausonius exchanged a last round of letters in which the older man expressed his bewilderment and anguish at Paulinus' inexplicable transformation.[5] Ausonius was a Christian and may well have been one from birth, but he could not understand what had impelled Paulinus to abandon their shared cultural environment. He accused Paulinus of 'impiety', meaning disregard of the obligations of friendship and also of the respect that Paulinus as a pupil owed his old teacher. Furthermore, he felt that Paulinus had removed himself from civilized surroundings. Ausonius wished upon whomsoever had come between them a life of solitary wandering in the wilderness, 'avoiding the society and tracks of men'. By implication, only those who were defective in mind (*mentis inops*) would do so and, like Rutilius twenty years or so later, Ausonius took the ill-fated Bellerophon to represent this sad condition.[6] 'Dearest Paulinus', he lamented, 'you have changed' (*Vertisti, Pauline, tuos, dulcissime, mores*).

Paulinus was wounded by the charge of impiety and replied by defining (or redefining) piety as a serious Christian was bound to do: it could mean nothing else but to do God's will. He picked up the reference to Bellerophon and rejected the imputation that he was in any sense deranged or subject to the *anxia Bellerophontis*. There were precedents among the pagan philosophers for withdrawal for the sake of study or composition (*pro studiis musisque suis*) and now those who sought Christ were doing likewise. It was not mental deficiency or brutishness that caused people 'to take up residence in desert places (*desertis habitare locis*)' but rather their vision of 'God and the deeps of truth (*deum verique profunda*)'. As Paulinus was certainly aware, it was scarcely novel or peculiar to Christians to denounce ordinary worldly affairs ('the din of the market-place') as vain and empty, for the Roman satirists had frequently done so, but he held up in their place a vision not just of a more rational existence but of eternity. The time was past when Ausonius could have wooed him with an appeal to the Muses.

The picture of Paulinus' new life at Nola which emerges from his writings, notably the verses that he wrote every year from 395 to 409 for the feast day of St Felix, hardly suggests solitude in the literal sense.[7] He and Therasia formed part of a small community of Roman notables who had embraced the religious life and lived together in dwellings around the shrine. They had frequent contact with the neighbouring peasants (for whom Felix sometimes did miracles) and with pilgrims and visitors. Alarmed by the apparent irrationality of the monks, Rutilius may well not have appreciated that they were in fact building a new form of community which was destined for a lengthy and immensely influential future in the post-Roman world.

Writing to Paulinus before the latter removed to Italy, Ausonius used deliberately heightened language to tax him with living in uncivilized surroundings. Paulinus rejected these strictures: Spain was not that barbaric, and anyway uncivilized surroundings or neighbours did not matter too much, for he who led a pure life would take no harm from them.[8] As Paulinus may well have known, this echoed much older Roman views, for example those of Seneca. He believed in fact that he was carrying an improved version of one Roman amenity with him into his new life. In a significant phrase, he suggested that the Christian valued *libera otia*, time and space free from 'vain cares'. Christians also sometimes laid claim to *philosophia*, applying the word to their quest for true wisdom. The monk, however, pursued *philosophia* and *otium* with a difference: not only sobriety and self-denial but the total and permanent abnegation of family ties, worldly careers and material luxury were essential to the pursuit of his ideal.[9]

Roman religion did not give the privileged position to celibacy, asceticism and contemplation that medieval Christianity was to do. To the Roman who upheld ideals of political and civic involvement, *otium* might mean little more than the episodes of 'leisure', dining and conversation, and (for the more cultivated) reading and writing, which punctuated *negotium*, occupation or business. There was a certain ambiguity about *otium*. It might imply inactivity, self-indulgence or idleness, although classical Latin offered several more disparaging words for those conditions, for example *pigritia* or *desidia* and also the obviously related *otiositas*. The adjective *otiosus* shared in this ambiguity: did it mean 'idle' or merely 'at leisure'? Wealth might make it possible for a Roman, cultivated or not, to give himself up to *otium*, but the high-minded did not approve of the neglect of public and civic duty. However profound an individual's commitment to literature or philosophy, it should be integrated into a larger, more diversified whole.

Roman thinkers sometimes discussed the competing claims of involvement in the busy world and of intellectual and philosophic *otium*. As far as posterity was to be concerned, Cicero and Seneca were the most important of them. Some of their pronouncements were quoted by participants in the long medieval debate between supporters of the active and the contemplative lives. Cicero's treatise *On Duties* (*De officiis*) was among the most widely read works of classical antiquity in the medieval period. At the beginning of the third book, Cicero recalls that, according to Cato,

> Publius Cornelius Scipio, the first of that family to be called Africanus, used to remark that he was never less idle than when he had nothing to do and never less lonely than when he was by himself.

The key words are 'numquam se minus otiosum esse quam cum otiosus, nec minus solum, quam cum solus esset'. More and less favourable meanings of *otiosus* are delicately contrasted and *solus* is used in two senses, which challenge the modern English translator.[10] It was a passage destined to raise echoes throughout the medieval centuries, and Edward Gibbon could still apply the description of Scipio's *otium* to himself.[11]

Cicero had given a slightly different version of the first part of Scipio's dictum in *De re publica* (i, c. 17), written perhaps ten years earlier than *De officiis* and now surviving only incomplete. Here, according to Cato, Scipio 'was never doing more than when he was doing nothing (*nunquam se plus agere quam nihil cum ageret*)'. Cato himself is praised (i, c.1) for rejecting the option of withdrawal. Although he might have enjoyed a delightful leisure at Tusculum (where Cicero himself spent much of his enforced retirement from politics) he chose, even in old age, 'to be tossed by the billows and storms of our public life'. Forced increasingly out of the political arena, Cicero himself turned to writing and the intensive study of literature and philosophy by way of compensation, but he could not rid himself of the feeling that this retirement could only be justified if its products were ultimately of some public use. He therefore valued Scipio's statement, for

> It shows that even in his leisure hours his thoughts were occupied with public business and that he used to commune with himself when alone; and so not only was he never unoccupied, but he sometimes had no need for company. The two conditions, then, that prompt others to idleness – leisure and solitude – only spurred him on.[12]

In this passage *otium* is invested with an entirely neutral meaning and is contrasted with idleness (here called *languor*). Scipio was not idle, but mentally girding himself for action. The vigour and creativity of his thought temporarily took the place of the exchange of ideas between civilized men. Cicero wished he could say of himself what Scipio did, but failing that he could take him as a model. He had been forced out of political and forensic activity and was perforce 'pursuing a life of leisure' (*otium persequimur*); for the same reason he had left the city 'and wandering around the countryside I am often alone'. Scipio had retreated into his *otium* from time to time and by choice; Cicero's had been forced upon him by the evils of the times and he was trying to make a virtue out of necessity.

St Ambrose, bishop of Milan (d. 397), much admired *De officiis*. He both borrowed its title and took it as the model for the three books of his own treatise on Christian duties. He may well have been responsible for much of the medieval familiarity and popularity of the description of Scipio's *otium*. Scipio, Ambrose observed, was not the first to make this use of retirement, for Moses before him 'spoke in silence and was busy *in otio*'. For the Christian, as Ambrose perceived, solitude was not what it seemed. The bishop asked rhetorically, 'When is the just man alone who is always with God? When is he solitary who is never separated from Christ?' Thus Ambrose fused Cicero with St Paul, 'Who shall separate us from the love of Christ?'[13]

Bishops had to eschew monastic retirement and embrace what they regarded as the active life. This provided one light in which to read Cicero. In a monastic environment it was natural to endorse his stress on the evils of the times, the virtues of retirement and the value of philosophy in inculcating a stoic indifference to suffering and misfortune. At all events, Cicero was believed to have stood aloof from the world and the passions, like a Christian ascetic *avant la lettre*. As a result Petrarch in the mid fourteenth century was in for a not altogether pleasant surprise when he discovered Cicero's letters to Atticus, Brutus and his brother Quintus in the ancient library at Verona, and in them the evidence of his intense and ultimately fatal political activity. Later in that century the further discovery of Cicero's other letters to his friends (*Ad Familiares*) confirmed him in his role as advocate of the active life, which was just what a new generation of Italian humanists wanted.

Seneca did not have to undergo a similar re-evaluation, although his medieval image was also subject to distortion and the reading of him was in some respects comparably slanted. His *Epistles* of ethical and philosophical counsel to his friend Lucilius had a wide medieval readership and he was even sometimes regarded as a Christian manqué.[14] His attitude to solitude was ambivalent, like Cicero's but for slightly different reasons. He was much interested in the question of whether solitude was in fact helpful to the pursuit of intellectual and moral self-improvement and was particularly fond of the idea that one's mental state should not be dependent on one's surroundings. In his 56th Epistle to Lucilius he prefaces a humorous description of the commotion which invaded his lodgings over a public bath-house with the words 'I cannot for the life of me see that quiet is as necessary to a person who has shut himself away to do some studying as it is generally thought to be.' Seneca in this vein was among the ancestors of those thinkers who explored the possibilities of creating what we might now term a virtual solitude inside themselves.

Marcus Aurelius was another: 'Are you distracted by outward cares? Then allow yourself a space of quiet, wherein you can add to your knowledge of the Good and learn to curb your restlessness.' To think that this could only be achieved in seclusion was, in the view of the philosopher-emperor, a gross error:

> Men seek for seclusion in the wilderness, by the seashore, or in the mountains – a dream you have cherished only too fondly yourself. But such fancies are wholly unworthy of a philosopher since at any moment you choose you can retire within yourself. Nowhere can a man find a quieter or more untroubled retreat than in his own soul.[15]

Seneca also stressed the converse possibility, that peaceful surroundings did not guarantee mental peace: 'I've seen for myself people sunk in gloom in cheerful and delightful country houses and people in completely secluded surroundings who looked as if they were run off their feet.' All the same, it was desirable to avoid crowds and spectacles: 'Retire into yourself as much as you can. Associate with people who are likely to improve you.'[16]

Company, then, should be carefully chosen; but company there should be. In the 9th Epistle, Seneca observed that the statement 'The wise man is content with himself' could easily be misinterpreted. The wise man sought retirement and enjoyed his own company, 'yet he would refuse to live if he had to live without any human company at all'. There was in man an inherent 'distaste for solitude' and 'craving for society'. This echoed Cicero's strongly held belief that society did not merely provide for the necessities of life but satisfied the demands of human nature; were a man provided with an abundance of everything he needed, he would still seek company.[17] Like Scipio as Cicero understood him, Seneca had 'only buried myself away behind closed doors in order to be able to be of use to more people'.[18] As to the true definition of *otium*, Seneca's judgement (in the 82nd Epistle) that without literary study it was 'death and entombment for a living man' proved popular with posterity, including Petrarch.[19]

Cicero and Seneca were agreed in regarding sociability as essential to mankind. For men with no pretensions to philosophy, this was even more obvious. The poet Ovid was no stoic. Exiled from Rome to the shores of the Black Sea in the year 8, he bitterly lamented (and possibly exaggerated) the barbarism of the place where he found himself, complaining that no one could expect him to write in such an environment. Writing poetry with no prospect of an audience to read it to, he observed, was like dancing by oneself. This outburst neatly expressed the social context in which many Romans expected to display the fruits of their creative leisure.

> An audience stimulates brilliance, to praise a talent
> swells it: fame indeed is the spur.

Who exists, here that I can recite my works to
save tow-headed natives, the Danube's barbarous crew?
Yet what should I do as a solitary, how kill my fruitless
leisure, how struggle through the day? [20]

Epistolary communication could not satisfy Ovid, but it was important for the Romans-turned-monks who in the years around 400 maintained contact with one another by this means. For later monastic generations the exchange of prose and verse compositions was the normal mode of 'publication' and also united in friendship monks who were far distant from one another; it was compatible with their stability, enclosure and 'solitude'. Paulinus and the monks who came after him did not demand a live audience and their *otium* was not a preparation for involvement in public life as the Romans had understood it. Superficially it might seem that it was more like an end in itself, but in fact it served purposes which, so the monk would have claimed, benefited not only himself but his fellow man. The life of prayer was not an abnegation of responsibility.

In its origins, however, and because of its penitential character, monastic or eremitical withdrawal implied rejection of the whole apparatus which sustained Romans in a 'civilized' way of life (including baths). The sacred could now be found in proximity to what the bemused Rutilius regarded as filth. Monasticism held up before young men of promise (like the one who had immured himself on the island of Gorgon) an ideal which was not based on the education, career structures, public service ideals and family relationships which Rutilius and his like took for granted. For all these reasons Rutilius would have had difficulty imagining that in a later age monks should be widely seen by historians as the conservators of much of the Roman cultural heritage, from book-copying to bee-keeping, gardening and viticulture, or that twelfth-century monks would borrow the words of Cicero and Seneca when describing and justifying their extraordinary way of life.

The younger Pliny might have been even more surprised. At the end of his life, as a special emissary of the Emperor Trajan to Bithynia and Pontus in the year 111, part of his time was occupied by the prosecution of Christians, for whom he clearly had no sympathy or understanding. His life had been spent in the world which three hundred years later Rutilius still thought must last for ever: legal practice and office-holding, political gossip and dinner parties, travel from town to country and from estate to estate, and the writing of literary works which were both aired at public readings and privately circulated among friends. These included carefully crafted epistles on subjects of interest, two of them devoted to elaborate descriptions of the settings in which Pliny liked to pass his leisure time and to study, notably his villas on the coast at Laurentinum, seventeen miles from Rome, and at Tusci at the foot of the Tuscan Apennines.

That *otium* was better enjoyed in the countryside than in the midst of the city was a commonplace. At Laurentinum Pliny speaks of the villa's outlook, both towards the sea and away from it, of its terrace, garden, covered arcade and swimming pool, of the openness of certain rooms to the sun. One corner captured the warmth to such a degree that it was used as 'the winter quarters and gymnasium of my household'. In this quarter too were the rooms used by his slaves and freedmen, which were presentable enough to accommodate guests if necessary. Pliny's sanctum was not here, however, but in a detached block linked to the main body of the house by a passage along one side of the garden. It contained his favourite rooms, built to his own specifications. They included a sun-parlour, with a view of both the terrace and the sea, and a bedroom 'which neither the voices of my household, the sea's murmur or the noise of a storm can penetrate':

> When I retire to this suite I feel as if I had left my house altogether and much enjoy the sensation: especially during the Saturnalia when the rest of the roof resounds with festive cries in the holiday freedom, for I am not disturbing my household's merrymaking nor they my work.[21]

There is nothing strange to a modern reader in this picture of a bookish individual's requirements and the way the design of his house satisfied them, even if most of us might reasonably envy Pliny the scale and setting of a house which he was pleased to regard as fairly modest. In his description of Tusci he devotes more space to the villa's surroundings and it is clear that the interplay between its internal and external features, garden, vineyard and broader landscape, was fundamental to the quality of the life that was lived in it.[22] Not only is the aspect of its various rooms lovingly described, but there are facilities for riding and games, for bathing and for dining both indoors and out. There are layers of seclusion: one bedroom 'no daylight, voice or sound can penetrate' and adjacent to this was 'an informal dining room where I entertain my personal friends'. This epistle ends with a rhapsodic statement of the joys of private life:

> I can enjoy a profounder peace there, more comfort and fewer cares; I need never wear a formal toga and there are no neighbours to disturb me; everywhere there is peace and quiet, which adds as much to the healthiness of the place as the clear sky and pure air. There I enjoy the best of health, both mental and physical, for I keep my mind in training with work and my body with hunting.

Generations of historians have tried to fix the point at which Roman civilization came to an end. One intriguing suggestion is that it was at the moment when people ceased to build, use or need houses like this.[23] Studies of Roman domestic architecture make it clear that the houses of the well-to-do and highly placed in society embraced a hierarchy of spaces, some accessible to clients and outsiders, some reserved for the master of the house and his intimates; places for the women of the family were naturally among the latter. Not all of this vanished totally with 'the fall of Rome', whenever we choose to locate it, but for much of what is commonly designated the medieval period we would listen in vain for the note that Pliny strikes here.

That in itself may be thought significant and revealing of a change in sensibility. Descriptions of the domestic environment become few and far between in the earlier middle ages. This does not necessarily mean that the lay elite did not value their personal time and space or appreciate beauty and comfort in their surroundings, rather that these were not seen as topics worthy of treatment by those who put pen to parchment. The aim of the spiritual man was as far as possible to transcend the limitations of material existence and, for those who knew or cared about the classics, the Stoic strain in pre-Christian thinking encouraged a studied indifference to physical conditions and bodily privations, provided that the moral life was in good shape. If writers celebrated architecture, it was likely to be church architecture.

It is in the twelfth century that signs of an interest in the details of upper-class living-space begin to appear in various literary genres. This was no isolated symptom. In a more populous society, human environments of all kinds, monasteries among them, left their mark on the written record. Urban expansion had the effect of sharpening awareness of issues of solitude and social involvement, and an increasing number of scholars outside the monastic setting, in the urban schools which became the universities of the later middle ages, meditated on this among other subjects, on the basis of an ever-richer accumulation of authorities ancient and modern.

In his *Verbum abbreviatum*, a 'popular manual of ethics' possibly written with preaching in mind,[24] the Parisian master Peter the Chanter (d. 1197) considered in three successive chapters 'bad singularity', 'good singularity' and the need to have good company and to avoid bad.[25] *Mala singularitas* was the desire to stand out from one's fellows for the sake of it, and among the authorities Peter quoted against it were Seneca's fifth epistle to Lucilius, St Paul and St Bernard of Clairvaux. Peter was insistent that philosophy inculcated 'a sense of community, humanity, sociability and association, from which singularity (*dissimilitudo*) will separate us'.[26] The individual should avoid being ridiculous and preserve the basic decencies (*faciles munditias*). *Bona singularitas* was, according to Peter, more often called *bona solitudo*. It depended above all on the society of good men; here Peter was able to claim the authority of Cato, Seneca, St Paul and St Augustine among others. The mixture of sources expresses the strength of what proved to be an enduring consensus.

Peter worked and wrote in a setting which would soon be that of the new orders of friars. The Dominicans in particular valued and revivified old ideas, such as those of Pope Gregory the Great, about the value of prayer and study in solitude as preparation for a more effective engagement with the world and pastoral care.[27] Gregory, read by many and immensely influential, had devoted a great deal of space, in several of his works, to both the primacy of the contemplative life and the necessity of engagement with one's neighbour; he also had much to say about inner and mental solitude.[28] Like many another prelate after him, Gregory on becoming pope lamented his lost solitude and keenly appreciated the need for an inner stronghold to which the pastor could retire to gain strength in the midst of tribulation. Among his many heirs was the Dominican archbishop of Florence Antonino (d. 1459) who declared, in reply to complaints about the bothersomeness of pastoral duty:

> Because of the anxiety that arises from the things of this world, it is impossible for many, indeed for almost all, human beings to enjoy the peace and quiet of a tranquil spirit, unless one creates for oneself some secret and hidden retreat in the mind, to which the irritations of business, the anxieties of responsibility, and the disquiet of all external occupations do not penetrate, and where, when it has finished with a host of undertakings, the mind, stripped immediately of all passions, can at once fly, as if to a stronghold and to what Paul calls the inner man.[29]

2

Pioneers of Solitude

Various explanations have been suggested and debated for the acceleration of Christian withdrawal from 'the world' which seems to have taken place around and after the year 300. These include, on the ideological level, a revulsion against a decaying and corrupt society; on the material level, economic distress in the eastern Mediterranean provinces of the Roman Empire and the desire to escape the taxman; and, on the social level, the breakdown of local structures of justice and protection which created a need for new mechanisms of social solidarity and assistance.

The extent to which the early monks were refugees from economic and social hardship has been questioned. For example, the community that Pachomius established at Tabennesi in Upper Egypt, which was a deserted village, may have appealed to its recruits as a familiar, viable type of rural settlement. Pachomius, it has been suggested, saw monasticism as retaining 'that supposedly classical quality, an emphasis on community'. The buildings revealed by archaeology at Egyptian monastic sites reinforce this impression, being 'entirely comparable to the better class of secular rural dwelling'.[1] It is also perhaps doubtful whether the men and women who adopted a strategy of religious withdrawal had anything like a modern historian's perception of a declining Roman Empire, a once-great structure disintegrating before their eyes, except insofar as they believed that the world as a whole was corrupt, transient and decaying. The bits of it that they knew were almost exclusively Roman territory, but deterioration was a condition of earthly life in general rather than of the Roman world in particular.

One explanation that seems worth considering has to do less with the decadence of Roman society than with the development of Christianity within it. The first Christians, it has been suggested, saw themselves as innately withdrawn from the world because they were an embattled minority, the elect. The Christianization of society as a whole, including the countryside, was bound to modify that mental framework. What did one now have to do to express a real sense of religious commitment? The answer might be to withdraw from 'the world' altogether.[2] This explanation would have commended itself to John Cassian, who believed that the very first Christians had lived the essentials of the cenobitic life, especially in their community of property. The admission to the faith of more and more 'foreigners', of whom the apostles demanded little more than that they forswear their pagan practices, created the situation in which the spiritual elite sought out the desert.[3] The monks went that extra mile or even more, literally and metaphorically, although many of them were in fact far from remote from the centres of civilization.

Rutilius spoke disapprovingly of Roman citizens who had become 'monks', but we might now be more inclined to call the individuals that he described 'hermits'. The boundary between the communal withdrawal from the world which is called cenobitic and a truly solitary religious life was more distinctly drawn in later centuries, when the word 'monk' came to be reserved almost exclusively for practitioners of the former and true solitaries were called hermits, anchorites or recluses.[4] The issue was then complicated by the reincorporation of certain elements of the eremitical life into cenobitic monasticism, for example by the Carthusians, but like other monks Carthusians dwelled together within an enclosure which excluded the outside world. This was by no means true of all early monks.

The broad distinction between 'cenobite' and 'anchorite' was already familiar to contemporaries of Rutilius. Pachomius, often seen as the first major lawgiver of cenobitic monasticism, died in 346, St Antony, regarded as the great pioneer of an authentically solitary existence on his 'inner mountain' near the Red Sea, in 356. The image of Antony as the hermit spectacularly persecuted by demons plays an important part in the *Life* that was written shortly after his death by Athanasius, patriarch of Alexandria, and greatly commended itself to western artists down to and including Hieronymus Bosch, but it did not exclude other less picturesque attributes.[5] Antony's isolation was by no means permanent or total and it is clear that a goodly part of his time was spent counselling and correcting monks who lived closer to settled society. His career well illustrates how the individual monk might move through a series of phases of greater or lesser physical solitude.

Late in the third century, when according to Athanasius 'there were few monasteries in Egypt' and no one had colonized 'the great desert', it was normal for an ascetic to live in the vicinity of his native village. Antony began in this way, seeking out any holy man he heard about. His first step beyond these limits was to take up residence among the tombs which lay a short way from the village. By so doing he breached the *cordon sanitaire* that traditionally separated the world of the living from that of the dead and challenged the demons on their own ground. Later he resolved to penetrate the desert and took up residence in an abandoned fortress. For twenty years he remained there, seeing nobody and never going out, although he had visitors who brought him food which he took in through a hole in the roof. As a result of this time of trial among the demons, he achieved perfect spiritual balance. From now on he attracted followers and 'monasteries' multiplied outside the inhabited zone. In Athanasius' famous phrase, 'the desert was made a city by monks', much to the chagrin of the devil, who saw himself deprived of his proper territory.

Antony himself now felt the need of another period of genuine solitude; people were seeking cures from him and disturbing his peace. A heavenly voice directed him to seek the 'inner mountain' near the Red Sea, to which he was guided by Saracen traders during a journey which lasted three days and nights. Even when he found his destined resting-place his isolation was not total, for not only did the Saracens call on him from time to time with bread, but certain brethren sought him out and, it seems, established a routine of monthly visits, bringing him gardening tools and other supplies. Antony also made several visits to the 'outer mountain' to advise and discipline the monks dwelling there, nearer to civilization. He exchanged visits with the monks of Nitria, an important settlement some distance south of Alexandria which was home to many of the most eminent ascetics at some point in their lives, and also with those of the no less important community of Scetis, further to the south.[6] It was during this last phase of his life that Antony told a layman that a monk who spent time in the outside world was like a fish out of water and must rush back 'to the mountain', like a fish to the sea.[7]

Athanasius' *Life* became the blueprint for countless later specimens of Latin hagiography, largely as a result of its early translation by Evagrius of Pontus, a scholar who lived as a monk in Egypt and wrote on spiritual subjects.[8] It was an outstanding item among the abundant literature about eastern monasticism that already by 400 had either been written in or translated into Latin, thus conveying vital knowledge to later western monks. In about 370 Rufinus of Aquileia (d. 410) founded a monastery on the Mount of Olives and in 394 a party of its monks made a pilgrimage to Egypt to seek out the great ascetics of the day. They described their findings in the so-called *History of the Monks of Egypt* and Rufinus himself translated it into Latin, making additions and amendments in the light of his own earlier travels in Egypt.[9] Palladius, whose career took him from monasteries in Egypt to a bishopric in Palestine, was a disciple and admirer of Evagrius of Pontus and has been variously described as the Herodotus or the Boswell of early monasticism. His *Lausiac History* (c. 419–20) contains a wealth of anecdote about monks great and small in Egypt and elsewhere, and became well known in the west; more than nine centuries later, Petrarch knew and used it.[10]

Of at least equal importance were the Latin writings of individuals who had first-hand knowledge of eastern monasticism. Almost at the moment that Rutilius was writing *De reditu suo*, John Cassian (d. c. 435) was active in southern Gaul, founding monasteries near Marseilles and putting into writing for the benefit of future generations his recollections of the ways of life he had seen, shared and studied during his travels in the eastern Mediterranean. By way of the *Conferences* and *Institutes*,[11] which were required reading (or listening) for generations of western monks, he transmitted not only his understanding of the underlying rationale of the religious life, in both its cenobitic and eremitical variants, but a number of anecdotes about the desert fathers. The acerbic St Jerome (d. 419–20) made the monastic *Rules* of Pachomius known to a western readership and also wrote about some of the personalities of eastern monasticism, for example the widely travelled Hilarion who died in Cyprus in 371.[12] The work of transmission and exposition continued well after 500. A Latin version of the *Apophthegmata* (*Sayings*) of the Desert Fathers which in fact antedates any known Greek collection was made early in the sixth century by two Roman clerics, John and Pelagius, and was known to the middle ages under the title *Vitae Patrum* (*Lives of the Fathers*).[13] While many Greek, Coptic or Syriac accounts of the eastern monks remained inaccessible to western readers until much more recent times, a respectable corpus of material was therefore communicated to western Christendom long before the theological and cultural gulf between the Greek and Roman churches became all but unbridgeable.

Athanasius described how, when Antony emerged from his twenty-year sojourn in the deserted fortress, all marvelled at the saint's unchanged appearance and how he had achieved and maintained an imperturbable equanimity of bearing. At this point Evagrius added a comment which can be rendered as follows: 'Solitude had not made him at all uncouth nor had the daily warfare with the enemy coarsened him.'[14] The choice of words suggests a conscious riposte to criticism of the kind voiced by Julian, Rutilius and even the Christian Ausonius. Antony and his admirers would also have rebutted the charge of misanthropy; the saint is supposed once to have said 'Our life and our death is with our neighbour. If we gain our brother, we have gained God, but if we scandalize our brother, we have sinned against Christ.'[15] Antony might, however, have differed from his contemporary, the Emperor Julian, in his opinion of what was socially beneficial.

Fundamental values were in question. Some of the eastern monks (like Evagrius) were highly educated men but claimed to attach little or no value to education. In 394, just at the moment when Paulinus abandoned his old life to become custodian of the shrine of St Felix at Nola, the Roman patrician Arsenius, friend and tutor to the imperial family, embraced the religious life in Egypt. Arsenius had received the standard classical education but asked why, with his background, he once sought advice from an old Egyptian monk, he replied: 'I have indeed been taught Latin and Greek, but I do not know even the alphabet of this peasant.' On another occasion, he said that the Egyptian peasants acquired their virtues from hard work.[16] His opinions might have perplexed fellow Romans who, like the Greeks before them, valued the products of manual labour but thought little of the producers.

Arsenius turned to religion at too advanced an age to embrace the monk's standard regime of manual labour. After some years an unnamed Egyptian monk visited him and was unimpressed when he saw the modest comforts – a little wine, a pillow for his head, sandals for his feet – which he enjoyed. Perceiving this, Arsenius questioned his visitor about his own previous life. He had been a herdsman, sleeping rough in the fields, eating what he could get and bathing in the river when he needed to. Gently Arsenius hinted that he himself had come down from a great height in order to embrace the religious ideal; he required some physical concessions in order to sustain the effort. Conscience-stricken, the other acknowledged that by contrast he had embraced an easier way of life in becoming a monk.[17] If there is a single explanation for the Christian 'flight' from the world, it has to comprehend both Arsenius and his visitor.

Rutilius rightly derived the word *monachos* from the root *monos*, 'alone', and seized on the monks' unattractive choice of dwelling-places. This might be an effective way of expressing their detachment from secular concerns, but possible habitats and styles of life were in fact very various. In Rome and other cities the religious aspirant might simply withdraw into his or her own house. Cassian professed to disapprove of such persons, classifying them among the deplorable 'sarabaites' as backsliders from true cenobitism who were not true anchorites either, and he suspected them of avaricious tendencies. He does not seem, however, to have ruled out the possibility that it could work: in the same *Conference* he goes on to praise a woman who lived in the house at Alexandria which her parents had left her and who devoted her substance to looking after the most cantankerous old widow the bishop could inflict on her.[18]

The lives of all classes unfolded largely within conventional frameworks determined by the structure of the family (and of the family dwelling), and by relationships with neighbours, patrons and clients in the physical setting of city or village. At the upper levels of lay society the cultivated man of letters would expect to enjoy peace and quiet in which to read and write, but like other men he spent much of his time in various more or less obligatory forms of social and political interaction. Upper-class women enjoyed seclusion if not solitude; the marriageable girl would be well guarded at home and respectable women did not go out without fit escort. Arsenius was familiar with these conventions. He once compared 'those who live in solitude without seeing anyone' to a young girl leading a 'hidden life' in her father's house before marriage; the esteem in which she was then held was diminished when she entered on married life.[19] The decision to detach themselves from ordinary society did not necessarily imply, for men or women, a total transformation in their environment or way of supporting themselves, but it did open up certain choices which the ordinary lay person did not have to make, and indeed had little opportunity to make.

What were the meanings and uses of solitude to the ascetic? Was he (or she) totally without company or, if accompanied, by whom, temporarily or permanently? At what distance were he, she or they located from settled, secular society and from other ascetics and what were their relationships with these others? What were the characteristics and amenities of the 'cell' and its immediate surroundings? What motivated monks to choose one form of 'solitude' or one kind of location over another, or indeed to change style of life or location (as many did) within the course of a lifetime?

After Antony and others had penetrated the desert in the years around 300, more remote hermitages and settlements came into being, but it is clear that many monks still settled sufficiently close to their original villages to be able to go back there if they chose. One prided himself on not having done so for many years, whereas others went back frequently. Abba Poemen commented that he himself had been accustomed to return every night and walk all around his village so as to avoid vainglory.[20] Macarius the Great at the beginning of his career lived as an anchorite actually within a village, with a servant to attend to his needs, until he was falsely accused of making a girl pregnant.[21] Genuine solitaries and loose associations of monks in small groupings lived cheek by jowl with one another and with *coenobia*. At the end of the fourth century, according to the *History of the Monks*, 'There is not a town or village in Egypt and the Thebaid which is not surrounded by hermitages as if by walls', while Oxyrhynchus is described as a town full of monks, with monasteries both inside and outside the walls, containing about ten thousand brothers and twenty thousand nuns.[22] Palladius spent four years at Antinoë in the Thebaid, where some twelve hundred men, including cave-dwelling anchorites, lived around the city.[23]

Enclosed communities existed: one monastery in the Thebaid housed one thousand monks within a high brick wall. There were wells and gardens and everything needful within this precinct, for none of the monks ever went out and they were guarded by a senior monk as gatekeeper, who let no one in unless he was prepared to stay for life.[24] Even at its most highly organized, however, the spatial and architectural setting of cenobites scarcely resembled, say, a Yorkshire Cistercian abbey of the thirteenth century. The individual cell remained an integral part of the layout. The imposing dormitories and refectories in which monks slept and ate together, which we tend to regard as typical monastic features, lay in the future.[25] Refectories seem to have developed earlier than dormitories. A community near Hermopolis, which consisted of about five hundred brothers, is said to have shared 'a common table'.[26] Palladius said that Pachomius had been instructed by an angel that there should be three monks to a cell but that meals should be taken in a single 'house'. In a Pachomian monastery the cells were grouped under the direction of a master; they had doors, and no monk could enter another cell without knocking, but no one was supposed to sleep in a locked cell. It is not clear, at least from the surviving *Rules*, whether Palladius was right about the number of monks to a cell.[27] In desert monasticism in general, solitary sleeping arrangements allowed for the possibility of strenuous vigils and nocturnal prayer which ceased to be a normal feature of classical cenobitic monasticism with its regulated, collective timetable and accommodation.

Individuals sometimes lived as anchorites within monastic communities. The monk Serapion once converted a courtesan, whom he installed in 'a monastery of virgins' with instructions that she should be allowed to have her own way. After a short period of increasing abstinence, she asked the superior (*amma*) to be so good as to enclose her completely in a cell and to put a little food and some work to do through the window.[28] Abba Motius had presided over more than one monastery but after trouble with one of the monks he withdrew to his native village, built a monastery there and lived within it as a recluse. Monks from his former monastery, including the troublemaker, came in search of him and knocked at his door, whereupon he put a ladder up to the window, recognized them and broke the door down with a hatchet in order to join them. His brief period of enclosure had evidently served its purpose, for he now abandoned it and in due season became a bishop and miracle-worker.[29]

In many non-cenobitic communities, the cells were widely scattered and the brethren came together in the church only on Saturdays and Sundays for the meeting called the *synaxis*, which centred on the celebration of the eucharist. There are several slightly varying descriptions of the community at Nitria on the southern shore of Lake Marea a short distance from Alexandria, where many of the great monks, including several who knew Antony himself, lived for some part of their lives. Writing of the years just before 400, Palladius said that there were nearly five thousand men living there, following different ways of life: 'Thus some live alone, others in pairs and some in groups.' He mentions the 'great church' and the guest-house where all visitors were accommodated for the entire duration of their stay, even if it lasted several years. Seven bakeries supplied the needs both of the inhabitants and of six hundred hermits dwelling in the great desert. There were pastry-cooks and doctors in residence, and 'wine was sold'; in fact there seems to have been a fair amount of commercial activity.[30]

When Rufinus translated the *History of the Monks*, he somewhat amended its original description of Nitria. He distinguished between the community at Nitria itself and the more remote settlement at Cellia ('the Cells') some ten miles away. According to his account, the settlement at Nitria consisted of about fifty dwellings not far from one another, variously inhabited by one, two or more brethren and placed under the direction of a single father. At Cellia the cells were more widely scattered, so that 'no one can see his neighbour nor can any voice be heard. They live alone in their cells and there is a huge silence and a great quiet there.' These were three or four miles apart, and it sometimes happened that a monk died in his cell and was not found for four days; only his absence from the *synaxis* would alert the others to the possibility that he was sick or dead. There is none the less a very strong insistence on the bonds of love which united the occupants of the Cells. So solicitous were the monks for the salvation of new recruits that they would eagerly offer them their own cells as temporary accommodation. A senior monk called Ammonius, who himself 'possessed beautifully constructed cells with a courtyard, a well and other necessary things', once did this and speedily mustered the other brethren to build a cell for the new arrival, which was done in a day.[31]

We obtain a possibly legendary insight into the foundation of Cellia from the story of a visit Antony paid to the formidable Abba Amoun at Nitria. Amoun said to him,

'By your prayers the number of the brethren increases and some of them want to build more cells where they may live in peace. How far away from here do you think we should build the cells?' At Antony's suggestion they ate at the ninth hour (mid-afternoon) and then walked out into the desert until sunset. The point they reached, about twelve miles away, was chosen for the new colony. Antony's reasoning was that the monks who remained at Nitria could do as he and Amoun had done, taking nourishment at the usual time and then walking out to visit the occupants of the cells: 'If they do this they will be able to keep in touch with each other without distraction of mind.'[32]

Thanks to the modern use of the word to describe a prisoner's place of confinement, 'cell' tends to conjure up a vision of a single, small, insalubrious room, but the reference to Ammonius' accommodation at Cellia suggests that this was by no means always the case.[33] Like the dwellings of anchorites at a much later period they often had an inner and outer room. One 'very famous hermit' was assailed by a harlot for a bet; when she presented herself at his cell, saying that she had lost her way in the desert, he reluctantly brought her into his courtyard (where she complained she was still at risk from wild beasts) and himself retired into his inner room and shut the door.[34] The monk Patermuthius was once a robber; one night he climbed on to the roof of an anchoress's dwelling, hoping to rob the inner chamber, where it was probably normal to keep any money or valuables, but he was unable to find a way to get either in or down. He was discovered by the anchoress after he had passed the night in reflection, and promptly asked her for directions to the nearest church.[35]

Cells could be two-storeyed: Abba Aaron, an extreme ascetic and wonder-worker who lived far to the south in Upper Egypt, had an 'upper room' which he seems to have used especially for prayer.[36] According to Palladius, John of Lycopolis in the Upper Thebaid had built himself three cells on his inaccessible mountaintop: 'one was for his bodily needs, he worked and ate in the second; in the third one he prayed'.[37] The cell was a workshop, both literally and metaphorically, and the spiritual trials the monk underwent within it were not usually imposed by the character of the space. Palladius relates, however, that Macarius of Alexandria (whom he depicts as something of an ascetic extremist) had a number of cells scattered about the desert, in Libya, at Scetis, Nitria and Cellia. Some of them were windowless, which was clearly not normal, and he sat in them in darkness during Lent; another was too small for him to stretch his feet out in. He received visitors in a more commodious apartment.[38]

Differing and overlapping interpretations of religious solitude were therefore being lived out in the 'desert', and issues that would remain debating points centuries later were also being rehearsed, among them the relationship between the cenobitic and the eremitical lives and the preferability of the one or the other, whether absolutely, in certain circumstances or for a given individual. The exponents of these varied styles of life shared the conviction that their faith imposed on them a quest for perfection which demanded the rejection of family ties, worldly careers and the ordinary involvements of social life. Whether it also implied individual physical isolation and the renunciation of all human contact was another matter and to some degree a matter of choice.

For many of the desert-dwellers poverty was of central importance. For Antony and others, the gospel precept, 'Go, sell all you have and give it to the poor and follow me' was their first call to the religious life. In practical terms poverty meant avoiding all superfluity, restricting material wants to the bare minimum. Where there was any kind of communal monastic organization the individual possession of property was strictly controlled; Cassian mused that only in the cenobium could a monk genuinely give no thought to the morrow.[39] Men and women who chose another ascetic path, although they would deny themselves all indulgences, did not necessarily give up all their property. The elder Melania thought it important not to wash, in itself a signal rejection of civilized Roman values,[40] but she remained true to her class in her use of her wealth as an instrument of patronage, endowing monks, monasteries and other charitable enterprises. Although her granddaughter, the younger Melania, sold off much of her property when she finally obtained her husband's consent that they should both adopt the religious life, she scarcely became destitute, retaining properties in Africa, Sicily and Campania with which to fund her monastic foundations. When Palladius last heard of her she was living with her mother, sometimes in Sicily, sometimes in Campania, with a household which included fifteen eunuchs and sixty serving women, free and unfree. In Campania she and her mother and husband were members of Paulinus' little community at Nola.[41]

At a lower social level the desert solitary, poor though he undoubtedly was, could not live entirely without means of subsistence and often kept small sums of money in the cell, occasionally pointing them out cheerfully to robbers. These were the product of manual labour, which occupied an important part in the thinking of the monks of Egypt. The *History of the Monks* emphasized the wonder-working powers of the desert saints, suggesting that when they lacked something they had no recourse to town, village, other brethren or kin but were supplied miraculously by the power of prayer. Other sources suggest a more prosaic reality. The same writer describes the huge community near Arsinoë which conducted a flourishing agricultural enterprise that supplied grain and woven goods to the poor as far away as Alexandria, even declaring that 'none of the fathers whom we have already mentioned throughout Egypt ever neglected this form of stewardship'.[42] It was believed that manual labour promoted humility and Antony, early in his ascetic career, remembered also that 'He who does not work, shall not eat'.[43] Monks went to market, were visited by itinerant traders and even hired themselves out as labourers at harvest-time. The dying Pambo of Nitria said that he did not remember having eaten bread which was not the fruit of his own labours, and this claim was echoed by others.[44] Inevitably this qualified their 'solitude', but there were differences of opinion or at least of emphasis.

Manual labour seems to have been less valued by the monks of Syria or at least by those who wrote about them. Among the ascetics described by Theodoret of Cyrrhus, only Theodosius, a native of Antioch who as a hermit practised extreme austerities, insisted on working with his hands; he imposed the same requirement on his followers when he became the leader of a community.[45] The Palestinian-born Silvanus, who for a time presided over a community at Sinai, once administered a neat rebuke to a visitor who reproved the dedication of his brethren to manual labour. Silvanus planted him in a cell with a book and nothing else and did not have him called to the meal. The moral was that 'Mary needs Martha': without the labours of Martha which put bread on the table Mary would not be free to sit rapt in contemplation. Silvanus himself once made a hundred necklaces from dried peas and traded them for an ass-load of loaves from Egypt.[46] Palladius thought it worthy of remark that the younger Melania, who retained such a respectable establishment when she and her mother retired into devout seclusion, made a point of sharing some of the work of her maidservants, whom she associated with her in her ascetic practices.[47]

This espousal of manual labour by persons of respectable social origins represented a significant breach with the cultural values of classical antiquity: it closed the gap between the life of the mind, as the monks understood it, and the work of the hands. In addition there was an awareness of the psychological value of repetitive manual tasks which harmonized with, and even assisted, the endless prayer which was the major objective of the religious life. It made possible some slight variation in the daily routine. Antony, assailed by the demon of *accidie*, that mixture of despondency, boredom and sense of futility which was the monk's occupational hazard, was once granted a vision of a man who looked just like himself. He was 'sitting at his work, getting up from his work to pray, then sitting down and plaiting a rope, then getting up again to pray'. The vision was an angel bearing the message 'Do this and you will be saved'.'[48]

The monks both enjoyed the possibilities and confronted the problems of all those who have been left alone to perform mechanical tasks, from the carpenter, cobbler or smith to the gardener or even the person who does the washing-up. Herders enjoyed built-in solitude. Jerome's Malchus, a Syrian hermit, was once captured and enslaved by Arabs. During this period he was employed as a shepherd:

> I found this occupation a comfort for I rarely saw my masters and my fellow slaves. I felt that I was rather like the holy Jacob and I reminded myself of Moses, both of whom had once been shepherds in the wilderness. I lived on fresh cheese and milk; I prayed without ceasing and sang the psalms I had learned in the monastery. I enjoyed my captivity and gave thanks to God for his judgement, because I had discovered in the desert the monk whom I had been about to lose in my own country.[49]

Malchus was forced into marriage with a fellow-slave whom he persuaded to live chastely with him. For any ascetic, the avoidance of sexual relationships was a *sine qua non* and in this sense all of them were 'alone'. There were occasional signs of anxiety about the presence of 'boys' in monastic communities, and kinship ties, especially with persons of the opposite sex, might also need to be strictly rationed. Links with parents, children and other kin left in the world could be troublesome when mothers and sisters tried to pay visits to monks or messengers came bearing news that a monk had come into an inheritance.

This detachment symbolized the monk's singleness of purpose more effectively even than the choice of a remote place of residence or the rejection of property (with which it was in fact often connected). However, not all natural relationships were broken. Numerous stories depict pairs or even larger numbers of brothers living the religious life together, and the younger Melania was not the only female adept to live with her mother. Occasionally we hear of a chaste marriage in which both partners were vowed to religion: Malchus has been mentioned, Amoun of Nitria entered upon such a marriage early in his career, and an angel once informed some Egyptian monks about a villager called Eucharistus who lived chastely with his wife, both performing works of charity and wearing hairshirts at night.[50]

Detachment from 'the world', then, rarely implied the complete isolation of the individual. Total solitude was difficult to achieve and certainly difficult to sustain over a long period. Many never sought or achieved it at all; for some it was a temporary time of trial. On the advice of Abba Poemen, a monk called Sarmatas often spent periods of forty days alone and treated this achievement as if it were nothing, which suggests that it was not regarded as common practice. Poemen asked Sarmatas what he thought he had achieved by inflicting this hardship on himself; with some reluctance, he conceded that he had obtained mastery over sleep.[51]

Extremes of ascetic privation could be attained by other means than solitude, as the saints of Syria demonstrated. The stylites represented a type of asceticism not often paralleled elsewhere. The posture of the all-weather pillar saint, such as the famous Simeon or his imitator Daniel, very obviously symbolized the approach to God and an exclusive dependence upon Him who alone made such extremes of endurance possible.[52] This spiritual power fuelled wonder-working and, so far as the lay community was concerned, the result was social, political and thaumaturgic effectiveness. When not engaged in prayer the stylites conducted a stream of interviews with petitioners to whom they offered counsel or healing. One stylite described by John Moschos in the sixth century had no ladder for his clients; when one of them wanted a confidential consultation, he bade him come round to one side of the pillar and immediately they were able to converse without being overheard.[53] The exponents of this mode of life were cultivating not so much solitude as singularity, perhaps a more accurate and also a less pejorative term than exhibitionism. Others who were not stylites lived in the open air, equally exposed to the scrutiny of their admirers: James of Cyrrhestica dwelled on a mountaintop near Cyrrhus and Theodoret describes him as having an attack of acute diarrhoea in full view of his public.[54]

The economic relationships of the Egyptian monks with secular society do not suggest that they normally stood in patron–client relationships with the laity or that they lived on almsgiving. In general, extremes of ascetic performance and wonder-working seem to have been less valued here than in Syria or Palestine. Occasionally the solitary's power to recall man's pre-lapsarian power over the brute creation is evoked. Antony's demons often manifested themselves in animal shape, but he also had trouble from real animals when he tried to grow vegetables in the desert. They came for the water which he used for his crops, and Antony treated them gently, rebuking them in the name of God until they went away.[55] A somewhat different spirit is evoked by the story of Theon, an anchorite near Oxyrhynchus, who

> used to go out from his cell at night and keep company with wild animals, giving them to drink from the water which he had. Certainly one could see the tracks of antelopes and wild asses and gazelle and other animals near his hermitage. These creatures delighted him always.[56]

As Antony's experience suggested, the monk who ventured into the desert well knew that he was not in fact alone. The presence of demons could be relied upon, but so too could that of God, and angels were not infrequent visitors. Solitude was not therefore what it might seem to a modern secularized consciousness. On the one hand it could be perilous, on the other, help was always at hand if only the monk was worthy to receive it and sometimes even if he was not. It was widely felt that the truly eremitical life was not for beginners. There was also a school of thought that it was in fact inferior to the cenobitic life, in which the individual submitted his will to the direction of a superior and in which he also experienced the delights of Christian fellowship. Both these attitudes became characteristic of later western monasticism, and both are explored in the early literature, sometimes not without humour.

The wider monastic community offered certain safeguards against the perils threatened by solitude if it was embraced by one who was not ready for it. Even outside the cenobitic framework there were at least loose systems of inspection and support. One hermit reported how the seniors used to visit the cells of new brothers to check that they had not suffered any harm from demons. There was a ritual process for cleansing them if such harm had occurred.[57] More vigorous measures were taken against one brother who immediately upon becoming a monk shut himself up and declared 'I am a solitary'. His neighbours descended upon him and threw him out of his cell, forcing him to do penance before them all and to admit 'I am not a solitary, I have only just begun to be a monk'.[58] There are occasional references to excommunication and other forms of discipline and punishment. The monks were for the most part not priests and we hear nothing about sacramental confession, but it was regarded as an integral part of the religious life to expose one's thoughts and deeds to fraternal or paternal scrutiny. One monk who kicked against this requirement was reminded that John the Dwarf had declared that 'The enemy rejoices over nothing so much as over those who do not manifest their thoughts'.[59]

Participation in the *synaxis* and in the eucharist was an important measure of the monk's fellowship with God and man. It was unusual not to attend it if it was physically possible to do so, although recluses had to make other arrangements. Mark the Egyptian was reputed not to have left his cell for thirty years and the priest brought the eucharist to him.[60] Paphnutius was at pains to explain how the monks who lived in the furthest reaches of Upper Egypt fulfilled their obligations. The farouche Onophrius dwelled beyond the reach of any priest, but he assured Paphnutius that 'an angel of God' administered the sacrament to him and to every dweller in the far desert on Saturdays and Sundays. Paphnutius was told the same story by four brothers, originally from Oxyrhynchus, who lived their separate lives in the desert but came together on those two days, receiving communion from an angel. Paphnutius himself once shared in this remarkable experience.[61] In more normal circumstances, Abba Motius counselled one brother to avoid singularity and a reputation for not attending the *synaxis* or the *agape* ('love-feast') which sometimes followed it. This was, he added, the best formula for not being bothered by others. Isaac the Theban, however, fled back to his cell immediately after receiving the eucharist so as not to dissipate the illumination which he had received from the sacrament.[62]

Joseph of Panephysis advised the brothers that they should speak freely with visitors, but when alone should weep.[63] Hospitality was an important yardstick of the monk's fellowship with others, sometimes forcing him to eat when he would not normally do so. When some visiting cenobites thus imposed on a certain solitary, they asked him if this did not upset him, but he replied 'I am upset when I do my own will'. Another went further when a visitor apologized for forcing him to break his rule: 'My rule is to welcome you with hospitality and to send you on your way in peace.'[64] Such situations could, however, give rise to sparring between practitioners of different ways of life. One hermit who dutifully served food to some cenobitic visitors discerned that they thought that he was living a fairly easy life; he sent a coded message to the next hermit along their route, 'Don't water the vegetables'. The other took the hint and gave his visitors a harder time.[65] The monk was supposed not only to offer hospitality but to receive it humbly when out and about. A hermit who was fasting visited another who had prepared some vegetable soup for visitors; the first-named took a single pea and chewed it, only to be rebuked privately by his host, who told him, 'If you want to keep your own rule, stay in your cell and never go out.'[66]

For some monks, solitude was in effect the preparation for leadership. Macarius the Great was once asked by certain brothers why he was prepared to mix so easily with them. He believed that this was a gift that had been granted to him by God as a reward for twelve years of 'service', and he was not now prepared to give it up.[67] His apprenticeship in solitude, like Antony's twenty-year sojourn in the deserted fortress, had so strengthened him mentally that he could now enjoy the company of the brethren without disturbing his inner equilibrium. A hunter was once shocked to see Antony chatting companionably with other monks; the saint answered his rebuke by inviting him to draw his bow and then to draw it again and then again. The hunter objected that the bow would snap and Antony replied that it was just so with the brethren if they were stretched beyond endurance.[68]

The obligation to associate with others sat more easily, however, on certain individuals. John the Dwarf assured a visitor that 'even if the whole of Scetis came to see me they would not separate me from the love of Christ', but others were less sanguine.[69] The past history of recruits to the ascetic life, as well as their individual temperaments, could help to determine what attitude they adopted to solitude. Arsenius, a refugee from Roman high society, needed to retain a few creature comforts, but his manner and style of life were otherwise austere. This may have been because he had to make a special effort to overcome the legacy of his former life, but it may equally well have been a latent severity and singularity of temperament that drove him to take up the option which (to the horror of Rutilius) the religious life was now offering. There are several testimonies to Arsenius' reluctance to meet people and, on one occasion, when asked why he avoided his fellows, he replied, 'God knows that I love you, but I cannot live with God and with other men.' This did not prevent him from attending the *synaxis*, and once he was put out when the brethren did not offer him his share of a bunch of withered dry figs on the presumption that he would not want it.[70]

The personality difference between Arsenius and the very approachable Abba Moses, a former slave and reputedly robber and even murderer, aroused contemporary comment. One observer asked God for an explanation: 'for Thy name's sake the one flees from men, and the other, for Thy name's sake, receives them with open arms'. He saw a vision of Arsenius in a boat on a river, accompanied in perfect peace by the Spirit of God, while Moses occupied another boat in the company of angels 'and they were all eating honey cakes'.[71] Moses' sociable and benevolent disposition however meant that he was so bothered by the brethren that he could get no peace. He sought advice from Macarius of Alexandria, who, perceiving that he was incapable of sending anyone away, advised him to retire to 'the interior desert', which he did. Moses is supposed to have declared that 'The man who flees and lives in solitude is like a bunch of grapes ripened by the sun, but he who remains among men is like an unripe grape'.[72]

Other individuals were temperamentally inclined to radical solitude. Theodore of Pherme, like Arsenius, was reluctant to meet people and was said to be 'like steel' when he did. 'The man who has learned the sweetness of the cell', he declared, 'flees from his neighbour, but not as though he despised him.'[73] A lesser figure, Isidore the

Priest, refused to go out to take a meal with another brother and, when visited, scuttled into the furthest corner of his cell so as to preserve the maximum distance from his visitor.[74] Sisoes, who received his monastic training at Scetis, found it overcrowded and departed for Antony's mountain, where he lived for seventy-two years. He was attended by a single disciple called Abraham who brought him his supplies from Pispir and was sometimes absent for considerable periods. During one of these absences, which lasted ten months, Sisoes went walking on the mountains and met a hunter who told him he had seen nobody for eleven months. At this Sisoes told himself 'You thought you had done something, but you have not even equalled this layman'. Apparently he accorded an innate spiritual value to the endurance of total solitude. In extreme old age he was forced to take up residence in the monastery of Clysma. Perceiving that this saddened him, a visitor pointed out that he would not now be able to cope in the wilderness. The old man replied: 'Was not the mere liberty of my soul enough for me in the desert?'[75] It may be fanciful to picture such an individual in, say, a Cluniac monastery of the twelfth century, but it is hard to think that he would not have found it acutely oppressive.

Not surprisingly, Sisoes valued silence, once declaring 'One form of pilgrimage is to keep the mouth closed'.[76] In later monastic history silence served to establish a kind of solitude for monks who spent their every hour, waking and sleeping, in the company of others. Abba Bessarion recommended silence to one brother who wanted to know how to conduct himself in the company of the brethren with whom he shared lodgings.[77] Macarius the Great dismissed an assembly at Scetis with the gnomic instruction to 'flee'. When the brethren asked whither they were supposed to flee, as they were already in the desert, he laid his finger to his lips and said, 'Flee that', retreating into his own cell and shutting the door.[78] Of Sisoes too we are told that when he was sitting in his cell he always closed the door; this may have been in allusion to Jesus' direction to avoid vainglorious self-advertisement when praying (Matthew 6:6).[79] Sometimes this text was interpreted metaphorically, as Cassian did:

> We pray in our room when we withdraw our hearts completely from the clatter of every thought and concern and disclose our prayers to the Lord in secret and, as it were, intimately. We pray with the door shut when, with closed lips and in total silence, we pray to the searcher not of voices but of hearts.[80]

If some of the great ascetics voluntarily emerged from their solitude from time to time, others found it breached willy-nilly when they acquired a reputation as wonder-workers. This happened to Antony and to others, among them Macarius the Great when he was living in Scetis. His answer was to build a tunnel from his cell half a mile long, with a cave at the end of it in which he could take refuge. Whenever a holy man was sought after in this way he needed assistants; Macarius had two disciples with him, one of whom coped with his visitors.[81] John of Lycopolis was visited on his mountaintop in the Thebaid by both Palladius and the party whose travels are related in the *History of the Monks*.[82] The approach to the hermitage was difficult, but it was so far from deterring hordes of suppliants that John authorized the building of a kind of reception area a little way from his cell, which Palladius said had been enlarged to accommodate about a hundred people and was opened on a Saturday and Sunday. The building and management of this hospice was clearly the responsibility of disciples. John's normal mode of receiving his visitors was to appear at the window of his cell, from which he rarely if ever emerged.

It was commonplace for senior monks to counsel younger men who were uncertain what form of life to adopt. This must sometimes have been an exasperating business. One particularly persistent questioner wondered whether he would not make better progress in a monastery than in the desert. He sought the opinions of Paphnutius, John the Dwarf and Arsenius in turn: they were unanimous that he must stay in his cell, not bothering too much about how much he ate, drank or slept. John was even prepared to advise that he should not pray, provided he stayed where he was.[83] In contrast, Joseph of Panephysis was once asked by a certain brother whether he should leave the monastery to live as a solitary, and replied that he should adopt whatever kind of life gave him peace. When the brother replied that he was at peace both in the monastery and alone, Joseph understandably intimated that he really had to make his own decision.[84] Theodore of Pherme was rather more forthright. An inmate of Cellia was ill at ease in his solitude and sought Theodore's advice. He advised him to 'be more humble in your aspirations, place yourself under obedience and live with others'. In due course the brother returned and told him that he could find no peace in the company of others, whereupon Theodore exclaimed, 'If you are not at peace either alone or with others, why have you become a monk? Is it not to suffer trials?' For himself, he added, perhaps with some complacency, he had been a monk for seventy years against the younger man's eight, and had not had a day's peace the whole time.[85]

This same Theodore refused to give any instructions to a disciple who was living with him, but always set the table himself: 'Am I a cenobite, that I should give him orders?'[86] Yet he was prepared to advise that someone who could not cope with solitude should place himself under obedience. Some saw obedience itself as among the greatest of virtues. Abba Rufus declared: 'He who remains sitting at the feet of his spiritual father receives a greater reward than he who lives alone in the desert.'[87] The reasoning was simple. The hermit followed his own will, just as the charitable person also did what gave him pleasure, whereas obedience entailed the sacrifice of will itself. Poemen said that the cenobitic life exacted humility, obedience and hard work, and warned a brother who wanted to live in 'the monastery' that 'you will not have the right even to drink a single cup there'.[88] 'He who dwells with brethren', said Matoes, 'must not be square, but round, so as to turn himself towards all.' He himself lived in solitude because of his weakness: 'those who live in the midst of men are the strong ones'.[89]

There were contrary views. At Shmoun in the Thebaid the monks liked to talk about their forebears (as they believed them to be), Elijah and John the Baptist. The future hermit Onophrius listened and asked the elders

> My fathers, aren't those who live in the desert the elect, more so than we? Look, we see each other every day, and we gather together for worship. When we're hungry we have the benefit of food prepared for us; when we're thirsty we have the benefit of water to drink. When we're weak the brothers help us and when we want a plate or a pot to eat from we serve each other out of love for God. Where will those who live in the desert on account of God find anyone if they run into trouble? Or if they are hungry where will they find food; if they are thirsty where will they find water to drink?[90]

This outburst could be read as an oblique repudiation of the counsel given in Ecclesiastes 4:10:

> Two are better than one, because they have a good reward for their toil. For if they fall, one will lift up the other; but woe to one who is alone and falls and does not have another to help. Again, if two lie together they keep warm; but how can one keep warm alone? And though one might prevail against another, two will withstand one.

Often reduced to 'woe to one who is alone and falls and does not have another to help', this saying was constantly on the minds and the lips of later monastic counsellors. To Onophrius, however, the dangers and deprivations of the genuinely eremitical life demonstrated its self-evident superiority, and he proceeded to act on this conviction, retreating into the remote desert.

Many hermits were aware of the hazards of self-determination. It was important not to make a fetish of self-imposed rules or to lay overmuch stress on mere ascetic achievement. John, abbot of a great monastery, went to visit his dear friend Paësius, who had been living in the desert for forty years. Asked what good it did him to live thus detached and undisturbed, Paësius replied that since he had lived in solitude the sun had never seen him eating; John responded that, for himself, it had never seen him angry.[91] Self-deception was all too easy. An unnamed brother who was dwelling in a community found that he was prey to anger, and resolved to leave and to live by himself, for (he thought) this would remove the causes of his irritability. He therefore took up residence in a cave. One day he filled his water jug and put it on the ground only for it to fall over. This happened again and then again, whereupon he picked it up and smashed it. At this he realized that 'Wherever you live you need effort and patience and above all God's help', and returned to his community.[92]

The belief expressed by one *abba*, that 'If you have not first of all lived rightly with men, you will not be able to live rightly in solitude',[93] would become part of the orthodoxy of western monasticism. Cassian was perhaps the major conduit through which this stream of thought passed westwards. In the nineteenth *Conference*, Abba John speaks of those who become 'so savage due to the unbroken silence of the desert that they are utterly distraught at the society of human beings'. This was evidently not a good thing and it was to be attributed to imperfect previous training in the monastery. Such people would not truly understand why they were in the desert and would mistakenly think that the mere rejection of human society was the height of religious perfection.[94]

Later monastic writers also made much of the virtue of stability, often meaning by this permanent residence in one place. The fathers were unanimously in favour of dogged perseverance in the cell: fasting, work, even prayer might be neglected, but the monk must not give in to discouragement, restlessness or the temptation to seek salvation outside the cell, whether this was in a cave, in the desert or within a *cenobium*. Stability of place reflected and encouraged stability of mind. One of the few women whose sayings are recorded, Syncletica (also sometimes called Matrona), recommended that if one found oneself in a monastery one should stay there, as a hen stays on her eggs which otherwise grow cold and fail to hatch. Similarly, 'as long as we are in the monastery, obedience is preferable to asceticism. The one teaches pride, the other humility'.[95] She further underlined the moral:

> There are many who live in the mountains and behave as if they were in the town, and they are wasting their time. It is possible to be a solitary in one's mind while living in a crowd, and it is possible for one who is a solitary to live in the crowd of his own thoughts.

Religious thinkers and others in many ages have played with the idea of creating a 'virtual solitude' in one's own head, arguably an indispensable technique for one who aspires to live the contemplative life in community. There is another version of Syncletica's dictum:

> Many solitaries living in the desert have been lost because they live like people in the world. It is better to live in a crowd and want to live a solitary life than to live in solitude and be longing all the time for company.[96]

The point of real solitude was not that it was inherently virtuous but that, rightly used, it facilitated the pursuit of virtue. Three friends became monks, one taking on the role of a peacemaker, the second choosing to visit the sick and the third embracing solitude. The first two found themselves worn out and disheartened and went to see the third. He listened to their troubles and then poured some water into a basin, inviting them to look into it. After a while he pointed out to them how clear it had become, so that they saw themselves mirrored in it: 'So it is with anyone who lives in a crowd: because of the turbulence he does not see his sins; but when he has been quiet, above all in solitude, then he recognizes his own faults.'[97]

The modern reader may well be struck by the consonance of much that the desert fathers have to say with the reflections of (for example) Seneca on the philosophic way of life. Seneca favoured stability in one place, which he saw as more important than what that place was like, and spoke of the moral perils of withdrawal from human society. The fathers too appreciated both the threats and the promises of solitude. It carried with it the risks of depression, self-indulgence in the senses of both laxity and excessive asceticism, self-deception and pride. On the other hand it made possible tranquillity, silence, self-knowledge and the uninterrupted contemplation of God. The monks of the desert left to posterity a rich legacy of reflections on the uses and indeed the meanings of solitude; and they inaugurated the long debate about the respective virtues of the solitary and the cenobitic lives.

3

The Western Desert

When a twelfth-century Cistercian spoke of the 'desert' which was the monk's proper habitat he did not have sand-dunes or date palms in mind, as we perhaps too readily tend to do. Unless he had been a pilgrim to the east, it is unlikely that he could have imagined such terrain. The physical characteristics of the 'desert' were of merely secondary importance for him, as for his Egyptian or Syrian spiritual ancestors. Heat by day, cold by night and shortage of water added usefully to the privations the latter had had to endure, but northern wind, cold and wet could do just as well. The *eremos* of the Greek sources, while sometimes rendered as *desertum* in the Latin the western monk read or heard, was also sometimes simply translated as *solitudo*. *Eremos*, *solitudo* and *desertum* alike described a condition as much as a kind of place.

Monastic solitude in the west gradually came to be understood almost exclusively as collective withdrawal from 'the world'. As an individual the monk was more completely screened from lay society (in theory, at least) than many of the desert-dwelling fathers had been, but he was also more completely exposed, at every moment of the day, to the company of his fellows. The individual isolation which some of the early monks had cultivated gradually ceased to be part of the normal monastic experience. The belief that the eremitical life was only for a qualified elite, and that entry to it should be tightly rationed and controlled, became characteristic of medieval western monasticism in later ages. The cenobitic choice was believed to bear the seal of approval of the desert fathers, largely because John Cassian, in transmitting their wisdom to future generations of monks, had tended to emphasize their teaching on discretion and obedience, for which the settled community provided the most obvious framework. Submission to the direction of a superior offered the best guarantees against self-will, whether that tended towards laxity or ascetic extremism.

It is not to be supposed that monasticism developed as it did in the west simply because of an ideological conviction in favour of cenobitism. Complex factors were involved, among them the development of the post-Roman agrarian economy and the involvement of great landowners, from kings and queens downwards, as patrons of monastic foundations.[1] Monks and nuns came to be more intimately involved in the political and economic structures of kingdoms and other territorial lordships than the loosely organized communities of the late antique east had been. The author of the *History of the Monks* wrote of the holy men of Egypt that 'the people depend upon the prayers of these monks as if on God himself'.[2] In the medieval west, monasteries took on this collective function within a different social and political framework. The monks fought against the devil as Antony had fought, but in a body and with the weapons of the liturgy, on behalf not only of themselves and their community but of patrons, benefactors and the world at large.

The authority of monastic superiors also took on a more sharply defined character. An abbot was supposed to be the spiritual guide and director of his monks as the senior monks of the desert had been, but no less was he a commanding officer whose word was law. The military metaphor is not idle. For much if not all of the medieval period the ruling class of western society was also its military class. The oft-quoted threefold division of society into 'Those who fight, those who pray and those who work', even if it never worked as tidily as it sounds, implicitly allotted a structural role to the monk which, although it was by definition quite distinct from that of the warrior, could easily be interpreted by analogy with it, especially if monks were the brothers, nephews and sons of fighting men. The order of cenobites, according to St Benedict, were 'fighting under a rule and an abbot'.[3] Given that an abbot was not infrequently a member of a great noble family, the manager of considerable landed estates and even called upon to attend at court, it may well sometimes have seemed that he was as much a representative of and participant in public authority as he was a member and product of a specifically religious society. The same, with obvious modifications, could also be said of female religious superiors.

This state of affairs took a long time to develop, and it is important not to exaggerate its rigidity. The paths of the hermit or of the recluse remained available to those who were determined to take them, but diverged more sharply from those of the monk or nun than had originally been the case in the late Roman east. For four centuries or more after the transplantation of the ideals of eastern monasticism to the west by Cassian and others, the organizational structure of religious communities remained loose by comparison with what it was to become, although the strong tendency, in both west and east, was to bring the community within the bounds of a single enclosure. The Carolingian rulers, striving to create a more ordered society under their command, were disposed to favour monastic reforms which tended towards a standardized observance. Gradually not only the written codes by which monks lived, which more and more commonly came to mean the sixth-century Rule of St Benedict, but the architectural layout within which they lived came to reflect and indeed facilitate this trend.

Benedict began the Rule with a brief account (c. 1) of the various classes of religious men. This owed much to the earlier discussions of Cassian and Jerome. The hermit, Benedict believed, must not be a beginner. He should serve a long apprenticeship in the cenobitic life and go forth thus fortified 'from the ranks of the brethren to the single combat of the hermit (*fraterna ex acie ad singularem pugnam heremi*)', managing henceforth without any human assistance. There were two detestable species of monk. The so-called Sarabaites lived 'enclosed in their sheepfolds' but 'without a shepherd', with no law except their own pleasure: 'whatever they think or choose, they call holy'. This might have served as a pejorative description of some loosely organized monasteries, in east or west, which did not have what Benedict would have regarded as a clear structure of command. He was expressing here, in heightened form, anxieties about the perils of self-determination which, as we have seen, were not unknown to the desert fathers. Worse still were the Gyrovagues who wandered 'from monastery to monastery (*per diversorum cellas*)', as some eastern monks had done and as Celtic monks also sometimes did.[4] They too were given up to the indulgence of their own wills. Benedict turned with relief to speak of 'the mighty race of the cenobites (*coenobitarum fortissimum genus*)'.

Benedict had a clear vision of the monastery as a stable and enclosed community. 'If it is possible', he declared in c. 66 of the Rule, 'the monastery should be so constituted that everything necessary, that is, water, mill, garden and different crafts (*artes*) can be provided within the monastery.' In c. 4 he says that 'The workshops (*officina*) where we diligently do all these things are the monastic enclosure (*claustra monasterii*) and stability in the community (*stabilitas in congregatione*)'. Benedict refers in passing to a number of specialized workshops or store-places (kitchen, cellar, *vestiarium*) but he often prescribes an activity without suggesting that there is a defined or specialized setting for it. The community is to be called together 'as often as there is anything important to be dealt with' (c. 3) but it is not stated where (in the developed monastic plan it would be the chapter house). After supper 'they should all sit together' (*sedeant omnes in unum*) to listen to holy reading, which should preferably be taken from 'the *Conferences* of Cassian or the *Lives of the Fathers*'. Then all together were to say compline (c. 42). A time is allocated to private reading (the *lectio divina*, c. 48), but no specific place. The seniors who are to see that it is being done properly are merely enjoined 'to go around the monastery' (*circumeant monasterium*). The monk was permitted to read on his bed during the post-prandial rest period, but he was to do so quietly so as not to disturb the others.

That Benedict prescribed communal eating arrangements may be inferred from what he says (c. 38) about the single monk who was to be appointed every week to read to the other brethren at mealtimes, but he gives no name to the room in which the meal (itself called *refectio*) was taken. An excommunicated monk was deprived of participation or fellowship in the monks' 'table (*mensa*)' (c. 24); in more serious cases (c. 25) he was suspended from both the table and the oratory. A little more precision is possible in respect of sleeping, the care of the sick and the reception of guests. Benedict says that the monks should sleep, one to a bed, 'in one place' (c.22), but he recognizes that the numbers of monks may not permit this to be in a single apartment and he does not use the term 'dormitory'. The all-purpose term *cella* does duty instead and the premises allocated to the sick, which would later be called the infirmary, also consist of a *cella* (c. 36).

The guest-house is similarly referred to (cc. 53, 58) as the *cella hospitum*. This, significantly, was to be served by a separate kitchen which was also the abbot's; this requirement that the abbot should eat with guests away from the community can be seen as the germ of the separate suites of lodgings which were later assigned to monastic superiors. The purpose was not simply to privilege the abbot, but to do honour to guests while preserving the seclusion of the monks. There were other *cellae*: one for the novices (c. 58) and one near the gate of the monastery for the wise old man who was to be stationed there (c. 66). There is no reference to cells for individual monks. It may be observed in this connection that Benedict seems to have envisaged that if the monk wanted to pray privately or individually (*peculiariter*), he would do so in the church (c. 52). He directed that the monks should leave the church promptly and in good order after the completion of the office so that any brother who wished to pray could do so.

If life and prayer were above all communal, punishment, as already noted, consisted first and foremost in exclusion from the community. The guilty party received his meal alone after the other brothers had eaten (c. 24). If he was suspended also from the church no one was to associate with or talk to him at all; he was to perform the work enjoined on him alone and take his meals alone (c. 25). The connotations of solitude are mostly negative; for the monk it means deprivation, for the hermit danger.

It would not be easy to infer from the Rule the picture of Benedict as a determined solitary which is given in the second book of the *Dialogues* attributed to Gregory the Great.[5] Authentic or not, this picture of the hermit turned monastic patriarch has a certain congruence with the lives of some of the desert fathers, which is unsurprising, as the *Dialogues* were written to provide a western equivalent of the *Vitae Patrum*. Benedict is supposed to have begun his religious life as a solitary, first living with his old nurse near the church of St Peter at Affile and then moving alone into 'the desert' at Subiaco. There was at least one monastery not far away and Benedict was well enough known to the inmates to be asked to become abbot. Having alienated the brethren by his strictness (and having survived a poisoning attempt) he returned joyfully to his 'solitude', or, to be more exact, 'alone, under the eye of the Onlooker from above, he dwelt with himself'. Gregory's interlocutor expresses puzzlement about the meaning of this phrase, which (whether or not Gregory intended it) echoes the *secum morari* of Seneca's second epistle to Lucilius, a commendation of stability in both residence and reading. In reply, Gregory explains the nature of true solitude as the preservation of that spiritual integrity which is imperilled by bad company: Benedict 'kept himself inside the cloister of his thought' while sometimes transcending himself when rapt in contemplation.[6]

Despite this retreat into himself, Benedict was soon founding monasteries in the vicinity and coming to be regarded as a supreme trainer of monks and educator of the young. Such glimpses as the *Dialogues* afford of his monastic setting as the author believed it to have been, suggest still a flexible pattern. There are references to individual cells for other monks as well as for Benedict himself,[7] but in one story the saint accommodates a visiting abbot in the lower room of the 'tower' at Cassino where he himself goes to rest, while their disciples sleep in 'a larger building' in front of the tower.[8] Eating arrangements are not made clear but, when planning a new foundation at Terracina, Gregory's Benedict uses the word 'refectory', which does not occur in the Rule.[9]

A similar fluidity seems to have characterized the monastic settlements which began to appear in the further reaches of north-western Europe. An Egyptian monk, transplanted in the sixth century to the island of Iona, off the west coast of Scotland, might have been disconcerted by the climate but would have found certain familiar features in the life lived by St Columba (d. 597) and his brethren, as it was described about a century later by the saint's biographer Adomnán.[10] Columba himself had both a hut (*tuguriolum*) raised on legs, which served as the workroom where he copied books,[11] and a 'house' or 'lodgings' where he slept.[12] Like many of the Egyptian fathers he had a servant, Diarmait, on hand, but other monks might sit, stand or study by him while he worked. It was normal in Irish monasticism for the abbot to have private accommodation, a mark of office and authority.[13]

If the abbot was a saint, an intruder might become the startled witness of the divine visitations he received in his lodgings. One night Columba's 'foster-son' Berchán disobeyed his injunction not to come to his hut and, looking through the keyhole, saw a 'heavenly vision' filling the house. A very similar story was told of Comgall, abbot of Bangor in Ulster: his personal servant, having settled him for the night and himself returned to the dormitory, thought he would go back to see if the saint was asleep and saw a great light filling the cell.[14] These private audiences with heavenly visitants depended on the saint's ability to achieve at least temporary solitude, and Columba had two ways of obtaining this: retirement into his own lodgings or into 'a place secluded from other people where he could pray alone' in the 'wilder parts of the island'. On one such occasion of retreat he gave strict orders that he was not to be followed, but a monk who was 'an artful scout' disobeyed and saw the saint in conference with angels.[15] This kind of story, told already of the desert fathers, was a hagiographic commonplace, often rounded off (as here) by the saint's stern direction to the witness that he should not disclose what he had seen until the saint himself was dead.

There were important communal buildings at Iona as at other Irish monasteries, which usually possessed a 'great house' where the brethren gathered for meals and other purposes. Adomnán pictures Columba 'sitting by the fire in the monastery' with another monk not far away from him reading a book; this would have been in the 'great house' of Iona.[16] The brethren at Iona apparently slept in 'chambers', but it has been suggested that these were cubicles within a common dormitory, for one morning Columba was able to address all the monks together while they were putting on their shoes to go out to their appointed tasks.[17] Other Irish monasteries are known to have had dormitories, as Comgall's at Bangor apparently did; there is also a reference to a refectory there.[18] Such apartments, if they were able to accommodate all the members of the community, were presumably comparable to those which Benedict knew or envisaged. They probably did not follow a standard plan but were disposed around an open space (not yet a symmetrically arranged cloister) which separated them from the church.[19]

In some Irish monasteries, the monks had individual cells, of which archaeological evidence has been found at several sites, although Adomnán makes no specific mention of them at Iona. Such cells might be used for any or all of the monks' activities; they accorded the occupant a degree of privacy, for example at night, which was unusual in early medieval society, but they may not always have been particularly comfortable or desirable.[20] Munnu, abbot of Taghmon, one day visited a member of the community who was 'a virtual hermit' (*quasi heremita*) and had a cell apart, which was also a carpenter's shop, for he was an expert woodworker and had a kiln in the cell for drying wood.[21] There are occasional references to separate 'cells' for particular groups, such as students or older monks.[22] Solitary living created some very specific problems. Sitting at the table alone in his cell the young St Ciaran said 'Benedicite', but in the absence of anyone to respond 'Dominus' he refused to eat anything. This went on until on the third day a voice from heaven supplied the response and then told him that it was sufficient for a solitary man to bless his food in the name of God and then eat.[23]

As in Egypt, contrasting imperatives were obeyed by contrasting personalities. St Coemgen, the founder of Glendalough, is depicted as a determined solitary who spent one period of indeterminate duration living in a hollow tree. Once he had established a 'great monastery' in his chosen valley he departed from it and built himself a little house a mile from the main site, with strict orders that the brothers should not seek him out except for urgent cause. He is credited with command over wild beasts who took water from him as the wild gazelles had taken it from Theon in the Egyptian desert. On several occasions Coemgen had to be hauled back into community life from an excessively harsh self-imposed isolation.[24] By contrast, St Cronan gave absolute priority to the demands of hospitality. Once some travellers were unable to find his monastery and had to spend the night on the open road; learning about this, he informed his monks that he would no longer inhabit a 'desert place where guests and the poor cannot easily find me'. The result was the foundation of Ros Cree.[25]

With the spread of monasticism came the literature and ideas of the fathers. The most celebrated of the early English hermits, Guthlac (d. 714), went from an early career as a warrior to the life of a monk at Repton in Mercia. After two years there he decided to seek 'the desert'.[26] His inspiration for this move was his reading about the 'solitary life of the first monks' (*priscorum monachorum solitaria vita*). The desert, in eastern England around the year 700, meant the fens, where fog rather than pitiless sun was likely to be the enemy. Guthlac had to take a fisherman's boat to reach his destination, the island of Crowland. Not long after his arrival he suffered a severe attack of depression, from which he was rescued when he called upon his patron St Bartholomew, and he then had to repel the bogus advice he was offered by two devils who quoted Moses, Elijah, Christ and the monks of Egypt at him in an effort to get him to cripple himself with fasting. Guthlac is clearly intended to recall the example of Antony and the rest in this very different setting. He was beset by devils in the shape of wild beasts, but he also exhibited command over real wild creatures – jackdaws whose mischievous kleptomaniac habits he proved able to control, swallows who would not build their nests without his permission, fish who came at his call to be fed. He had a number of companions: one, Beccel, was tempted by a devil to slay him when he came to tonsure him as he did every twenty days. Suitably reproved, he survived to witness and describe the saint's death.

There was no need for hermitages such as Guthlac's to follow a standard pattern, although in their simplicity they were likely more or less to resemble one another. Monastic architecture, on the other hand, gradually developed to become a suitable container for a life lived by day and night according to the Benedictine Rule as it achieved ever more widespread acceptance and high-level backing from the Carolingians and other rulers as the industry standard for monasticism. An early ninth-century description of the abbey of Fontenelle speaks of a dormitory 208 feet long and a refectory. Both ran from north to south towards the abbey church and they were linked by a building, evidently running from west to east parallel to the church, called the *domus maior*, which seems to have contained a warming-room and a 'chamber' of uncertain purpose. These three buildings were fronted by porticoes; the result was in effect a cloister, although the arrangement of the buildings around it was not quite the one which later became familiar and the ensemble lay to the north of the church rather than the more customary (though not invariable) south. Abbot Ansegis (822–33) in addition built to the north of the church a *domus*, in effect a chapter-house, in which the brethren took counsel.[27]

The cloister, the arcaded quadrangular walkway bordered on one side by the church and on the others by the various monastic offices, is perhaps the most characteristic feature in our mental picture of a monastery, but no such feature was to be found in the monasteries known to St Benedict himself in the sixth century or to the other monks of his day. Although the Latin word *claustrum* is used in early sources, it often means the monastic enclosure as a whole, just as we still use 'cloister' to signify the monastic life in general. The cloister seems to have evolved only gradually to meet the requirements of the Rule and there is some debate as to when it can first be certainly identified, although the much-discussed St Gall plan, which is loosely contemporary with the regime of Ansegis at Fontenelle, certainly includes one.[28]

It is not altogether surprising that when, around 850, Hildemar, monk of Corbie, composed a commentary on the Rule at the Lombard monastery of Civate, he felt the need to clarify and amplify St Benedict's topography. It was by now possible for him to suppose that when he had used the word *claustra* Benedict meant (sometimes, at least) the cloister and he quoted a current view that it should be at least one hundred feet square. He also pointed out that Benedict could not have meant the infirmary to consist of only one *cella*, a single apartment. The sick must be able to vomit, eat, evacuate their bowels or, indeed, die in suitable accommodation; and the abbot must have a separate cell so that, if sick himself, he could talk to visitors without disturbing other invalids. This personal infirmary would be suitable for the entertainment of convalescent monks who could get out of bed to eat.[29]

With the passage of time the monk came to inhabit a more developed and articulated set of spaces than virtually any other member, lay or ecclesiastical, of early medieval society. In the Benedictine framework the excesses of fasting and other bodily austerities which were open to solitaries, including the avoidance of sleep, were brought under multiple controls. There was not only the authority of the abbot and other superior officers but the constant presence of one's fellows to reckon with. Communities organized in this way took on an increasing liturgical burden which was, in large part, a condition of the close relationships between monasteries and the landowning families that provided not only the greater part of their endowments but a significant part of their personnel. Such patrons sought to share in the prayers of the monks and often to receive burial among them, sometimes taking the habit towards the end of their lives. The monastic endeavour was focused at least as much on liturgical intercession and the performance of the eucharist as on individual spiritual development, and monastic buildings (including churches of increasing size and splendour) reflected that priority.

One symptom of this enlarged secular involvement was the practice of the oblation of children, often the children of patrons and benefactors, who were deemed to be as irrevocably bound to the community as if they had entered it of their own free will.[30] Many of the desert fathers were deeply suspicious of the presence of children within monasteries; but St Benedict devoted a chapter of the Rule (c. 59) to the reception of oblates and in several other chapters acknowledged the presence of 'boys' and provided for their special requirements.[31] An early medieval monastery or nunnery would commonly embrace both children and grown individuals who had not chosen the religious life and had equally little choice about how they were to live it. Whatever their social origins, this was the only mode of existence they had ever known; their recollections of secular domesticity may well have been hazy. Monasteries were never populated solely by oblates, however, and the impulses to reform and reorganization which so strongly marked western monasticism from the tenth century onwards were mostly driven by men with varied previous life histories, who entered the cloister as adults in fulfilment of their individual religious needs.

There were several hazards in the intimate involvement with lay patrons and benefactors which came to characterize western monasticism after the seventh century. At worst it could lead to the effective secularisation of monasteries and their landed endowments and to the dissolution of the common life into a looser form of corporate organization. So-called monks lived in individual accommodation, disposing of their share of community funds as private property and eventually ceasing to regard themselves, or to be regarded, as monks at all. The capacity of monasticism to provide a framework for the development of the interior spiritual life was obviously seriously impaired in these circumstances, but that was not the only problem. For many reformers the great evil was subjection to secular authority, which both dissipated monastic economic resources and destroyed the common life which guaranteed the performance and quality of the prayer that it was the purpose of a monastery to offer. Founded early in the tenth century, the great Burgundian abbey of Cluny was made subject to no authority except that of the pope.[32] Cluny stood for monastic independence from secular toils and it affirmed the necessity of the common life, but this was a life focused with increasing intensity on the performance of the liturgy, for which the architecture of its successive great churches provided a fitting receptacle. For the individual monk the long hours spent in choir amounted to a demanding way of life, not least physically.

Cluny was not the only tenth-century model of monastic reform, but in the course of time its influence came to be immense. Most contemporary reformers seem to have been looking in the same general direction. The re-establishment of the common life was their chief priority and they assumed the central importance of the liturgy; after all, St Benedict himself had said that nothing was to come before the *Opus Dei*. There was clearly no thought that the *Rule* itself was being violated by these trends and the eremitical impulse was very far from extinct. The call of 'the desert' and solitude had to be reinterpreted in a variety of changing geographical and social settings in which the communal ideal was by and large dominant.

One way of achieving this end was to enclose the aspirant solitary in a *cella retrusionis* built, in effect, on to a monastic church. Grimlaic, author of a rule for such solitaries written perhaps c.900, states firmly that 'monk or solitary, it's one and the same'. Grimlaic had the precepts and practices of the Desert Fathers very much in mind, but although his solitaries were and remained members of the monastic community in which they had served their probation, his counsels for their accommodation and way of life in many respects look forward to the rules for anchorites, male and female, of a later age.[33] The *cella retrusionis* was to be small and strictly enclosed against the outside world. It was to provide for all the solitary's needs. If he was a priest it should include an oratory consecrated by the bishop and adjacent to the church, with a window which permitted participation in the liturgical and prayer life of the brethren but which also had curtains to prevent unwonted intrusion. The cell should also incorporate a garden in which the solitary could both cultivate vegetables and take the air, which was understood to be beneficial. Outside the enclosure (*septa retrusionis*) proper, there was to be another *cellula* in which the solitary's disciples could gather at appropriate times to minister to his needs through the window.[34]

This solitary's solitude then was far from absolute or uninterrupted. It was Grimlaic's strong recommendation that two or three should dwell in adjacent cells, all of them contiguous to the church, with windows permitting communication and mutual exhortation between the solitaries. Thus the well-known hazards of real solitude could be avoided.[35] Grimlaic had little time for solitaries who wanted merely to retreat into a life of private study and uninterrupted quiet; he who had received great gifts from God was under an obligation to take on a teaching role.[36] He should also entertain pilgrims or the poor at his 'little table' when he had the means to do so. These would be derived from his manual labour or the offerings of the faithful.[37]

The intermeshing of the personal impulse to eremitical solitude with the reform of cenobitic monasticism can be illustrated by the life-histories of some of the individuals who were involved in the refoundation in 933 of the ancient abbey of Gorze, originally founded by St Chrodegang in 748 a few miles west of Metz. The story of its refoundation is told in the *Vita* of its second abbot, John of Gorze (d. 974).[38] John was born to prosperous parents in the rural surroundings of Pont à Mousson, now a small industrial town on the east bank of the Moselle between Metz and Nancy. His story unfolds within an approximately equilateral triangle formed by three cities, Metz and Toul on the Moselle and Verdun on the Meuse. This triangle lay on the south-western edge of one of the major regions of European medieval urbanization, which included the southern Netherlands and the Rhineland. Tiny though we might think these cities, it seems that for some at least of their inhabitants they were quite big enough to threaten their spiritual calm.

John was educated for a time at the abbey of St Mihiel on the Meuse south of Verdun (a reminder that in addition to nurturing oblates some monasteries, at least, also took in boarders who received their education from the monks). For some time after his father's death he managed the paternal household, obtaining practical experience which was valuable to him later on, but eventually he embraced the clerical life in Metz, serving a church which belonged to the nunnery of St Peter and living in a house nearby. Here he got to know the saintly young nun Geisa. Accidentally catching a glimpse of the hair-shirt she wore under her upper garment was for John a life-changing experience, but he was puzzled as to what next step to take, for scarcely any monastery, 'even in Italy', properly observed the regular life. Inspired by two men who were famed in Metz for 'continent life', Roland, who presided over the singing school at the church of St Stephen, and Warimbert, a priest at St Salvator, he withdrew into what he intended to be permanent enclosure in a cell (*retrusionis cellula*) at St Salvator, but became discontented with its setting 'in the middle of the city' and hankered after 'the deeps of the forest'.

It was in this unsettled period of his life that John became acquainted with another learned recluse, Humbert, who had established a *reclusoria* for himself at Verdun, some forty miles to the west of Metz. Here Humbert had gained such a reputation that religious women of the town came to receive 'the word of doctrine or other instruction' from his window. John enrolled himself among his disciples and henceforth abstained from eating flesh. It was while frequenting Humbert that John got to know about a hermit called Lanbert who lived in the forest of Argonne to the southwest of Verdun and decided to join forces with him. In so doing he made a false move, for Lanbert

> was completely rustic in behaviour and knowledge (*moribus et scientia rusticanus*) and but for the fact that the enormous labours which he inflicted on himself, to an excessive and unreasonable degree, earned him some religious merit, he seemed totally stupid and savage (*stolidus et agrestis*), to the extent that if any weaker-minded persons happened to see him they could scarcely contain their laughter. The last thing he thought of was covering his body and private parts; similarly his way of eating and drinking were far removed from that of other mortals.

Lanbert was excessively filthy and his behaviour was unpredictable and impulsive. He would suddenly leave the hermitage and wander around the neighbouring villages and towns, returning as suddenly to his cell; he fasted immoderately, without a fixed timetable. The use of the adjectives *rusticanus* and *agrestis* to describe him, with their echoes of classical cultural attitudes, is entirely characteristic of the religious literature of the central middle ages. Whether or not Lanbert was actually illiterate, the contrast between him and the educated John was extreme. The spiritual man might abjure urban life (as John wished to do), but it was not in order to embrace barbarism, but rather to establish a kind of *urbs in rure*, as the devil complained that St Antony had done.

After a time in Lanbert's company John felt compelled to retreat to a cell of his own. Here he was visited by Humbert and a Breton called Andreas, a refugee from the incursions of the Vikings on his homeland. They prevailed upon him to abandon Lanbert and join with them in a pilgrimage to Rome, which also took in the shrine of the Archangel Michael on Monte Gargano in Apulia and (significantly) St Benedict's Monte Cassino. On their return, John and Humbert would have joined forces in the religious life had they been able to find 'a place suitable to their desires'. Pending the discovery of such a place, Humbert returned to Verdun and John stayed in his own house at Metz, where he lived a life indistinguishable from that of a monk, but with extreme discretion: all his austerities were confined 'to the interior of the house, with God alone as witness, and scarcely anyone in the household was aware' of them.

At this point another cast member is introduced, Einald, who was a recluse at Toul and had once been archdeacon of the church of that city. His cell was adjacent to 'the cloister of the clerks' (presumably the cathedral community). So far was he from dwelling in the wilderness that when he once heard a voice from heaven he thought it was the sound of boys reciting in the neighbouring schools. Here he spent 'three years of extreme and arduous continence, rarely going out except to celebrate mass in the church or for nocturnal prayer. He was content with just one servant who was sent out to get necessities'. Like John in his house at Metz, and indeed like any anchorite, Einald was dependent on the ministrations of others. He was surprised to receive a visit from Humbert, whom he knew to be leading a life of permanent enclosure at Verdun. Like John earlier, Humbert had been driven to abandon his cell by the desire to become a hermit, and he proposed to Einald that they should embrace this life together and thus 'serve God much better than in the city crowds, free from all the annoyances of men'. Einald agreed to Humbert's proposition and they took up residence in a clearing across the Moselle, but such was the 'awfulness of the place' that no amount of labour could make it habitable, nor could they obtain necessary supplies. No more than the desert fathers could a hermit near the Moselle live by prayer alone. By mutual agreement they returned to their respective cells, but stayed in touch.

It was at this point that Humbert mentioned John to Einald, remarking that he was an expert at keeping his activities secret from others. John was invited to meet them and described the life he was now living at Metz. He saw nobody outside a like-minded coterie which consisted of Geisa and some of the other nuns of St Peter's; Salecho, the clerk of St Martin's across the Moselle; and Randinus, priest of St Stephen's outside the southern gate of the city, where it seems they all frequently met because of the greater seclusion of the place. Roland and Warimbert, who had earlier inspired him, were dead. The events that led to the revival of the community at Gorze under the aegis of Adalbero, bishop of Metz, now unfolded. In 933 Einald became the first abbot, while John's earlier experience as a household manager was put to good use in his capacity as cellarer. Einald died around 968 and John succeeded him as abbot.

In praising John and his companions, the author of the *Vita* made the point that monasticism in the Mosan region, as elsewhere in the earlier tenth century, was in a decayed condition. Motivated individuals however were determined to satisfy their religious impulses, even if they encountered difficulties and frustrations in the process. John led a form of the religious life in his own house and the other Metz clerks with whom he associated were perhaps doing something similar. He, Humbert and Einald all spent periods in anchoritic cells and all made abortive attempts to become hermits. Whether Lanbert was the only hermit in the forest of Argonne when

John joined him is not clear. He does, however, seem to be the only person mentioned in the narrative who led a completely solitary existence. While he is not explicitly condemned for that reason, there is a strong implication that total isolation made a disordered way of life possible.

Gorze was situated in a forested area on the west bank of the Moselle; such a site probably answered the collective needs of a community which included former aspirants to eremitical solitude. Some individuals used the community as a staging-post on the way to a greater austerity. A former archdeacon of Metz, Blidulfus, after a period at Gorze, withdrew 'to the remoter parts of the Vosges' with a companion, Gundelach, who had once been a monk at Fulda. When he died Gundelach buried him in 'the oratory of his cell' and remained there until his own death. The reverse trajectory was followed by Angilramn, a would-be fugitive from Gorze, who returned in floods of tears and passed his time in a hut (*tugurium*), significantly likened to a *cella solitaria*, near the tomb of St Chrodegang. As soon as the communal *synaxis* was over he returned to this cell and shut the door, spending his nights and days in tears, groans and genuflexions. Angilramn was driven by penitence above all: he was seeking not freedom but an enclosure in which to expiate his faults.[39]

We get only a rather general impression from the *Vita* of what the settlement at Gorze was like. It seems that the previous buildings were ruinous and John is given a lot of the credit for managing the restoration of the site. Within four years all the monks' quarters 'within' were completed and he bent his mind 'to enclosing them all with an exterior wall like a castle (*in modum castri*)', hiring craftsmen from all quarters and completely girding the *claustrum* with a wall which is again likened to that of a 'castle'.[40] It looks as if *claustrum* here means the monastic buildings as a whole. There is a notably strong emphasis on the 'inside' and the 'outside'; the monks' collective solitude was girded against the outside world, to the extent that Gorze looked as if it could withstand assault. The buildings of another reformed monastery of the period, Fleury, were similarly contained *intra ambitum castri*. Here there was certainly a cloister, for a well-educated but presumptuous monk called Walter was once sitting in it with the others when he was seized by an impious compulsion to emend the copy of the Rule which he had in his hands.[41]

The eremitical impulses felt by individuals from a variety of backgrounds were an important source of monastic renewal. St Romuald (d. 1027) was described by his hagiographer and follower Peter Damian as an aristocrat with a taste for hunting, who even in his sinful youth saw the religious possibilities of the wilderness:

> As often as he found a pleasant spot in the woods, his spirit burned with desire for the desert (*eremi desiderium*) and he said to himself, 'Oh, how well hermits could have lived in the depths of these groves! How fitly could they find refuge here from all worldly perturbation!'[42]

Romuald's conversion was precipitated by his refusal to get involved in a murderous family feud, from which he took refuge in the church of Sant' Apollinare in Classe at Ravenna.[43] From this moment on he was in search of solitude in good earnest. His life centred on Ravenna and its region, but he is often remembered as the founder of Camaldoli near Arezzo in Tuscany, where he established six cells, each inhabited by a single hermit. In August 1027 the bishop of Arezzo granted the church of San Salvatore at Camaldoli to the hermit Pietro, whom Romuald had put in charge of the little group. Other gifts were attached to this grant, on condition that the brothers never 'transferred themselves to any life except the eremitical, solitary and contemplative' and never converted the holy place 'into a monastery of cenobites'.[44]

Romuald himself migrated from place to place, leaving behind him a number of foundations but no written rule or structure by which his successors could live in the longer term. One of his foundations was on Monte Pietralata, where, according to Peter Damian, Romuald spent seven years of enclosure and rigorous fasting in imitation of St Hilarion, attracting flocks of penitents who wanted to live in imitation of the Egyptian fathers.[45] Damian, born in 1007, was another native of Ravenna and entered the monastery of Fonte Avellana, on Monte Catria north-west of Gubbio, in 1035. Fonte Avellana, as described by Damian's biographer, did indeed somewhat resemble a recreation of Nitria in the Italian Apennine landscape. Some of the brethren lived near the church, two to a cell; others dwelled higher up the mountainside in strict seclusion, meeting with the others only on Sundays and principal feasts. The life lived by the professed monks was strictly contemplative and ascetic, for the brunt of the community's manual labour was borne by lay brothers; Damian himself was waited upon by a servant in his cell.[46]

Counsellors to those who undertook the solitary life rapidly realized that it could propose a number of knotty problems. Damian devoted a whole treatise to a question which he said he had been asked by 'followers of the eremitic life':

> whether, since they live alone in their cells, it is right for them to say *Dominus vobiscum, Jube, domne, benedicere*, and the like; and whether, despite the fact that they are by themselves, they should say the responses, as the custom of the Church demands.

(St Ciaran had had the same problem.) Damian concluded unequivocally that the solitary need have no fear on this account,

> for although he is separated in space from the congregation of the faithful, yet he is bound together with them all by love in the unity of faith; although they are absent in the flesh, they are near at hand in the mystic unity of the Church.[47]

This leads him into a eulogy of the cell, adorned with multiple metaphors: it is variously paradise, warehouse, market place, workshop, prison, bath, fishpool, bridal couch and more besides.

Damian was familiar with the cell as a physical reality; but he was also a convinced proponent of the Benedictine doctrine that the truly eremitical life could only be embraced under the most stringent safeguards. In his treatise *On the Perfection of Monks* he told the sad story of his scribe Silvester. The 'boy', as Damian called him, was actually engaged in taking down the treatise when the devil

> put it into his head that he should seek the solitude of the upper hermitage, where he would rarely, if ever, see any of his fellow men; when we offered him the chance of becoming a true recluse, however, he replied that he did not at all want to become a completely enclosed hermit, but wished to live somewhere where he could be free and alone, and his comings and goings would not be watched over.

Silvester interpreted his constant floods of tears as a sign of divine approval, and when he was in fact given permission to dwell in solitude, he 'cut himself off completely and used to wander in vagabond fashion to other places'. Finally he damaged a book which was precious to Damian and, fending off the punishment (imprisonment) which was due to him for this outrage, drew a knife and threatened to harm 'either himself or anyone else who came near him'.[48]

Poor Silvester, we may think, was totally unfitted to be a monk; probably emotionally unstable, he may even have been driven over the edge by the pressures of the life. What Damian saw at work was the prompting of the devil. Solitude, as the fathers of the desert well knew, gave scope to self-will. The liberty which Abba Sisoes had lamented when old age drove him back to the monastery could only be permitted to an elite few. The pleasures of freedom of movement might even need to be expiated:

> He who takes pleasure in an unaccustomed journey on horseback should confine himself within the narrow walls of his cell, and then the cloisters of the monastery will seem like a market-place to him.[49]

Damian insisted on the sovereign value of communal norms and strongly urged the monastic superior to conform to them:

> Do not shudder at the idea of dining at the monastic table, nor take pleasure in private banquets; you must not think that those who share with you the common table of the altar are unfit to partake of bodily nourishment with you.[50]

This note would be sounded with increasing desperation by critics of the later medieval religious life.

4

Living in the World

Throughout the world's history, ordinary individuals, male and female, have spent their lives in a temporal and spatial framework determined by the needs, wealth and social standing of the family into which they were born. The technologies at their disposal have limited not only the ways in which they can make a living but the ways in which they can spend their free time. In pre-modern society both depended to a much greater extent than they now do on constant face-to-face interaction with others. Few people in the early medieval domestic environment had much need, or for that matter desire or opportunity, to pursue the literate occupations which were usually performed by a professional clerical elite, including monks. Not only were the supply of books and the ability to read them restricted; so too was the lighting (not to mention the heating) which now makes private reading feasible by day and night. Leisure moments were passed either in the open air and in daylight, or in a domestic setting in which space, light and heat were shared. One could be either spectator or participant in pastimes involving physical activity, such as hunting, jousting, feasting or dancing; one could listen to music or story-telling. Conversation could take place anywhere between two people or more, and board games, including chess when it was introduced to Europe (by the tenth century), could be enjoyed equally privately. Chess is likely to have appealed to a social elite, including clergy, who possessed suitable domestic accommodation, and there is ample evidence, in manuscript illumination and elsewhere, that many women played it. While chess and other board games helped supply the need for ways of passing the time indoors and in bad weather, they also provided opportunities for gambling and sometimes outright violence.[1]

For the great, almost constantly surrounded by servants and suitors, the boundaries between private and public spaces could be very fluid. Einhard relates that Charlemagne saw only friends while he was dressing, but if the count of the palace informed him of an unresolved dispute he would order the parties to be brought before him at once and hear the case 'as if he were sitting in court'.[2] One might be disposed to regard this as a stock story illustrating the emperor ceaselessly at work as father of his people, but most early medieval government was centred on the household; a more formal 'court' would simply have taken place in another, more public apartment which was perhaps more regularly used for the purpose. The 'town houses' of lords great and small who resided habitually in the countryside might be so used. Aimon of Fleury related around 1100 how the rapacious Gauzfredus, lay advocate of a *villa* of the monks of Fleury, was in his house within the walls of Troyes hearing cases between the peasants when he was deservedly attacked by a rabid black dog.[3]

For centuries after the fall of Rome there were few buildings, churches apart, which were exclusively designed for the discharge of public functions. They multiplied first in non-monarchical states such as the Italian cities, where the need was felt to create a public space which did not belong to any one person or family but to the 'commune'. The building of public palaces does not antedate the later thirteenth century; earlier, urban magistrates used churches for their meetings. Down to the twelfth century the single most important figure in many Italian cities (as indeed elsewhere in Europe) was the bishop, and the palaces which manifested the bishop's presence in the city were complex and evolving combinations of the public and the residential.[4] Where monarchical regimes existed, the prince's personal and social existence could scarcely be disentangled from his exercise of power.

There was all the more reason therefore why he had to be visibly distinguished among the surrounding company. The isolation of the king on his throne visually singled out an individual on whom power had been conferred from on high. At the end of the tenth century, the young emperor Otto III, the son of a Byzantine princess, is said to have dined sitting alone at an almost semicircular table, slightly elevated above the rest of the company.[5] This is a far remove from privacy: the individual is quite deliberately exposed to view, yet isolated so as to accentuate his uniqueness. To some degree this was true of all who exercised power at any level. The prerogative of occupying a chair while others stood was (and sometimes still is) a significant marker which accounts, historically, for the word 'chairman', while 'individuals, including peasants, in their own homes might occupy a distinctive seat which they could not aspire to in their feudal lord's hall'.[6]

The more private side of Otto III's self-image is commemorated today in the magnificent gospel-book which was made for his personal use, and he is also recorded as having frequented Romuald and his monks.[7] His successor Henry II (in due course venerated as a saint) emulated him in both his patronage and his piety, and like him doubtless used his private apartments for prayer and devout reading. Like their Roman precursors and like their successors and other lesser lords for centuries to come, such men and their womenfolk inhabited a number of spaces hierarchically arranged from the most public to the most private. In the course of time, with the development of government and the multiplication of its personnel, a degree of physical separation between 'offices of state' and the ruler's dwelling-space, both private and ceremonial, came into being; but bureaucracy was only part of the business of ruling, which required almost constant exposure and accessibility to the people who mattered.

In this connection it is worth remembering that abbots as well as bishops were rulers, who not only commanded their communities but often belonged by birth to the ruling stratum of secular society and by virtue of their office remained in contact with it. In requiring them to dine with visitors, St Benedict saw them as the point of contact with the outside world. For monks, clergy and laity alike, sociability was not only a duty; it was taken for granted, as the Romans had taken it for granted, as a condition of membership in society, with all its benefits in terms of mutual support and protection. The framework of the lives of early medieval kings and nobles differed in a number of respects, however, from that of their Roman predecessors. They did not receive the same education and the material setting of their lives, in town and country, had also changed. With these changes came a whole scenic apparatus which formed the imaginative backdrop for centuries of European literature.

The social life evoked in *Beowulf* centres on Heorot, the magnificent 'mead-hall' built by Hrothgar the Dane, which is not only a building but, for the poet (or poets) and his audience, a symbol of social order itself. It is menaced by the monster Grendel who comes by night and devours the thegns who sleep within. One of their reactions is understandably to seek safer chambers (*bure*) among the outbuildings which clearly cluster around the hall but are not further described. Grendel has succeeded not only in getting easy meals but in disrupting the sociability of the community, indeed threatening society itself. When the hero Beowulf arrives to offer his services against the monster, he is received in the hall, which is perfectly safe by daylight. Its lord, Hrothgar, does not himself sleep there, but retires 'out of the hall' to share the bed of his consort Wealtheow, leaving Beowulf to make good his boasts, which he does by inflicting mortal wounds on Grendel in single combat in the mead-hall itself. Fortunately it is well built, for it trembles under the impact of their confrontation. When Hrothgar emerges in the morning to learn of the hero's triumph, it is from 'the woman's chamber' (*bryd-bure*) that he comes. Beowulf is feasted and congratulated in the hall which, it is for the moment presumed, he has delivered from mortal peril. Alas, on the following night Grendel's mother comes to take revenge for the destruction of her child, which she does by seizing the most beloved of Hrothgar's thegns. It is essential to the narrative that Beowulf should not be present when this happens; we are told parenthetically that he had been assigned lodgings 'elsewhere', but not precisely where and what they were.[8]

The pattern that is sketched here in a work which can perhaps be dated to the eighth century, although it took its final written form somewhat later, lasted through the medieval centuries and beyond. The lord's hall was the centre of conviviality and hospitality; it was also the place for solemn audience and the doing of justice and estate business, within which the master of the house displayed his availability and his superior status simultaneously. Great houses in England are not infrequently still simply called 'the Hall'. It was surrounded by other living rooms and also the specialized offices such as kitchens and stables, which, in monasteries and larger secular dwellings alike, were scattered around the domestic quarters. When, in the twelfth-century romance *Erec et Enide* by Chrétien of Troyes, Erec arrives at the house of Enide's father, an impoverished vavasour, she and her mother are summoned from a 'workshop' (*ouvreour*) where they have been busy at some unspecified task, probably weaving.[9]

For most of the medieval period, the users of written language and the small number of people whose lives they described disposed of a very limited range of terms to describe their living spaces. An unspecialized vocabulary reflected what was in general a somewhat unspecialised use of space, aided by the sparseness and portability of most furniture. Large beds were among the exceptions to the rule that few pieces of furniture occupied a fixed place.[10] The *literati* would have been familiar with the existence of classical words for the various components of a dwelling house but, although they continued in use in Latin texts, surprisingly few of them gave birth to vernacular derivatives.

Special words for dining-rooms, such as *cenaculum* or *triclinium*, sank virtually without trace. The former, which had already taken on the sense of an upstairs room in classical Roman usage, would have been familiar to the literate from the gospel accounts of the preliminaries to the Last Supper (in Italian *cenacolo* denotes a painting of that subject). The descendants of the monastic *refectorium* and *dormitorium* survive in institutional contexts. The word *cubiculum* was well known from both classical and biblical examples and much used in Latin texts, but it did not determine the vernacular terms that gradually came into being to designate bedchambers. For a long time, in fact, there was no word which exclusively meant 'bedroom'.[11] Most rooms which contained beds, even permanently, might also be used for other purposes than sleeping.

Foremost in frequency and importance among the words used to describe living rooms in general and bedrooms in particular were the late Latin *camera* and its descendants. A derivative of the Greek *kamara* (meaning a vault), *camera* was rarely used in classical Latin but has had a varied progeny in the modern European languages. The most familiar of its present English descendants is an abbreviation of *camera obscura*. This suggests its basic connotation of an enclosed space, which led to its use for any kind of private apartment or, suitably qualified, for one set aside for some specialized purpose, as still in a wide variety of terms from the German *Schatzkammer* (treasury) to the English 'torture chamber'. In French and Italian, *chambre* and *camera* remain standard words for bedrooms. They can be loosely contrasted with another class of terms which denote apartments in which either more public or more specialized activities are conducted or (such as *salle à manger* or *salle de bain*). For Chrétien de Troyes in the 1170s, the word *sale* clearly signifies the 'great hall'.

In the course of time other words came into being to describe private living-rooms. One of the earliest to designate the principal withdrawing- or sitting-room of a well-to-do household was the 'solar'.[12] The 'talking room', *parlatorium*, originated in the monastic setting, but this was formed from an Old French root which triumphed over the more authentically Latin (although not classical) *locutorium*. The parlour spread to lay society and both word and thing have lasted down to modern times in English. When scholars, clerical or lay, decided that they needed a room dedicated to the purposes of study and a special word with which to describe it, they gave a new meaning to a familiar Latin word and created vernacular equivalents for it.[13] 'Chamber' in its various linguistic incarnations remained an all-purpose term, loosely corresponding to the modern English word 'room'.[14] There were household servants who took their job descriptions from the apartments on which they attended; the poverty of Enide's father is underlined by the fact that he has no *chamberiere* in his employment.

In the history of English medieval royal government the *camera* became virtually a department of state, whose officers (headed by the chamberlain) were responsible for making certain types of payment on the king's behalf. This role obviously developed from the primitive function of the chamber as a store for valuables. References to the early medieval royal bedchamber and its personnel, and also to the chambers of bishops, which were in many ways similar, evoke something close to an institution, certainly a space or set of spaces rather more complex and more highly populated than we might expect a mere bedroom to be. We owe a number of these glimpses to the desire of biographers or hagiographers to emphasize the fact that their subjects lived out their piety in private as well as in public, and sometimes also that the austerity and self-denial of their private conduct belied the grandeur of their public image. Another motive was the desire to illuminate the relationships between great people by showing them communing in a setting from which lesser mortals were excluded.

In about 971, returning to Germany from Rome, Bishop Ulrich of Augsburg (later the first saint to be formally canonized by the pope himself) heard that the Emperor Otto I was at Ravenna and decided to wait upon him:

> He sent a messenger ahead to announce his arrival and following hard on the messenger's heels arrived at the door of the emperor's bedchamber (*ad hostium cubiculi imperatoris*). But when the emperor learned that he was so close at hand, with one shoe on and the other foot still unshod, out of humility and divine love, he made haste to receive him affectionately. The empress was summoned and they had an enjoyable conversation in the bedchamber.[15]

It was clearly not headline news that Otto the Great had his own bedroom. The aim of the passage was rather to convey to the reader the intimacy between the emperor and the bishop. A similar purpose underlies the description of Adalbert, bishop of Prague (d. 977), constantly in attendance on the imperial chamber, as a *dulcissimus cubicularius*.[16]

We learn more about Ulrich of Augsburg's use of his own bedchamber. Every day during Lent, when compline and other prayers had been said after the evening meal, he 'sought the privacy of his bedchamber (*secreta cubiculi sui*) and avoided all conversation, unless it was with God and his saints' until the following morning.[17] At Augsburg he would dine abstemiously with the household and then enjoy psalm-singing or listening to sacred reading, either in the church or in his bedroom. When he re-entered his chamber after mass, he would not repose on his bed before the hour of vespers but sat on a chair with his shoes still on, changing his position from time to time on his cushion or reclining against the back of the chair. There was the usual company in the chamber: when Ulrich awoke from a deep sleep there were people sitting around him and listening (*assidentes et audientes*).[18] The reader is clearly meant to understand that this was a great and holy man who, when plagued by infirmity towards the end of his life, indulged only sparingly in the comforts that were available to him.

Another member of this political and spiritual elite was Otto the Great's brother, Bruno, archbishop of Cologne (d. 965). His biographer Ruotger applied Cicero's description of Scipio (or St Ambrose's quotation of it) to him, remarking that 'When he was at leisure, no one ever seemed busier; nor when he was busy, did he ever abandon leisure'.[19] The piety of Matilda, mother to Bruno and Otto, was well known. She slept in a *cellula* which every night 'she filled with the melody of divine song'. This was adjacent to the church, but also so situated that she could see travellers arriving from far off and attend to their needs. When the queen sensed that 'everyone in the bedroom with her' was asleep she awoke her maid (*cubicularis puella*) and went stealthily out into the church, where 'she completed the entire psalter before cockcrow, unless she was prevented by the shortness of the night'.[20]

There is a somewhat similar description of Wenceslas of Bohemia awaking his *puer cubicularis*, seizing an old psalter and spending the night wandering up and down in the palace gardens barefoot, singing psalms. He had a little room tucked away in the palace which was very dear to him and this was evidently sometimes used as a place of prayer.[21] Some stress is laid on his difficulty in obtaining privacy for his devotions. He had a series of prayers copied into a little book which he secretly kept with him and when worldly business permitted he would recite twelve or more of them, although this was often possible only in his private apartments.[22] Wenceslas thus sought to find a place for his religious exercises within the space allocated to him as a great prince; that this was sometimes difficult underlined his sanctity. Like Matilda, we may note, he was accompanied in his nocturnal devotions, even if only by a single servant.

Biography at this period was a compliment reserved for those distinguished by rank or piety, and Matilda and Wenceslas qualified on both counts. Their *Lives* give us glimpses of literate devout practices which do not differ essentially from those of men and women of varied ranks in the later middle ages. The psalms recited by Matilda and the prayers that Wenceslas had chosen (or that his spiritual advisers had chosen for him) later came together to form the books of hours which nourished the devotions of a more urbanized and more literate society in the fifteenth century, when even some non-noble families possessed private chapels. Patronage and piety of this kind were more restricted in social scope around the year 1000, as was the ownership of the buildings in which private devotions could be easily pursued, but they were never entirely restricted to the clergy.

In the ninth century the Lady Dhuoda, wife of Bernard of Septimania, exhorted her sixteen-year-old son William to make prayer and devout reading an integral part of his life. She instructed him how to pray while lying in bed and on rising in the morning; he was also to keep the canonical hours. As for his reading, 'You already have books – and you will have them – in which to read, ponder, contemplate, study and understand.' The spirit of wisdom would come upon him, 'If you love God with your whole heart and study carefully the volumes of his scriptures in the Old and New Testaments, and if you do this with appropriate concentration.' Dhuoda could apparently presume that William was sufficiently competent in the use of books to be able to use chapter-headings as signposts to their contents.[23] She and her son also both inhabited premises in which they could make space for prayer and reading, quite probably in the company and with the assistance of household clerks; it is a fair supposition that the bedchamber was at the centre of this activity. If lay aristocrats had books in their homes we might expect their clerical counterparts to do so, but unexpected uses were sometimes made of them. Bishop Gerard of Toul had saints' lives copied into 'smallish books' (*modicis libellis*) which he took to bed with him, scattering them in fact all over the bed, but not, as we might suppose, with the intention of reading them. His hope was that when he turned over in his sleep the books would turn with him, 'believing that with the aid of the saints whose acts were contained in them, he would be guarded from all the evil assaults of the Enemy'.[24]

The convention by which non-monastic clergy were and are called 'seculars' may seem confusing to anyone who supposes that there was a simple division in the middle ages between clergy and laity, but in some important respects the secular clergy did indeed more closely resemble the laity. Whereas monks inhabited a complex set of communal spaces which had developed to accommodate a very specific timetable of activities, the secular clergy, from popes and bishops downwards, lived in houses which resembled those of laypeople of corresponding rank. There is no reason to suppose that the house which John of Gorze occupied in early tenth-century Metz differed from the ones which may have been owned by the more prosperous laymen of the city. The most pious and learned bishops are sometimes described in terms which suggest that they straddled two worlds of secular and monastic habits. The canonist-bishop Burchard of Worms had an oratory and 'cell' built for him a couple of miles from the city. Here he retreated when he had disposed of worldly business; we are specifically told that he did a great deal of work on his canonical collection in this cell.[25] He would often shut himself in the oratory praying, 'and what he did inside is not known to us, but only to God'.

It is rare to be afforded a detailed look at ordinary dwelling houses in town or country, for there was little incentive to describe something so commonplace, but one is provided by Ralph Tortarius, the latest of the four authors who recorded the miracles of St Benedict at Fleury between the ninth century and the early twelfth. The setting is a rural *castrum* belonging to the seigneurs of Châtillon-sur-Loing, who were determined enemies of the monks of La Cour Marigny, which belonged to Fleury. A member of this family, Seguinus, one day carried off some pigs from land near Marigny. The aggrieved owners were directed to him and found him in his wooden tower house, which Ralf regarded as a mark of his status as a *vir potens*. Seguinus had an upper room, a *solarium*, where he 'passed the time with his *familia*, talking, feasting and sleeping at night'. Underneath this was a cellar which contained a variety of food-stores. The floor of the solar, 'as is usual', was made of small beams, which were somewhat broader than they were thick, and quite long.

The point of this detail becomes apparent. Seguinus received the deputation with predictable hostility, expressing his earnest desire to set fire to the monastery. Scarcely had he uttered this abomination than the beam on which he was standing up-ended itself, and he fell in such a way that his head got wedged between two of the chests in the cellar, with the rest of his body sprawled across one of them. He had broken his neck and died. Having given all these circumstantial particulars, Ralf noted that this reprised one of the ancient miracles of St Benedict, as recounted by St Gregory, in which a *solarium* where the saint's enemy Florentius was standing was demolished, leaving the rest of the house intact.[26] The description of the house here helps to characterize Seguinus as one of the breed of petty local *potentes* who were a constant menace to the monks. The upstairs room, set apart for the private pursuits of the master and his intimates, with cellars beneath, was and would remain for centuries a standard feature of domestic architecture, in wood and in stone.

There were words with which domestic apartments could be described if there was need to do so, but often they did not carry precise or distinct meanings. The clerk Lambert of Ardres, writing in the years just before and after 1200, displayed considerable interest in the building works of the counts of Guines and the lords of Ardres a hundred years and more earlier.[27] Several of them had devoted attention to domestic as well as to military and ecclesiastical building. Lambert was impressed by the complexity of the round house which Count Baldwin (d. 1091) built over the existing keep at Guines and sought words from the classical vocabulary with which to describe the variety of its apartments: apart from *cameras* it had *habitacula et diversoria multa ... et diverticula*, 'so that it seemed little different from the labyrinth, that is, the house of Daedalus'. The chapel, which was 'like the glory of Solomon', stood outside the gate of the house.[28]

If this house was labyrinthine, it was far surpassed by the wooden structure erected by Arnold the Old (d. c. 1138) over the keep at Ardres. Lambert puts the description of this wonderful edifice into the mouth of Walter of Le Clud, a bastard son of Baldwin of Ardres (d. 1147) and as an old man a member of the household of Lambert's patron Arnold II (d. 1220). Walter recites the history of the lords of Ardres to the assembled household during a rainy spell which is keeping them all indoors. Other members of the entourage had already regaled the company with much concerning the Roman Emperors, Arthur, Jerusalem and Antioch. Echoing Lambert's earlier reference, Walter likens Louis, the 'architect or carpenter' from Bourbourg who built the house, to Daedalus. It was an 'inescapable labyrinth' in which the master-craftsman linked 'storeroom to storeroom, chamber to chamber, and cubby-hole to cubby-hole, and connected the granaries to the cellars'.[29]

Sheer height, as well as complexity, was a distinguishing feature of the house, which had three storeys. The lowest contained cellars and storerooms (*cellaria et granaria*), in which foodstuffs and other materials and tools were kept. The second floor contained 'the common living spaces of the inhabitants (*habitatio et communis inhabitantium conversatio*)', including, on one side, the premises of the bakers. On the other side, where the butlers also had their quarters, was the 'great chamber' of the lord and his wife, with a side chamber (*latibulum*) adjacent to it where their younger children and attendants slept and therefore glossed as *puerorum camera vel dormitorium*. Lambert adds that the great chamber contained 'a more private apartment (*diversorium*)', presumably some kind of alcove, where a fire could be made at dawn or dusk 'in illness, or for bleeding or keeping the servants or weaning children warm'. Also on this floor, presumably on the other side with the bakers, was the kitchen, which was itself divided into two levels. On the lower of the two, pigs and chickens awaiting slaughter evidently added to the noise and vitality of the household, while the preparation of 'the lord's very refined food' took place on the upper level. The third storey contained bedchambers (*solariorum diversoria*), on one side those which were available to the grown sons of the house when they wished to use them, on the other those allocated to the lord's daughters, as was befitting. Somewhere on this floor, too, the servants and guards, 'ever ready' to keep watch over the house, could snatch some sleep.

The whole structure was linked and articulated by stairs and passageways, and the house opened on to a loggia or gallery (it is not specified on which floor). Lambert/Walter fancifully derives the word 'loggia' from *logos*, 'word', which he regards as an appropriate etymology, for it was here that family members delighted to sit and converse. From the loggia one could reach the chapel, which was built high up on the eastern side of the house. Like its counterpart at Guines, it inevitably 'resembled the tabernacle of Solomon in its carving and painting'.[30] To Walter the house was in itself an heirloom which deserved description, not so much for the benefit of members of the family, who had known it all their lives, as for that of their visitors. Small wonder, he said, that the latter could never get to know all its rooms, for even those, like himself, who had been brought up in it could not fully reckon up 'the number of doors, gates, little entries, and windows'.

It is evident that to Lambert this was the setting for as civilized an existence as the age could afford. We might now regard the presence of the pigs and chickens as a trifle intrusive and we might also be unable to suppress a touch of anxiety about a fire made in the great chamber of a wooden structure, but the house was clearly an effective machine for living as far as its occupants were concerned. The framework within which Walter's story-telling is placed itself tells us a great deal about their culture and values. The weather was preventing the male members of the household from getting out into the open air. Lambert relates that as Walter began to speak it was still raining, but the wind was abating, 'as if to let us listen'; even indoors, the outdoors was not far away. No sooner had Walter finished than the skies cleared and Arnold leapt from his seat; happy though he had been to listen to the story, he was now like one released from prison and he instantly went out through the village with his companions, simply, it appears, to stretch his legs.

It is in such a setting that Lambert's eulogy of the learning and literary patronage of Baldwin of Guines, himself 'completely illiterate' but possessor of a fine library, has to be appreciated.[31] Such people formed the audience for Chrétien's romances, and his descriptions of both outdoor and indoor settings would have been meaningful to them. They were physically active and their contact with bookish culture was effected principally by ear: they needed a place to hear reading or story-telling (if the loggia was an open gallery, it would have done very well in warmer weather), rather than places in which to read for themselves. Evidence of balconies designed to make it possible to take the air and enjoy the view can be found elsewhere. At Richmond Castle in Yorkshire, built by the Breton Count Alan who had fought with the Conqueror at Hastings, there are the remains of one of the earliest halls in England, now known as Scolland's Hall. The hall proper was on an upper storey with a small solar chamber at its east end. This had a fireplace and next to it a doorway which now gives puzzlingly on to vacancy. The presence of square sockets in the outside wall suggests that there was a wooden gallery, reached through the otherwise mysterious doorway and overlooking what was perhaps already a garden in the late eleventh century.

Lambert does not mention a hall at Ardres. Doubtless one already existed in the keep to which the ingenious carpenter had added the superstructure. The new building was supplying a need for a greater number and variety of specialized workrooms and living spaces. Writing a little earlier than Lambert, Chrétien de Troyes supplies a domestic *mise en scène* for his romances which has the *sale* at its centre, with numerous *chambres* and other apartments, serving multiple purposes, disposed around it. *Lancelot* begins at the Ascensiontide feast at Caerleon, and here the queen and many courteous ladies, 'ben parlant an lengue françoise', are present in the hall with the king and his *barons*.[32] At the beginning of *Le Chevalier au Lion*, however, Arthur causes something of a stir by leaving the assembled company at his Pentecostal feast at Cardigan and joining the queen in a *chambre* where he falls asleep. There is adverse comment; he has never been known to do such a thing at such a great feast.[33]

The *chambre*, like the *bryd-bure* of *Beowulf*, has clear associations with the women of the household, probably functioning as a drawing-room, especially when the going got rough in the hall. In *Erec et Enide* the ladies titivate themselves in chambers ('les dames es chambres s'atillent') while the young men attend to the horses.[34] The knights, after dining, assemble wherever the ladies bid them to discuss the latest news, to talk of love or to tell stories. More than once it is specified that women receive or take leave of visitors in a *chambre*. *Loges* and their uses are also mentioned quite frequently. In one episode of *Erec et Enide*, Gawain and Kay are in a loggia outside the *sale*, where they have been followed by a large company, and from this vantage point they are the first to see some new arrivals; Guinevere ascends to a *loge* in a tower to watch Lancelot in single combat.[35]

Chrétien de Troyes was writing for a partly female clientele and he shows women exercising a certain power of social command. The widowed châtelaine who takes Yvain (the killer of her late lord) as her new husband displays her superior status and freedom to dispose of herself, leading him by the hand into the *sale* where her 'people' are and seating herself on a bench at the top of the hall to announce her decision.[36] More fantastic is the setting of the mysterious and forward damsel who takes Lancelot to her castle, where she lives (alone) in some style: she has had 'asez des beles chanbres' constructed for her personal use and also a 'sale molt grant et pleniere' which is tile-roofed.[37] The appointments are admirable, but the fact that there was not a servant in sight should have alerted Lancelot to the fact that this was not a normal household. He and the damsel dine *à deux*, after which a number of rather unexpected things happen. On more than one occasion in *Lancelot* beds are prepared in the *sale*, which reflects the fact that this too was a multi-purpose apartment, but it was presumably unusual for a flaming lance to descend from the ceiling during the night and threaten to pinion the guest to the mattress, just as, even in earlier times, it was unusual for a carnivorous monster (or his mother) to crawl out of a swamp to devour members of the company.

Chrétien has a number of ways of qualifying *chambre*, including the diminutives *cambrete* and *petite chambrete*. Yvain's lion is accommodated in a *cambrete*.[38] Guinevere has a *chambre domainne* and takes Enid into 'a withdrawing room', *une chambre a recelee*, where she can dress.[39] Occasionally stress is laid not merely on the decorative splendour of an apartment but on its other merits. The wounded Erec is taken by Guivret and his sisters into 'a delightful room, airy and far away from people'. Sickness was an acceptable excuse for seclusion in the secular as in the monastic environment. On an earlier occasion, Erec is 'well lodged' and his host stipulates that he shall have a bed to himself, so that no one will be able to touch his wounds.[40] The convalescent Yvain is put in 'a quiet room', *une cambre coie*; on another occasion he and Gawain, after a punishing duel, are both taken *en enfremerie et en mue*, that is to a room apart.[41] In a similar context, the bruised and exhausted Lancelot is brought by a maiden to a manor which she especially delights in because of its various amenities, among them that it is *sains et molt privez*.[42] Bleeding takes place (as at Ardres) 'en ses chambres priveement'.[43] Gottfried von Strassburg describes how Tristan and Isolde and a handful of other intimates are bled together with King Mark and rest pleasurably with him in his chamber.[44] In monastic life too bleeding was an occasion on which the monk was accommodated apart and permitted a more lavish diet.

In the first decade of the fourteenth century, the Sieur de Joinville dictated his memoirs of Louis IX of France, whom he had known and served and accompanied on his first crusade nearly sixty years earlier. Scattered throughout the work are snapshots of the king in particular places. At a meeting of the king's counsellors in Acre, Joinville made himself unpopular by opposing the advice of the majority. When the tables were laid, Joinville sat next to the king as he usually did but Louis said nothing to him during the meal and he thought he was out of favour.

> While the king was hearing grace I went over to a barred window in an embrasure at the head of his bed. I passed my arms through the bars of the window…While I was standing there the king came up to me, and leaning on my shoulders put both his hands on my head. I thought it was Philippe de Nemours, who had already plagued me too much that day because of the advice that I had given. So I exclaimed: 'Stop bothering me, my good Philippe!' By chance, as I was turning my head, the king's hand slid down over my face and I recognized who it was by the emerald ring on his finger.[45]

These are an old man's spoken reminiscences, but consciously or not Joinville here paints himself and the king like characters in a romance. Chrétien's Lancelot stands pensively at one window while Gawain talks confidentially with a damsel at an adjacent one, and from this vantage-point they all see Guinevere led captive.[46] Joinville and his contemporaries were doubtless familiar with such stories and their mode of scene-painting. It is to him also that we owe the picture of Louis and his wife Marguerite contriving to meet on a staircase (*une viz*) between their two rooms in the castle of Pontoise and being alerted to the approach of the Queen Mother.[47] Joinville uses such details to convince the reader of the quality of his information: he knew that what he said was true because (very often) he had been there and had seen with his own eyes. Minor incidents in which he was himself involved are invested with the same particularity, as when Eudes de Châteauroux, legate on the Holy Land, 'led me into a private room (*garderobe*), where no one else was with us, and shutting the door took both my hands in his and began to weep very bitterly'.[48]

Hagiography too had its scenic requirements. The dramatic twelfth-century story of Christina of Markyate is an example. Christina had vowed her virginity to Christ and had to resist the advances of no less a person than Ranulf Flambard, bishop of Durham and justiciar of the kingdom. The bishop slept in a chamber, hung with tapestries, in the house where he used to stay with Christina's aunt, his ex-mistress, whom he had married off to a citizen of Huntingdon; into this he had Christina brought while her father and mother were getting drunk in the hall. The chamber of course had a door which could be bolted, evidently from both sides, for Christina neatly turned the tables on the lustful bishop by bolting it shut with him inside. Christina had her own chamber in her parents' house; this too was a scenic necessity, for when she was forcibly married, at Ranulf's behest, to a young man called Buhrtred, she several times had to resist his advances in this room, once hiding behind the tapestries which decorated the walls. In a dream Christina envisaged the sanctum in which she hoped to find rest as a *solarium* which could only be reached by so steep and difficult a staircase that she needed the Virgin's assistance to get up it.[49]

Scene-setting was an important constituent of narrative art, fictional and otherwise. To the poet of *Beowulf* the setting was a fundamental component of the drama he was narrating. Chrétien embroiders colourful detail onto a backcloth of life in a noble household as his audience would have known it; like the hearers of *Beowulf*, they would have been able to measure the distance between the plausible and everyday on the one hand and the fantastic on the other. Some saints lived their lives in the world the audience knew but contrived to transcend it, which gave them a special exemplary importance. The ways in which their lives were described by hagiographers accordingly sometimes display more than a little kinship with contemporary works of fiction.

5

In Search of Lost Solitude

For the pioneers of the new religious orders which came into being in the eleventh and early twelfth centuries, as for the desert fathers whom they had very much in mind, solitude was a means to an end, the uninterrupted contemplation and praise of God. They tried to set a distance, physical and moral, between themselves and 'the world', adopting different means and architectural solutions in order to do so. The Cistercians and Carthusians eschewed the practice of child oblation and, although some of their recruits were little more than young adolescents, others had followed a variety of paths before they committed themselves to religion. They therefore had some experience of family life, of the households of magnates lay and ecclesiastical, of the urban environment and not infrequently of the disputes which convulsed ecclesiastical politics.

One notable example was the founding father of the Carthusians, Bruno, who was born at Cologne a little before 1030 and studied at the cathedral school of Reims before becoming master of the schools there around 1056.[1] Appointed chancellor of the see of Reims in 1074, he retired in 1083 with two companions to live as a hermit at Sèche-Fontaine on the borders of Champagne and Burgundy. When his companions decided to embrace the cenobitic life, he sought out the site which was to be that of the Chartreuse, high in the Alps above Grenoble. In 1088 one of his former pupils became pope as Urban II and two years later Bruno went to Rome to do homage to him. When in the summer of that year Urban was forced to leave Rome, Bruno became a hermit at La Torre in the diocese of Squillace in Calabria, where he died in October 1101. From Calabria Bruno wrote a letter to Raoul le Vert, provost of Reims, which included a rhapsodic description of his retreat and a justification of his withdrawal.[2]

Bruno, who had spent most of forty years in the scholastic environment, was not now squatting in isolation on a mountainside. He enjoyed the company of 'religious and often learned brothers' who with him were awaiting the return of the Lord. Words could not do justice to the fertile and well-watered expanse of plain, rich in trees and gardens, which they inhabited. These in themselves were not the *divina* which must be the wise man's real pleasures, but unremitting spiritual exercises were wearying to the weak mind. In words which recall St Antony's rebuke to the censorious hunter, Bruno declared that 'If a bow is persistently drawn it becomes weakened and less fit for its purpose'. The peace and beauty of the surroundings made it possible to breathe:

> What profit and divine pleasure solitude and the silence of the hermitage bestow on their lovers, only those know who have experienced it. Here strong men are able to retreat into themselves and live with themselves, to cultivate the plants of the virtues and happily feed on the fruits of paradise... Here a busy leisure is enjoyed and there is repose in peaceful action.

Bruno's education had not gone to waste: the paradoxical phrase 'busy leisure' (*otium negotiosum*) and the simple reference to 'living with themselves' (*habitare secum*) locate this apologia firmly in a literary tradition which drew on the vocabulary of Cicero and Seneca. It is also an example of the monastic version of the Latin pastoral convention and has been likened to the equally lyrical description of the setting of Rievaulx in its Yorkshire dale, written half a century later by the Cistercian Walter Daniel, who also seems to be evoking a real rather than a merely symbolic landscape.[3]

Bruno's project in the French Alps was revived a few years after his death under the leadership of Guigo I (d. 1136), who became prior of the Chartreuse in 1109, while still in his twenties. Among other writings, in 1127 he compiled the *Customs* of what was now becoming an order.[4] Early in the century Guibert, abbot of Nogent, described the Chartreuse in his memoirs, possibly deriving his information from hearsay rather than from personal information.[5] At the time there were thirteen monks, each inhabiting a cell around the cloister which, Guibert observed, was 'quite suitable for common use' but was not in fact used, as Benedictines or Cistercians used it, for meditation, perambulation and miscellaneous other activities. Each monk spent his life working, praying, eating and sleeping in his cell, eating with his fellows only on Sundays and feast days. His work took him no further than to the little enclosed garden which adjoined his cell and provided him with some of his food. Other supplies, such as bread, were put through a hatch in the outer wall of the cell by a lay-brother.

The gardens are still to be seen at Mount Grace in Yorkshire, which, although a late fourteenth-century foundation, followed a plan not changed greatly since the twelfth. The lay-brothers (or *conversi*), as in other orders, were not committed to the full rigours of the monastic life and were responsible for relations with the outside world, but, like the full monks and unlike their Cistercian counterparts, they lived in separate cells, as can also be seen at Mount Grace. The Carthusians thus provided a firm architectural framework for the individual monk's isolation and created a distinctive kind of monastic space. The contemporaneous Italian communities of the congregations of Camaldoli and Vallombrosa were physically loose structures, 'only colonies or villages of hermits, not monasteries'. To that extent they resembled the ancient Egyptian monasteries more closely than did a Charterhouse (which has been likened to a housing estate).[6]

For the Carthusians, to call the cell the monk's workshop was more than metaphor. The *Customs* enumerated a long list of *utensiles* that were issued to the 'inhabitant of the cell', rather like the kit issued to an army recruit.[7] In addition to his bedding, garments and other accessories, he received a comprehensive inventory of pens and stationery, including chalk, two razors for scraping parchment and a ruler. If an illiterate craftsman were recruited to the order, which rarely happened, he should be taught to read and meanwhile have the tools of his own trade provided for him. The books the monk drew from the store (*armarium*) were to be treated with great care, for they were 'in a manner of speaking the everlasting food of our souls', and the copying of books, which was foremost among the crafts the monks practised, enabled them to 'preach' with their hands since they could not do so with their mouths. Everything needful for cooking, washing-up and making a fire was provided. A mattock was supplied for work in the garden. Every individual received this abundance of stores lest he should be compelled to leave his cell to get something.

Guigo was clearly anxious that it should not be thought that his monks were over-provided with material goods, for poverty was in his view integral to solitude. In his *Meditations* he reminded the reader, very much in the spirit of the Egyptian fathers, that 'poverty and lowliness (*vilitas*) can create solitude in the middle of cities, while riches can fill deserts with crowds'.[8] Good use could be made of *otium* in such a setting. Guigo told an anonymous correspondent that 'I think him happy above all who humbly chooses to be rusticated in the hermitage, who loves to philosophize studiously at leisure (*in otio*), who longs to sit alone in silence'. Later he explains how the soul under this regime

> is both continuously at leisure and never idle (*continua in otio, quod nunquam est otiosa*). She so multiplies her duties, that she more often lacks time than a variety of things to do (*variae actionis negotium*), and more often complains of the deceits of time than of the tedium of the work.[9]

Manual labour (including the all-important business of book-production) was an integral part of this programme. It had many merits, as an English Carthusian, Adam of Dryburgh, explained later in the century. The fourth component of the 'quadripartite exercise of the cell' to which he devoted a treatise, it obviated boredom (*fastidium*) and idleness and produced useful results. It was not however undertaken at the individual's whim. The prior prescribed what it was to be, and it had its established place within the timetable framed by the liturgical hours. The hours from Terce to Sext in the winter and from Prime to Terce in the summer were allocated to manual work, with the addition, in summer, of the interval between Nones and Vespers. All these periods were to be punctuated with brief outbursts of prayer. The remaining hours were devoted to spiritual exercises, prayer, reading and meditation.[10] The physical circumstances of the Carthusian's life meant that (like the desert fathers of old) he had greater freedom, within the four walls of his cell, to choose how he spent a given moment. This relative freedom represented both an opportunity and a formidable challenge.

The contemporaneous but somewhat differently motivated Cistercian reform of cenobitic Benedictine monasticism similarly drew recruits both from already established convents and from 'the world'. In 1112 the young nobleman Bernard entered the mother-house of Cîteaux in Burgundy. Within three years, he was chosen to establish a daughter-house at Clairvaux, and as its abbot he rapidly became an adviser, inspiration and authority on all aspects of monastic life. Like Bruno, Bernard was not a monk from the cradle. Such men had personal reasons for embracing the monastic life and something with which to compare it. Bernard had a great deal to say about solitude and he was read and quoted, on this as on other subjects, by his admirers and followers. His most celebrated utterance on the virtues of monastic withdrawal is the treatise *De consideratione*, addressed to Eugenius III, the first Cistercian to become Pope and, as Bernard saw it, much in need of his counsel amidst the pressures of his great office.[11] Another succinct and representative treatment of the subject is to be found in the latter part of his fortieth sermon on *The Song of Songs*, on the text 'Thy cheeks are beautiful as the turtle-dove's'.[12]

Having established (not without some difficulty) the mystical significance of the plural 'cheeks', Bernard turns to the turtle-dove, a bird which was reputed to remain solitary if it once lost its mate.

> Sit, then, solitary as the turtle-dove. Have nothing to do with crowds, nothing to do with the masses of mankind; forget also thine own people and thy father's house; so shall the King have pleasure in thy beauty [Psalm 45:10-11]. O holy soul, remain alone, so as to preserve thyself for him alone, whom thou has chosen to thyself from among all others.

The monk had not perfected his withdrawal simply by becoming a monk. There was more to do:

> Avoid appearing in public, shun even those who dwell in the house with you, withdraw yourself from friends and intimates, yea, even from him who minsters to you. Do you not know that you have a Bridegroom who is diffident, and not willing to honour you with his presence when others are present? Withdraw thyself therefore; I do not mean in body, but withdraw in mind, in intention, in devotion, in spirit. For the Lord Christ, who presents himself to you, is a Spirit, and He requires solitude of spirit, not of body, although this last is sometimes not without its uses when you are able to maintain it, and especially in the time of prayer. You thus observe the precept of the Bridegroom, and the practice he advises: 'Thou, when thou prayest, enter into thy closet, and when thou hast shut the door, pray [Matthew 6:6].'

The essentially interior meaning of solitude is further elaborated for the benefit of men who in fact lived in a closely packed community:

> For the rest, the only solitude prescribed to you is solitude of mind and spirit. You are alone if you are not thinking of common things, if you are not interested in things present to you, if you think little of that which many estimate highly, if you despise what all others desire,

> if you avoid disputes, do not take to heart losses, nor bear injuries in mind. Otherwise you are not really alone, though there be no one with you. Do you not perceive that it is possible for you to be alone when you are in the company of many persons, and to be in company with many persons when you are alone? However large be the throng of men in which you find yourself, you are alone if only you take care not to listen eagerly to the conversation around you, nor to judge of it rashly.

Knowingly or not, Bernard was here echoing Stoic opinion about the possibility and desirability of what we might term 'virtual' solitude. Throughout the passage, he melds this implicit reference to a classical tradition of thought about the withdrawal of the sage with a catena of familiar biblical quotations. This typifies the manner in which Cistercian authors, assuming an audience of enclosed cenobites, approached the subject of monastic solitude.

Among those who applied to Bernard for counsel was Guerric, a refugee from the conflicts which agitated the city of Tournai in the early years of the century.[13] There were frequent altercations between the citizens and the numerous clerical students at the urban schools, and discontent was also caused by the efforts of Odo, abbot of St Martin's, to impose a stricter life on his community. Guerric, born probably in the 1070s, was first a student and then a master at the cathedral school, but retreated from the surrounding turbulence into his house near the church, 'in which he remained enclosed, intent on sacred exercises and stimulated by sacred desires, always either reading or writing or meditating'. Hugh, a monk of St Martin's and later abbot of Marchienne, visited him often: 'Oh, how often, he shared in heavenly secrets alone with him in that house of his.' According to Hugh's biographer they removed themselves by this means far from the city; when Hugh sought Guerric's company, he came, metaphorically, 'from the ends of earth to hear the wisdom of Solomon'.

Guerric predictably aspired to a more perfect life, but a visit to Bernard of Clairvaux diverted him from his first intention of becoming a hermit. Bernard urged Guerric to take up residence at Clairvaux, lest the malice of the world should change his mind, and added: 'Woe to him who is alone, for if he falls, he has no one to raise him up. Brother aiding brother is like a well-founded city.'[14] Guerric took his advice, but not until he was already fifty. In 1138 he became the second abbot of Igny, a daughter-house of Clairvaux. By now he was in his sixties and like his mentor Bernard was too frail to pursue the full common life; he died in 1157, leaving behind him a corpus of sermons in which he showed himself to be an eloquent and sensitive commentator on monastic solitude.

In his fourth Advent sermon, on the text 'A voice crying in the wilderness, Prepare ye the way of the Lord', Guerric speaks of the special consecration conferred on 'the desert' by John the Baptist and then by Christ Himself:

> By a marvellous favour of divine dispensation it has been provided that in these deserts of ours we have the peace of solitude but do not lack the consolation of a pleasing and holy

> company. Although everyone is able to sit alone in silence [Lamentations 3:28], for he suffers no interruption, it is not [a case of] 'Woe to him who is alone, for he has no one to comfort him or to raise him up if he should fall' [Ecclesiastes 4:10]. We are in a crowd of men; but we lack a crowd. We live as if in a city; but we suffer no noise, except that, provided only that we have silence within as without, we hear the 'voice crying in the desert'. For the words of the wise, says Solomon, are heard in silence, more than the shouting of a ruler among fools [Ecclesiastes 9:17] ... Happy he therefore who has thus distanced himself, fleeing the tumult of the world, who has retreated so far into the secrecy and solitude of a tranquil mind, that he deserves to hear not only the voice of the Word but the Word itself, not John but Jesus.[15]

Elsewhere Guerric comments on the apparent but deceptive sterility of the desert: the eremitical solitude is in fact 'the paradise of beatitude'. He echoes this sentiment in a sermon on the Baptist, who made the desert bloom and whom all solitaries took as their example.[16]

True solitude was not, however, what one might superficially expect. In his fifth Advent sermon, Guerric adverted (echoing Bernard) to the perils of the solitary life as too many led it: they went astray and almost all were proud, because they wrongly thought of themselves as genuine solitaries. One of the temptations of this deluded way of life was over-reliance on personal prayer. Guerric cautioned the brethren against believing that 'what you offer to Him in secret psalms or prayers' could be acceptable to God if one was negligent in the recitation of the psalms according to the Rule.[17] To restore the Benedictine Rule was bound to mean affirming the supreme position of the *Opus Dei*, the formal celebration of the liturgy, in the life of the community, but it is clear that there is also a warning here against a form of self-indulgence. In insisting on the importance of community, Guerric was obedient to the vocation he had embraced and to his duties as an abbot. The 'solitude' of the individual monk was a condition of interior peace and wholeness, sustained by the loving support of one's fellows; it did not mean following one's own bent in isolation. If this solitude was to be secure, it must be rooted in a community which was itself effectively separated from the world.[18]

Among the ancient truths that counsellors such as Guerric reaffirmed was the supreme value of silence. This was not easily come by in the world and it was an important constituent of the monk's artificial solitude. The monk was constantly in the company of his fellows but was not supposed to indulge in idle conversation. When Aelred of Rievaulx first learned about the Cistercian way of life, he was told 'they do not talk together'.[19] This did not prevent him from casting some of his works in dialogue form, ostensibly relating conversations with his favourite monks in the cloister. The Benedictine Hugues de Fouilloy (d. *c.* 1172) offered an interpretation of the rule of silence in his treatise *De claustro animae*, citing Psalm 140, 'Set a guard over my mouth, O Lord; keep watch over the door of my lips'. The Psalmist, he observes, says 'door', not 'wall'. Were it the latter, it would amount to a permanent prohibition on speech, but a door can be opened, and there are occasions, for example in prayer, confession and reading, when speech is permitted. What is prohibited is idle chatter, *confabulatio*.[20]

The psychological pressures of such a life were potentially considerable and for some individuals problems arose, which included the classic bugbear of *accidie*. Guerric recommends that *accidie* should be combated by a spiritual visit to Bethlehem to behold the living Word of God in the crib; he expounds the profound silence of the speaking Word and its special message for those bound by their vows to a silence in which they were above all to listen.[21] Elsewhere he declares

> the discipline of silence nourishes the human spirit, shapes and strengthens it ... This mystery is not hidden from you, my brothers, for your experience and profession is my witness how the peaceful and retiring spirit is strengthened in silence, how it grows fat and flourishes, and how by contrast it is weakened as if by a kind of paralysis and dissipated by words....[22]

Guerric goes on to deal with the question 'with what employment the mind is to be occupied in silence'. It was all too likely that the individual monk would not always or instantly know how he was to fill the wide psychic spaces that were opened up before him. Anyone can waste time, but the monk, sealed into his inner solitude within the collective solitude of the monastic enclosure, faced the risk in an unusually acute form. In this connection Guerric cites Suetonius' *Life* of the Emperor Titus, who always repented a wasted day. He urges the monk to cast up a daily personal account of what he has gained and lost, punishing himself for negligence.[23] Reading was one valuable resource in this silent existence. Just as fervent prayer lit the lamp of wisdom, so frequent reading lit the lamp of knowledge.[24]

In a number of respects the monastic experience of reading differed radically from what is usual for us. We read either for information or for recreation; to say that someone is reading 'to improve his mind' is regarded as faintly flippant. For the monk, the improvement of the mind in the most fundamental and far-reaching sense was the essential purpose of reading. He read a very limited range of texts and may often have done so slowly and with some difficulty; fluent Latinity was not universal. What he learned from his reading did not consist of discrete items of knowledge. He enjoyed (or was meant to enjoy) recreation in the process, but that meant a true re-creation of the self, rather than mere relaxation.[25] This was simultaneously an individual or solitary occupation and a communal one, in that the monk did not normally retreat into a private space in order to read. The cloister was the usual setting for reading, meditation and a number of other activities. Another Cistercian, Isaac of Stella, sardonically pictured monks who slump (*conquiniscunt*) over their books in the cloister.[26] The modern experience of reading in a library or within the family circle may give the best clue to the way in which activities that may be thought of as solitary can be carried on in the midst of people.

The physical environment occupied by the monks is of little explicit concern to Bernard or to Guerric. This was not merely because they focused their attention on the interior life that was to be lived in the metaphorical desert, but because they knew, and knew that their readers or hearers knew, precisely what that environment was like. This did not of course mean that real monastic spaces were not important and indeed carefully designed.[27] An unusually sharp sense, less of the specific architectural setting of the monastery than of the impact of material circumstances on monastic 'solitude', emerges from the sermons of Isaac of Stella. This was partly a consequence of personal experience.

Of English origin, Isaac came to France to study and enrolled himself as a monk at L'Etoile in the diocese of Poitiers, some time before it became Cistercian as a 'daughter' of Pontigny in 1145. He later became abbot, and his support of Thomas Becket, when the latter took refuge at Pontigny in 1164, brought upon him (as upon other Cistercians) the displeasure of Henry II. It may have been because of this that he had to leave L'Etoile, probably in 1167, becoming for a time abbot of a community at Notre Dame des Châteliers on the Ile de Ré; at all events, his absence from L'Etoile was enforced.[28] In several of his sermons Isaac seems to refer to the real isolation of himself and his brothers, and this predicament certainly provided him with an opportunity to give sharply pointed treatment to some standard themes, although it is not entirely certain which of the sermons were composed during the sojourn on Ré.[29] Given the prevailing fondness for metaphor it was not actually necessary for him to be immured on an island to tell the brethren that they had 'entered a solitude not merely of place but of the spirit'.[30] The fourteenth sermon, which contains the fullest treatment of the problem of solitude, certainly belongs, however, to the Ré period.[31]

'Wisdom', Isaac declares, 'is learned in leisure, not in idleness.' Here, as so often, the Latin pun is unavailable in English: 'Sapientia quidem in otio sed non in otiositate discitur.' Isaac proceeds to use the sisters Martha and Mary, as so many spiritual writers did, to signify the active and the contemplative lives. Mary became the type of the contemplative, and therefore of the solitary, not so much because of her legendary history as a penitent and anchoress in a cave in southern France as because she had withdrawn from household duties to sit at Christ's feet and hear His words, while Martha busied herself 'about many things'. That Martha's labours were meritorious and even necessary was not entirely forgotten, but Mary had chosen the better part, and the monk was supposed to have done likewise.[32] Isaac however perceived that all too many were in fact falling between two stools.

> How many today, freed from useful external toil, are slothful and despondent (*desides et accediosi*) within; sure of their necessities, they are intent on mindless thoughts and chatter. They have abandoned Martha's cares and have by no means discovered Mary's devotion.

Isaac enlarges on the shortcomings of these backsliders and expounds to his audience the significance of *lectio*, *meditatio* and *oratio*. He then evokes their present predicament:

> Therefore, dearly beloved, we have brought you into this remote, arid and rugged solitude; artfully, for here you can be humble, but you cannot be rich; into this solitude of solitudes, I say, lying far away in the sea, having almost no contact with the world, so that, devoid of all worldly, almost of all human comfort, you can be at peace from the world; for now you have no world anywhere besides this little island, the last of all lands.

This then is a real desolation, not the rich poetic solitude of St Bruno's Calabrian valley or Walter Daniel's Yorkshire dale. Once Isaac had been 'desirous of flight and thirsting for solitude'; now he had come to this vast and remote desert (*eremum*) and very few of his previous confederates had followed him. Solitude had been heaped on solitude, silence upon silence; but among the things they had to be thankful for was that not only did 'this our exile' leave them free to pray, meditate and read but that they had to work to provide their bodily necessities.

Similar themes are developed in the following sermon.[33] 'The discipline of your profession' and the 'hidden desert' together constitute the monks' cross. Their solitude detaches them from others, the discipline of obedience detaches them from themselves; but they retain two freedoms, peace and work. There are many things which may get them down, including the isolation and the deep stillness, but by means of reading, meditation and prayer they may be able to awaken 'the sleeping Christ'. From the eighteenth sermon it appears that they were poorly off for books, especially scriptural commentaries.[34] They had learned from books about 'the virtue of solitude, the fruits of peace, the grace of poverty'. Isaac implies that now they had a real opportunity to experience all these things, for they had left not merely 'home and fleshly kinship' behind them, as they had done when they had first entered the religious life, but also the religious community they had once known with its spiritual amenities, including its library. 'Losing the whole world and almost the human race, embracing the naked cross of the naked Christ, naked and shipwrecked, we few have escaped to this remote island, enclosed by the sea.' It was this situation that compelled Isaac to expound the gospel and not always (he said) to take the usual line of interpretation.

The theme that the monk did not always take advantage of the opportunities that were on offer is hammered home elsewhere. Those who out of spiritual infirmity were unable to appreciate the *otium*, *quies* and *solitudo* they had supposedly longed for were likened to invalids who were unable to eat the nourishing foods that had been carefully prepared for them.[35] Isaac was well aware that he was trying to get the brethren to make a virtue out of harsh necessity. As monks, they had chosen solitude; now they had got it. What better opportunity to show that they knew how to make spiritual use of it? Whatever the external circumstances, furthermore, this remained a shared solitude. Isaac was insistent on the mutuality of the monastic life, the bearing of one another's burdens. He was also conscious that this life might seem to outsiders self-contradictory: monks separated themselves from 'the common life of men', yet formed their own *conventicula* apart. The justification was classically biblical. Separation from men was necessary because 'evil talk corrupts good morals'; but monks lived

> together thus, because we are not yet fit for solitude; together thus so that if anyone should fall, there will not be lacking one to lift him up. Together thus, because 'brother aiding brother' shall be exalted like a city fortified and strong. Together thus, finally, because it is good and pleasant for brothers to dwell together in unity.[36]

For Cistercians and Benedictines alike the individual monk's cell was a thing of the future, regarded by many when it appeared as a sign of relaxation and decadence, but it had always been recognized that old age and sickness justified separate accommodation. Aelred of Rievaulx was afflicted by the stone and arthritis in his last ten years and the Cistercian General Chapter granted him privileges which, according to Walter Daniel, he accepted with shame and reluctance. He took measures to bridge the gap between the retirement that he was thus permitted and the life of the community, building a *mausoleum* adjacent to the infirmary in which he lived, attended by two monks but eschewing all luxury. Walter was keen to point out that Aelred dedicated this 'hut' (*tugurium*) to the well-being of the brethren, for they came to sit in it with him, even on his bed, to hear his spiritual counsels. One wonders about the size of the hut when one reads that there were sometimes twenty or thirty of them in it at a time, still more when Walter says that there were sometimes a hundred monks with Aelred as his death approached. It was big enough, at all events, to permit the insertion of an internal cubicle in one corner, closed off by a wooden partition. Here Aelred kept his crucifix and relics and prayed more often than he slept in his bed; here too he wrote 'many things worthy of recollection'. Walter refers to it variously as his *mansio*, his *secretarium* and his *oratoriolum*. Aelred used to sit in a hole excavated in the ground, remembering that he was dust, weeping and praying.[37]

Such a space was obviously conducive to personal prayer, study and literary composition as well as to convalescence. In a work that in modern times has been entitled *Of Affliction and Reading*, the Benedictine Peter of Celle makes several references to the *cella* (rather than the cloister) as the setting for devout reading.[38] What he meant by *cella* is not entirely clear, but it is possible that he intended the treatise for 'eremitical or quasi-eremitical religious' who would actually have possessed individual 'cells'.[39] Peter was on close terms with the Carthusians of Mont-Dieu north-east of Reims, and he sometimes took temporary refuge there, so it is possible that his remarks in this treatise were based on his own luxurious experience of a retreat in such a cell. This would make sense of his reference to himself, in a eulogy of solitude at the end of the work, as 'a new and infrequent dweller in my room'.[40]

In 1145 the Mont-Dieu community had received the dedication of perhaps the finest of all expositions of the meaning and uses of monastic solitude, the so-called *Golden Epistle* by the Cistercian William of St-Thierry, the biographer of St Bernard (to whom the *Epistle* was long attributed).[41] A native of Liège, William received a cathedral education, probably at Laon, and became first a Benedictine monk at St-Niçaise at Reims and then abbot of St-Thierry nearby. Although much that he had to say was equally applicable to all practitioners of the monastic life, he frequently refers to the real cell which was the Carthusian's habitat, as well as to the metaphorical cell which any monk could be said to occupy. Although the monk was exhorted to preserve lifelong stability in his cell, he was also reminded that he was a pilgrim on earth who should not be putting down roots in comfortable lodgings. From time to time William distinguishes this 'exterior' cell, which the soul has to share with the body, from the inner cell of conscience. In this mode the real closed door of the cell signifies the vigilance of the interior guard: just as the bodily senses are preserved from distraction by the closed door, so the 'interior senses' are kept directed to their internal purpose.[42] Much of Hugues de Fouilloy's *De claustro animae* is devoted to metaphorical exposition of this kind. As the title indicates, the soul itself has a 'cloister', which is identified with contemplation; it also has its dormitory, refectory, guest-house and oratory.[43]

The problems of solitude took a particularly acute form in the real cell. *Pietas*, that is, a genuine sentiment of religious devotion, was an absolute requirement. William declares

> If any of you does not have this in his conscience, display it in his life, practise it in his cell, he should be called not a solitary but a man alone; nor is the cell a cell to him, but an enclosure (*reclusio*) and a prison.

William's essentially Latin verbal wit does not always permit easy translation into English; Italian would do better here with the phrase *non solitarius, sed solus*. *Solus* might seem to denote an objectively verifiable bodily state rather than a frame of mind, but here it is juxtaposed with *solitarius* to indicate alternative psychological possibilities, negative and positive, which might arise in the same situation. Such juxtapositions continue:

> For he is truly alone with whom God is not. He is truly shut in, who is not free in God. Solitude and enclosure are unhappy words. The cell must not be an enforced enclosure, but the dwelling-place of peace; the closed door not a hiding-place but a private place (*secretum*). For he with whom God is is never less alone than when he is alone. Then he is free to enjoy his happiness; then he is himself, to enjoy God in him, and himself in God.[44]

First the reader is deftly reminded of the universal availability of God and therefore of the contingent, ambivalent nature of solitude; then, like others before and after him, William bends Cicero (or St Ambrose) to his purpose.[45]

He goes on to deal with the familiar problems involved in embracing the solitary life, among them how the beginner is to knuckle down to it and occupy his time. The common life provides the indispensable framework which makes it all possible; communal norms, including for example the permitted issue of clothes and food, must be observed. Manual labour is valuable not as a pleasure or as an end in itself but as a means of refreshing the spirit for more important things.[46] The object of the exercise is to learn 'to stay in [one] place, to endure the cell, to live with oneself'.[47] The Senecan sentiment that one cannot escape from oneself by moving ceaselessly from place to place was obviously adaptable for monastic purposes. William returns to the all-important issue of fitness for 'living with oneself', which is also Senecan. 'He who lives with himself', William warns, 'has only himself, such as he is, with him.' Therefore 'A bad man can never safely live with himself, because he lives with a bad man and no one is more harmful to him than he is to himself.' An extreme case is represented by the insane and the excessively melancholy (*nimium dolentes*) and those who for whatever reason are not fully sound in mind, who are usually kept under guard and not left to themselves, lest they abuse their solitude. There are multiple echoes here of Seneca's tenth epistle.[48]

In the end we discover that to be either *solitarius vel solus* is but a preliminary stage. Both words suggest the absence of something – at the crudest level, company – in contrast to *unus* and its progeny, which imply simple totality and self-sufficiency. At the end of the religious quest 'he who hitherto has been *solitarius vel solus* is made one, and his bodily solitude is transformed into unity of mind'. Obviously this signifies unity with God, but also the total unification of the human being in the pursuit and fulfilment of that objective. In terms of process, 'a man should begin to know himself perfectly, and by progress in knowledge of himself ascend to the knowledge of God'.[49]

The semantic ambiguities of solitude and the familiar Ciceronian or Ambrosian allusions were further exploited in a Carthusian context by Adam of Dryburgh:

> You must not think that, when you are alone in the cell, you are alone in it. For you are never less alone than when you are alone in it, so to speak, if you are in it in the way you should be. Are you alone when, enclosed in the interior bedchamber of a pure, cleansed mind, with your door closed against everything useless, you pray in spirit to your God?[50]

For Adam, as for William of St Thierry, this insistence on how the Carthusian should understand his solitude was prompted, at least in part, by an awareness that it was not in fact necessarily easy to get it right. The perpetual solitude (*iugis solitudo*) of the cell was the chief excellence of the order, offering enticing prospects of all kinds of spiritual delight, and it could be likened to Paradise itself, but it might also generate psychological difficulties:

> Often when you are alone in the cell a certain inertia, a languor of spirit, an inner tedium (*taedium cordis*) seizes you, you feel a really heavy boredom inside; you are a burden to yourself, the inward pleasure which you usually experience fails you.[51]

The answer had to be fortitude, perseverance and the faith that the clouds would ultimately lift. The monk must not leave the cell. Here Adam echoes St Antony ('The inhabitant of the cell cannot live spiritually outside the cell for longer than a fish can physically live out of water'). As often as the monk rashly leaves the cell and stays out of it for no good reason, he returns as if he was beginning all over again (*quasi novus inhabitator*) 'and finds that he has returned a different person from what he was before he went forth'.[52]

It is apparent that monastic superiors and writers were well aware of the stresses of monastic life and of the human weaknesses that made men as likely to experience moral and psychological difficulties inside the cloister as outside it. This understanding is often expressed in purely human terms, with the necessary proviso that human nature was seen theologically as poised between the grim reality of original sin and the resplendent promise of redemption. No one would have denied, however, that as a consequence of the Fall humanity had to contend with a personal Enemy and his staff, who were not only busy in the secular world, but were perfectly capable of invading even sanctified solitudes and wreaking havoc. Some writers were especially concerned with their activities and inclined to blame them when things went wrong. Isaac of Stella had an extremely loquacious personal demon which chattered temptingly about the delights of the world and Isaac's own good points, including his family, learning, eloquence and elegance. 'What am I to say? Often he so distracts and occupies my ears that I have no freedom to read or to listen to someone reading.'[53]

Isaac would have sympathized with a Cistercian of a later generation, Richalm abbot of Schönthal in Franconia, who in a work cast in the form of a dialogue with a disciple ('N') expounded the various ways in which demons could invade and subvert the monk's tranquillity.[54] They would stealthily approach someone who was reading and gradually induce uncomfortable sensations on his skin, like those of a cauterizing iron, until he threw the book away and left his place. Richalm suffered leg pains which often caused him to speak when he should not have done; he would have to sit down and then he would start to chat, successfully distracted from his reading. The only answer was to bathe the leg with holy water.

Reading was a problem. Richalm complained that the demons made him read aloud and not just 'with the book and in thought, as is my custom'; he believed that to the extent that he did this he lost the inward understanding of the text. When he sat down to listen to spiritual reading, the demons sent sleep upon him, and also fleas. Their reasoning, on the latter count, was subtle. Hunting for fleas under one's habit warmed the hands; warm hands encouraged sleep. Richalm thought it best to keep his hands cold. He had been sitting listening to reading a short while before he summoned 'N', thinking to himself that 'there is nothing better than that a man should concentrate on everything in peace and quiet'. At this point the demons intervened and distracted his attention, so that the pleasure of listening to *lectio sacra* was denied him, like Isaac of Stella half a century or more earlier. The demons induced monks to sleep during reading so that they would not sleep at night, which of course exposed them to the humdrum annoyances of insomnia if not to actual night terrors (also caused by demons), and presumably made it more likely that they would again fall asleep during the day. When Richalm sat in discussion (*in colloquio*) with his monks he always had his book open before him; the demons tried to get him to shut it and if he did idle chatter immediately broke out among the monks.

Distractions of all kinds were the demons' favoured weapon. It was as a result of their endeavours that 'even in the largest convent scarcely one or two can be found who willingly sit in the cloister, who willingly concentrate on interior things'. The demons had their distinct preferences as to what the monks should read if they were permitted to do so. Something exciting like the Book of Kings was from their point of view much to be preferred to the *Moralia* of St Gregory or the works of St Bernard, which would presumably recall the monk's mind to what he was really supposed to be doing. One monk who used to try to read the *Moralia* daily was the object of their assiduous attentions and on another occasion they were successful in partly sabotaging a proposal to copy the *Sermons* of St Bernard.

As anybody who is left alone to perform a task well knows, and as Seneca knew, peace and quiet do not guarantee concentration. The task in question does not have to be an intellectual one, but there can be little doubt that it is regrettably easy to fall asleep over a book and just as easy for one's attention to wander from what someone else is saying or reading; both reading and listening require a great deal of effort. In Richalm's view, something had to account for the difficulty monks experienced in making effective use of their time and space, and there was no doubt who or what it was. He was very insistent on the numberlessness of the demons and it was this that really alarmed 'N'. Even now, the two of them were sitting alone, companionably talking, and all the while they might be surrounded. What, he asked, did Richalm advise, given that the monks were rarely together in their reading, but each went severally to their tasks? From this remark it would seem that for 'N' the individual solitude of the monk was a reality. At any one moment the brethren were going about their business cocooned in silence; 'N' seems to have been more conscious of the hostile presence of the invisible demons than of the brother who would pick him up if he happened to fall.

Religious community had never been the answer to every problem. For Guibert of Nogent a century earlier, it had not assuaged the terror of nightmares:

> To this emotion, crowds or solitude are the same, since the company of others is no defense against such fear, and dwelling alone either leaves it as bad as before or makes it worse.[55]

These terrors have their place in the picture of monastic life given in the 1220s by another Cistercian, Caesarius of Heisterbach.

If Palladius was the Boswell of the desert, Caesarius might lay claim to that title in respect of the ecclesiastical world which his monastery, a little to the south-east of Bonn, shared with the clergy of that city and other neighbouring religious communities. Caesarius had been a student at Reims and became a monk during the civil wars which followed the premature death of the Emperor Henry VI in 1197.[56] His world was far from hermetically sealed. There were a hundred and one routes by which anecdotes could flow into the cloister. His information came partly along the grapevine of his own order and partly from local acquaintances, for example Hermann, dean of the church of Bonn, who had once been a parish priest in Cologne. His reach extended northwards to Cologne, south-west to the abbey of Himmerod near Bernkastel, and westwards into Flanders and Brabant, where for example he knew the monks of Villers, one of whom, Godfrey, had once been a Benedictine at St Pantaleon in Cologne. Another Godfrey, now a monk of Heisterbach, had been *scholasticus* at St Andrea in Cologne; lay-brothers and monks alike had pursued various previous occupations in the world.

In describing monastic life, Caesarius gives us what might be termed a collection of Cistercian folklore, illustrating the terrors and superstitions of the monks as well as their aspirations and hopes of paradise. Spiritual hazards lurked under the same bush as spiritual opportunities; this was never more true than when monks were alone. Walter, abbot of Villers, once prayed alone in the abbey church, as St Benedict had provided, and thanks to the prayers of one of his monks found himself suddenly possessed of the gift of tears which he had longed for. Another monk, praying alone before the altar, was visited with such abundant tears that he flooded the earth; but the devil put into his mind the thought, 'I wish someone was here to see this grace' and followed this up by manifesting himself beside him in the form of a black (that is, Benedictine) monk. To his credit, the Cistercian was as much disturbed by *horror mentis* as by the Benedictine habit, and he escaped by making the sign of the Cross; but the incident showed why the Lord had said 'When you are going to pray, go into your room and close the door on yourself, that is, avoid human praise.'[57]

In general, there is more emphasis on the risks than on the benefits of solitude. The devil freely perambulated the monastic space and he could even pursue quarry which he had marked out for himself into the cloister. Once he falsely told a parish priest that he would die after a year. When the time was up the unfortunate man, overcome with shame because the whole parish had got to know about the bogus prophecy, became a monk. He had completed his novitiate when the devil again appeared to him, unrecognized, and told him that God had marked him out for great things; he must therefore husband his strength and not overdo indulgence either in prayer or manual labour. He was to ask the prior to assign him solitary tasks so that the devil could more easily confer with him. Eventually the devil decided to bring his design to its climax and came to the monk's bed by night, instructing him to go to the privy (*ad cameram privatam*) and hang himself from a beam so that he could receive his reward. Fortunately the monk came to his senses and repelled the devil with the sign of the cross, rushing to the prior's bed and insisting that he must confess at once. Even when the prior had listened and imposed a penance on him, the poor man's trials were not over. Before returning to bed, he had to go to the privy in good earnest. There the devil, enraged by his confession, tried to shoot him with a bow and arrow and had to be fought off once more.[58]

Solitude, whether at prayer, at work or in the privy, could be dangerous, but it could also provide an opening for grace and entirely beneficent visions. This was the experience of a couple of lay-brothers who were in charge of granges, where evidently they sometimes went out to work alone. A *conversus* called Conrad, while alone at Dollendorf, not far from Heisterbach, thought he was going to die of heart failure; falling into ecstasy, as Caesarius put it, he received a vision of Christ on the Cross, and was told that all his works except one (which was not specified) were acceptable to God. Henry, a *conversus* of Himmerod who figures in several stories, had a series of rather mysterious but edifying experiences while alone at Hart. These began when he was perambulating a field, going over his prayers (*orationes suas ruminando*) and saw beneath a pear tree a white-haired, bearded man who proved to have remarkable powers and insights: Caesarius did not know whether he was man or angel.[59]

A similar workaday situation might just as easily have been productive of evil, for the possible effects of solitude were unpredictable; they depended on one's spiritual condition and the individual was not always the best judge of that. The sick in the infirmary were sometimes left alone, at least with one another. A *conversus* of Himmerod, who in the world had been an oppressor of the poor and had taken the habit more out of fear of hell than love of heaven, was dying in the lay-brothers' infirmary, 'lying alone on his bed', when another *conversus* called Ludo, who was in the bed opposite, saw vultures gathering rather ostentatiously around him and got rid of them. 'This vision shows', Caesarius explains, 'how valuable the prayer of brothers who are present is to the dying.'[60]

A worthier invalid, to whom solitude *in articulo mortis* was beneficial rather than threatening, was Meynerius, formerly a canon of St Simeon of Trier, who spent more than thirty years at Himmerod, holding a succession of important offices. When he fell ill the abbot, considering his labours and grieving at his imminent death,

> had him put in a secluded place and deputed four people to serve him. He rejoiced at the solitude but lamented the honour that was shown him, saying to the abbot, 'These brothers

> are wearied by watching and working, and they are not necessary to me. Solitude is pleasing to me, nor am I less alone, than when I am alone. He is not alone whose overseer and guardian is the Lord. If I am without human ministrations I do not believe that I will lack heavenly protection.'

The abbot took no notice of the Ciceronian echo, so Meynerius himself dismissed his attendants and extinguished the lamp. Visited later by the Prior, he explained that he had been celebrating mass all night long, describing in rhapsodic terms what he had seen and heard.[61] His experience was illustrative of a general rule: to the worthy, solitude might be the gateway to union with God but for the generality of mankind its risks were likely to outweigh its benefits.

6

In the Midst of People

It is apparent from the pages of Caesarius of Heisterbach that there were a number of ways to live the religious life in the early thirteenth-century Rhineland. His information network brought him news of recluses, male and female, as well as of pious layfolk, whom he designated *religiosus* or *religiosa*. This use of the word is a sign of the thirteenth-century times. With increasing frequency it described individuals who did not live under a formal rule but were recognizably committed to a godly life. It is possible to distinguish between those who had taken vows and accepted formal enclosure as recluses, male or female, and those whose commitment was less formal and who continued to live in ordinary surroundings, although the issue is complicated because the same individual not infrequently moved from one status to another in the course of time, while the status of the hermit remained ambiguous and fluid.

Caesarius discusses a number of true recluses. There was, for example, Heyleka, whom he calls 'a recluse of our order'. Her anchorhold was adjacent to the collegiate church of St Andrea in Cologne, where the saintly dean Einsfrid supported her from his prebend for as long as he lived.[1] There were recluses in smaller population centres. One of Caesarius' informants, the ingenuous Godescalc, a former canon of Cologne who had become a monk at Heisterbach, was a native of Volmarstein, a *castrum* some miles south of Dortmund. Here there lived an *inclusa* called Bertradis, who built up a local reputation as a fortune-teller on the strength of information passed to her by a demon whom she mistakenly took to be a heavenly visitant. News of this reached Hermann, a male recluse at Arnsberg some fourteen miles to the east of Volmarstein, and he sent her a friendly warning and instructions as to how to test the demon.[2] This was but one example of the hazards that lay in wait for the unwary solitary, for Godescalc also told Caesarius how this same Hermann was once brought what he took to be some fish, only to discover, when the time came to prepare it, that it was horse dung. What we might take to be a malodorous practical joke by a neighbour was naturally taken to be the work of a demon.[3]

If recluses were at least as vulnerable as monks to the pranks of demons, they were also liable to the psychological afflictions of monastic enclosure. A girl in the province of Würzburg had resisted offers of marriage and had herself formally veiled by the bishop and enclosed in a cell. The abbot of Bronnbach was deputed to visit her and discovered that she was in a poor frame of mind. 'I am living badly,' she said, 'I am doing badly and why and for what purpose I am enclosed here, I have no idea.'

The abbot suggested that it was for the sake of God and the kingdom of heaven. She replied, 'Who knows if there is a God, if there are angels with him, souls or a kingdom of heaven? Who sees them? Who has returned from there and told us what they have seen?' The abbot was shocked, but she went on, 'I speak as it seems to me. Unless I see these things I cannot believe.' She asked to be allowed to leave her cell, but agreed to remain there for a further seven days. When the abbot came back she was doing well: 'Never better'. She had had a frightening yet consoling vision of her own body on the floor of her cell, while her real self was viewing paradise.[4]

This young woman, after a distinctly shaky start when she clearly became prey to severe depression, seems to have found herself sailing on calm waters within a remarkably short space of time. Whatever the motivation of the would-be recluse, we might well think that stringent tests of mental fitness were needed before a candidate could be safely admitted to live in genuine solitude. Monastic counsellors seem, however, to have had other anxieties at the forefront of their minds. Bernard of Clairvaux was once invited to pass judgement on the desire of a nun of St Mary at Troyes to set up by herself. Her abbess and the other sisters had tried to dissuade her but to no avail. Bernard was unimpressed by her manifesto, although it was, superficially, couched in the appropriate terms.

> 'Is it not wise,' you say, 'to fly riches, crowded towns, and delicate meats? Would not my modesty be safer in a desert where I could live in peace with a few others or even quite alone, so as to please him alone to whom I have pledged myself?'

Bernard's answer was discouraging:

> For anyone wishing to lead a bad life the desert supplies ample opportunity. The woods afford cover and solitude assures silence. No one can censure the evil no one sees. Where there is no fear of blame the tempter approaches more boldly and evil is committed with greater freedom. In the convent, if you would do good there is no one to stop you; if you would do evil, you are not able. Soon everyone would know about it, it would soon be blamed and corrected, just as on the other hand all would admire, respect and imitate the good they saw. Therefore you see, my daughter, that in a convent a greater glory awaits your deserts, and a more prompt correction your faults, for amongst others you set an example by a good life and give offence by a bad one.

In effect, Bernard excluded the possibility that the 'desert' could ever be the right option. If the nun was a good woman, she was needed in the convent; if she was not, she needed it. It was perhaps natural that he should project an optimistic view of the efficacy of conventual discipline, but he had a shrewder blow yet to deliver. He noted that, according to his information, the nun had shown no desire to leave the convent before it was reformed: 'only when Religion began to flourish there did you suddenly become holy and, fired by an unexpected fervour, begin to think of the desert.' For Bernard, at least, the hand of the tempter was plain to see.[5]

Around the year 1160 Bernard's disciple and admirer, Aelred of Rievaulx, composed a manual of advice for his sister, who was a recluse. He recognized the validity of the eremitical option, but with significant qualifications:

> There are some for whom it is dangerous to live amidst a lot of people. There are also some for whom it is, if not dangerous, harmful. There are also many who have to fear neither of these, but judge that to live in seclusion (*secretius habitare*) is more fruitful.

Some of the ancients therefore made this choice, which implied supporting themselves by manual labour. Those who thought this course unsafe because of the freedom inherent in solitude and the power of 'wandering' that it conferred, thought it 'better to be enclosed and contained within a cell with no way out'. His sister was one of these.[6] Recluses in these degenerate days were, however, not what they once had been.

> Many, either not knowing or not caring about the rules of this way of life, think it sufficient to contain their limbs within four walls, while not only is the mind unloosed in wandering and dissipated in cares and anxieties, but the tongue wanders all day through towns and villages, through fairs and markets, over the lives and customs and works of men, seeking out things which are not only useless but shameful. You will scarcely find a single recluse at the present day before whose window some garrulous old crone or gossiping woman is not sitting who keeps her busy with stories, regales her with rumours and slanders, describes the appearance, face and conduct of this or that monk or clerk or some other man ...

Aelred dwells somewhat obsessively on the likely content of these poisonous confabulations. When the time comes to go, the recluse has been thoroughly titillated, while the old crone departs laden with foodstuffs. Now the misguided anchoress is unable to settle down, inwardly rehearsing the mental pictures with which she has been filled. As night falls, everything becomes more sinister. The cell becomes a brothel (*prostibulum*), the door is opened by some means or other, 'and either she goes out or the adulterer comes in'. It is all very sad, but too true of many, men as well as women, in this age.[7]

Despite this last phrase, it is evident that many of these strictures were directed at female recluses, and not solely because Aelred was addressing himself to his sister. The desert fathers had counselled silence, and garrulity came to be associated (and has continued to be associated) peculiarly with women. The temptation to 'wander' in thought and speech was very real; nor was the recluse to permit herself to be distracted by money-making on the pretext of the need to do works of charity, for this should not be her concern. She was to provide for her own subsistence by the work of her hands or, if unable to do so, should arrange for one day's food at a time to be brought to her. To avoid offering charity or hospitality obviated the need for a large household. She was to choose an old woman with good references as custodian of the cell, with a girl under her who could bear burdens such as wood or water and cook beans, vegetables and potions if they should prove necessary. This girl was to be strictly controlled and children were to be kept away: 'There are some recluses who are occupied in teaching children and turn their cell into a school. She sits at the window, they sit in the anteroom (*in porticu*).' The possible attachments that might result are clearly condemned as 'carnal'.[8]

Having given this vivid if perhaps highly coloured picture of life as he would have it believed all too many anchoresses actually lived it, Aelred sketches ways in which the recluse could import the essentials of the monastic vocation into her cell. Silence was productive of peace and 'much fruit': 'Let her sit alone, let her keep silence, listening to Christ and speaking with Christ.' Confession was to be made at infrequent intervals (*raro*) to an old and worthy priest. Aelred's concern seems to slide rather easily from the positive spiritual benefits of silence to the need for the recluse to preserve her reputation by speaking with few. There were to be no affectionate exchanges of gifts with men and no making of purses or girdles for young monks or clerks, as frequently happened (the anchoress's manual skills were naturally thought likely to incline to needlework). Her work was rather to be directed to making useful things for her own upkeep, the surplus going either to the church or to the poor. The aim was perfect tranquillity of mind. The foolish and the talkative would be deterred when they saw that the recluse put a high value on silence.

Much of the treatise is devoted to the daily timetable which, as we have seen, posed problems for the cloistered monk as well as for the recluse. The individual who had withdrawn from secular life and confined himself or herself to an enclosed space, whether it was the larger enclosure of the monastery or the smaller enclosure of the cell, was threatened by the lack of the usual occupations of everyday life: 'idleness is the enemy of the soul'. Among other evils, it fomented *accidie* and melancholy; 'it breeds a revulsion from peace, it instils a horror of the cell'.[9] It must be dispelled by a variety of occupations, prayer among them. Aelred adapts the Benedictine rule to the recluse's needs. At the nocturnal vigils she was to pass from spontaneous prayer (which was not to be too long) to the Office of the Virgin, adding commemorations of the saints. She was to sing psalms for as long as they pleased her, but when this became burdensome,

> switch to reading, and if this becomes boring, rise up for prayer, and when tired by this change to manual work, so that by means a salutary alternation you may refresh your spirit and dispel *accidie*.

This guiding principle, already familiar to the desert fathers, is reiterated subsequently. The period between the midday meal and vespers was to be occupied in this way, and then

> After a short interval, let her privately read to herself something from the *Lives of the Fathers*, or the *Institutes* or miracles, so that a certain compunction may arise from this, and in some fervour of spirit let her say compline and with a heart full of devotion compose her limbs for bed.[10]

Does the phrase *secretius sibi legat* mean 'silently' or simply 'privately', in the sense of not being in the presence or hearing of the recluse's companion or maidservant? At all events, the recluse was educated enough to be able to participate in the culture of monastic spirituality inherited from Christian antiquity.

The third section of the treatise is devoted to meditation. Here was another means by which the religious solitary could introduce variety into his or her place of confinement. The recluse should 'first, with the blessed Mary, enter the bedroom and open the books in which the Virgin's conception and the advent of Christ are prophesied'. She is to accompany the Virgin on the Visitation, on the journey to Bethlehem and on the Flight into Egypt. Later, she is told 'Now enter the house of the Pharisee and wait upon the Lord who is reclining there; approach his feet with that most blessed sinner [Mary Magdalen]'. The hardworking Martha and Mary had already been introduced into the treatise when Aelred discussed the problem of practical charity; they appear again when the recluse is exhorted to enter the house at Bethany with Christ.[11] Step by step she is taken through the scenes of Christ's life and death; the contemplation of the risen Saviour is held up before her as a most delicious pleasure. What the pilgrim could hope to experience by contemplating the actual scenes of the birth, life and passion of Christ, the monk, nun or recluse (to whom in theory pilgrimage was debarred) might attain by such means. Like the recitation of the Office of the Virgin which Aelred had commended to his sister, this kind of meditation, the imaginative outgrowth of prayer and reading, was destined in the later medieval centuries to be exported from the monastic setting to the devout laity.

Despite the theoretical reservations of monastic lawgivers, many anchorites lived in the penumbra of monastic houses and earned the admiration, even the veneration, of monks as well as the support, active and passive, of the neighbouring laity. The *Life* of Christina of Markyate substantiates that point and also suggests just how many individuals, male and female, might be living the religious life in a small area of twelfth-century England and how often there were blood ties between them.[12] The Roger with whom Christina found refuge was a monk of St Albans who lived as a hermit in a wooded area of Watling Street between St Albans and Dunstable but still preserved obedience to his abbot.[13] Not only had he made the transition, with permission, from the monastic life to the eremitical, but he had become a highly regarded spiritual adviser. Christina was directed to him by his kinsman Eadwin, another hermit. Offered the choice of several places of refuge, she settled on Flamstead, some two miles from both St Albans and Roger's hermitage, where a recluse called Alfwen, much loved by Roger for her holiness, was already installed.

At least five hermits lived with Roger himself, for they acted as witnesses when Christina's husband Burhtred appeared and solemnly renounced his marital rights over her. Godescalc of Caddington and his wife lived 'a praiseworthy married life' under Roger's direction, and he entrusted to them the task of escorting Christina to an interview with Archbishop Thurstan of York at Redbourn.[14] Christina herself had both a brother, Gregory, who was a monk at St Albans, and a sister, Margaret, who joined the community which grew up at Markyate.[15]

At Flamstead Christina was accommodated in a very secluded and uncomfortable chamber which was scarcely big enough for her.[16] After two years, Roger decided to have her cell brought closer to his, despite Alfwen's opposition, and so mutually convinced were he and Christina of each other's holy intentions that they henceforth dwelled together. For four years Christina remained immured in a tiny 'prison' (*carcer*) adjoining Roger's cell and near his oratory; the entrance to it was sealed by a plank which Roger removed only in the evening, so that only then could she relieve herself, and so tiny was it that she could not even wear extra clothing in winter. It is little wonder that in this extreme penitential enclosure she developed a variety of infirmities which, as is customary in hagiography, served only to increase her merit.[17]

It was not until Roger died that Christina received formal consecration from the bishop of Lincoln.[18] This was the prelude to the establishment of a formal religious community for herself and the companions whom she had attracted. By this time she had established herself as an adviser to Geoffrey, abbot of St Albans; she was put on to his case by a holy monk called Alvered who had clearly previously established friendly relations with her. Like other recluses she received numerous visitors. It is implied that she did sometimes leave her enclosure: with her sister Margaret she attended her brother's burial at St Albans and she probably visited the monastery at other times, for she loved it as the burial place not only of the saint himself but of her mentor Roger.[19] Roger himself seems not have left his hermitage, although another hermit in the St Albans penumbra, Siger of Northaw, walked to the monastery every night to attend the services.[20]

Wulfric of Haselbury (d. 1154) was a close contemporary of Christina and, for all the obvious differences between them, not least their gender and the fact that Wulfric was an ordained priest, there are also points of comparison. Like Christina (whose given name was Theodora) Wulfric was English.[21] Like Christina, he entered on the solitary life without official authorization, and like her he earned the approbation of cloistered monks, in his case principally Cistercians. His *Life* was written by John, abbot of Forde in Somerset.[22] Although one of John's chief informants was a black monk, Walter of Glastonbury, much of Wulfric's network of holy contacts was Cistercian.[23] The scribe who assisted him, Richard, evidently a married man with a son, later became a monk and *cantor* at Forde; Henry, abbot of Waverley, evidently knew Wulfric, for he compared him to St Bernard, and further testimonies are quoted from the abbot of Tintern among others.

Born in Compton Martin in Somerset, Wulfric was still keen on hunting, although he was a priest, when a strange encounter with an angel in disguise changed his life. During the first phase of his conversion he remained in the world but embraced abstinence and 'with all his heart defended his solitude and holiness of spirit in the hall itself and amidst solemn feasts', an achievement as marvellous as it was difficult. He then removed to Haselbury, thirty miles east of Exeter, and, in a cell adjacent to a church which he had once served,

> not introduced by a bishop as is the custom, with no ceremony of benediction, but with the favour and authority of the Holy Spirit (*familiari Spiritus Sancti auctoritate*), he buried himself to Christ.[24]

In describing Wulfric's religious strategy, John of Forde had at his back a well-established Cistercian tradition of thinking about the true nature of solitude. That its essence was *interior* solitude was axiomatic:

> Just to condemn the body to prison confinement (*carceralibus angustiis*) while the soul remains outside, as is the way of many, is wretched madness; this is Jewish solitude, the shadow and not the truth.

Needless to say, this was not Wulfric's approach. In his confines he discovered 'immense latitude' (*summam latitudinem*) and developed his thoughts 'as freely as secretly', while God rained manna from heaven upon the *vir solitarius*.[25]

In fact Wulfric's solitude was heavily qualified. With some humour John describes his relationship with the priest Brihtric, who served the church to which his cell was attached. Brihtric was a simple married man, whose son Osbern eventually succeeded him in the care of the church. He was so inspired by Wulfric's example that he spent as much time as he possibly could in prayer in the church, rushing home for meals and rushing back again. Wulfric used to say that Brihtric 'was the real anchorite in this place, while he himself, who was perpetually involved in conversation, could more truly be called the parish priest'.[26] It was with reference more to the spiritual productivity of Wulfric's prayers and vigils than to these external contacts that John, using language by now familiar to us, asked rhetorically: 'Who can describe how busy was the quiet of his little cell (*quam negotiosum fuerat interim otium cellulae illius*)?' He adds another verbal paradox: 'How great a noise there was in the silence, what great peace amidst the noise! Was not this cell the *cella vinaria*, which has made the city of God itself rejoice?'[27]

It is one of the most interesting features of the *Life* that it gives at least some impression of what Wulfric's anchorhold was like.[28] It possessed a door into the chancel of the church, through which it was the holy man's habit to pass to celebrate vigils before the altar of St Michael. One day Wulfric sent his only servant to the smith's to obtain a *stapellum* (probably a bolt) which was necessary for the closure of the door. The servant locked the outer door and took the key with him. While he was away, a white-haired visitor knocked 'in the usual way' at Wulfric's window and they talked of holy things. The visitor asked if Wulfric had confessed all his sins: he replied, 'Yes, I think so', whereupon his visitor reminded him of another, remarking, 'Your place in heaven is prepared; all you lack is a bolt,' and promptly vanished. When the servant returned, Wulfric asked to be assured that he had in fact locked the outer door before he went on his errand.[29] The window, as it had been for some of the desert fathers, was the usual channel of communication with outsiders, but a crowd of people once came to the door (*ad ostium*) for Wulfric's blessing.[30] He tried to be sparing of speech in his consultations and, when the essential business had been done, he 'closed the window and retired to the innermost part of his cell'.[31]

Like Christina's *Vita*, Wulfric's reveals the existence of a loose community of religious enthusiasts in one corner of twelfth-century England. One day Wulfric sent his servant to bring 'my sister' to him. The servant was a trifle bemused as to who was meant, but found a West Saxon woman in 'the women's cemetery'. She told Wulfric that she was about to go on an overseas pilgrimage, but he informed her that her destiny was rather to live as an anchoress for sixteen years at Wareham, having first spent two years in the town as a mattress-maker. This was Matilda, who became known also to 'John the anchorite of Winterbourne which is in Dorset'. There were also 'the venerable *inclusa* of Wareham, Cristina', Odolina of Crewkerne and Aldida of Sturminster Newton. Evidently there was no shortage of women leading the solitary life in twelfth-century Dorset and Somerset. At a lower level of commitment, there were 'religious women', such as Joanna, wife of the lord of Haselbury, who sent servants to the cell with gifts of bread, pasties and wine.[32]

In the early thirteenth century there is further testimony to the popularity of the anchoritic way of life among Englishwomen in the form of vernacular literature for the use of female recluses, most famously the treatise *Ancrene Wisse*.[33] This draws on numerous sources (including Aelred) and may have been written by a canon of the Augustinian priory of Wigmore in Herefordshire.[34] The author sees the women to whom he addressed himself as constituting an 'order'; they were united by the life they led just as if they all lived in the same convent, 'in Oxford, London, Shrewsbury or Chester'. It was expected that the anchoress would be in touch with others by way of their maidservants, who might be permitted to stay for a couple of nights. Despite the seeming rigour of her enclosure, therefore, the life of the anchoress was in some important respects intermediate between that of the nun and the pious laywoman, including the beguines and tertiaries who will concern us later.

The tone of *Ancrene Wisse* is suitably austere, but somewhat less so than Aelred's manual, although the two authors agree on many obvious points. This author's treatment of breaches of the solitude and silence of the anchorhold is more humorous and less melodramatic than Aelred's:

> It is said of anchoresses that almost every one of them has some old woman to feed her ears, a gossip who tells her all the local tid-bits, a magpie who cackles about all that she sees and hears, so that the saying now runs, 'You can hear the news from a mill or a market, from a smithy or an anchorhouse'. Christ knows this is a sorry saying! – that an anchorhouse, which should be the loneliest place of all, can be compared to these three places that are most full of gossip.[35]

He is also in agreement with Aelred that the anchoress should not teach children or indulge in profitable economic activities. She should be very careful about disciplining her servants, but not too fussy about her attire. Her maidservants should be sober in dress and comportment and perform simple religious exercises within their capacity. At several points the regular monastic life is held up as the measure of what the anchoress should and should not do, but there are important distinctions. Her profession should cover only obedience, chastity and stability, leaving most externals, such as dress, diet and even what prayers she should say, open to negotiation. Virtues such as charity are anyway not optional.

The audience for *Ancrene Wisse* was presumed to be literate. Having gone to the trouble of writing the book, its author wanted it to be read repeatedly. He enthusiastically commended reading, in English or French, to the anchoress, to the extent of representing it as an alternative to prayer which in fact nourished and led to prayer. Quoting Jerome, he urged that she should always have 'holy reading' in her hands; sleep would come upon her and her drooping head would come to rest on the sacred page. He refers also to the English 'book of St Margaret' that she had in her possession.[36] He made available to his readers traditional concepts of solitude and its justifications, citing the pioneers of this way of life: Jacob, Moses, Elijah, Jeremiah, John the Baptist, the Desert Fathers. It is his frequent technique to quote the Latin scriptures and immediately translate into English, thus making plain his idea of the vernacular equivalents for the Latin terminology of the religious life.

What were the key words? 'Solitary life' is *anlich lif* and one who is 'solitary' may be *bi him ane*. A 'solitary place' is *anlich stude*, and 'sitting by oneself' (as envisaged by Jeremiah in Lamentations 3:28) *anlich sittung*. Words of ultimately Latin origin such as 'temptation', 'meditation' and 'recluse' were taken to be part of the anchoress's vocabulary and *silentium* had already given birth to 'silence', although the equivalent adjective remained the Germanic *stille*. The anchoress herself is most often called 'ancre', which enables the author to pun happily on the identical word for 'anchor'; her place of retreat is an *ancre hus*. Privacy's forerunner 'privity' (more exactly, *privite*) makes several appearances, sometimes signifying 'secrecy' more nearly than 'privacy' as we intend it. Urging the anchoress to keep her good deeds to herself, the author declares with memorable terseness, 'Bosom is privite'.[37]

It has very reasonably been urged that the solitude of the anchorite was not intended to resemble privacy as we understand it, but was an imprisonment, entered into for the sake of a more perfect penance, a deliberate self-deprivation of the sociability and support networks of normal life. It has also been suggested that while earlier guides to the enclosed life stress its penitential character, a change is observable from the early fourteenth century: a greater, more positive stress comes to be laid on the possibility of mystical advance in the knowledge of God, and the word 'contemplative' comes into use.[38] Much of course depends not only on how we now react to medieval texts but on how we suppose that they were read by their intended public and what conventions governed the description of situations and motivations. That individuals may have sought enclosure precisely in order to get away from social and familial obligations is hard to prove or disprove, however likely we may think it, for it was unlikely to be said. What precisely did the girl in the diocese of Würzburg – who had resisted marriage but was initially so unhappy in her enclosure – hope to achieve?

It is commonplace for spiritual writers commending solitude to insist on the woes of everyday human life, if only as an inducement to embrace religion. Marriage, child-birth and family life are made to sound anything but alluring, while the advertised counter-attractions include spiritual peace and a greater closeness to God. There are differences in tone between writers: the author of *Ancrene Wisse* may several times remind his reader that she is 'dead to the world', as the rite of enclosure made clear, but he is often much less forbidding, as when he commends washing: 'Wash yourself whenever it is necessary and as often as you like, and your things too. Dirt was never dear to God, though poverty and plainness are precious to him.'

The physical layout of the *ancre hus* envisaged in *Ancrene Wisse* is a little unclear. The author either had a standard arrangement in mind or was visualizing the cell of one particular woman with whom he was acquainted. It seems that (like Wulfric's) the anchorhold was divided into two principal parts, an inner sanctum where the recluse was intended to spend most of her time and which contained her bed, altars and images, and an outer 'parlour', occupied by her principal maidservant, who presumably slept there. Into this parlour the anchoress herself would come only when it was strictly necessary for her to do so. An important part is played in the text by windows both literal and metaphorical (in the latter case, the recluse's eyes), which represent her point of contact with the world outside her retreat and outside herself. There was a window into the church from the inner room; the anchoress was cautioned that she should not talk with anyone at this window, for its sole purpose was to enable her to see the Holy Sacrament. Then there was a 'parlour window' and a 'house window' and the author sometimes also speaks of a 'window' without qualification. The windows were to be tightly covered with black cloth with a white cross; black cloth kept its colour better and was more wind-resistant.

There have been divergent interpretations of where these windows were.[39] The parlour window may have been in the party wall between the parlour and the inner room and the house window in the external wall of the inner room. Alternatively, the parlour window was in an outside wall while the house window communicated between the inner room and the parlour. The author advises 'use the house window for talking sometimes with your women; for others, the parlor window'. Unless the maids were standing in the street, this seems to favour the interpretation that the 'house window' was in the party wall, permitting communication with the 'ancre hus' in the narrow sense, the recluse's inner sanctum.[40] The parlour window, wherever it was, should be the smallest and narrowest of all, because it was here that the anchoress communicated with callers. The author's insistence on the need to secure the cloth at the parlour window very firmly, and also on the dangers of looking out of it, seems to imply that this window gave on to the outside world (hence also the advantages of wind-resistance).

The anchoress was not to go to the parlour window unless she had found out from her maid who it was who wanted to speak with her. If that window was in an outside wall, this prior consultation could take place through the house window and the anchoress, if satisfied, would presumably enter the parlour in order to speak to the visitor. At all events there must surely have been an exterior window in the parlour where the maid spent her time and was permitted to entertain visitors. The anchoress should not go into the parlour to eat with guests, but might open her window from time to time to make friendly signals to them. Neither here nor when he forbids her to play 'worldly games' at her window with her maid does the author specify whether this is the 'parlour' or the 'house' window, but the reference to using the house window for communication with the maids seems to favour the latter. It was clearly possible for a caller to see into the inner room, for if a man's devotion impelled him to see the anchoress's altar she might draw the cloth aside to permit him to do so, veiling herself closely in the meantime. She was advised how to cope with the shocking possibility that he might cast his eyes towards her bed and ask her where she slept. This window was evidently not so small and narrow that it did not permit a fairly extensive view of the inner room. If a man made so bold as to reach out his hand towards the cloth she should shut the window at once. This window had either to be in an external wall of the inner cell or in the party wall; in the latter case this wolf in devotee's clothing must have obtained admission to the parlour. Wulfric, we have seen, was able to converse through a window with a visitor while his servant was out and the outer door was locked.

These trivial details may seem to have nothing to do with the quality of the interior life; but every solitary had to occupy a real physical environment. It might be the object of the exercise to transcend environmental limitations, but the difficulty of so doing was recognized at every turn. Bodily necessities had to be met. The varied company and clientele which clustered around such a cell, ranging from the recluse's servant or servants to pious visitors and the beneficiaries of the healing or prophetic powers which a recluse sometimes dispensed, must sometimes have amounted to a substantial qualification of anchoritic solitude; but solitude should probably always be evaluated in relation to a particular state of society.

The essential feature of the life adopted by Christina of Markyate, by Wulfric or by the anchoress of *Ancrene Wisse* was its detachment from the workaday obligations of the layman and laywoman. These varied according to the subject's rank and gender, but might include war, statecraft, litigation, marketing, trade, household management and childbirth, all of them bothersome and some of them dangerous. This withdrawal constituted one meaning of 'solitude', as it had done for almost a thousand years. By adopting this course, anchorites male and female opened up for themselves possibilities akin to those which we now find in privacy: the freedom to choose how to spend their time and with it the risk of depression and boredom. In this too they resembled the desert monk or the Carthusian. To a large extent (as the sad proverbial tales of gossiping anchoresses revealed) the degree of their solitude and the quality of their inner life depended on themselves; hence the reservations with which they were regarded by some cenobites.

If proper procedures were followed, the anxieties Bernard had articulated were met by thorough examination of the candidate before she was enclosed. In January 1436 Beatrice Franke, hitherto a nun of Stainfield Priory, entered an anchorhold adjacent to the parish church of Winterton in Lincolnshire. First her prioress certified the sincerity of her intention to lead a stricter life and to obtain 'more freedom to contemplate [her] Creator'; William Gray, bishop of Lincoln, echoed these words and authorized the abbot of Thornton to examine Beatrice before performing the rite of enclosure. The abbot in his turn pronounced himself satisfied that she was not wavering, but had desired the solitary life almost from infancy, and recorded 'shutting up the aforesaid sister Beatrice in a building and enclosure constructed on the north side of the said church and making fast the door thereof with bolts, bars and keys'. She was left, the abbot believed, 'in peace and calm of spirit'.[41]

Why did Beatrice choose Winterton, which is over thirty miles distant from Stainfield? Was she in fact returning to a place where she (or her family) was already known? Were her necessary servants recruited locally or brought with her? Directly or indirectly, members of the village community would certainly play a part in meeting her various needs; life might have been difficult for her if they had been hostile to her vocation. The bishop's instructions to the abbot in fact included a direction to ascertain whether 'the consent and agreement of the general folk among whom she will have her conversation are forthcoming in this behalf'. The relationship is nicely illustrated in the predella that is all that remains of an altarpiece celebrating Giulia (d. 1367), a recluse of Certaldo in Tuscany; it shows children bringing bread to her window and receiving flowers (miraculously always available in the cell) in return.[42] The window gives directly on to the street.

There are several surviving examples and some modern reconstructions of anchorholds. That of the celebrated Julian of Norwich, long since destroyed, has been reconstructed conjecturally in a position against the south side of the church from which the occupant could see the high altar. Another East Anglian example is similarly built on to the south side of the church of St Nicholas at King's Lynn. The 'Anker's House' at Chester-le-Street was differently arranged; at the north-west corner of the church, it is on two storeys. The anchorite lived in the upper room, reached by a ladder, and his only view of the church was obtained through an exceedingly narrow squint. This was a collegiate church and the anchorite's view was not of the chancel where the canons celebrated mass but of the altar in the south aisle where mass was celebrated for the parishioners.[43]

Anchorites were both male and female; the hermit was almost invariably male and could be both more obviously detached from the everyday social world and economically self-supporting. Because he could turn up anywhere, he was a useful character in fiction. An example is the hermit whom Chretien's Yvain, run mad out of disappointed love, discovers in the middle of a forest, dwelling in a house which is 'very small and lowly'. Yvain is stark naked; he has been killing beasts with his bare hands and eating the flesh raw. The hermit's first reaction to this startling apparition is to retire post-haste in terror into his *maisonnete*, but he has sufficient self-command to extend charity to the unfortunate madman, putting bread and pure water out on a windowsill for him. Bread and water had ancient religious meanings, but one senses here that they also signify civilization itself; the hermit in the forest is a mediator between the world which Yvain has abandoned in despair and the total savagery into which he has now fallen. Yvain's longing for the bread is strongly emphasized, even though, as Chretien ironically comments, it is unlikely that he had ever tasted any so coarse: this was not made of finely milled flour, but of 'barley kneaded with straw'. When he has eaten and drunk he plunges back into the forest in search of game and the hermit, watching him go, prays earnestly that he won't come back again. There is no creature, however, that will not return where it has received benefits, and Yvain returns daily. The bread and the water are regularly put out for him and the hermit makes the effort to skin the venison he kills and to cook a goodly part of it (unlike Yvain, he evidently has a fire, another sign of civilization). He tries also to sell the skins and buy barley or wheaten bread. This hermit is no spiritual superman and he is not the sole agent of Yvain's redemption, but he is important in helping to arrest his decline and his little house is a staging post on the way out of the wilderness.[44]

Yvain's hermit clearly did not live a hundred miles from a market. Many eremitical vocations originated in a revulsion against the growing commercialism of the world but, unless the environment favoured total self-sufficiency, the lives that resulted had to be lived within reach of settled society. A number of individuals from urban backgrounds rejected mercantile wealth in favour of poverty and its concomitant, religious solitude, before Francis of Assisi so famously did so early in the thirteenth century. The most remarkable of Francis's Italian forerunners was Ranieri of Pisa (d. 1160) who, like his English near-contemporary and counterpart Godric of Finchale, felt the first stirrings of his conversion while still engaged in trade.[45]

The first major influence on Ranieri was a holy man called Albert, a Corsican who when Ranieri first heard of him had his *habitaculum* with the monks of San Vito in Pisa; he dwelled in the abbey hospital and received 'food and clothing' from the abbot.[46] The first signs of Ranieri's conversion under Albert's influence were greeted with dismay by his parents, for he was their only son, but he was not yet ready to make the decisive move and in 1140, aged about twenty-five, he went to Jerusalem with a load of cheeses which he hoped to sell during the forthcoming Lenten fast. An intolerable stench arising from the cheeses however notified him that these intentions were misplaced. In a series of stages he detached himself from his normal company and conduct, eventually 'hiding' for eight days on the walls of Jerusalem with 'the solitaries who live there', until his original companions and compatriots went away.[47] Here he remained until he returned to Pisa in 1153.

As a hermit in Jerusalem Ranieri was often invited to eat with one of the other solitaries on the walls and used to drink wine with him, only for the invitation to be cancelled when he received a divine injunction to drink no more wine. God consoled Ranieri: he would henceforth have a *habitaculum* of his own 'where I shall give you my own dinner'.[48] What this meant in practical terms was that Ranieri found lodgings with a *religiosa matrona* who cooked for him, and he did not leave her house until he returned to Pisa, obedient to Christ's words: 'In whatever house you enter, remain there and do not leave it, and do not move from house to house' (Matthew 10:11; Luke 9:14). This did not mean that Ranieri never left the house, for he continued to receive alms at the church of the Holy Sepulchre; the point was stability of residence. When Ranieri at last returned to Pisa he took up residence in the monastery of San Vito, where Albert had originally illuminated his mind, and became much sought after as a healer, especially of the possessed. Monasteries often had male and female devotees dwelling within their precincts or at their gates who in some measure shared in the conventual life.

Ranieri's life was lived in two major Mediterranean cities, Jerusalem and Pisa. The course followed by his English counterpart Godric of Finchale was strongly marked by his very different physical environment. In early life he was 'at once merchant and pilgrim', according to his biographer Reginald, monk of Durham; he frequently visited Lindisfarne and Farne Island, and began to conceive the desire to abandon the mercantile life when he heard about Cuthbert's *vita solitaria* and the marvels he had performed.[49] On his return from a pilgrimage to Rome he began to lead a form of religious life in his parents' house: 'night and day he never ceased from divine conversation and prayer'. His mother and father greeted his vocation more kindly than Ranieri's had done, his mother in fact deciding to accompany him on a second Roman pilgrimage. It was after their return from this journey that Godric definitively decided to obey the gospel precept: 'If you want to be perfect, go and sell everything that you have and give to the poor and come and follow Me.' After a while he found a suitable place of retreat at Eskedale Side in the parish of Whitby, but was bothered by the lords of the place and transplanted himself to the vicinity of Durham. Here he acquired some basic instruction by joining the children at their lessons and in due course settled in the 'horrid solitude' of Finchale beside the Wear, receiving the cession of a plot of land from the bishop, none other than the Ranulf who had so pestered Christina of Markyate.

For a long time Godric had no companion and tried to avoid seeing anyone. His 'house' was dug out of the ground and covered with sods. There was some sort of roof with a cross-beam, for we learn that the 'serpents and worms' which were attracted by his fire used to lie along it when the warmer weather came. Eventually, demonstrating his power over nature as his predecessors among the eastern and Celtic saints, and also Cuthbert, had done, Godric dismissed them. The local people sought him out with offers of food and other good things but he always refused, preferring to consort with the wild beasts rather than with men.[50] In the course of time he erected a rough wooden structure which he called the chapel of St Mary, with an adjacent *domus* in which he lived and kept his necessary tools. At some point he acquired a servant, who would bring a large pot into the chapel, where none but he was permitted to enter; closing the door, Godric filled it with water and immersed himself in it to quell the stirrings of the flesh.[51]

Meanwhile, as so often happened, a community was growing around the hermit. Godric had *famuli* who were often with him in the fields, and a small boy who ran errands into the outside world. There was a guesthouse: Godric was unwilling to send guests away unfed. When his sister expressed her wish to lead a solitary life with him, he assented and built her a *cellula secretior* a short distance from the oratory. The little group was reliant on visiting priests to perform the sacraments, and Godric's sister rarely entered the oratory unless it was to hear mass on such an occasion.[52] The increasing resort of the faithful to Godric impelled the building of a larger *cellula*, accompanied by a church which was dedicated to St John the Baptist. Adjacent to this a *domus* was built in two sections, in one of which Godric was wont to talk with his *domestici* and to receive visiting friends. The larger section, which was thatched, was dedicated to other necessary purposes. The entire construction was wooden and vulnerable to fire; it must have resembled many a contemporary farmhouse.[53]

As he aged, Godric was scarcely able to get out of what Reginald calls the *mansiuncula* of his oratory. The care of the community was made over entirely to the priors of Durham, who deputed individual monks, including Reginald, to perform tours of duty there. Godric's efforts to avoid conversation were partly frustrated by his infirmity and need for attendance but he evidently continued to seek solitude, in the church and elsewhere, whenever he could. Clearly he retained a sharp sense that it was essential to the eremitical vocation to maintain mental concentration on the spiritual objective. When Prior Thomas sent Reginald to ask questions about the saint's life (he was obviously earmarked to write the *Vita* before Godric died), he gleaned only self-accusations, among them the saint's declaration that he was 'no solitary, but one who roams in thought over every kind of uncleanness'.[54] As for the desert fathers, the solitary was defined not by his external mode of living, but by his internal focus on one thing only.

Christina of Markyate had a brother and a sister who embraced the religious life; Godric's sister joined him; another northern hermit of slightly later date, Robert of Knaresborough (d. 1218), had two brothers who followed religious vocations.[55] One was a lay brother at the Cistercian abbey of Newminster and another, Walter, a senior cleric (*maior*), presumably a canon, of the church of York.[56] Robert himself was ordained subdeacon and spent some time with his brother at Newminster, winning praise from the abbot, before returning to the parental home and then joining forces with a hermit who was living in a cave at Knaresborough, 'in a place of horror and vast emptiness' (*in loco horroris et vaste solitudinis*).[57] It was here that after numerous vicissitudes Robert would eventually return and die.

> Besyde Knaresburgh in a skerre
> In a creves closed hym ferre
> And full devoutely he lay
> In contemplacioun nyght and day
> In service of our Savioure
> Als solitary close day and houre.[58]

This was the age of Robin Hood, and Robert's fellow-hermit was not quite what he seemed. He had aroused the wrath of Richard I and was in hiding from the king's agents; one wonders how many other hermits could be similarly explained. When Richard died he went back to his vomit, that is to his wife and children.

The early *Life* now comments that Robert 'had not yet learnt how to sit alone and in silence'; this interesting judgement is not repeated in the other sources.[59] He found succour from a widow called Helena who gave him a nearby church dedicated to St Hilda, where he lived a life of great austerity until robbers stripped him of his sustenance (according to the later *Life* this consisted of bread and cheese). He now moved to 'Spofforth town' (a little south east of Harrogate), where he began to achieve local celebrity as a saint, and from there to Headley, a small abbey where the monks identified him as *homo singularis*, unlike them in dress and life, and drove him out. He returned to the church of St Hilda and the benevolent widow extended substantial help to him, employing workmen to build him 'an honest hall' and a barn. Like Godric's, this presumably resembled a peasant farmhouse. Four servants were hired, two to work the land, one to go about the country to gather alms and the fourth to attend on Robert personally.[60]

Like Godric early in his career, Robert now had trouble with the local lord, Willliam de Stuteville, who happened by and observed the new building. To him Robert was an impostor and 'a receiver of thieves and robbers'. It is not clear whether this was William's opinion of hermits in general or of Robert in particular. Had he perhaps heard about his dubious previous associate? At all events Robert was driven out and returned to the site near Knaresborough where he had previously lived. Here there was no shelter but a chapel dedicated to St Giles (of which there seems now to be no trace), so Robert built himself a wooden hut against the cliff and settled down, as he hoped, to the peaceful contemplation of God, away from 'popular tumult' (*plebis strepitus*), which one would not suppose to have been all that great in early thirteenth-century Knaresborough. He was mistaken: crowds came bearing gifts and bestowed on him a little field (*agellum*) near the river which he could cultivate 'with his own ploughs'. At this point William de Stuteville reappeared and saw a plume of smoke rising from the hermitage. Once again he resolved to destroy it, but this time he was warned by a vision and became a changed man, endowing Robert with land 'between the cliff and Grimbald Kirkston', together with two oxen, horses and cows.[61]

Robert now received a visit from his brother Walter, canon of York. He regarded Robert's habitation as 'too cramped and confined and bare and bereft of all conveniences' and tried to persuade him to join a community living under a proper rule but, finding him resolved on his solitude, decided to be helpful. He sent to York for craftsmen who built the chapel, which was dedicated to the Holy Cross, and made certain improvements to the *domus* so that Robert could accommodate the poor and pilgrims. Up to this moment Robert had had servants but no fully-fledged companion. He now engaged one 'To beilde [help] hym with his besiness' so that he could devote himself to religion, or (in the words of the *Metrical Life*), 'haunte hys halynes'.[62] The cave is still to be seen, buried in trees on a steep slope above the river Nidd, and it is the only site which can genuinely be connected with the saint. Without a torch its depths are impenetrable, but ledges and recesses have been hollowed out in two of its corners. Robert presumably prayed in here before the little chapel, whose outlines can be seen on the tiny flat space in front of the cave, was built for him. A kind of stone bench runs along the outside of the cave. Robert was buried before the altar of the chapel.[63]

Although these glimpses of Robert's setting have a certain vividness the character of his inner life is barely indicated in the sources. The fleeting suggestion in the fragmentary early *Life* that he had something to learn about solitary living is not elaborated. Reginald's account of Godric is altogether more developed and gives a clearer sense of a tradition of spirituality and pious practice within which the saint tried to locate himself or (perhaps more accurately) could be located by an informed observer. Undoubtedly Reginald was writing, as most hagiographers did, primarily to establish the credentials of a saint, and undoubtedly he knew about the desert fathers, whether or not Godric himself did. The *Lives* of Robert seem to have been written more simply for an audience that would be impressed by the plain fact that this man had overcome adversity in his determination to live as other men did not.

The religious solitude of monks, nuns, hermits and anchorites alike meant withdrawal from the normal round of social and familial obligations, but recluses and, often, hermits lived in a more obvious condition of proximity to, and even dependence on, the local lay population. Their living accommodation also was intermediate in character between the fully-fledged convent behind its perimeter wall and the ordinary dwelling-house or farmhouse. The presence of a chapel or oratory as an adjunct to the living space was a distinguishing feature. In human terms hermits and anchorites often constituted the centre of a small group or affinity of servants, helpers, devotees and disciples, some of whom were themselves subjected to a degree of religious discipline. Some of those who lived on the outer edge of the circle might be leading entirely normal social lives but were classifiable as devout. Wulfric of Haselbury and Robert of Knaresborough both received help, in Robert's case substantial help, from pious women. There was nothing extraordinary in that, and the phrase *religiosa femina*, when used by John of Forde to describe the Joanna who sent provisions to Wulfric, seems to have no technical meaning. In a different environment, and with the passage of time, it could take on a rather more specific significance.

7

In Chamber and in Hall

In about 1290 a two-storeyed stone extension was built to an existing hall block at Old Soar in Kent, between the North Downs and the Weald. It may have been the work of members of a prominent local family, the Culpepers. The ground floor of the new block was probably used for storage. A door a few steps above ground level gave access to the hall from the staircase which led to the three apartments on the upper floor: a solar or great chamber with a fine timber roof, a spacious garderobe and a chapel. The hall has been replaced by an eighteenth-century brick house, but evidence survives to indicate that it was aisled and timber-roofed, with a dais for the high table against the east wall, which the new extension abutted.[1] Here we may imagine the Culpepers presiding over the traditional functions of business and sociability to which they were committed as landowners.

The builders of the new block were doing what had been done at Ardres two centuries earlier: creating space apart for their private use. Stripped of its original furnishings and somewhat battered by the centuries, it is now a shell in which only traces of their private life can be discerned. An aperture in the west wall may have made it possible for the *paterfamilias* to see what was going on in the adjacent hall; a similar feature is to be found in other manor houses. Small valuables could be stored in locked cupboards in both this and the opposite fireplace wall. The fireplace has lost its chimney-hood, but (provided it drew properly) it would have made the apartment not only warmer but less smoky than the hall, almost certainly heated by the customary central hearth. The tall windows to north and south were originally not glazed but shuttered. The one to the north had window seats of polished marble, doubtless rendered more comfortable by cushions, which are frequently mentioned in late medieval inventories of domestic possessions. Here it was possible to sit and converse, listen to music or story-telling, gaze out over the surrounding countryside or perhaps even read by the available light. As this chamber was doubtless also used for sleeping, we need to supply in imagination a bed, stools, probably wall-hangings; a table could easily have been put up if the family wished to take a meal together.

At almost the same moment, far to the west in Shropshire, the wool-merchant Laurence of Ludlow was in search of similar amenities but on a more sumptuous scale. Edward I's forcible pacification of Wales made it possible for Laurence to build his manor-house at Stokesay (miscalled a castle) with only vestigial fortifications.

Here he provided himself with a great hall, with the traditional central hearth and magnificent timbered roof, but there were also spacious living rooms in the north and south towers, whether intended for guests or for members of the family, with fireplaces, window-seats and latrines. The lordly hall and the sophisticated private accommodation were alike essential to the self-image of a man who had 'arrived'.[2] At a true castle some sixty miles to the north, Chepstow, which had already been so added to and altered as to offer all the amenities the noble heart could desire, Marten's Tower was built at a very similar period with a private chapel and rooms on each floor with fireplace and latrine. The upper classes, both lay and ecclesiastical, were engaged in an ongoing quest for civilized private living.

The basic division of the secular household between 'hall' and 'chamber' continued to be reflected in the literature of the later middle ages.[3] The word 'chamber' appears in the written English language around 1300, at about the time that Old Soar and Stokesay were built. Phrases like 'in chamber or in hall' are commonly used to distinguish the living quarters of a house from the kitchen and other offices. In *Mum and the Sothsegger* it is declared that the 'sothsegger' (truth-teller) is 'To be cherisshid of chief in chambre or in halle'.[4] Sometimes the old English word 'bour' takes the place of 'chamber' in these doublets, possibly implying a greater privacy and seclusion and often associated with the women's apartments, a sense which sits well with its use in *Beowulf*. The phrase 'bright in bower' is a stock description for a marriageable maiden.[5] Not all bowers, however, belonged to women. In *Piers Plowman* Covetise explains that his wife got away with selling small beer to those who thought they were buying the best quality because 'The beste ale lay in my bour or in my bedchamber'. Both were screened from public access; it was easy to adulterate the beer or to substitute small beer for it on its way to the customer.[6]

'Chamber' too might have feminine connotations. In the fifteenth-century version of *Guy of Warwick* 'Knyghtys sate in the halle, Ladyes in the chaumbur alle',[7] and this distinction is attested elsewhere in the poem. When Guy's lord directs him to wait upon his daughter and her damsels in the chamber where they are eating, he falls hopelessly in love with the young lady. The archaic English custom, still not quite dead, which requires the women to follow the lady of the house in withdrawing from the dining room after dinner and leaving the men to their drink is a survival of this division of leisure. It was however a poet's assumption that the mistress of the household, who played a wider strategic role than her daughters and the other women, would preside at feasts, perhaps exercising a civilizing influence on the proceedings. In the description of Arthur's New Year Court with which *Gawain and the Green Knight* begins, Guinevere is seated on the dais under a canopy of Toulouse cloth.

Gawain offers some colourful imaginative pictures of the movement of a household's life between hall and chamber. As Gawain approaches the castle where he is to have such an interesting stay, he sees it glittering white and bristling with chimney-pots (line 798). We may imagine it, girded by its moat, as bearing some resemblance to Bodiam in East Sussex, built in the 1380s.[8] Chimneyed fireplaces were not new, but evidence for them and references to them multiply in the fourteenth century.[9] They give the 'chambers' in the castle of *Gawain* a certain style and luxury, but the hall remains the principal reception room. It is here that Gawain is introduced when he arrives; a fire burns on the hearth, presumably in the centre of the floor.[10] He is greeted by the lord, who emerges from his chamber, and is then taken 'to a bright bower' with a chimneyed fireplace in which charcoal is burning. A chair (later called a 'settle', line 882) is set for him before this fire; the host's own chamber also has such a fireplace. Gawain's secluded bedchamber is another necessary element in the story. It has a door which can be locked or bolted, for the lady of the house does just that when she softly enters the room on her repeated missions to seduce her guest.

Thus far, the private chamber or bower is not specifically associated with the women of the house but, after service in the chapel, it is they who take Gawain 'to chamber, to chimney' (line 978), where they send for spice-cakes and wine. Games of an unspecified nature take place in the hall, which presumably had more room for music and dancing. The host enters the hall (here called the *sale*) on his return from the hunt, and summons the ladies down from the *loghe* to inspect his bag. Later, when they have played in the hall for as long as they desire, the lord invites Gawain to his chamber and they go and stand by the fireplace (line 1030). The picture is not so much one of a stark demarcation of ladies in the chamber and knights in the hall as of a movement between more and less private apartments, in obedience to a well-understood code which governed who went where, when and with whom. Bodiam Castle, which abounds in rooms of different sizes, with and without fireplaces, conveys a strong sense that distinct spaces were allocated to the different groups that might at any one moment be present (the lord and his family, guests of rank, the garrison, household and estate servants), even if it is not possible to recapture every detail of how that allocation was carried out.

The mid-fourteenth-century core of the Kentish manor house known as Ightham Mote is approximately contemporaneous with *Gawain*. The domestic layout that was accumulated piecemeal at Old Soar, barely three miles away, can be recognized here, as at the heart of numerous manor houses and farmhouses elsewhere in England. At one end of the central hall, which rises to the full height of the building, is a service area; at the other, on an upper floor, there were private apartments (now reached by a seventeenth-century staircase), including a chapel. This hall is smaller than the one which once stood at Old Soar and has no raised dais for the high table, but it did have a chimneyed fireplace (the present one is Elizabethan). At Penshurst, some eight miles from Ightham, Sir John Pulteney, London merchant made good, built himself in the 1340s a great hall of impressive dimensions, complete with dais and the traditional central hearth.[11] Pulteney's self-image probably demanded grandeur as much as comfort. He also had his solar or great chamber (now much altered) over an undercroft to the west of the hall.

This was a pattern which was capable of innumerable variations of detail and was adaptable to the aspirations and ambitions of both the hugely and the modestly wealthy. Less grand than Ightham or Old Soar, and several degrees less grand than Penshurst, is the fifteenth-century Kentish farmhouse called Bayleaf, which originally stood at Chiddingstone near Edenbridge.[12] Here the owner, presumably a yeoman, had his lofty 'great hall' with its central hearth and his private apartments, including an upper chamber with garderobe, at one end. Adapted to changing needs and tastes in the following centuries, the 'Wealden' houses of which Bayleaf is a representative still stand in large numbers. This arrangement represented only one of many possible ways in which better-off householders could supply their wants and advertise their status. In the fifteenth century, at Gainsborough Old Hall in Lincolnshire, the central block occupied by great hall and solar was flanked by east and west wings which provided extra accommodation. It was a distinctive feature of both these wings that access to the rooms on the upper floors was from a corridor on the inner, courtyard side; they did not, as was more common, simply open one into another.[13] Such corridors, often regarded as a later architectural development, occur occasionally in late medieval buildings. In urban houses they may have been 'created accidentally when the house was built down one side of the plot',[14] but however they originated they offered the possibility of greater seclusion to the occupants of the several chambers.

Everywhere in Europe, great (and aspiring) men possessed grand apartments in which they could at need entertain lavishly and withdrawing-rooms into which they could retreat to enjoy moments of leisure with a more select company. The scale and elaboration of what was built depended not only on the owner's wealth but on his social position and ambitions, while the uses to which similar apartments were put varied in different societies. The 'great hall' has been described as a distinctively English concept, not because English halls were necessarily larger or more splendid than comparable rooms in France or elsewhere, but because they were differently used. In England it was customary, at least on certain occasions, for the lord and lady to dine at the high table in the hall, together not only with their special guests but with the entire household and clients and visitors of all ranks. The high table was so called because of its raised position on the dais; clear visual expression was thus given both to hierarchy and to hospitality. In France (in households of sufficient grandeur), the *grande salle* was strictly reserved for nobility and clergy.[15] Halls rising through two storeys were unknown in France, but in England they were possessed by householders of modest standing, such as the farmer who owned Bayleaf.

In the Norse society recreated or imagined in the sagas many of the leading men were both farmers and warriors, and their dwellings accordingly had to supply multiple needs. Evocations of the domestic setting are scattered throughout the saga literature and archaeology has amplified the picture. Stone building was rare in this environment and accommodation for the most part extended horizontally rather than vertically, although there are references to cellars and also to loft rooms that were not just used for storage. In *Egil's Saga* (written between 1220 and 1240) Egil has a private conversation with his confidant Arinbjorn in an upper room in the latter's house and remains there all night, composing a poem in praise of King Eirik.[16] In *Njal's Saga* the ill-fated Gunnar sleeps with his wife Hallgerd and her mother in a loft room above the main room.[17]

More often, a couple would occupy a 'bed closet' on ground level, inserted into the main room of the house and provided with a door that could be secured from the inside, although it was also possible for a bed to be screened only by curtains. An eleventh-century farmhouse excavated at Stöng in Iceland had a 'hall' with a central hearth and benches along the walls which served for both sitting and sleeping; a 'bed-closet' was inserted between the benches on one side of the hall. Attached to one end of the hall was a living-room which broadly resembled the main hall on a smaller scale, with benches around the sides. Spaces could be added horizontally as required; at Stöng there were a latrine and storeroom off the hall.[18]

There is no indication of an upper floor in this house, but storage and other facilities could be provided in buildings separate from the main farmhouse. In *Laxdaela Saga*, written in the second half of the thirteenth century but set over two hundred years earlier, it is remarked that 'in those days it was fashionable to have outdoor privies some distance from the farmhouse'. In the same work there is a reference to an 'outbuilding used for the storage of fine possessions'.[19] Some outhouses had fireplaces and could be used for the accommodation of unexpected or unwelcome guests; one householder who offered such grudging hospitality (and no ale) to Egil and his companions did not outlive their visit.[20] Egil's brother Thorolf entertains King Harald Fairhair to a feast; as he possesses no hall big enough for the number of guests he proposes to invite he fits out a barn or granary for the occasion, with benches at which the drink can be served and shields hung all round the building for that obligatory touch of virile *noblesse*. The touchy king is not best pleased by this display, suspecting that Thorolf means not so much to do him honour as to threaten him by advertising the size of his following, and Thorolf's enemies are quick to insinuate that he had in fact planned to kill the king but did not want his own fine house burnt down in the process.[21]

There were different words for the principal apartment in these houses, variously rendered in English as 'hall', 'main room', 'living room' or 'fire-room'. Where the kitchen was a separate room or building, it was sometimes called the 'fire-room', while 'main room' might designate an additional living room, similarly fitted with benches, as at Stöng.[22] The thirteenth-century author of *Eyrbyggja Saga* described a farmhouse which possessed a 'large living-room with a bed closet behind it, as was usual in those days'. It was in this room that people sat for hours before mealtimes by the principal fire. It also had panelling, and sounds very much like the 'hall'.[23] The normal routine in this household was somewhat disturbed when a party of drowned men invaded their own funeral feast, walking through 'the main room, which had two doors, and into the living room', where the fire was burning and the feast took place. The living were understandably discomfited by this turn of events and fled into another room, which had no fire. On subsequent nights they had to light two fires, one in the 'living room' for the drowned men.[24] Here the 'main room' was evidently distinct from the 'living room', as at Stöng.

Provision was made for status and privacy within this framework. The householder's high-seat, with its ornamental carved posts, was placed in the centre of the 'upper' bench, which ran along the right-hand side of the hall as one entered; the 'lower' bench was not lower in terms of elevation but opposite, and the guest of honour sat in the middle of that. The cross-bench or dais which ran across the far end of the room was the women's domain. The bride and her attendants would sit there at wedding-feasts and on other occasions women congregated there to sew, spin and talk. A sick woman might lie on the 'cross-bench' during the daytime.[25] In *Gisli's Saga*, Thorkel stretches out in the 'fire-room' after breakfast and overhears the women gossiping as they sew in the 'women's area' on the south side. We are told that this room was 100 feet long and 60 feet wide.[26]

Women of standing seem sometimes to have had their own apartments, but it is not always entirely clear whether they were located in separate buildings or simply partitioned off from the hall. In *Egil's Saga* Bjorn's mother has a private room in which she sits with the other women, including Thora, Bjorn's intended bride; when he takes Thora away the women are warned not to talk about this in the more public part of the house.[27] In *Njal's Saga* Hallgerd often uses a private room, where on one occasion she gossips mischievously with some beggar-women and also with at least one man, Sigmund. He makes some scurrilous verses about a neighbour, only to be overheard by Hallgerd's husband, Gunnar, outside the door.[28] In the saga which bears his name, Kormak is received in the hall at Gnupsdal where the fire burns; Steingerd comes from her room and, hearing strange voices, peers over a half-door into the hall. It seems that she is standing in a 'narrow, dark passage' which runs around the hall, presumably separating it from the more private apartments and also perhaps from storerooms. The following morning, finding no one in the hall, Kormak hears the voices of Steingerd and her women in 'an inner room' (perhaps her own) where she is combing her hair.[29]

The bed-closet often features in these narratives. The old might spend most of their time in one; in *Laxdaela Saga* the formidable Unn the Deep-Minded in her old age retired early, slept until noon and was not to be disturbed during that time.[30] Egil, pretending to be mortally ill, shut himself up in his bed-closet; he was, however, prepared to admit his daughter, who lay down on the other bed before inveigling him back into circulation. When old and blind, he spent his time getting under the feet of the women as he tried to get warm near the central hearth, retiring to his bed when they rebuked him.[31]

The houses of the sagas broadly conform to the 'longhouse' type which was characteristic of much of northern Europe. At Stöng the animals were clearly stabled elsewhere in the farm enclosure, but in many German houses their stalls were to be found under the roof of the hall (generating warmth as well as odour) with the family's living accommodation screened off at the other end. The ceiling space of such halls might be floored over, to provide storage for grain rather than space for people. As indicated in the sagas, two-storeyed living accommodation was not unknown. It has been suggested that the appearance of upper rooms in Germany was influenced by the spread of urban fashions among the more prosperous peasantry, for this space-saving feature had early become characteristic of town-house building.[32] Wherever and whenever it appeared, it was dependent on the involvement of professional carpenters and other specialist craftsmen.

Much rural housing in England was single-storey.[33] Descriptions in manorial court records of houses built or planned in late medieval Worcestershire reveal very little explicit evidence of upper storeys, although houses of three or more bays were not uncommon.[34] Long houses with accommodation at one end for cattle continued to be built in this region, but became rarer after about 1350 in England as a whole. For the more affluent, the trend was towards a two- or three-bay dwelling, divided by walls or partitions. The 'Wealden' house and its many equivalents elsewhere were born when upper rooms were inserted into the end bays. The central bay, often open to the roof as in grander houses, was the 'hall'. In *The Nun's Priest's Tale*, Chaucer describes the poor widow's cottage as having both 'hall' and 'bour'. Both are 'sooty' and the character of the 'hall' is clarified when we learn that the cock Chantecleer roosts in it with Pertelote and the rest of his harem. The contrasting 'bour' was presumably used as a bedroom by the widow and her two daughters.[35] Perhaps Chaucer's language is not as tongue-in-cheek as it might seem, for peasant dwellings were in fact described in fourteenth- and fifteenth-century documents as consisting of 'hall' (*aula*) and 'chambers'.[36]

In several areas of England (as elsewhere) there seem to be signs of thirteenth-century changes in both style and method of building, which drew added strength from the shifts in income distribution and in the balance of power between lords and tenants which followed the fourteenth-century plagues. This resulted in more substantial structures, which may have made a reasonable amount of living-space available to their inhabitants.[37] Obviously the quality of the accommodation – lighting, heating, ventilation – would not have been up to the expectations of the higher social classes. Heating was (and is) crucial to comfort; the shortcomings of the central open fire, particularly in a large space, were evident, but alternatives were not necessarily easy to devise. In central Europe the introduction of the enclosed stove was epoch-making. The thirteenth-century Bavarian *Minnesinger* Neidhart von

Reuental evokes its impact on peasant social life, with neighbours coming in to dance in the heated parlour, the *Stube*.[38]

Generalization about peasant dwellings anywhere in Europe is hazardous in view of the variations not only in the status and affluence of different members of this very diverse class, but in local building traditions and available materials. Everywhere gradations of affluence among the rural classes were reflected in their housing. Farm building in Tuscany, as in most of Italy, was in stone, and it would therefore be considerations of cost rather than of building technique that inhibited the vertical growth of a house. A tiny peasant dwelling might be built in two storeys because of the cramped nature of the site and was not necessarily a more desirable residence just for that reason. One such house, at Radda in Chianti, possessed one room on each floor, measuring 3 metres by 2.10, and little more than 2 metres high.[39]

Inventories of the possessions of peasant proprietors in the territory of fifteenth-century Florence list what was to be found in the different rooms and thus reveal the scope of the dwellings they occupied.[40] In 1430, for example, the recently deceased Nanino di Dietisalvi had lived with his wife and five children in a house which boasted a cellar (*cella* or *cellarium*), *camerae* and *salae*, as well as a dovecot, threshing-floor, garden and other rural appurtenances. The inventory identifies one *camera* as belonging to Nanino's widow Caterina (who herself died within a few days of him) and another as being occupied by their four sons. Caterina had presumably occupied the former with her husband, for a locked chest containing all his papers was listed among its contents. It is not clear whether these bedrooms were on an upper floor, but there was a *sala de super* used for storage.[41] A house left by Maso di Pitacco in 1458 had a *cella*, two *chamerette* above the 'hall' (or *sala*), a chamber where Maso himself used to sleep and, it seems, a dining room ('sala dove si mangia') which is listed separately from the *sala*.[42]

Whatever the size of the peasant family (typically four or five strong but sometimes more) or of their dwelling-house, it had to suffice for their needs all the year round. Florentine citizens resembled other European medieval (and indeed modern) elites in possessing more than one residence. Already in the early fourteenth century the chronicler Giovanni Villani commented disapprovingly on the opulence of Florentine upper-class building activity in the countryside, remarking that visitors noted a similarity to the way ancient Rome was girded by villas and palaces.[43] A house on the road to Pistoia which Bartolomeo Corbinelli left to his wife and seven children in 1446 had a loggia, courtyard and kitchens, chambers and a *sala* on both floors.[44] Such rural *case signorili*, even if they were functioning farms, were not only predictably superior to the dwellings of the peasantry but were occupied by the proprietors for only part of the year.

In the fifteenth century Florence witnessed a development of elite housing styles in both town and country. Both the urban *palazzo* and the rural or suburban villa were deliberately intended to be the prerogative of a tiny minority, some of whom, at least, had Rome in mind. In 1452, under the title *De re aedificatoria*, the humanist Leon Battista Alberti provided a theoretical handbook for patrons and builders, intended to update the Roman treatise of Vitruvius.[45] Here he carefully distinguished between the amenities that were appropriate to houses in urban and rural surroundings and to those that belonged to men of different ranks, while identifying a common core of values to be embraced by anyone of any standing. It has been supposed that his criticism of rural building in 'the castle style' was directed against the early Medicean villas, which retained some of the features of the fortified rural residences of earlier times, even while they exhibited up-to-the-minute architectural features and were built with regard for aesthetic considerations such as the beauty of the view.[46] It is supposed that the owners of such villas would have been more or less aware of the ideas Petrarch adumbrated in *De vita solitaria*,[47] and may well have valued their country houses as havens of peace, the more so because they had political and commercial entanglements that could not be permanently avoided. This aspect of the villa as retreat (and as reminiscence of the world of the Roman elite) attained a further development in its use as a setting for the philosophical discussions that were favoured in the circle of Lorenzo de' Medici.

The monumentality of the urban *palazzo* of the new age had as much to do with creating a magnificent frame for the patron's self-image as it did with providing a comfortable, functional living-space. The façade was of considerable importance, while the living rooms might represent quite a small proportion of the total bulk of the palace. They were not overcrowded in relation to the probable size of the household, even including servants, who were less numerous than we might think. The spaces thus created (or left) had to be filled up with *objets d'art* and with furniture, which it seems may have expanded to fill the space available, being 'notable for its massiveness and the architectural quality of its forms'.[48] The head of household had his private apartments, which could be elaborate, comprising, as in Cosimo de Medici's palace, suites of bedchambers and anterooms which, at least for the master himself, included a study.[49] In the rest of the house, specialization of function was largely absent, as it had been in the past and was in other European societies; beds might be found throughout. In time, a demand for greater specialization of function manifested itself and was gradually reflected in the remodelling of *palazzi* and modifications in the plan of new ones.

In much of Europe the principal residences of the powerful had traditionally been in rural rather than urban surroundings, but with the growth of governing powers which centred themselves in cities they had to build in town. In the late twelfth century William fitz Stephen described how all the great men of England had 'lordly habitations' in London, which they occupied when summoned by the king or their own business.[50] In around 1360, the Augustinian Prior of St Oswald at Nostell built a hospice for the accommodation of the priors and canons when they had business in York and for the entertainment of their visitors. Later it became the dwelling of a private citizen and, currently being reconstructed in York under the name of Barley Hall, it is a unique urban survival in England.[51]

The principal feature surviving from St Oswald's hospice is a block of five first-floor chambers, with an attic floor above. The imposing 'Great Chamber', a large reception room with a crown-post roof, could be reached by a staircase from the courtyard. The hospice had its great hall, at right angles to the chamber block, but the reconstructed hall that can now be seen was probably the work of the tenant to whom the house was leased, about a century after it was built, when Nostell Priory fell on hard times. This tenant was William Snawsell, goldsmith, member of parliament and, in 1468, lord mayor of York, who in 1466 was paying an annual rent of fifty-six shillings and four pence for the property. His great hall (if it is indeed his) was somewhat larger than its predecessor but followed the same general pattern, with raised dais, central hearth and fine tiled floor. Whoever carried the work out was determined to have the dais, for that end of the hall was a deliberate insertion into the chamber block and cut through some structural timbers.

This change of use and ownership which thus overtook a monastic hospice well illustrates the flexibility of medieval dwellings. If Snawsell required a nursery or a study, he could easily adapt pre-existing spaces. One chamber has been interpreted and furnished as a 'parlour' used by the master of the house as a private writing-office, and Snawsell probably entertained important guests in the Great Chamber as Prior Dereford had done before him. Monastic officials would have been familiar with such buildings on their own territory; Prior Dereford built a Great Chamber at Nostell itself. The separate lodgings occupied by abbots and priors and also monastic guest-houses obeyed very similar principles, while almshouses, hospitals, colleges and guildhalls display features in common with both monastic and domestic buildings and underwent their own developments.[52]

There was a general trend towards the provision of a more differentiated interior space and more individualized accommodation. It became increasingly common for individual cubicles to be partitioned off within monastic infirmaries, and hospitals and almshouses manifested a similar tendency, until by about 1500 many were being built with separate cubicles opening off what in effect was a central corridor.[53] Inns too in the fifteenth century responded to what we may presume was a demand (and a willingness to pay) for greater privacy; at the New Inn in Gloucester, for example, a gallery around the central courtyard, in effect performing the function of a corridor, gave access to forty or more chambers which were large enough to accommodate at least four guests. The degree of privacy afforded was, of course, relative, the yardstick being the communal dormitories of earlier inns, such as the one at the Chequer of the Hope in Canterbury which could sleep one hundred people. On the ground floor of the New Inn there were separate parlours for eating, drinking and socializing.[54]

Among urban dwellings built for single families, the so-called 'Medieval Merchant's House' at 58 French Street, Southampton has been described as 'perhaps the earliest complete medieval town-house surviving in England'.[55] Recently restored to its mid-fourteenth-century appearance, the property consists of two floors above a cellar. It has been a common feature of urban living to live over (or behind) the shop and here a shop, on the ground floor, opens on to the street and also gives on to a short passageway which leads back through the house. The principal room is behind the shop, opening off the passage through a screen. It is in effect a reduced version of the great hall of a grander dwelling, open to the roof. As now reconstructed, it has a fireplace with a brick chimney-breast in the north wall. It was once believed that there was no sign of a medieval fireplace in this wall and that there must have been a central hearth. The more recent view is that a forerunner of the present reconstructed fireplace was inserted in the north wall during the fourteenth century, as open fires became less popular in town-houses and 'wall fire-places with proper chimneys' became common. It had 'a flue lined with imported Flemish brick and a prominent plastered hood painted to resemble brickwork', presumably a cheap simulation of a more expensive and fashionable solution.[56]

The ground floor is completed by an 'inner room' behind the hall, which has been construed as a parlour or counting-house where the merchant transacted private business. A stairway from the hall leads to a first-floor gallery running along its south side, with a chamber at either end. The one at the eastern end, over the shop, survives in nearly its original condition. This was not closed off from the gallery, so intrusions and draughts can have been excluded only by the use of screens or curtains fixed to the tie-beam which crosses the room. The much more altered western chamber was the master bedroom; it had a door, but like its opposite number was unheated until modern times.

Excavations in Southampton have revealed the degree of luxury which such people might enjoy, for example, their fine imported tableware. The successive owners of the French Street property wanted a hall in which to receive their guests, adequate sleeping accommodation for the household, a private room in which the master of the house could do his accounts and conduct business, and (in due course) a fireplace in the modern manner. Similar aspirations are documented elsewhere. In 1308 the London skinner William of Hanigton entered into a contract with the carpenter Simon of Canterbury for the rebuilding or enlargement of a house which cannot now be precisely located. His hall was to have an 'oriole' or window recess behind the high table. At one end of the hall, separated from it by a larder, there was to be a chamber with a heated fireplace, at the other a stable, both with solars above them. It looks as if William's hall was going to be two storeys high and certainly the house altogether had many of the attributes of grander dwellings.[57]

Two-storey halls were not invariable in houses in London or elsewhere, in town or country. They were understandably absent when storeys were added above a range of shops. In 1310 a contract for a range of three shops in Cornmarket provided for two storeys to be built above them, with chimneyed *sales* on the first floor along with the buttery, pantry and kitchen, and *beles chambres* (with privies) on the second.[58] The 'halls' here look like principal 'reception rooms', distinct from the presumably more private rooms above. Elsewhere open halls are not invariably present even where there was ample room for them. A citizen of Bury St Edmunds who died in 1468 built himself (or at least ordered) a house which was to have a hall, parlour and kitchen on the ground floor but be 'all soleryd over' on the upper floor. A house contracted for in the Kentish village of Cranbrook in 1500 was similarly to be 'lofted over' throughout.[59]

The house in Norwich now known as Dragon Hall well illustrates how a fifteenth-century merchant might adapt and build for show. When Robert Toppes (d. 1467) bought a fourteenth-century hall house which fronted on to an alleyway which led from King Street (a prestigious address) down to the River Wensum, he inserted a grand new hall at first-floor level, thereby creating a frontage on King Street itself. Internally, an imposing wooden staircase led to it from the previously existing ground-floor hall. This new hall was not however intended for domestic living, but for the display of goods (probably woollens) and probably for the transaction of private business at the northern end where there was a fireplace.[60] Even in Italy, monumental staircases were a post-medieval feature of grand residences.

Different householders doubtless had differently mixed motives, aspiring to comfort and privacy on the one hand, self-advertisement and conformity to fashion or some ideal scale of values on the other. The provision of separate sleeping accommodation for individuals would depend not merely on the availability of space and money, but on the belief that it was desirable, perhaps even necessary to the family's reputation. It has been suggested that before the fifteenth century London householders set a greater value on providing themselves with 'small extra sitting-rooms' than with numerous bedrooms for individuals. Chambers identifiable as bedrooms multiplied in some later fifteenth-century houses, but the process does not seem to have been even.[61]

It is one thing to know how and what people built, another to know how they experienced their domestic environment. There are some clues in late medieval literature, but the diaries, letters and biographies which might give us a more intimate impression of the relationship between people and their living space are largely lacking. Wills and inventories taken on death sometimes afford indirect insights into the ways rooms were used and even valued, inasmuch as they describe what furnishings were to be found where in a house.

One of the most familiar English examples is the inventory of Sir John Fastolf's goods taken in 1459. This listed quantities of plate that had been deposited in the abbeys of St Benet at Hulme and Bermondsey, but also plate, fabrics and furnishings found at Caister, Sir John's Norfolk castle.[62] Apart from both Great Hall (*magna aula*) and 'winter hall' (*aula hyemalis*), there were numerous chambers, distinguished in the inventory in a variety of ways. Some were described as having been occupied by servants (porter, cook or gardener), or by named individuals such as Thomas Fastolf, the knight's distant cousin, his stepson Stephen Scrope or his secretary William Worcester; some were distinguished topographically, for example 'the Chamber over the Draught Brigge' or 'the utmost chamber nexte Winter Halle'. Scattered throughout the house there were touches of refinement, such as lavender pillows, a coverlet with four white roses at every corner and one in the middle, and a bedspread which depicted in one corner a gentlewoman 'with a whelp in hir honde and an Awnus Day [Agnus Dei] abought hir nec'. As befitted a knight of Fastolf's pretensions, he possessed numerous figured tapestries, including one for the west side of the hall which depicted the siege of Falaise and one 'of the Morysch daunce' which hung in the winter hall.

In late medieval York inventories, terms such as *aula* or *camera* are sometimes used generically to indicate either a category of furnishing or the entire contents of a particular apartment.[63] A lay testator might bequeath his 'hall' and his 'chapel', his 'kitchen' or his 'brewhouse' to his principal heir. In 1345 Richard de la Pole left his wife 'my chamber in its entirety, apart from the silver vessels and my arms', which were to be divided among his sons.[64] The hall virtually never contained a bed, but beds and linen were often found in all the other living rooms. On the other hand, while hangings, table-tops and trestles, benches, chairs, chests, cupboards and 'counters' (tables made for the purpose of writing or accounting) were all standard hall furniture, all might appear in other rooms.

The number of chambers naturally varied with the size and affluence of the household and this sometimes made it necessary for testators or inventory-makers (as at Caister) to find ways of distinguishing one from another. Some listed a 'first' or 'great' chamber, followed by 'second', 'third' and even 'fourth' chambers. This style was adopted for the inventory of the possessions of Martin Collins, treasurer of York, who at the time of his death in 1508 had several residences.[65] The *magna camera*, as at Barley Hall, functioned not only as a principal reception room but very probably also as a dining room of somewhat less public character than the hall; given the rarity of permanent dining-tables as we now know them, meals could be taken almost anywhere. The terms 'exterior' and 'interior' chamber also occur: Thomas Farnylawe, chancellor of York, in 1378 left his nephew 'the bed in which I used to lie in the outer chamber'.[66] There are several references to a testator's 'own' chamber. In 1373 the will of archbishop John Thoresby of York was made at his manor of Thorp, 'in a certain room in which the reverend father used to sleep'.[67] Rather more poetically, John Clifford, treasurer of York, in 1392 made his will 'within the chamber of my repose and quiet (*infra cameram requiescionis et quietis meae*) in my dwelling house' in the cathedral close.[68] Such phrasing seems to hint that Clifford used this particular apartment not only as a bedroom but as a private sanctum. More than one testator mentioned a chest or coffer standing by his bedside,[69] and in 1505 John Brecknock of Doncaster left to the Carmelites some 'bokes which lye in a little chest undre my chambre window'.

In the will he made on 14 February 1453, Sir Thomas Wombwell not only referred to his own chamber but gave names to several others. To his son, heir and chief executor John he left, as was customary, the *ornamenta* and vestments pertaining to his chapel and also all the *necessaria* of his hall, together with half of the contents of his kitchen and brewhouse. John also received 'the whole of my bed in my own chamber which I occupy', another bed and bed-stuff that were to be found 'in the chamber called Hightower' and all the *apparatus* in the parlour. Sir Thomas's second wife, Joanna, was assured of the possession of the jewels and other items she had brought with her to their marriage and was also to receive, besides money and livestock, two 'hanging beds' with all their furnishings, 'which are usually in two chambers, viz, the lady chamber and the new chamber'. To another son, Thomas, was bequeathed a bed that was to be found in 'the chamber called the parlour chamber', together with all his *utensilia et necessaria* in the two chambers which he normally used. Sir Thomas may have been referring to suites of rooms – bedchamber and 'drawing' or 'sitting' room – that his wife and son effectively treated as theirs, and the younger Thomas was guaranteed the continued possession of what he probably regarded as his own belongings.

There were numerous other ways of differentiating rooms. Thomas Creke, citizen of Beverley, who died in 1465, possessed both a 'little chamber' and a 'gest-chambre'.[70] The widow Alice Sothill, who made her will in October 1500, mentions, in addition to her parlour, great chamber and wine-cellar, the 'little chamber', the 'green chamber', which had a fireplace, and an upper chamber called 'my lady chamber'.[71] Few wills are as lavish with terms designating different rooms as that of John Brompton, merchant of Beverley, made in 1444.[72] Brompton clearly lived in some style. Among the numerous furnishings of his hall were hangings, a long table specifically for the upper part of the room, and a standing counter near the entrance to the parlour. Elsewhere in the house there was a *magna camera*, and a 'withdraw-yngechaumbre', 'forechamber', 'waterhouse chamber' and 'menychaumbre', all of them containing beds. The parlour contained both beds and an 'everyday' table, which suggests that informal meals were taken there. The parlour may often have been used as a private room into which the master of the house could conveniently retreat to discuss business with a visitor, but its uses and furnishings were clearly as varied as those of any other room in the house.

On 5 April 1435 Margaret Blackburn dictated the final codicil to her will in 'a certain upper room in the upper part of the hall in the dwelling of John Bolton, citizen and merchant of York, in Skeldergate'. Bolton was the husband of her daughter Alicia.[73] Among her many bequests to Alicia was 'a Flemish chest with images carved outside', a water-heater, a brass mortar, 'six new cushions with gryphons' and six cushion-covers of arras-work. Chests, the all-purpose storage places for garments and valuables of all kinds, variously described and often of Flemish make, were frequent possessions and evidently valued bequests among York testators. Margaret's son Nicholas was to have the iron-bound chest in which she had kept her silver; to her other son-in-law, Brian Sandford, went 'a big plain chest painted red' and to his wife, her daughter Isabella 'another smaller chest, carved outside like a window', which vividly evokes the Gothic tracery to be seen on several extant examples. The Sandfords' son John received 'a small chest painted green', and John Bolton 'an iron-bound chest standing on four iron wheels'. There was plentiful linen, some of Flemish manufacture, among the bequests: Isabella was to have 'a very good table-cloth diapered with roses'. Several legatees received table-cloths, towels and pairs of sheets and also basins, some of them specifically finger-bowls. Among the numerous bequests to Margaret's maidservant Johanna Escrik were two small round basins 'for the chamber'.

The Blackburns, Boltons and Snawsells were considerable people, and there were many like them in the cities of Europe. They were able and willing to adorn their dwellings with good-quality objects which they evidently prized and which were beyond the reach of the generality of the population. If 'Flemish chests' were the prized possessions of York citizens, the Flemish themselves, like other northerners, prized the new Italian majolica tableware.[74] The smaller-scale panel painting of the period, for example the portable altarpiece, Italian, Flemish or other, was itself an object of private consumption, designed for the domestic setting, although not solely for lay patrons. The citizens of York by the end of the fifteenth century may not have achieved the levels of luxury and refinement of their Florentine contemporaries, or other Italians for that matter, but they were not inhabiting a different planet.

Had Margaret Blackburn been living with her son-in-law for a time before her death, perhaps occupying the upper room in the house in Skeldergate? The arrangements that were made for the housing of the elderly and the widowed, at all levels of society, sometimes shed light on domestic arrangements. The abbot who had outlived his competence might be assigned private lodgings within the monastery, which was not always good news for his successor; the invalid monk might obtain a permanent place in the infirmary. The agreements that old peasant couples or widows made with their offspring sometimes specify that they are to be allocated a certain quantity or type of living space.[75] In an agreement made at Cranfield in Bedfordshire in 1294, John, son of Elyas and Christina of Brickendon, undertook to provide his parents with 'honourable sustenance in food and drink as long as they live'. They were to have 'lodging on the chief messuage', but

> if it chance (which God forbid) that quarrels and discords arise in time to come between the parties, so that they cannot dwell together peaceably in one house, the aforesaid John will find for the same Elyas and Christiana, or for whichever one of them survives the other, a house in his courtyard, with a curtilage, where they can honourably dwell.[76]

This may have meant that John would if necessary build them a house in his farmyard or that one of the existing outhouses was convertible for the purpose. A new building was certainly not out of the question. Thomas Brid of Halesowen in 1281 undertook to build his mother 'a house thirty feet long and fourteen feet wide and having three doors and two windows'.[77]

In other such contracts, the widowed spouse was to lodge in his or her child's house and inter-generational discord was not envisaged. In 1320 the widowed Petronilla of Teye, of Dunmow in Essex, was to have a room, with garderobe, at the eastern end of her son's house, together with a modest quantity of livestock.[78] What could be allotted to a widow presumably depended not only on the goodwill of the children but on what room they could reasonably be expected to spare and therefore on their general level of affluence. The widow of Simon Welling of Wymondham was to continue to live in his house but was guaranteed only the right of entry, 'a place by the fire, and a bed'.[79] A widow of South Elmham in October 1407 demanded the use of a 'chamber' and a 'solar' in her late husband's house, with free entry and exit for herself and her friends for life.[80]

Similar arrangements were made by the citizens of fourteenth-century Ghent.[81] The elderly seem to have felt that they needed to make adequate financial arrangements for their sustenance and that they could not necessarily rely on the pure goodwill of their heirs. Where house-sharing arrangements were made with sons or daughters, the possibility of disagreement might be allowed for. The widow of Gillis Van den Rietgavere surrendered to her daughter and son-in-law all her dower rights in the daughter's property and all her own property in return for lifetime support. Were relations to sour, the young couple were to keep the property and grant her a lifetime annuity which would more than suffice to keep her. In 1390 Jan de Zomer and his wife neatly foisted the care of his mother on to his wife's daughter (presumably by a previous marriage); they gave her a house in which the old lady was to have an apartment. A variant strategy was to import a female family member, often a niece, into the house to look after old couples or individuals in the expectation of inheriting some of their property. Some agreements did not involve family members. Margriet Van Huesdine in 1354 declared that she retained no rights in a house which Willem Arnoutssone had just bought from her and had 'no property in it except a bed, old chests and chairs and ten torn pillows'; Willem was however to permit her to live there for as long as she liked. Mergriet Van Scerdruwe too sold her house but reserved the use of an apartment for her lifetime, with free access for all her friends to visit her.

It has probably always been true that there is a greater and more varied pool of accommodation available in a town than in the rural environment and a wider variety of people potentially inhabiting it. Ghent doubtless exemplified features to be found in other late medieval (and more modern) cities:

> The city rather favours solitude: the solitude of the young in search of work; the solitude of widows or of old couples whose children have set up independent households or are already dead; the solitude even of the married couple caring only for its own children and not displaying, by a common residence, solidarity with brothers or other kin.[82]

The voluminous records of the *catasto*, the Florentine tax assessment carried out in 1427, make it possible to get some idea of how the hearth, the actual household unit, was constituted in both town and country.

There were over 8000 households headed by 'solitaries', amounting to 13.61 per cent of the total number surveyed.[83] About half of these solitaries are identifiable as widowers or widows, 60 of them male and nearly 4000 female. Many other widows, in town and country alike, were living with their children; widowed females were much more likely than males to be doing so. There were anyway many more widows than widowers, which suggests not only the effects of a wide difference in age between male and female at the time of marriage, but a strong tendency on the part of women to refuse or avoid a second (or perhaps third or fourth) marriage. A substantially higher proportion of the population of the city of Florence was made up by single men and single and widowed women than was the case in the countryside.[84] The number of urban single males was swelled by the younger sons of patrician families, who were married late in life if at all, and might remain under the paternal roof for a considerable period, as of course their sisters also did until marriage, if they were not lodged in a convent. Other single persons were servants, male and female, some of whom 'lived in' while others were likely to be lodgers in someone else's house.

Single people, especially women, who were not living some version of the religious life dwell rather in the shadows of our picture of the middle ages, but clearly they existed. Their numbers were probably always small as a proportion of the total population, but may well have been larger than we sometimes assume.[85] It has been suggested, for example, that once a determined effort is made to find single women in thirteenth-century Paris, they begin to become visible.[86] Similarly, in fourteenth-century Ghent, 'Unattached women of all ages are found living alone in apartments or houses throughout the city.' One Lisbette Steppe lived in the sixth part of a house next door to her father's, but separate from it. Other lone women were to be found in hostels and inns, where they might come to grief.[87] The prostitute was simply the extreme illustration of the obvious truth that women should not be permitted to remain alone.

The tendency for women to opt for single status or for continued widowhood can be identified in many places.[88] It may well have been partially dependent on favourable economic circumstances, for example the labour shortages which followed the plagues of the later fourteenth century, and everywhere the urban environment rather than the rural favoured women who wanted to exercise that choice. Running a farm might pose real practical difficulties for the unattached woman. Among its other attractions the city boasted a wealth of religious institutions, including houses of friars, which might provide support and occupation for the pious widow. Eleanor Wandesford of Kirklington made her will on 2 October 1472 in 'a certain *bassa camera* or parlour' in the Dominican convent at York, which suggests a degree of intimacy with the friars.[89]

Tax assessments and manorial court records provide welcome evidence of household structure. Literature and the fine arts offer attractive detail but pose numerous problems to the historian who wants to use them as sources for 'private life'. We may plausibly contend that Chrétien in the twelfth century or Langland in the fourteenth afford us authentic glimpses of the life that was lived in the great houses of their day; but artists and writers alike are quite capable of bringing disparate and even incompatible elements together in their pictures to create a setting which will work for the story they want to tell and which convinces, impresses, amuses or gratifies the expectations of the viewer or reader. At what point did the great hall and its rituals become a familiar, conventional backdrop to the story, which the fourteenth- or fifteenth-century audience simply expected to find in place, rather as a modern cinema or pantomime audience may expect its mental picture of the Sleeping Beauty's castle to be realized before its eyes? Some, at least, of the audience for the late medieval romances may have had little more first-hand acquaintance with the noble world of the great hall than P.G. Wodehouse's readers have with the country house surroundings of Bertie and Aunt Dahlia; but they knew how they expected such characters to live.

Among late medieval authors Chaucer exhibits a particularly acute sense of place and interior space. It may be risky to treat his scene-painting as the mere reflection of reality, but he certainly contrives it with great deliberation in order to make his stories work. The Oxford carpenter in the *Miller's Tale* is able to let a room to a student (with unfortunate results for himself). He is not simply a realistic type, the 'rich gome [churl]' who has prospered and has a big house; it is necessary to the comic narrative for his rascally lodger Nicholas to have a room by himself. The Miller of the *Reeve's Tale*, by contrast, has to put a bed for two unexpected guests into the same room with himself, his wife and daughter; this is equally essential to the dénouement. Both scenarios were real possibilities, and therefore Chaucer is working on a base level of plausibility, but he is not giving us sociological data on real carpenters or real millers. Yet it is beyond question that he had an exceptionally rich vocabulary of domestic spaces and furnishings and that he sometimes requires his readers and hearers to follow him closely in visualizing a complex *mise-en-scène* according to his directions.

This is especially noticeable in *Troilus and Criseyde*. Several times in the course of the poem the layout of rooms in relation to one another and the need to manoeuvre the characters among them acquire critical narrative importance. Chaucer is also notably alert to the need to make it clear when his principal characters are genuinely alone, or *tête-à-tête*, and not accompanied (and potentially overheard) by servants, which would be normal for people of their rank.[90] The *tête-à-têtes* are perhaps the more interesting, for the episodes of genuine solitude are mostly contrivances enabling the lovers to lament and soliloquize. As Chaucer well knew, lovers for centuries had fled to their chambers to weep, and there are several examples here. On one occasion Pandarus overhears Troilus' lamentations when he comes into his chamber unexpectedly, and he later tells Criseyde 'as I was comynge, Al sodeynly he lefte his complaynynge'.

More interesting is the description of Troilus' reaction to the news that Criseyde is going to leave Troy. He rushes home from 'Parliament' and enters his chamber 'alone, except for one or two of his men'; these he dismisses peremptorily, saying he is going to sleep. He shuts all the doors and windows and then sits down on the side of the bed, having created the necessary preparations for his outpouring of grief. The specific need to dismiss all retainers from his presence serves as a kind of realistic punctuation mark in the otherwise predictable flow of his actions and utterances.

Chaucer carefully draws attention to this necessity on several occasions. Pandarus several times calls upon Criseyde in her own house when he is working to win her favour for Troilus. On the first occasion, he finds her with her nieces and women in 'a paved parlour', listening to reading; she sits him down with them, and when the story is over he intimates that he wishes to speak confidentially to her. Thereupon,

> everi wight that aboute hem tho
> That herde that, gan fer away to stoned

until it was clear that they had said what they wanted to say. On another visit Pandarus and Criseyde go arm in arm down the stairs from the chamber into the garden, where Pandarus delivers her a letter from Troilus. On yet another they dine together; after the meal, Pandarus 'slily' wanders over to the window which overlooks the street and asks Criseyde who has done up the house opposite. She joins him at the window and they sit there together making small talk until Pandarus, seeing 'that here folk weren aweye', seizes his moment to ask how she liked the letter and to urge her to reply. It may be noted that when she does so she retires into a 'closet' which, it would seem, opened off the chamber in which they were talking. Pandarus too has a closet, in which he contrives that Criseyde shall sleep on the fateful night when he introduces Troilus into her bed. Chaucer was one of the first to use this word, yet another equivalent for 'bower', in English; he is also an early user of 'parlour'.

In another ingenious piece of scene-setting, the movements of the characters from space to space are still more exactly plotted on a timescale. Troilus is abed in his house, feeling sorry for himself: Pandarus introduces a party which includes Criseyde,

Helen and Deiphebus, ostensibly on business. Troilus produces from beside 'his bed's head' a letter and a 'treatise' on which Hector has asked his opinion. Helen and Deiphebus together saunter out of the room, down the stairs into the garden, reading the letter as they go; they take most of an hour about it, during which time Pandarus is able to inveigle Criseyde into an interview with Troilus. This ends when Helen and Deiphebus come back up the stairs from the garden.

By far the most elaborate episode is Pandarus's stage-managed introduction of Troilus to Criseyde's bed, although the details are not made entirely clear. Pandarus invites Criseyde to an elegant supper in his house; she comes with her niece Antigone, 'a certain number' of manservants and nine or ten of her women. (Not only in royal households was hospitality an expensive business.) Pandarus obtains the assistance of the elements: a storm breaks and he is able to persuade Criseyde that she and her whole party would be well advised to bed down in his house. She is unaware that Troilus has been observing the supper-party and subsequent recreations from a 'stewe', that is a small heated room, which we must suppose is above the chamber and has a window or spy-hole giving on to it. Evidently Pandarus had hopes of a favourable outcome even without the intervention of the weather, but as it happens all other sounds are drowned by the thunder and rain. Pandarus puts Criseyde in his own closet, with her women in a 'middle chamber' outside it, which, if there were nine or ten of them, must have been sizeable. When all is still, Pandarus enters the 'stew' and assuages Troilus's nerves: he then admits him into the closet by a secret trap-door. It would appear that Pandarus himself then settles down to sleep in front of the fire in the same room; and we must presume also that when Troilus leaves in the morning he does so via the trap-door and the stew, rather than by walking out over the waiting women in the middle chamber, but these details are not precisely clarified.

Here and elsewhere, Chaucer seems to appeal to a willingness on the part of his audience to visualize a setting. This imaginative procedure was also encouraged by devotional practice. The Tuscan Franciscan friar who late in the thirteenth century composed the *Meditations on the Life of Christ* to assist the contemplative life of a nun, and ended by achieving a much wider readership in several languages, not only visualized the Passion of Christ in exhaustive detail but invited his reader to imagine apocryphal incidents in the saviour's early life. As a child He brought water for His parents: the fountain from which He drew it is still to be seen. Later He continued to give every assistance to His hard-working mother, who had no servants: 'Did He not help to set the table, put the beds in order and do the other intimate things in the household?' Thus the scriptural message that Christ came 'to serve and not to be served' (Matthew 20:28) is fleshed out in the most homely manner. The reader is asked to imagine that the Holy Family had a small house and slept in 'three beds in one small room, as humble and simple as that of any poor man of the people'.[91] A wide variety of literary texts were located in settings of increasing particularity and concreteness.

The same applies to visual representations. In late medieval painting architectural features are often both idealised and highly stylized; painters frequently (as they must) cut away the wall of a house or a room to reveal the action within as if on a stage set. Realism is uneven and a detail which looks like a realistic touch may carry symbolic meaning. On the wall behind the Virgin Mary in an Annunciation by a follower of Robert Campin there is a woodcut of St Christopher: is this a matter-of-fact representation of something one might have seen in a fifteenth-century Flemish household, a reference to the fact that Mary too is about to become a Christ-bearer – or both?[92] Much anachronism is relatively easy to allow for; we would not mistake Mary's room in the painting just mentioned for a room in a house in Nazareth in the Roman period, just as we are unlikely to deduce from *Sir Gawain* that there were chimneys in Arthurian Britain. This Virgin belongs not only to fifteenth century Flanders, but to a comfortable social stratum; her emblematic lilies stand on the table in a fine jug of Hispano-Moresque ware.

It is not always so easy for the unwary to know when old motifs are being copied or old descriptions recycled. Nevertheless, it is clear that art and literature alike often do describe places and things accurately and informatively and can therefore be valued as source material for certain features of domestic life, from window-boxes to baby-walking frames, that are unlikely simply to be artistic inventions. Artists (especially the Flemish) and writers seem to have shared with their patrons and audiences a keen interest in such mundane objects and more generally in the domestic interior.

The relationship between people, space and objects may have been different in fifteenth-century Florence and in fifteenth-century York or Bruges or Lübeck, but measuring such differences (if they existed) presents its difficulties. How did the citizens of these places view themselves, their needs, desires and status, in relation to their domestic setting? The more affluent dwelling afforded its occupants greater opportunities to pursue a variety of occupations, but it is hard to know precisely what advantage individuals took of those opportunities or how important (if at all) privacy as we now know it was to them. In the countryside, superior peasant dwellings offered a marginal increase in the space available to each member of the family, but it cannot have been easy for them to get away from one another, should that thought even have entered their heads. A peasant boy anywhere in Europe who against the odds succeeded in getting an education, acquiring a patron and rising in the social scale by means of intellectual attainments would eventually come to inhabit a rather different physical environment. He would need to do so, for his father's house was not designed to nurture literate activity.

8

Religion in the Home

There was a two-way interchange between secular society and those who lived different varieties of the religious life. Many monastic settlements had in the course of the centuries become the nuclei of urban settlements of various sizes or had effectively been absorbed into growing cities. The inhabitants of such cities were familiar not only with the urban clergy and with formally constituted religious communities in their midst, but with individuals who were trying to live the religious life in a domestic or quasi-domestic setting. Caesarius of Heisterbach tells a number of stories about laypeople who achieved divine recognition of the religious lives that they lived in their domestic surroundings.

An 'honourable and religious widow' of Liblar near Cologne lived with her son and his wife, who were somewhat neglectful of her. She was a friend of Henry, abbot of Heisterbach, and like the widow of the gospel she was never away from church, always fasting and praying. When she was dying, she asked her maid to fetch a priest. The maid notified the daughter-in-law, who said offhandedly, 'She's already had communion this week, and as far as I can see she's still alive – but go and call him.' When the priest eventually came the widow told him that she had in the meantime been personally communicated by Christ and would not now accept the sacrament from any mere man.[1]

Similarly, a *religiosa femina* of Brabant who desired ardently to receive communion was brusquely told by the priest that 'lay women could not communicate according to their liking but at a certain time'. The true 'high priest' took note of this and that very night, as the woman lay in her bed praying, the Saviour came in splendour into the bedroom, carrying in His own hands the pyx from the church and accompanied by a wondrous fragrance and hymning angels. He communicated her Himself and departed. Unknown to her the whole transaction had been witnessed by another *religiosa femina*, her companion, who was sleeping in the same room. As a check, she went to the priest and asked him to count the hosts in his pyx, assuaging his panic, when he found he was one short, by telling him what had happened.[2] In yet another story Caesarius tells of a maiden of Nivelles who 'left her father's house and her parents for the love of Christ and joined with certain religious women of that province, with whom, supporting herself with the work of her hands, she spent her time in prayer and fasting'. The devil was envious of the virtue of these women and decided to abstract a goose from the house of the maiden's father and introduce it into the *triclinium* in which she was sitting with the other women. The idea, apparently, was to tempt them, although it could also have been to get them accused of theft.[3]

Although Caesarius does not use the word in these passages, these women were clearly beguines, living the religious life in a largely domestic setting. In another story Walter, abbot of Villers, tells how as a new-made monk in quest of the gift of tears he obtained permission to visit a house of Cistercian nuns whose inmates had a reputation for holiness and effective prayers. An *honesta femina* who was offering him overnight hospitality asked him 'in jest' why he wanted to visit 'those beguines (*istas beginnas*)' and then and there produced from a bedroom (*de cubiculo suo*) a woman whose prayers proved just as efficacious. The term 'beguine' seems here to be applied derogatively although humorously to the nuns, while the woman who emerges from the bedroom looks very much like a beguine in good sooth.[4]

All these stories are located in Brabant. Beguines were certainly not confined to the lands which now constitute Belgium, but they were at their strongest there.[5] The surviving beguinages to be seen in many Belgian cities now mostly present a seventeenth- or eighteenth-century appearance but usually go back to thirteenth-century origins. One of the most atmospheric is tucked behind the parish church of Anderlecht, now part of Brussels. Founded in 1252, it had only eight residents at the end of the fifteenth century and could scarcely have accommodated more, if they were to have any space to themselves. Like the inmates of some other beguinages, the sisters of Anderlecht worked as nurses elsewhere in the neighbourhood.[6] Beguines were not enclosed as nuns were, nor did they take binding lifelong vows. At the end of the fourteenth century, the so-called Ménagier de Paris made several references, in the advice manual he wrote for his young wife, to a beguine called Agnes who seems to have been at her side to give her advice on household management.[7]

The beguinages probably made it easier for some single women to live respectably and usefully, but this did not commend them to conservatives who believed in a strict demarcation of 'orders' and were suspicious of women who were insufficiently supervised and not clearly definable as either nuns or laity. At much the same time and place as the Ménagier was writing, Jean Gerson, chancellor of the University of Paris from 1395 until his death in 1429, expressed strong doubts about the orthodoxy of beguines 'and others living in little communities (*in conventiculis*)' while recommending to his own sisters and other laywomen a way of life which sounds rather similar.[8] There was ongoing pressure on the beguines to become more regularized and institutionalized, and it was far from unknown for individual beguines to become enclosed nuns in the fullness of time. From the beginning, they often had close and mutually admiring contacts with nuns and monks of the established orders, notably Cistercians and Dominicans, and with high-ranking ecclesiastics such as Jacques de Vitry.

It is not clear whether the pious widow of whom Caesarius speaks had taken formal vows, but the same adjective, *religiosa*, is applied to her as to the 'beguines' and indeed the 'holy nuns'. The degree of acceptance that devout laypeople achieved, in some quarters at least, is reflected in the supple definition offered by the canonist Hostiensis (Henry of Susa) in 1253:

> In a general sense, one calls 'religious' those who live in a holy and religious manner in their own homes, not because they submit themselves to a precise rule, but by virtue of their way of life, which is harder and more austere than that of other laypeople who live in an entirely worldly fashion.[9]

Yet even the admirers of layfolk who achieved a reputation not only for holy living but for sanctity sometimes betrayed difficulty in remodelling ancient concepts to fit new situations, especially when they were dealing with women.

Marie of Oignies (d. 1213), the archetypal beguine, began her religious career when she and her husband jointly decided to devote themselves to nursing lepers at Willambroux near Nivelles. In the preface to his *Life* of Marie, Jacques de Vitry is openly scornful of the critics of the *sanctae mulieres*, whom they slander only because they feel themselves rebuked by the holiness of their lives. He has surprisingly little to say, however, about the more novel features of the way of life Marie adopted, preferring to stress her prayer and fasting, her attachment to silence and solitude, her tumultuous weeping and ecstasies and devotion to the sacrament.[10] The *Vita* was dedicated to Fulk, the bishop of heresy-ridden Toulouse, and Jacques makes several references to the Albigensian crusade, representing Marie as a passionate supporter of it. She was intended to be an icon of orthodoxy, and on several occasions Jacques stresses that her austerities are to be admired rather than imitated.

A saint had to meet established standards; it was therefore desirable to describe Marie as nearly as possible in terms of traditional 'monastic' spirituality. That she should in the end leave Nivelles to live a more retired life at the priory of Oignies fits with this pattern, just as Jacques's insistence on her precocious piety as a little girl fits a standard hagiographical model. There are occasional references to her servant and her 'friends', but the pious company which she gathered about her is left in the shadows. Implicitly Marie's way of life is justified because its fruits resemble those of a more familiar regimen. Other hagiographers made similar assumptions and responded to similar expectations. One result is that they display a variable degree of interest in the real-life background their subjects inhabited; what mattered was that the men and women in question were successful in transforming the mundane into the 'desert'.

It is quite impossible to compute the numbers of women who lived informal religious lives, within their families or in groups, in their own homes or in houses close to the churches where they received communion and spiritual direction. As the mendicants established themselves as a force in Italian urban life in the course of the thirteenth century, their third orders provided a framework in which both men and women could find a niche and even obtain a reputation for sanctity while continuing to live in 'the world'.[11] The *Lives* of such persons occasionally provide information about the way they utilized the domestic setting for religious purposes. One example is the *Life* of the Florentine Umiliana de' Cerchi, written by the Franciscan Vito da Cortona a few years after her death at the age of twenty-seven in 1246.[12]

As a youthful widow who refused to remarry, Umiliana was defrauded of her dowry by her father. She wanted to enter a community of Poor Clares, but this was not God's will and she set about living a life of asceticism and prayer in a room in her father's tower-house. In describing her way of life Vito clearly felt the need to explain how it conformed to the antique model. Referring to the original community of Franciscan nuns presided over by St Clare near Assisi, he asked rhetorically:

> What austerities did she sustain less than the holy sisters of San Damiano? What did she lack of the monastic life, who lived in such continuous silence and observance? What less did she possess than the holy hermits, who found herself a solitude in the midst of the city and converted her bedchamber into a prison-cell?

The point is later underlined: 'Having established her little cell, her prison rather, in her father's tower, she transformed that prison into an oratory, as far as she could, and was content there to exert herself to do the best she could.'

Vito wished to advertise the availability of a new way of life which was as good as the old, and he needed therefore to show that in essential respects it was similar:

> Some leave the world and their paternal home, and fleeing into solitude fight for the Lord; she brought solitude into her father's house, and fighting nobly defeated the world and vice in the midst of worldly things.

This reiterated likening of the converted bedchamber to a 'prison' assures the reader that Umiliana's enclosure equalled that of the nun that God did not permit her to be. It was not however total. Her chamber became an 'oratory' in as much as it was a place of prayer, but she had to go out to church, she visited spiritual friends as well as receiving visits from them and, although her charitable activities were curtailed by her loss of income, she continued to carry out some errands of mercy. She knew other female recluses, among them Gisla of Mugello, who experienced a number of occupational hazards and temptations in her efforts to lead the religious life at home. First Gisla was bothered by noisy neighbours, so that she could not concentrate on prayer; but when she told Umiliana that she would have to leave her house 'God took pity on her and the disturbances ceased'. Then she was tempted by the devil to live in complete solitude, but Umiliana knew that this was dangerous for women and prayed for her until God liberated her from the temptation.[13]

Other women lived lives which similarly combined the domestic simulation of solitude with churchgoing and pious visiting. Benevenuta Boiani of Cividale del Friuli (d. 1292) ultimately entered a Dominican convent, but earlier pursued her vocation in her father's house, which clearly provided a godly environment.[14] She used the garden for prayer, weather permitting, and her *cubiculum*, which she shared with her almost equally pious sister Maria, when it did not. She and Maria are pictured sitting in the courtyard of the house exclaiming at the beauties of the starry sky and the works of God. One winter evening her father left the fireside, where he had been taking his ease with the family 'as is the way of secular men', in order to complete the Hours of the Blessed Virgin, which he recited every day. Finding himself outside Benevenuta's room he heard voices; in obedience to Christ's own precept she closed the door when performing her religious exercises. Her father was probably within his rights to open the door and go in, where he found her alone. She had been conversing with Saints Catherine, Agnes and Margaret, who disappeared as soon as the door was opened. Maria, who slept with her, testified that she heard voices and saw a light shining in the chamber, as Umiliana's maidservant also did.

Benevenuta's domesticity, like Umiliana's, was invaded by demons, who bothered her in both house and garden. This was the price that had been paid by the solitary throughout Christian history for the holy visitations and consolations which were dependent on solitude. The divine and the diabolical alike set the seal of authenticity on the experience of the home-dwelling religious. The gifts of spiritual discernment and healing were certainly not the peculiar rewards of the solitary or of women, but they were especially appropriate to persons whose gender limited their opportunities for active charity or proselytization. These were the means by which women like Benevenuta and Umiliana exerted influence on the people around them (although charity too was important to Umiliana, above all when she was a married woman with material resources at her disposal). Thus the solitary and the woman could 'preach', as Vito said of Umiliana: 'What about her preaching, in which she preached more by deeds than by words and does not cease to preach now the body is dead, and will preach in perpetuity?'

It was not solely women who took the opportunity to live what Vito called 'a new way of holy life' in the thirteenth century; but it is not surprising that they have attracted a disproportionate amount of attention. Religious opportunities were historically much more restricted for women than for men, and such as they were they had hitherto been conditional (in theory at least) on the most severe seclusion. Secular women too lived more restricted lives than their male counterparts and they spent a high proportion of their time within four walls, especially if they were of respectable social status. That the opportunity of leading a religious life should be extended to the domestic environment was obviously good news for pious women but, as the *Lives* of Marie of Oignies, Umiliana and Benevenuta all indicate, there was a tendency for descriptions of how they exploited those opportunities to emphasize their emulation of monastic seclusion and austerities.

Benevenuta's near-contemporary the Franciscan tertiary Pilingotto of Urbino (d. 1304) in some respects lived a very similar life but with differences which owe something to his gender.[15] It seems not unlikely that he was simple-minded. In early life he proved his uselessness as a cloth-dealer and turned to contemplation instead, but he retained his masculine freedom of movement, endlessly going from church to church. There was an embarrassing incident one Passion Sunday when he went to the cathedral with a rope around his neck, carrying a home-made banner, and fell into an ecstasy on the steps of the altar of the Virgin. Rumours spread that he had set out to hang himself and his family had to come to take him home. His kin seem to have been prepared to tolerate his religiosity but retained him at home when he wanted to become a hermit. He therefore embraced a domestic version of the solitary life: 'He did not wander around the squares and streets, he did not go from house to house, but stayed in his house, wishing only to serve the true and living God.' The embarrassing incidents were not entirely at an end. As he acquired a reputation for sanctity, Pilingotto wondered what he could do to humiliate himself. His answer was to go to the main piazza one freezing Friday and shackle himself to the public pillory until he was half-dead with the cold; once again his family had to come and take him home. Later in life he devotedly served his infirm mother, doing the household tasks himself like a hired servant.

The *Lives* of contemporary lay holy men such as Pier Pettinaio of Siena (d. 1289)[16] or Rigo of Bolzano (d. 1315)[17] similarly suggest that, despite a strong emphasis on private prayer, fasting and other austerities, they remained free to wander around the city, even by night (Pier was once apprehended by the town watch) and to fall into ecstasies in public places, as Rigo did in the portico of the cathedral of Treviso. It is largely for this reason that their *Lives* do not tell us as much as those of Umiliana or Benevenuta do about their domestic environment as such. The bishop of Treviso who wrote Rigo's *Life* however gives some idea of the lodgings which the saint had in the house of a notary: 'a little room at the far end of the house, beyond a courtyard', where 'for a long time until his death he lived a life of abstinence and penitence'. Here he received divine visitations. The notary's wife, 'who as is usual with women' spent more time in the house than her husband did, played the indispensable part of aural witness, for she heard voices inside the room and asked Rigo about them, but he admitted nothing.

The servant-saint Zita (d. 1278), housekeeper to a wealthy family of Lucca, is represented as enjoying a greater freedom of movement than female saints of higher social rank.[18] Although her sanctity was principally displayed within the household and the neighbourhood, she was an assiduous performer of little local pilgrimages, which we are asked to believe she accomplished entirely alone; Umiliana would not have been so represented. Zita had a bed of her own, which she rarely used, but it does not seem that she had her own room. She prayed all the time (sometimes to the detriment of her housework) but when she wanted greater seclusion she had to seek out a rather ill-defined part of the house, from which observers saw a light shining.

Umiliana's vocation was obstructed by her father and brothers, but she was aided and abetted in her charities and devotions by other women in her family, notably her sister-in-law. Benevenuta's story suggests that sanctity could draw sustenance from kin and friends who were themselves devout. Marie of Oignies had the backing of her husband who, although hardly mentioned by Jacques de Vitry after the first few chapters of the *Vita*, was still around to give his consent to her move from Nivelles to Oignies. Opposition from the family made good copy for hagiographers, for it was obviously the acid test of a saint's early resolve. A girl's refusal to get married was paradigmatic, not least because it recalled the example of the early martyrs. Catherine de' Benincasa (d. 1380), the daughter of a Sienese dyer, was a conspicuous example. The account of her early life that her confessor Raymond of Capua included in his *Vita* is firmly located in the physical setting of the family home.[19] Like Marie of Oignies, Catherine was precociously pious as a child and developed the habit of saying the Hail Mary whenever she went upstairs, kneeling on every step to do so. This had the unexpected result that she was sometimes conveyed upstairs so fast that her mother was quite frightened. As she grew older and became determined never to take a mortal husband, even cutting off all her hair to damage her marriage prospects, the family recognized that her possession of her own bedchamber was giving her unwelcome opportunities for spiritual communion:

> It was decided that from now on Catherine was not to have a room of her own and was to be kept busy doing housework so that she would have no opportunity for praying and uniting herself with her bridegroom.[20]

Catherine's strategies for coping with this reverse were both psychological and practical:

> Under the inspiration of the Holy Spirit she began to build up in her mind a secret cell which she vowed she would never leave for anything in the world. She had begun by having a room in a house, which she could go out of and come into at will; now having made herself an inner cell which no one could take away from her, she had no need ever to come out of it again.

Raymond of Capua would certainly have been aware of the classical and monastic tradition of thinking about virtual solitude and this may colour his account, although he gives Catherine the credit for the insight:

> Catherine built for herself a cell not made with human hands, helped inwardly by Christ, and so was untroubled about losing a room with walls built by men. I remember – it has just come into my mind – that whenever I used to find myself pressed with too much business, or had to go on a journey, Catherine would say again and again, 'Make yourself a cell in your own mind from which you need never come out.'

She therefore perfected the technique of thinking about Christ as she worked in the kitchen or waited at the table, neatly and painlessly heaping coals of fire on her family's heads by imagining her father as Our Lord, her mother (improbably) as the Virgin Mary and her brothers as the Apostles.

Her need for a place in which to pray she met by making use of her brother Stefano's bedroom, both while he was out during the day and when he was asleep at night. She had to leave the door open, for she was forbidden ever to shut herself away anywhere. Her father came into the room one day to look for something and saw her in the corner praying with a snow-white dove hovering above her head. This was the beginning of the end of the family's resistance. Catherine was now permitted to have 'a little room of her own in which she could pray and scourge herself as much as she liked as though she were living in solitude'. 'In this little room were revived the ancient deeds of the holy Fathers of Egypt' (of whom, Raymond declares, Catherine was entirely ignorant).[21] She spent her entire time in her 'cell' except when she went to church: 'She established a desert within the walls of her own home and solitude in the midst of people.'[22]

The concept is familiar, and so too are Catherine's austerities, her floods of tears and divine and diabolical visitations. Like Umiliana's, her cell was invaded by demons of the most troublesome kind. So far her style of sanctity basically resembles Umiliana's or Marie's. It was not surprising that it should be marked by gifts of spiritual discernment and counsel, and the *Vita* might be thought unusual only in the particularity with which Raymond evokes Catherine's domestic environment. Unlike Umiliana, however, Catherine at Christ's specific command took on a public, apostolic role to which he devotes the second part of the *Vita*, deliberately contrasting it with the first, 'which was made up of silence and seclusion'.[23] This took her, reluctantly as Raymond describes it, far beyond the confines of the household in Siena.

Catherine, the daughter of a Sienese dyer, was illiterate when she embraced the religious life. She tried to learn to read so that she could 'say the psalms and sing your praises in the Canonical Hours'. After experiencing considerable difficulty, she was prepared to accept that she might have to do without, but with the aid of a miracle she acquired the ability to decipher the Latin words and 'say them properly'.[24] In the same city a century earlier, however, the aristocratic mother of the future Dominican *beatus* Ambrogio Sansedoni (d. 1287) is supposed to have read the Hours of the Blessed Virgin in the presence of her child, provoking him to uncontrollable weeping until the book was handed to him.[25] Literacy was most likely to be found in upper-class surroundings, and it was not the only available stimulant to devotion in the home. It is not clear whether Umiliana was literate, but she kept in her room an image of the Virgin and Child before which she kept a light continually burning.[26]

Jean Gerson believed that a life of prayer and contemplation was attainable by men and women who were living in the world, unequipped with Latin learning. When he embarked on his ecclesiastical and academic career, Gerson left on the family farm near Reims not only his parents but several sisters, one of whom, Marion, had been married and widowed. Between about 1395 and 1408 he directed a stream of advice to them about the avoidance of marriage, the preservation of virginity and the way to lead a holy life in their domestic surroundings.[27] The household constituted a devout community embracing both parents and children. There seems to have been no question of installing the girls in a regular convent, perhaps because the family could not provide the necessary dowries; that they could remain under their brother's watchful eye and continue to look after their parents were consoling benefits. Gerson's father Arnoul told him that his sisters 'love God and fear sin, and they fast one or two days a week and recite daily their hours to our Lady; Marion has learned the hours since the death of her husband'. Gerson was delighted by this and wanted the girls to learn to read French so that he could send them *livres de devocion*. They had doubtless learned their Hours by ear, but the ability to read their own language would open a range of supplementary material to them. A letter written in the winter of 1399–1400 suggests that they had made progress: although 'you have sufficient letters and books so that you can always be learning how to serve God and have spiritual consolations, you can now profit from even more of these'.[28] One of the 'Eleven Rules' which he laid down for the guidance of their lives prescribed daily reading aloud from a good book.[29]

In 1400 Gerson produced a generalized and considered version of his advice, in the form of a vernacular treatise, *The Mountain of Contemplation*.[30] He addressed this to a broader public of *simples gens*, but he was still thinking more of women than of men. While contemplation was available to people dwelling in the workaday world, Gerson conceded, on the authority of St Gregory, that some individuals were temperamentally wedded to practical activity and unfitted for contemplation.[31] Women of the rank to which he was addressing himself would have to work in one sense or another and to strike a balance between action and contemplation, not only because they had to consider the needs of others but in order to prepare themselves for the ascent into contemplation. It was not given to many to launch straight into solitude in youth as St Benedict did. Besides, the objective,

> the way of hermitage or reclusion ... is found not only in the woods and deserted places, but anywhere that one can pursue it in escaping from the confusion of the world and all its cares and obligations.

Gerson explained that it was the established practice of the religious orders to inflict considerable burdens of labour and sleeplessness on new entrants, precisely 'in order to keep them from thinking on their own about anything else'. The well-tried seniors 'have more room in themselves for being alone and at leisure'. In reality every individual was obliged to mix the two elements of action and contemplation, to be both Martha and Mary, and, as Gerson had already acknowledged, for some people constant external occupation was a moral and psychological necessity.[32]

For the dweller in the world who sought contemplation time and space were practical issues. Gerson here drew on an established repertoire of thinking about real and virtual solitude, with much of which we are already familiar: 'the main hiding place and silence should be within the soul rather than outside of it'. This was achievable in a variety of different ways, and to be physically alone did not necessarily proof the individual against 'herself, with her fantasies, thoughts, and bouts of melancholy'. St Jerome had humbly confessed to difficulties with lurid imaginings 'when he was in the desert without any companions except for wild beasts and scorpions'. With the obligatory nod to Cicero (or St Ambrose) Gerson however affirmed that the truly contemplative soul 'is never less alone than when it is alone'.[33]

Real solitude could be helpful, especially for 'beginners' and those who had not yet mastered the techniques of withdrawal while in company. They might seek out woods, forests, 'deserts', the fields, 'the hidden parts of churches or of their own dwelling places' as inclination, and presumably opportunity, afforded. Here again there was no fixed rule. For some people any noise was distracting, for others the sound of chant induced a salutary state of mind. Other duties might make it impracticable to linger overlong in church; it was therefore good to learn to make a virtue of necessity and 'to make a habit of being in one's lodgings, in one's room if one has one's own, or somewhere else within'. Gerson quotes the example of an invalid who learned to treasure her confinement to her sickroom because it enabled her to concentrate her mind on God and herself. However, it was not wise to rely on the possibility of physical solitude or to insist on being in a particular place: 'wherever one is, in the fields, in town, even in the bath, as St John Chrysostom said, one can try to return to oneself and to withdraw from the world'. Benefit and renewal could also be derived from 'diversity and change of place or places' and the silence of night-time was helpful.[34] Gerson repeatedly insists on the need to consult one's own temperament. For certain individuals 'it would be a minor form of hell for them to be without company or to be in a fixed place for even a short while'; similarly anyone prone to depression or irritability should seek constant work and companionship rather than the life of contemplation.[35]

Unlike a monastic counsellor such as William of St-Thierry, Gerson was addressing himself to people who had and would retain a certain power of choice and freedom of movement. They might have a problem finding peace and quiet and had to be advised how to get the best out of their everyday environment and their customary religious practices. He was unwilling to recommend that his sisters should give up the pilgrimages to male and female saints which they undertook to obtain benefits both for themselves and for their friends alive and dead.[36] Such popular devotional exercises had their place in a mixed spiritual economy. The women he was addressing had to learn to take opportunities for spiritual advancement as they arose; their physical and economic environment was not presumed to be conducive to unbroken contemplation. To constitute themselves into an informal community, as his sisters had done, would ensure mutual support and encouragement.

Despite Gerson's enthusiasm for virginity, there is no reason why there should not have been widows (like his sister Marion) among his readership. Certainly there were numerous widows among those who tried to live a devout life at home. The pious routines followed in the household of one very high-ranking widow, Cicely duchess of York, the mother of two kings, are well known.[37] Widows often took formal vows of continence and, while some may have taken lodgings in convents, many doubtless continued to live in their own or a relative's household, like the widow in the story told by Caesarius of Heisterbach.[38] Just as some saints found early nurture and encouragement in godly homes, some widows had lived in an atmosphere of piety in their husbands' lifetimes. This may well have been the case with Joan, the widow of Thomas Wombwell, who took her vows promptly on the death of her husband early in 1452.[39]

The possession of private chapels is one of a number of rough indicators of the growth of domestic religious practice among the laity in the fourteenth and fifteenth centuries. Another, not unconnected, is provided by licences to private individuals to possess portable altars, which become numerous in the papal registers after about 1300. As objects, portable altars were very far from new, but now not only the secular and regular clergy and the higher nobility but substantial numbers of individuals of lesser rank, including married couples, were obtaining permission to use them. Individuals, rather than premises, were licensed. For landowners who were frequently on the move the portability of the altar was a large part of its point, and there is no reason to suppose that every recipient of such a grant possessed a private chapel, in the sense of a distinct and permanent structure, in all or even any of his residences.

Such altars (sometimes called *superaltaria*) might be set up on tables in any suitable room, which further illustrates the adaptability of the medieval dwelling-space. The will of William Duffield, canon residentiary of York, Southwell and Beverley, made in 1452, reveals that he had chapels in his houses at York and Beverley, but not at Cawood, where there was 'a table with high trestles for celebrating masses'.[40] A few years later John Dautre, citizen and lawyer of York, referred to 'a chest in the *bassa camera* on which I have made my altar' and again to 'the altar *in bassa camera*'.[41] Purpose-built private chapels, however, there were, and like portable altars they were not only to be found in the houses of the great. Dautre's equally pious contemporary John Baret, citizen of Bury of St Edmunds, may not already have possessed a chapel of his own when he obtained a licence for a portable altar from Pope Eugenius IV in 1444, but he did by the time he made his will in 1463.[42]

The spread of the private chapel below the ranks of the highest nobility had begun in England much earlier. There is one on the first floor of the tower-block built around 1290 at Old Soar in Kent.[43] Its present aspect is slightly misleading in that it now communicates directly with the solar through a rough opening made in the eighteenth century when it was used as a grain-store; originally the chapel was reached via an external staircase to a now blocked doorway. Private chapels had to be licensed by the diocesan and the usual pretext on which petitioners requested such a licence was the distance of their dwelling from the parish church; Old Soar is some four miles from the church of Wrotham. There is no private chapel at Stokesay Castle, built at a very similar date, for the parish church of St John is adjacent to the house.

The contemporaneous register of Oliver Sutton, bishop of Lincoln, contains a number of licences for private chapels, in which the bishop spelled out the uses to which they might and might not be put.[44] Every effort was made to safeguard the sacramental and financial rights of the parish church. All offerings had to go to the rector of the parish; and while a priest might celebrate mass in the chapel, he might not actually administer the sacrament to those present, who must include only the petitioner's immediate household. It was occasionally specified that guests were included, but it was not permissible to invite the neighbours in. All family members were to fulfil their obligations at the parish church on the major festivals of the year and chapels were not to advertise their presence by exhibiting a bell-tower or other *insignia*.

What then was the point of having a private chapel? Oliver Sutton ruled a far-flung and largely rural diocese, and most of his petitioners claimed to live too far from the parish church for comfort, at least in winter, although the distances invoked were sometimes as little as one mile. In principle town-dwellers should have had no such claim, but Sutton also granted private chapels to Oxford masters and students. A century and a half later John Baret, who was in fact a devoted parishioner of St Mary in Bury, would have had equally little physical difficulty in getting to church. Clearly there was a desire to have the comforts and possibly also the décor of religion close at hand, whether we interpret this as proceeding from pure devotion or the desire for a spiritual marker of superior social status. Baret in his will envisaged that his niece, who was going to continue to occupy rooms in his house, should be free to go into the chapel to perform her devotions. It may have seemed obvious that if something of the visual appearance and apparatus of a church was available in the dwelling-place, private prayer would be best offered there. The ability to have mass celebrated under one's own roof, even if only the priest could communicate, was of value in an age which increasingly prized the very sight of the sacrament. The restrictions on what was permitted were in fact relaxed in the course of time. The privilege received by John Baret in 1444 included the administration of the eucharist and the performance of baptisms by either his own 'or other fit priest'. Not every possessor of a private chapel, still less every possessor of a portable altar, was in a position to maintain a chaplain, let alone a staff of chaplains; many must have relied upon a friendly visiting priest.

There were marked differences between cultures. It has been said that private chapels in Florence were rare before (and even after) Cosimo de' Medici built one in his *palazzo* in the late 1440s, although there is evidence that Oliviero de' Cerchi (of the family which had produced Umiliana) possessed one in the 1290s. Cosimo and his wife had received the grant of a portable altar from Pope Martin V some twenty years before the chapel was built; this too has been described as a 'rare privilege'.[45] If this was so in Florence, it certainly was not in England at the same period, and as we have seen not all English petitioners were stranded in remote countryside. Prominent Florentine laymen seem to have felt a strong, indeed a competitive, commitment to the public, civic arena in which they displayed their piety and their patronage; it was in the city's churches that they built, furnished and decorated chapels which bore the family name. The palazzo built by Cosimo's Florentine contemporary Giovanni Rucellai was hard up against the church of San Pancrazio and it was in the church, not within the body of the palace, that he built a chapel containing a replica of the Holy Sepulchre. It was here that as an old man in 1481 he went every Friday to a special mass.[46]

This did not mean that Florentines, or other Italians, did not perform domestic devotions, rather that they were informal and there was rarely specialized accommodation for them. Portable altarpieces and other images, like Umiliana's Virgin and Child, could be accommodated in any convenient place. The Florentine merchant Giovanni Morelli evidently had some kind of image of the Crucifixion; haunted by the memory of his dead son, he conducted an anguished private ritual in his bedchamber, addressing his prayers to the Crucified Christ, Mary and St John.[47] The bedroom everywhere continued to play a part in domestic religion. Cicely, duchess of York, maintained a chapel and a staff of chaplains, as befitted her rank, but she performed certain devotions in her chamber. This was anyway the natural and immediate setting for the prayers with which the devout were enjoined to begin and end the day. A late fifteenth-century English book of hours included prayers which 'ougt for to be sayd or ye departe out of your chambre at your uprysyng'.[48] The dining table too could be sanctified, as it was in Cicely's household, by holy reading at mealtimes.

To listen to such reading was to do what monks did (or were supposed to do) in the refectory. While the domestic practice of religion can legitimately be described as private, it would be mistaken to suppose that it conflicted with public observance or to postulate a dichotomy between the religion of the clergy and the religion of the laity. The devout laity imported into their domestic space not novelties but words and images which were already familiar to them. The Psalms, the Hours of the Virgin and the other constituents of private prayer books were common property. Certain books which found their way into the hands of the laity had originated in a clerical milieu: the *Meditations on the Life of Christ*, written by a Franciscan for the use of a nun, became an immensely popular handbook of lay devotion when rendered into English by the Carthusian Nicholas Love in 1410.[49]

From the point of view of the individual family member, participation in the rituals that were prescribed by the head of the household must often have been a supplementary obligation, like Victorian family prayers, rather than a spontaneous expression of personal devotion. In the mid-fifteenth century the Florentine humanist Leon Battista Alberti, sketching the ideal country villa, envisaged that there should be adjacent to the entrance

> A chapel dedicated to God, with its Altar, where Strangers and Guests may offer their Devotions, beginning their friendship by Religion; and where the Father of the Family may put up his Prayers for the Peace of his House and the Welfare of his Relations.[50]

This *paterfamilias* was rather self-consciously re-enacting the role of his Roman prototype; but perhaps he had moments, like Cosimo de' Medici when he meditated on the afterlife, when his chapel served a more genuinely private purpose. If he had no chapel his bedchamber might do.

Umiliana de' Cerchi, Benevenuta Boiani or Catherine of Siena withdrew into a space apart within the household. Because they were saints, what we might be tempted to call their privacy had to be likened to the solitude of ancient tradition. There were subtle differences between their several situations. Umiliana sealed herself away quasi-permanently, in self-defence against a hostile family; Catherine initially did something similar, but emerged at Christ's command to take on a wider role; Benvenuta had no family opposition to counter but shared a cosy domestic piety with father and sister, withdrawing when it was necessary to do so in order to converse with the saints. Outside these elite ranks, Giovanni Morelli at a moment of crisis withdrew into something we might recognise as privacy. Cicely of York did so more routinely when she prayed in her chamber, alone or with her clerks. When she presided at table and directed the devotions of her dependants she showed another face. Where there was no chapel in a household – and often even when there was – the bedchamber as a place of prayer manifested another aspect of its multi-purpose usefulness.

Much late medieval religious art is set against a domestic background. In Flemish fifteenth-century painting the Virgin is depicted as a girl of the bourgeoisie reading her prayer-book in a well-appointed bedroom or sitting room at the moment of the Angel's arrival.[51] Donors are depicted as if at prayer before the Virgin in their own chambers. The infant Jesus practises walking in a wheeled frame in the carpenter's workshop; the Last Supper takes place in a dining-room somewhat less idealized and more fully furnished than is usual in Florentine frescoes. In Italian painting the birth of the Virgin or of the Baptist is a favourite occasion for depicting the bedchamber, often with its stone fireplace. All this is to be regarded less as a sacralization of the domestic space itself than as a means of conveying the message that 'These things really happened on this earth and can legitimately be imagined as taking place in settings which are familiar to you.' The *Meditations on the Life of Christ* went well beyond the warrant of scripture to encourage such visualization. At bottom a profound and vital truth was being affirmed: the reality of the Incarnation. Many of the images which affirmed it in the fourteenth and fifteenth centuries held up a mirror to the more comfortable and well-appointed domestic world which was the habitat of the artist's audience and in which the more prosperous members of society very often lived a part of their religious lives.[52]

9

Men of Letters

In *The House of Fame* (lines 652–660) the Eagle pokes fun at Chaucer's incurable attachment to the written word. He can think of nothing better to do when he comes home from work:

> For when thy labour doon al ys,
> And hast mad alle thy rekenynges,
> In stede of reste and newe thynges,
> Thou goost hom to thy hous anoon;
> And also domb as any stoon
> Thou sittest at another book
> Tyl fully daswed ys thy look,
> And lyvest thus as an heremyte,
> Although thyn abstynence ys lyte.

The Eagle evidently thinks that Chaucer should get out more. The constant reader bears a superficial likeness to a religious, for ordinary worldly men did not hide themselves away like this, but Chaucer does not have their 'abstinence'. If the Eagle is right, he also belonged to the growing army of silent readers, 'domb as any stoon'. Perhaps his friend the French poet Eustace Deschamps was another; at all events, he was (or wished to be) so attached to his book collection that he wrote a *ballade* with the refrain 'I'll never lend a book again no matter what', which must strike a chord with many a modern reader.[1] The condition was incurable, and among its consequences were the development of behaviour patterns which were not those of the knight, merchant or peasant. If they had belonged anywhere, it was in the cloister; but they were now invading the domestic space.

The habit of silent reading seems to have evolved as part of a complex package of developments, both nourishing and nourished by changes in scribal conventions, text layout, book-production and modes of study.[2] Alongside readers who were engaged in the prayerful contemplation of texts, there were others who were subjecting them to analytical scrutiny and yet others who were simply seeking recreation. Chivalric romances or Chaucer's works could still be read aloud to an assembled company, just as monks were still supposed to listen to reading at mealtimes, but alternative modes of private reading became more widespread. Readers in pre-modern society always remained relatively few, however; their numbers were limited by the restricted spread of literacy, the scarcity and high cost of books and the shortage of space and light (especially in domestic surroundings), as well as by the pressures of company and occupation.

The books that the scholar or the literate layperson read in the later centuries of the pre-print age were the products of the cumulative development of the codex, that is, the book in its now familiar shape, during more than a thousand years of Christian history. Books were produced in an array of sizes, some of them far from portable, but the small, closely written volume, such as the gospel books which were owned by some early Irish monks, may now look to us like the future: personal rather than communal possessions, designed to be carried about and consulted or mulled over by the individual at any convenient moment. In a series of stages after *c.* 1100 books were increasingly designed to serve the professional needs of the academic, lawyer or preacher, and, somewhat later, the devotional or recreational needs of the layperson. A legible script and a clear layout of the page as of the volume as a whole were important considerations, and finding devices made their appearance: contents lists, alphabetical indexes, running headings, rubrication and folio numbers. The manner in which text and illustrations were integrated or related on the page was another feature of this development of the book and emphasized its character as an object that was interpreted above all by means of the eye.

There has been much discussion of the development of the habit of silent reading. St Augustine records that St Ambrose 'never read aloud'. Observing him so deeply engaged with his book, visitors would sometimes go away, unwilling to interrupt his precious moments of recreation. Augustine evidently regarded this habit as worthy of remark and offered several possible explanations for it. As a bishop and therefore a great man, Ambrose was never alone; to read silently was, perhaps, a way of avoiding interruption from companions who might want him to explain a passage he had just read out. Alternatively, and in Augustine's view very probably, he simply wished to spare his voice.[3] It may indeed have been the case that a man who spent so much of his time addressing others was attracted by the opportunity of silent communion with another mind, but Ambrose was surely not the only man of his time so situated.

Also often quoted in this connection is c. 48 of the Rule of St Benedict: if a monk wishes to read on his bed during the rest period he should do so quietly so as to avoid disturbing the others. This seems to presuppose that he was expected to vocalize as he read. The Benedictine Peter of Celle declared in his treatise on *The School of the Cloister*, written in 1179, that reading was 'chained' to silence; but how complete was the silence?[4] Herbert, a monk of St Albans who became abbot of Selby in Yorkshire for a few years in the 1120s, was a true and observant monk: 'He would sit alone (*solitarius*) in the cloister, keeping silence, reciting the psalms, praying. He read and gathered flowers from the scriptures.' (As a result the administration of the abbey went to wrack and ruin.)[5] Hugues de Fouilloy pairs *lectio* and *silentium* (both of which were neglected by overfed monks), but there was a time and place for speech: the mouth could legitimately be opened in the cloister 'at the hour appointed for reading'. This might suggest either vocalization by a solitary reader or monks listening to reading in a group (as they did in the refectory).[6]

Everyone may have been used to a certain level of noise:

> In the late antique library and early medieval monastery, where readers had read aloud, each reader's own voice had acted as a neurophysiological screen, blocking out the sounds of the adjacent readers.[7]

When today we use the telephone in an office or on a train a similar mechanism must come into play; yet silence is demanded of readers in open-plan libraries and we also read silently even when completely alone. The Eagle implies that Chaucer had already developed this logically unnecessary habit.

The all-purpose Latin word *legere*, 'to read', did not necessarily denote a silent, predominantly visual process and 'reading', in English, may still imply 'reading aloud'. Addressing Robert of Gloucester, William of Malmesbury declared that although the earl was so beset by business, 'you set aside some time for yourself when you can either read yourself or listen to readers (*aut ipsi legere aut legentes possitis audire*)'.[8] Interesting as a tribute to a literate layman, this does not of itself tell us whether Robert vocalized or read silently. St Anselm (d. 1109) prefaced his *Prayers and Meditations*, a copy of which he sent to Countess Matilda of Tuscany, with the caution that the contents 'non sunt legendae in tumultu, sed in quiete, non cursim et velociter'. This has been translated as 'not to be read in a turmoil, but quietly, not skimmed or hurried through'.[9] To read aloud *cursim et velociter* would be to gabble, and it seems probable, if not quite certain, that Anselm was recommending an eye–brain and not a vocal procedure. He also drew attention to the division of his text into paragraphs, which was intended to make it easier for the reader to 'begin and leave off wherever he chooses'. Anselm sent seven of his prayers to Adela of Blois, the daughter of William the Conqueror, telling her that there were 'certain things' in the prayers to St Stephen and Mary Magdalen which had greater power 'to inflame love' if they were said *intimo corde*, when leisure permitted. This could mean 'in', 'with' or 'from' one's inmost heart and it is hard to know whether it necessarily implies a silent process.[10]

There was clearly a widespread awareness by the early twelfth century of the variety of ways in which it was possible to read and of the ambiguities of the related terminology. It has been suggested that around this time the vocabulary of reading shifted in a manner which may indicate a shift in actual reading habits. Words such as *inspicere*, from which 'inspect' obviously derives, began to be used to describe the perusal of texts. Expounding the meaning of the triple process *lectio, meditatio, oratio*, Guigo II, prior of the Chartreuse, defined reading as 'the careful inspection of writings with mental concentration (*sedula scripturarum cum animi intentione inspectio*)'.[11] He asked rhetorically what profit there was in spending time in continual reading and 'going through (*transcurrere*) the deeds and writings of the saints' unless by means of 'mastication and rumination' the sap was extracted and transmitted to the innermost heart, with consequent impact upon one's actual conduct. How are we to achieve these things and be put on our guard against falsehood and error unless first we are instructed by reading or by listening? Listening does in some measure apply to reading; hence we are accustomed to say that we have read not only those books which we have read to ourselves or to others, but those which we have heard from our masters.

There are three possibilities: reading to oneself (perhaps silently), reading to others, and listening. Having been instructed by hearing Christ's *lectio* the woman of Samaria meditated upon it and proceeded to prayer.[12]

The regular canon Hugh of St Victor and the secular clerk John of Salisbury explicitly distinguished between different meanings of the word 'to read'. Hugh expounded a threefold definition which reflected academic practice:

> Reading consists of forming our minds upon rules and precepts taken from books (*ex his quae scripta sunt*) and it is of three types: the teacher's, the learner's and the independent reader's (*per se inspicientis*). For we say, 'I am reading the book *to* him', 'I am reading the book *under* him', and 'I am reading the book'.[13]

John, more simply, distinguished two meanings: 'The word "reading" is equivocal. It may refer either to the activity of teaching or being taught, or to the occupation of studying written things by oneself.' There was *praelectio* (lecture or exposition) and *lectio* (the individual's scrutiny of a text).[14] Hugh was notably concerned with punctuation and visual aids to the comprehension of text, and both he and John quoted the advice, attributed to Bernard of Chartres, that the studious should seek among other aids to scholarship 'a quiet life' and 'silent scrutiny'.[15] John enlarged on his understanding of this advice:

> The practice of study is most profitable when the virtue in everything which a man reads or hears gains strength from the silent scrutiny of true judgment within himself; for there the reason examines all things and weighs the fruit of all things in the balance.[16]

Here the 'silent scrutiny' seems not (or not necessarily) to be a part of the reading process as such but of the subsequent mulling-over which is necessary for the value of reading to be realized. Perhaps some of Seneca's twelfth-century admirers noticed a passage in which he distinguishes 'reading' from 'hearing'. In his 66th epistle, written in acknowledgement of a new book by his correspondent Lucilius, he apologizes for not sending an instant verdict, saying that although he has in fact read the work through he has not come to a settled opinion, 'just as if I have heard it read aloud and not read it myself (*tamquam audierim illa, non legerim*)'. He implies that personal visual inspection, silent or not, is important to concentration. Early in the thirteenth century the Cistercian Richalm of Schönthal too associated silent reading with concentration. He may not have been physically alone as he read, but it seems that he was accustomed to weaving himself a cocoon of silence.[17]

Practice was evidently variable and influenced by circumstances. Pope Innocent III was as literate an individual as any alive in the year 1200; in the words of Gerald of Wales 'he was abundantly lettered and loved literature'.[18] Gerald however also testifies that, when the pope was investigating the papal records, he sometimes had documents read to him. On one occasion when Gerald waited on him in his chamber, a volume of the papal registers was brought and the list of churches that were subject to Canterbury was read out (*lectum fuit*). 'When he had heard this' (*quo audito*), the pope gave his opinion. On another evening, Innocent handed the transcript of a letter to Cardinal Ugolino, who was sitting by him, to read aloud (*ad legendum*); again the pope commented when he had 'carefully listened'. The habit of verification by reading aloud must have been so engrained as to be habitual and indeed necessary when a large number of people, perhaps including illiterates, needed to be informed of the contents of a document. Here, however, it has been argued that the pope must simply have wanted to concentrate better, for the only other people present were Ugolino and Gerald, who had provided the transcript.[19] If so, the contrast with our present habits is instructive. On yet another occasion Gerald describes how Innocent, consulting the records of Eugenius III's dealings with France, quickly found the letter he was locking for 'and joyfully inspected and read it' (*inspexit et legit*). This might mean that, having first perused the letter silently (*inspexit*), Innocent then read it aloud (*legit*); that the two processes were simultaneous; or, perhaps least likely, that *inspexit* and *legit* were merely synonyms.[20]

The key issue is perhaps not whether readers muttered to themselves as they scanned a text but whether their principal reliance was on their own eyes. Reading was not necessarily silent, private or solitary, but it could be any or all of these things and was then inevitably 'inspection'. It did not exclude mumbling or the use of other modes in other situations: a clerk or secretary reading to his master, sociable or ceremonial reading aloud. In the mid-fourteenth century, the bibliophile bishop of Durham, Richard of Bury (d.1346), said that it was his daily custom to 'read or hear' books (*legere vel audire*); the procedures were distinct, but both counted as 'readings' (*lectiones*).[21] Large *de luxe* volumes which could only be read at a lectern continued to be produced and may have been intended not only for the personal enjoyment of their calligraphy and illuminations but for reading aloud to the household. The dukes of Burgundy, assiduous patrons of book-production, read or were read to in all manner of situations both public and private.[22] Many of the editions printed by the first printers represented the book as it had developed since 1100 to cater for a constituency beyond the monastic or the aristocratic. How these books were used could vary, as it still does. We read aloud to small children and to the sick, thus unconsciously recalling a situation in which it must have been much more common for the literate individual, the holder of the magic key, to read to those who could not. When early in the fifteenth century seven Londoners were arrested on suspicion of studying heretical texts it was found that only one of them could read.[23]

Writing, or at least writing swiftly and legibly, was a still more restricted and arcane skill. Just as men who could read often listened to reading, so men who were capable of writing were accustomed to giving dictation; literary composition was not a strictly solitary pursuit. It has been suggested that writing for oneself made it easier to write erotica. As a young monk Guibert of Nogent composed erotic poetry in secret, which he recited to like-minded companions, albeit disguising his authorship, but he did not elude discovery by his master. Later he 'secretly' defied his abbot's injunction to discontinue work on a biblical commentary.[24] As he explained in the prologue to a late exegetical work, he had always been not only the composer (*dictator*) of his works but his own *notarius*. When his eyesight failed, he lamented his enforced reliance on 'voice' and 'memory', where he had been used to 'hand' and 'eye'. For him this was an irksome transformation, for he had been used to revising, in the literal sense of that word, repairing omissions and polishing style, as he went along; now he had to reckon with the impatience of his scribe.[25]

Richard of Bury humorously pointed out certain advantages that books had over human teachers: what a convenient, easy and secret (*arcana*) source of learning they were, 'how safely, without shame, we expose the poverty of our ignorance' to them. They did not use the rod, harsh words or anger; they did not sleep or evade questions; they did not reproach one's errors or mock one's ignorance.[26] To the old-fashioned schoolmaster, these might not have seemed like recommendations. Books, as Richard was not the first to notice, brought the world to one's door:

> How highly the marvellous power of books is to be estimated, when through them we perceive the boundaries of the world and of time, and contemplate both things which are and things which are not as if in an eternal mirror.[27]

The capacity of the book to represent indifferently both the imaginary or non-existent and the real, both the false and the true, could of course be seen as much as a threat as a promise. If books opened a window on the world, and as they multiplied in number, even before the age of print, it mattered increasingly who was looking through the window and what they saw out there.

Heresy and heretical writings had never been a matter of indifference, but before the later twelfth century it was scarcely necessary to worry about the possibility that laymen might get hold of heretical writings or of vernacular translations of the scriptures. Thereafter and until the Reformation (and indeed beyond), this was intermittently a problem for the ecclesiastical authorities in several parts of Europe.[28] The potential complexity of the issues involved was revealed when, in the summer of 1199, Innocent III was informed by the bishop of Metz that

> Both in his city and in his diocese a multitude of laymen and women, led to a large extent by a desire of understanding the scriptures, have had translated for themselves the gospels, epistles of St Paul, the Psalter, the Moralisation on Job, and many other books in the French tongue.[29]

The writings were in themselves unimpeachable; but who had translated them, and who was reading them and with what purpose in mind? From the beginning, this desire on the part of the laity (or some laity) to understand Holy Writ was believed to imply a desire to challenge the authority of the priesthood and to arrogate to themselves the role of preaching and expressing opinions on scripture. As it was represented to Innocent, and as he was evidently prepared to believe, these suspect persons were gathering in 'secret conventicles'. To the spokesmen of the official church, the orthodoxy they defended was always the consensus, which held its head up in the light of day. The presumed heretics of Metz were guilty, among other things, of withdrawing into secrecy and 'refusing the fellowship of those who do not receive the said translation'.[30]

In 1229 a council at Toulouse, in the heart of Cathar country, ruled that 'Lay people shall not have books of scripture, except the Psalter and the divine office; and they shall not have these books in the vulgar tongue'.[31] This implied permission to possess the Psalter and the divine office – in Latin – became a more or less general rule. The many women (and men) in the following centuries who owned and used Psalters and books of hours were not necessarily learned in Latin, even though the contents of their prayer-books remained for the most part in that language.[32] If prayers were read with the aid of a chaplain, they could be followed rather than independently read, and the devout doubtless learnt to recognize on the page Latin words whose sound was familiar to them. Such edifying matter could safely be supplemented by vernacular translations of saints' lives or specially composed devotional tractates. In the late fourteenth century the Ménagier de Paris provided French prayers and French translations of Latin prayers for his wife, as well as a commentary on the Mass and the Seven Deadly Sins.[33] He evidently expected her to be able to read these and the vernacular religious works which he owned, as well as what he had to say about cooking, gardening and household management.

Since the twelfth century, female literacy (and indeed lay literacy in general) had been promoted not only by translations but by the multiplication of original vernacular texts. There is evidence that women of rank were expected to learn their letters and read their psalter even when, possibly, this was less important for their menfolk. Their somewhat more leisured and secluded mode of life gave them, at least potentially, cultural opportunities which the great ladies who read St Anselm's prayers and meditations exploited. Eleanor of Aquitaine, like her daughter Marie, countess of Champagne, was part of the audience for Chrétien's romances, but she is shown on her effigy at Fontevraud with her prayer-book in her hands, a mode of representation appropriate to both her rank and her gender.[34] The image of the woman reading her psalter in fact penetrated the romances: the lady whom Chrétien's Yvain has just widowed 'read her psalms in a psalter, illuminated in letters of gold'.[35] Fourteenth-century Saxon law codes classified 'Psalters and all books related to the service of God that women are wont to read' among the personal possessions that a widow would claim on the death of her husband.[36] The Virgin was imagined to have been reading at the moment of the Annunciation; to judge from a motif especially popular in the art of northern Europe, she had learnt from her mother St Anne.[37]

When, very early in the fourteenth century, Dante started work on the *Convivio*, a compendium of philosophical knowledge in Italian, he intended it for an audience of 'noble people, not only men but women' who were literate in the vernacular but not in Latin.[38] The precise connotation of 'noble' here is uncertain, but access to literacy in general, and for women in particular, was to a large extent class-bound. Christine de Pizan assumes that the daughter of a 'princess' will be taught to read and commends the reading of the lives of the virgin saints to young girls further down the social scale 'if they can'. The artisan's wife should put her children to school, but no such counsel is given to the peasant woman.[39] In Tuscan mercantile society it was clearly not the invariable rule that girls were taught to read: where women were not expected to help run the family business, they did not need even mercantile 'pragmatic' literacy. Margherita, the wife of the Merchant of Prato, learned when she was over thirty, so that she could read her husband's letters and write to him when he was away. She probably learned from a psalter, and had difficulty reading a business letter written in quite a different hand.[40]

In Italian society there was no controversy about the need to keep respectable girls in seclusion from about the age of twelve as they awaited marriage, but their parents were theoretically obliged to keep them busy at every hour of the day. This was the training a good wife needed, but Giovanni Boccaccio, who wrote the *Decameron* specifically for a female audience, hints that it was not always what she got. As a lifelong servant of love who had compassion on the sufferings of lovers both male and female, he took pity in particular on lovesick girls. Apart from their other sufferings

> they are forced to follow the whims, fancies and dictates of their fathers, mothers, brothers and husbands, so that they spend most of their time cooped up within the narrow confines of their rooms, where they sit in apparent idleness, wishing one thing and at the same time wishing its opposite, and reflecting on various matters which cannot possibly always be pleasant to contemplate.

Boccaccio therefore wrote the *Decameron* as a remedy for depression, which men were better able to alleviate by external activity, such as hunting, riding, fishing, gambling or business, while other (perhaps older) women could divert themselves 'with their reels, their needles and their spindles'. In his epilogue to the work, he defended himself against the inevitable critics of its improprieties and mischievously characterized his readership. His stories were harmless, even edifying, if properly read, and 'the lady who is forever saying her prayers or baking pies and cakes for her father confessor' did not have to read them. Anyway, he was not the author, just the reporter. Perhaps some of them were too long, but

> It has not escaped my memory that I offered these exertions of mine to ladies with time on their hands ... Brevity is all very well for students, who endeavour to use their time profitably rather than while away, but not for you, ladies, who have as much time to spare as you fail to consume in the pleasures of love. And besides, since none of you goes to study in Athens, or Bologna, or Paris, you have need of a lengthier form of address than those who have sharpened their wits with the aid of their studies.[41]

Three-quarters of a century later, the Franciscan preacher Bernardino of Siena vigorously endorsed the need to keep young girls both secluded and busy around the house. He did, however, concede some usefulness to reading: a girl could not be expected to do without any pleasure and that could be provided (so Bernardino believed) by the Scriptures.[42] In a sermon which was effectively devoted to the education of *fanciulle*, he clearly envisaged that preaching would be the major vehicle of their religious instruction, but he also held up the Virgin of the Annunciation as a model for imitation:

> Now let us say where the Angel found her. Where do you think she was? At the windows or about some other business of vanity? Oh no! She was shut up in her room, and she was reading, so as to set you an example, girl, that you should never take delight in standing in the doorway or at the window, but stay in the house, saying Ave Marias and Paternosters, and if you know how to read, read good and holy things; learn the office of Our Lady and amuse yourself with that.[43]

In the medieval social context, it was not merely the *damnosa hereditas* of Eve, reinforced by the contemptuous pessimism and fanciful physiology of the ancients, which sealed women's educational fate. Women and men alike had their place in a society of prescribed roles and functions; most were unable to transgress their allotted boundaries and the choices available to individuals of all ranks were, in general, more restricted than we may find it easy to imagine. The fourteenth-century Dominican Jacopo Passavanti acknowledged that all Christians needed to know the truths that were necessary to their salvation, but clearly expected the mass of believers to get this information by ear from their priests and preachers. There was a limit to what even 'the unlettered parish priest' needed to know: 'But each one ought to know, and study to know, as much as befits his office, and the status which he holds.'[44]

It was consistent with such views that while the higher social ranks were increasingly expected to be literate they were not expected to be scholars. Kings were by definition exponents of the active, not the contemplative or intellectual, life; certain kinds of knowledge were more appropriate to them than others. In Dante's *Paradiso* (xiii, 95–108), St Bonaventure discourses on the nature of the wisdom which Solomon asked of God. This was not knowledge of philosophy or mathematics but *regal prudenza*, that is, what he needed to know 'that he might be a sufficient king'. William of Malmesbury had commended Robert of Gloucester for not neglecting warfare for letters, nor letters for warfare, but he does not tell us what the earl read.[45] Three centuries later, the 'Lollard knight' Sir John Oldcastle was not only guilty of heretical belief but was also offending against the duties of his class:

> It is unkindly for a knight
> That should the kingës castle keep,
> To babble the Bible day and night
> In resting time when he should sleep.[46]

In the fifteenth century the East Anglian Augustinian friar John Capgrave produced an intriguing fiction which cast a woman as both a ruler and a scholar and imagined the problems that might result. The precocious learning of St Katherine of Alexandria enabled her to vanquish the emperor's pagan philosophers in debate. In its basic form, this story was little more than one version of a venerable commonplace, the divinely inspired eloquence of the Christian who made fools of the worldly wise. Other female martyr-saints, like their male counterparts, denounced pagan religion as absurdity and contrary to reason, but unusual emphasis was laid on Katherine's bluestocking tendencies. The Latin *Life*, from which most others took their cue, stated that her noble father had her so well educated at an early age that no one could better her in disputation.[47] Capgrave elaborated colourfully on these hints.[48]

Katherine's troubles begin when she becomes queen on the death of her indulgent father, who had equipped her lavishly with all the amenities she needed to progress in learning. The people grumble (i, lines 862–65):

> Wee have a queen, she cometh among no men,
> She loveth not ellis, but bookys and scole;
> Lete alle oure enemys in londe ryde or ren,
> She is evere in stody and evere-more soole.

These complaints are focussed not on Katherine's inappropriate behaviour as a woman but on her failure as a ruler. It is left to her mother (often the fiercest enemy of a daughter's spiritual vocation) to put the former view (i, lines 976–77):

> To leve allone in stody, it was never seyn
> That any lady ony tyme dede soo.

Katherine must endear herself to the people who matter by conforming to their customs and expectations. She should therefore take up the outdoor life (ii, lines 125–26):

> Ye must now leve your stody and your bookes
> And take youre solace be feeldes and be brookes.

Katherine is less than enchanted by this prospect, which seems to her also to involve an unwelcome preoccupation with new clothes (ii, lines 186–86):

> I muste leve stody and wash myn booke in myre,
> Ryde oute on huntynge, use al newe a-tyre!...

So far, Katherine has been told only that as a queen she cannot shut herself up in her study. It is left to the Earl of Joppa to denounce learning itself from the viewpoint of the man in the street (ii, lines 468–69). Books

> ... dulle a mannys mende,
> A-peyre his body, his eyne thei make blynde.

In practical terms, 'stody' will be the ruin of Katherine as a queen (lines 474–80); therefore

> ... for youre puples sake,
> Chaunge now your lyf and lete youre book be stille.
> Looke no lengere up-on tho letterys blake!

Katherine is prepared to defend herself and learning in a long speech (lines 535–60): how else are we to obtain the knowledge of history which guides our policy? Hercules prince of Paphon comes up with the solution. She must take a husband who will rule on her behalf (lines 600–601):

> Thanne may ye have your bookys in youre hande
> And stodyen youre fylle, it shal not greven us.

A number of the problems of individual withdrawal and self-determination are illustrated in this holy fable. Katherine's wealth (or her father's) makes it possible to retreat into a solitude equipped with every facility, but her rank makes it impracticable and undesirable. Katherine's mother injects an objection to female learning, and the earl of Joppa an objection to book-learning as such, but the essential argument is less about what is appropriate to Katherine's gender than about what is demanded of her as a ruler. This means, in practical reality, participating in the social diversions of the nobility. For Capgrave, who would probably have been startled to encounter a real-life Katherine, her learning is justified because she is a saint who is going to use it to confront and vanquish pagan error. She thus lays claim to a status which has prior claims over mere secular rulership; what she could not do (and in fact did not want to do) was to combine the two.

By a slow process of seepage during the later medieval centuries, individuals who had not traditionally had access to books obtained it. Many were less suspect than the 'heretics' of Metz in 1199, but they still represented a solvent, forming niches for themselves within or alongside traditional structures, and, even when they were of respectable birth (like St Katherine), they might exhibit modes of behaviour that were regarded as unconventional. Dante Alighieri was clearly not easy to get on with. Recording his death in 1321, the Florentine chronicler Giovanni Villani summed up a contemporary view of his character: 'This Dante, because of his wisdom, was somewhat arrogant, fastidious and disdainful and, rather like a philosopher, awkward, not knowing very well how to talk to ordinary people.'[49] The word translated here as 'ordinary people' is *laici*; we still use 'layman' to describe one who is ignorant of a particular branch of knowledge. Dante himself was a layman in the more traditional sense, but he was clearly not clubbable by the customary standards of the Florentine guild community.

The same could be said of his friend and fellow-poet, Guido Cavalcanti. Like Dante, Cavalcanti was not too proud to get involved in Florentine politics and as a result he died in exile in the summer of 1300. He resembled his friend also in his attitude to the everyday social world. According to the contemporary chronicler Dino Compagni he was 'courteous and bold, but disdainful, solitary and intent on study'.[50] This was an early use of the adjective *solitario* to describe a personality type; here it may also have implied singularity, an unusual and wilfully unconventional kind of character.

Later in the fourteenth century, Boccaccio told a story about Cavalcanti which illustrated his personality in action. Messer Betto Brunelleschi, the leading light of one of the Florentine *brigate* (social clubs of free-spending young patricians), went to great lengths to enrol Cavalcanti among his following but failed to do so. Cavalcanti was a catch because of his charm and wit and above all his wealth, which enabled him to give lavish entertainment to anyone he thought worth the trouble, but he resisted all Betto's blandishments. Betto and his companions supposed that 'this was because of his passion for speculative reasoning, which occasionally made him appear somewhat remote from his fellow beings'. It was believed, furthermore, that his speculations were Epicurean, dangerously focused on the problem of the existence of God. One day Betto and his coterie decided to make mock of Cavalcanti when they saw him walking among the tombs which lay between the cathedral and the baptistery; like a romantic poet *avant la lettre* he was fond of this particular walk. Riding up to him they cried, 'Guido, you spurn our company; but supposing you find that God doesn't exist, what good will it do you?' Cavalcanti promptly replied, 'Gentlemen, in your own house you may say whatever you like to me', and made his getaway by vaulting lightly over an adjacent tombstone. Betto explained to his puzzled companions that the graveyard was the house of the dead and therefore their house, because 'by comparison with himself and other men of learning all men who are as uncouth and unlettered as ourselves are worse off than the dead'.[51]

Sdegnoso, in Villani's description of Dante and Compagni's of Cavalcanti, is close to 'snobbish'; Dante and Cavalcanti were, perhaps, intellectual snobs. The studious Pope John XXI displayed a slightly different but equally typical characteristic: 'although he was Supreme Pontiff and his rank was the highest, he did not deign to associate with his inferiors, whatever their standing, whether rich or poor, as long as they were educated (*literatus*).' This, to the hostile Ptolemy of Lucca, was John's sole virtue; he was also prone to glory in his own cleverness.[52] The intellectual makes his own rules. He chooses his company to suit himself, rather than allowing it to be predetermined by rank or connection. Still more seriously, he may be conducting researches into dangerous topics, as both Cavalcanti and John XXI were supposed to be doing.

The ordinary man's propensity to believe both that one should not probe the unknown and that too much study turns the wits is humorously exploited in *The Miller's Tale*. Nicholas's convoluted stratagem to seduce the wife of his landlord the carpenter involves shutting himself up in his room for several days until the alarmed carpenter sends up a servant, who peers through a hole in the door (apparently used as a cat-flap) and sees Nicholas seemingly in a trance. The prospective cuckold draws the obvious conclusions. Nicholas is away with the fairies or (as the carpenter puts it) with the elves and wights:

> This man is falle, with his astronomye,
> In some woodnesse or in some agonye,
> I thoghte ay wel how that it sholde be!
> Men sholde nat knowe of Goddes pryvetee
> Ye, blessed be alwey a lewed man
> That noght but oonly his bileve kan!

As Cavalcanti inquired into God's existence, so Nicholas is inquiring into 'God's privity', his secret purposes; this is not a fit occupation for the sensible person. The carpenter does not realize that Nicholas's feet are in fact very firmly on the earth and his eyes keenly focused on his landlord's sprightly wife Alison.

Dante and Cavalcanti may have been regarded as eccentric or unapproachable, but they were not apparently accused of being outright mad. In the poetic conventions with which they were familiar, love could inflict varied forms of disablement on a man, from near-derangement through unsociable moping to an elevated isolation brought about by contemplation of the superior merits of the beloved. When creating his literary persona, Dante carefully fused the stereotypical image of the lover and poet, consumed with love for Beatrice, with that of the philosopher. In the *Vita nuova*, written in 1293–4, he depicts himself as that superior kind of lover who is led by passionate introspection into intense experiences which are essentially solitary.[53]

Sometimes he is truly alone. He receives his initial vision of Love in his chamber and retires thither to lament when Beatrice denies him her salutation and again when he is mocked by certain ladies in her company; he receives poetic inspiration walking along the riverside; he sits drawing an angel on a tablet for some time before he realizes that be is being watched; he stands recalling the past and realises that a woman is looking at him from a window.

His solitude may however be entirely psychological, as it is when he is forced to take a journey from Florence. 'I was in the company of a great many people, outwardly at least' (which is irksome to him), but this does not prevent him receiving another vision of Love, after which he rides on, 'somewhat altered in my appearance, very pensive and sighing a great deal'. This of course is proper lover-like behaviour and Dante also exploits the convention that the lover should try to conceal his feelings from outsiders. This is a thought-filled isolation, psychological if not always physical, and it generates poetry which, because Beatrice is so much more than an ordinary Florentine girl, can be interpreted (in the later treatise *Convivio*) as bearing a freight of genuinely philosophical meanings.

Dante experienced one incidental consequence of his intellectual preoccupations: eye-strain and an awareness of defective vision. He records a bout of severe eye trouble in the 1290s: 'by greatly tiring my sight through devoting myself to reading I so weakened the visual spirits that all the stars appeared to me to be covered by a kind of white haze'. The remedy was 'long rest in cool, dark places' and bathing the eyes.[54] The invention of spectacles for long sight (presbyopia) around 1280 looks like another sign of the times. Obviously it depended on multiple developments in optics and glass technology, and not just on the desire of the elderly to be able to continue to read for themselves, but it proved useful to people such as the poet Petrarch (d. 1374), who reluctantly had to use spectacles when he passed sixty.[55]

Dante and Cavalcanti were laymen, Petrarch a clerical amphibian. The son of a notary, he studied but disliked law, and in 1330 took minor orders. Although thus theoretically committed to celibacy, he lived an essentially secular life and fathered two children; his daughter Francesca looked after him in his old age.[56] In the year of Francesca's birth, 1343, Petrarch's brother Gerardo entered the Carthusian monastery of Montrieux. By this time, according to the autobiographical account which he later addressed 'To Posterity', Petrarch himself had conceived a profound distaste for the urban environment and above all for the Babylon that was Avignon, currently the papal capital. He discovered nearby 'a tiny and solitary and delightful valley', Vaucluse, and 'transferred my books and myself there'.[57]

In 1346, Petrarch dedicated to his friend and nearly exact contemporary Philippe de Cabassoles, bishop of Cavaillon in southern France, the first recension of what he said he had intended to be a letter but had turned into a book, a lengthy treatise 'On the Solitary Life', *De vita solitaria*.[58] The title recalls a traditional subject, the Christian pursuit of religious retirement, and this is indeed a large part of the subject-matter. As befits an author who is frequently designated the father of renaissance humanism, however, it covers a wider ground. *De vita solitaria* is in many ways a remarkable work, not least because it is virtually a summation of what had been written on the subject by both pagans and Christians since antiquity. It would be an exaggeration to say that Petrarch had read everything, but of what was available to him he had read a considerable amount. Here we find Seneca's counsels to Lucilius and that *leitmotiv* of thinking about solitude, Cicero on Scipio Africanus; here too are the forebodings of Ecclesiastes, the heroics of the Desert Fathers and even (a late addition to the work) Peter Damian's *Life* of St Romuald.[59]

Petrarch's eagerness to achieve a synthesis of Christian and pagan authorities is everywhere apparent. At the end of the work he expresses his gratification that he has so often been able to include 'the glorious name of Christ' alongside the examples of the ancients, 'whom in many respects I am accustomed to follow'. He acknowledges, as he must, that pagans are in the last resort to be found wanting but, although he lists the Old Testament patriarchs and the Christian saints who sought the desert, from John the Baptist through the Desert Fathers to Bernard and Francis, he conveys rather little sense of the distinctively spiritual character of Christian eremitical solitude, aside from the fact that it makes it easier to establish contact with God. Unquestionably a Christian, he was not of a mystical or other-worldly disposition but was inclined to regard human life as a time of moral trial, an opportunity for a self-improvement which could be interpreted in both Christian and non-Christian terms.

Given that man is above all a moral being, solitude must in Petrarch's view be the preferred option for anyone who would achieve anything worthwhile, from scholarship to salvation:

> Whether we are in search of God, of ourselves and the honourable studies whereby we achieve the one and the other, or of a mind which is akin to our own, we must retreat as far as possible from crowds of people and the turmoil of the cities.[60]

A similarly inclusive formulation occurs towards the end of the work:

> Whether therefore we wish to serve God, which is the one liberty and the one felicity; or whether we wish to exercise our talents in good arts, which ranks next as a worthy task; or whether we want through meditation and writing to bequeath the memory of ourselves

> to posterity and thus hold back the flight of the days and extend this brief span of life; or whether it is our intention to attempt all these things, let us, I beg, flee forthwith and pass whatever little time there may be left in solitude.[61]

Petrarch's solitude is distinctly rural. Excluded from his list of legitimate pursuits are the money-grubbing and power-seeking which he relegates to the 'city'. The *occupati*, that is those who are engaged in futile and probably immoral activities, have at their disposal 'the baths, the brothels, the palaces, the taverns'; the right-minded, by contrast, have 'the woods, the mountains, the meadows and the springs'.[62] Petrarch is at his most literary when developing this antithesis. His caricature of the urban *occupatus*, reeling from one unsavoury bout of drunkenness and gluttony and one episode of toadying, chicanery and spoliation of widows and orphans to the next, owes a great deal to the Roman satirists, while the picture of the happy *otiosus*, giving thanks to God in delightful surroundings, merges Christian commonplaces with the idyllic pastoralism of the poets.

A salient characteristic of the benighted *occupatus* is that he is unfree. Petrarch was insistently concerned with freedom. It was both the objective and the consequence of solitude; but what was it? From what did Petrarch wish to be liberated? Here, as at several other points, there are both affinities and discernible contrasts between his ideas and the monastic and eremitical conceptions with which he was familiar from his reading, as also from his contacts with monks, not least the confrères of his Carthusian brother. Jesus had declared (John 8:32) 'You will know the truth and the truth will make you free'; St Paul had said (Corinthians 3:17), 'Where the Spirit of the Lord is, there is freedom.' In the monastic tradition it had commonly been believed that only in the cloister could men on earth achieve or at least approach a freedom which did not mean emancipation from all constraints or the right to determine one's own course of action, but liberation from the vain entanglements of the flesh and the world. Because the will of fallen mankind was perverted, the goal was achieved by way of obedience to the will of the superior who stood in the place of Christ. At the end of *De vita solitaria*, Petrarch acknowledges that the service of God is the true freedom, but elsewhere in the treatise he defines freedom in a different, and to us more familiar, way which owes as much to classical as to Christian precedent.

The town-dwelling *occupatus* is besieged by cares, clients and 'friends' (who are simultaneously enemies). By contrast the *solitarius atque otiosus* is as free as air: he is not endlessly bothered by people who want to see him and therefore 'his doorway is vacant and he has the freedom to stay in or to go out as the spirit moves him'. His liberated way of life is characterized by moderation, if not asceticism; he eats sparingly, but for that very reason well, and he sleeps well too. It is above all the absence of constraints imposed by others that defines this happy condition. To live as the *occupatus* does is to have nothing to call one's own: one's very face, one's mind belong to others. 'They do not weep or laugh according to their own judgement but take on someone else's feelings, abandoning their own, they do, think and live what is alien.'

Petrarch was at one with the monk in fleeing from this world, but, as he was well aware, unlike the monk he did not seek salvation in the abandonment of his own will. He might talk about the solitaries as friends of God who were experiencing a foretaste of heaven, but he himself was a sinner. Perhaps he was simply motivated by the love of literature to seek out a place that was friendly to 'leisure and letters'; perhaps, less nobly, there was something in his character that caused him to avoid the populace; perhaps, even, he was only too well aware of his own life and wanted to get away from the 'many-tongued witness' to his defects. At all events, there could be no doubt of the high value he put on the freedoms to be enjoyed in rural retirement, and he appealed to Philippe de Cabassoles to admit that he valued them too:

> to live as you wish, to go where you wish, to stay where you wish, to rest on the purple cushions of the flowers in spring, in autumn among heaps of fallen leaves, to fool winter by staying in the sun, summer by staying in the shade, to feel neither except to the extent that you wish. In either, to be yourself and wherever you are to be with yourself, far from evil, far from the example of the wicked, not to be pushed, bothered, crowded and badgered, not to be dragged to a banquet when you prefer to remain hungry, not to be forced to talk when you wish to remain silent.[63]

Amid the other delights of the countryside, Petrarch was even prepared to permit the occasional indulgence in hunting, fishing or hawking; perhaps this seemed odd, 'but I know that some very intelligent people have thought that hunting is conducive to thought and study, that is because of the solitude and the shadows of the grove and the silence of those who are handling the nets'. This was especially true if one just followed a hunt as a spectator.[64] Even more relaxed, the two Scipios had both been lovers of solitude; they liked to lay aside their insignia after a battle and to go alone or with a single friend to Literno, Formia or Gaeta. What a splendid spectacle it was to see these servants of the republic 'wandering alone, at leisure and free of humble cares, over the hills and shores, often gathering different shells and beach pebbles, black and white'.[65]

The essence of the solitary's liberty, as far as Petrarch himself was concerned, was intellectual. He was free 'to send the memory back and to wander through all centuries and all lands, to go about and converse with all the great men there have been'. Thus he was enabled to forget present evils and sometimes himself; to meditate intensely on heavenly things and, to speak of the more commonplace occupations, 'to devote oneself to reading and writing, alternating the one as relaxation with the other, to read what our forebears have written, to write what those who come after may read ...'[66] The desert solitary or twelfth-century Cistercian might have recognized this insistence on variety and diversion, but (despite Petrarch's recurrent emphasis on the possibilities of holy contemplation) there is much else here that might not have commanded their understanding or acceptance.

William of St-Thierry had given thought to the problem of suitability for the religious life while maintaining, as he was bound to do, its indisputable superiority to any other. Petrarch, similarly confident that his kind of solitary had chosen the better part, was insistent on the need for self-knowledge but saw the appropriate qualifications in terms of his own interests and predilections:

> There are those to whom the solitary life is harder than death and seems to bring death with it. This applies above all those who are ignorant of letters and who, if they lack someone to talk to, do not know what to talk about with themselves or with their books, and are therefore dumb. Solitude without literature is exile, prison, torture. Add literature and it is homeland, freedom, delight. For there is Cicero's well-known saying about leisure, 'What is sweeter than a literary leisure?' and Seneca, no less familiar, 'Leisure without letters is death and living burial for a man'.[67]

In quoting these two authorities, Petrarch was well aware of the ambiguities in their views of solitude. He begged leave to differ from Seneca when the latter urged that 'location does not do much for one's tranquillity', pointing out that the philosopher himself in other passages seemed to acknowledge that healthy or unhealthy places did have some importance. Petrarch is prepared to admit that location is not all-important, but the mind unaided cannot do everything. Both Seneca and Quintilian offered advice about creating an imaginary solitude in unpropitious circumstances. Petrarch had followed this advice in the past and if circumstances changed he would do it again, but he preferred the real thing.[68]

Quintilian had objected that pleasant places might be more enjoyable than actually conducive to study, quoting the opinion of Demosthenes that one worked best in a place where one could see or hear nothing, rather than open to the distractions of a beautiful view.[69] Confronted with these authoritative judgements, Petrarch points out that both Demosthenes and Quintilian were orators, the least retired type of intellectual. He might well in fact have quoted Cicero's own criticism of Demosthenes, that 'he had learned to speak in the presence of others, but not much with himself'.[70] Petrarch anyway is not making rules for everyone, even though he himself is never more inspired than by woods and mountains. He is not commanding the learned to write their books in these bucolic surroundings, but it might be a good idea for them to refresh themselves in such an environment and then retire to write.

One objector to solitude was easily disposed of. Petrarch was familiar with Ovid's noisy complaints about his Black Sea exile, and observes, primly tongue in cheek, that the poet had many faults: had he been a better person 'he would have had a more illustrious reputation with serious people and either would not have experienced that Pontic exile and the solitudes of Istria or would have put up with them with more equanimity'.[71] There were however more formidable adversaries and more profound objections to the effect that solitude was unhelpful, or at least unnecessary, to the scholar and positively inimical to the pursuit of virtue. Seneca's reservations on this score were well known. Here again Petrarch invokes the inapplicability or inadvisability of general rules. If Seneca were to say that solitude is invariably a fomenter of vice, he would be wrong, but that is not in fact what he is saying: '"No imprudent person", he says, "should be left to themselves." Who is there who does not see that this is true?' Anyone who is not master of himself is on the road to ruin if left to his own devices, wherever he is; neither solitude nor the city is friendly to him. Petrarch is thus able to satisfy himself that he and Seneca are fundamentally in agreement, pointing out that the latter, after all, recommended solitude to Lucilius because he was worthy of it.[72]

Cicero presented Petrarch with slightly different problems of exegesis. It is well known that Petrarch was somewhat discomfited by his discovery, by way of Cicero's private letters, that the great orator's withdrawal from public life into scholarly retirement had not been his first choice but had been forced on him by the disasters of the expiring Roman republic. In a letter addressed to his hero, Petrarch reproaches him with his failure to follow his own better inclinations and 'grow old in rural tranquillity'.[73] Cicero's reluctant seclusion had produced the late works of philosophy from which his medieval readers had derived their image of him as the unimpassioned sage. Regretfully knowing better, Petrarch sets out to elucidate his hero's personal development. He sees in Cicero a personality in some respects akin to Demosthenes. Both were by profession forensic orators, a line of business that could only find its fulfilment in the city. Demosthenes put solitude to use in the service of his profession, studying in a room without a view so as to avoid distraction and practising elocution against a background of waves crashing on a beach. Cicero, for his part, eventually learned to prefer his solitude to the depressing and dangerous spectacle of politics and acknowledged that he was much more productive and had written more in his enforced retirement than in years of *occupatio*.

This productivity included the three books of the treatise 'On Duties', *De officiis*. Petrarch remarked that St Ambrose had not only imitated the name of the *De officiis* and the number of its books in a work of his own, but had appropriated Scipio's formulation of the value of *otium*, applying it to Moses, Elijah and the rest, 'who he thinks were busy in their leisure and accompanied in their solitude, long before Africanus'. How indeed can we think that Moses was ever alone when he spoke face to face with God, and how can we think him *otiosus*? Similar reasoning is applied to Elijah and Elisha. Petrarch is at pains, however, to point out that, although the prophets did indeed have chronological priority, the words were first spoken in praise of Africanus.

This little piece of scholarly elucidation serves to emphasize Petrarch's syncretism. He is eager both to demonstrate his own understanding of the sources and to legitimate Scipio's claims. We should also notice his exploitation of the ambiguities of *otium* and *otiosus*. Monastic writers had had their own reasons to stress the productive character of the monk's *otium*, but their conception of useful outcomes naturally differed somewhat from Cicero's. It was congenial to Cicero to commend Scipio Africanus for his use of his 'leisure'; by implication, at least, it served as a springboard for action. With due modesty Petrarch applies the formula to himself, by way of apologia for his own preference for solitude:

> For as long as I can remember being chained in this bodily prison I seem only to have lived when I have lived alone and at leisure ... I too have never been less idle than when at leisure, nor less alone than when alone, but I have always been idle except when at leisure, and always alone except when alone.[74]

This was a partial answer to the familiar accusation that solitude was socially useless if not actually antisocial. Very early in the treatise Petrarch acknowledged that he loved his fellow-man as he was bound to do, but he hated their sins (and his own) as well as the cares and anxieties which accompanied life among large numbers of people.[75] He conceded the principle that a man might be able to combine *occupatio* useful to his fellow-men with the virtues of solitude. Given that possibility, he would voluntarily abandon the solitude which was pleasing only to himself and apply himself to what he could do that was useful to others. This was Cicero's advice in *De officiis*; this was the better part. In fact Petrarch was sceptical about how many, if any, actually brought off this feat of uniting social service with personal moral progress. He was more concerned with the moral condition of the individual, especially himself, and what external circumstances were conducive to his tranquillity and inner improvement.[76]

Petrarch's reading would have informed him that this emphasis on what is necessary to the individual had been a familiar theme of Christian literature from Athanasius's *Life* of Antony onwards. To this extent, and also to the extent that one of the objectives of the *vita solitaria* was a salvation which was deemed more difficult to attain amidst the haunts of men, he can be said to endorse the Christian rather than the Ciceronian option, Mary rather than Martha.[77] It is obvious from the nature of his interests, his reading and his own works, however, that this was not the whole story. Petrarch was not Erasmus, still less Montaigne, but in temperament he had about him much of the 'man of letters', and it was to secure the freedom to be what he was that he sought retirement. He does not engage in elaborate justification of the work which he did there; in his heart of hearts, like most writers and scholars, he probably thought it was self-evident and did not greatly care if it was not. His persistent emphasis on freedom and, in effect, on choice distinguishes him from the more pessimistic lawgivers of the monastic life.

What, however, did he mean by being alone? For him, as for his monastic predecessors, 'solitude' was something of a term of art. In the autobiographical sketch which he addressed to posterity he expressed his distaste for banquets but added: 'to dine with friends is such a pleasure that I have regarded nothing more agreeable than their arrival and I have never willingly taken food without a companion.'[78] Towards the end of *De vita solitaria* he urged Philippe de Cabassoles, in emotional language, to join him in the solitary life which he had pioneered:

> I cannot be alone, but I have made a beginning and will easily persevere if only a leader and companion in the solitary life should be with me. If I may say something of what is in my mind, you will be not only the supporter of my peace, but yourself my peace; not only the comfort of my solitude, but in a way yourself my solitude; then indeed I shall seem to be the complete solitary, when I am with you.[79]

This paradoxical formulation expressed a very old idea, evoking as it did a community, in this instance a very small community, of the like-minded.

Petrarch therefore felt that he could easily confront the familiar warnings of Ecclesiastes 4:10 on the dangers of isolation, including for consideration the preceding verse, 'It is better for two to be together rather than none, for they have the consolation of their company.' Critics had thrown these and similar sayings in his teeth, which he said they would not have done if they had really been listening to what he was saying. He had been reminded of Aristotle's dictum that man was a social animal and that he who does not communicate with others is either beast or god, 'as if I proscribed or barred human society or had freely chosen to prefer to be beast or god'. Cicero in *De officiis* had thought that society arose not so much from necessity as from a natural human impulse, and that even someone abounding in resources and not subject to necessity would eschew solitude and seek out 'a companion in his study'. So far was Petrarch from disagreeing that he would advocate seeking not merely a single 'companion in solitude and study' (*solitudinis et socium studi)*, but several such companions.[80] The Petrarchan solitary does not, however, have to accommodate himself to companions who have been chosen for him. If Petrarch had had the word at his disposal, he might well have spoken of privacy rather than of solitude.

10

Studies

If lovers and poets required rooms to which they could retire and indulge in outbursts of grief and lyricism, scholars required somewhere to work. A variety of spaces were adaptable to their purposes. Cicero makes several references to his 'library' and, in a letter to a friend, M. Marius, imagines him enjoying 'light reading' (*lectiuncula*) in a *cubiculum* overlooking the bay of Stabiae.[1] The Emperor Augustus possessed a 'special place' (*locus singularis*), high up in his house on the Palatine, to which he retired if he had anything to do 'privately and without interruption' (*secreto aut sine interpellatione*). According to Suetonius, he called it his 'Syracuse' or 'little workshop' (*technyphion*), with apparent reference to the 'study' of Archimedes. It was distinct from the bedroom (*cubiculum*) which he used for over forty years. Suetonius describes how the emperor used to retreat after dinner to a *lecticula lucubratoria* (literally, 'a couch for study by lamplight') before retiring to bed late at night.[2] In his villa at Laurentinum the younger Pliny had one wall of a sunny apsidal *cubiculum* fitted out, 'to resemble a library' (*in bibliothecae speciem*), with the books which he read repeatedly.[3]

Cubiculum thus described a room which might well be used for sleeping but was adaptable for other purposes. It might have seemed ready-made for continued use in the sense of a scholar's or student's workroom. Shortly before 800, Alcuin of York used a closely related word when he imagined the students (*scholastici*) in the cathedral school of Bishop Beornrad of Utrecht reading the verse version of his *Life* of St Willibrord *in secreto cubili*.[4] It proved however to be the even more flexible *cella* that carried all before it in religious contexts, while in secular usage *cubiculum* was superseded by derivatives of *camera*.

Members of religious communities needed on the one hand to read and meditate, on the other to write, less often in the sense of original composition than in that of book-copying. The Benedictine Rule did not designate any particular space for these activities. The *bibliotheca* of c. 48 was almost certainly a mere book-store or cupboard rather than a place to work, a later development.[5] The physical requirements of writing are more complex than those of reading and space had to be provided somewhere in the monastery not only for book-storage but for the materials required by scribes and the surfaces on which they could write. The Carthusians facilitated book-copying by providing and equipping the separate eremitical cell. For Benedictines and Cistercians the cloister was the multi-purpose focus of the monk's waking life when he was not in church and the principal location for his work. In the early twelfth century, a visitor to the cloister of St Martin's at Tournai might have seen twelve young monks 'sitting on chairs and silently writing on carefully and cunningly made tables'.[6]

Individual accommodation was not however unknown. Nicholas, for a while the secretary of St Bernard and emissary between him and Peter the Venerable of Cluny, was privileged to possess an office (*scriptoriolum*) which he described rapturously in a letter written to a friend in praise of the life of Clairvaux.[7] It had been allotted to him, he said, for the purposes of 'reading, writing, composing and meditating, praying and adoring the majesty of the Lord'.[8] It was surrounded by other 'celestial workshops' which concealed it from view. Its door opened on to the novices' quarters; to one side lay the monks' cloister, to the other the infirmary. Nicholas significantly described the cloister as the place where the monks

> under the strictest discipline one by one peruse the books of divine eloquence, not so as to make a show of the treasures of their learning but in order to arouse delight, compunction and devotion.

His own sanctum was furnished with the choicest sacred books, but he clearly used it for more than reading or writing letters: 'Here, alone, I often enter the solitude of my heart, depressed by the weight of an unhappy conscience.' He put himself on trial in the hope that the most terrible of judges would not do so. Whether or not Nicholas had to brave the wrath of God, he certainly aroused Bernard's, for he left Clairvaux at last under a cloud of suspicion, pursued by the abbot's denunciations.

The more frequent provision of accommodation specifically intended for study, both for the community as a whole and for the individual, is a suggestive indication of the changes that overtook the late medieval religious life. In origin it depended not only on what is clearly a very ancient belief that peace and quiet are necessary to intellectual work, but on a change in the character of the learning that was deemed appropriate to the professed religious.

In the early thirteenth century a religious order appeared which gave priority to the pursuit of the theological learning that could nourish preaching, combat error and enlighten the world. An occupation hitherto chiefly identified with the secular clerks of the 'schools' was installed at the heart of the religious vocation. The Dominicans, more properly the Order of Preachers, preserved many features of the traditional common life and their early convents were built, like traditional monasteries, with refectories, dormitories and cloisters.[9] In some respects, however, they abandoned or modified traditional monastic norms. Already in the early *Constitutions* special provision was made for the needs of the order's students, and in the course of time this had its effect not only on the routines followed by the brethren but on their physical environment.

The General Chapter of the recently formed order which met at Bologna in 1221 gave particular attention to education. As a general principle, the conventual superior was to grant whatever dispensations were necessary to safeguard student activity and the student-master was to have a say in the allocation of a 'place' in which they could assemble 'to put forward doubts or questions or to conduct discussions in his presence'. The individual student, or at least the more promising, received further consideration, for special accommodation might be allocated to him:

> A cell shall not be given to all the students, but only to those among them who can draw profit from it in the judgement of their master. If someone fails to make progress in his studies, his cell shall be given to another and he shall be employed on other tasks. In the cells those who wish may study, write, pray, sleep and even keep vigil during the night for reason of their studies.[10]

These cells were already being constructed in the early days of the order. In the Toulouse convent a range of cells, where the brethren were able both to sleep and to study, was built above the cloister adjacent to the church.[11] A friar of Santa Sabina in Rome related how he had been praying by his bed when he heard the tread of heavenly visitants in the dormitory who sprinkled all the cells, including his.[12] Numerous regulations about cells and the entitlement to them followed during the thirteenth century and after, and concern was recurrently expressed that the privileges enjoyed by students and *lectores* should not detach them from the common life of the community. By the mid-thirteenth century the *lector*, who was responsible for instructing the brethren at the level of the individual house, was permitted to have a room to himself if the conventual prior judged it would be helpful to him, but in 1255 the General Chapter felt it necessary to stipulate that this was to be within the dormitory (*infra clausuram dormitorii*). At the Oxford General Chapter in 1280 it was directed that neither conventual priors nor *lectores* who were not actually engaged in teaching should have *camerae speciales*; active *lectores* could have them where it was convenient, 'according to their needs', but it was repeated that this should be within the dormitory.[13]

To judge from a case which came before the General Chapter in 1301, *lectores* did indeed occasionally get above themselves. The Swedish brother Goffredus was disciplined because, not content with his *camera lectoris*, he had occupied the chamber allocated to the provincial prior and refused to give it up, even though the Danish provincial prior and a sick man had had to be put in the common dormitory as a result.[14] The preservation of the common life remained a preoccupation; students were not to be emancipated from its basic requirements. In 1286 it was stipulated that 'all the brethren of the convent and visitors and students shall sleep in the dormitory, the sick and those being bled however excepted, and shall be bound to rise with the convent to say matins'.[15] The student's cell was not to be a secret hideaway. In 1289, priors were enjoined 'that they should so organize and arrange cells in which there are beds that chair, bed and desk (*pulpitus*) may be clearly visible to passers-by'.[16] These efforts to prevent the screening of cells from outside scrutiny continued into the fifteenth century, at least as far as novices were concerned.[17] Those who were privileged to receive cells were accorded only a qualified privacy, which nonetheless was obviously considered to be significant.

For the friars in general, as for the monks before them, the cloister supposedly remained the place where reading was routinely done:

> When they are sitting in the cloister, they should behave as good religious, each one reading his own book, except for those who are singing something from the antiphonars, graduals or hymnbooks, and those who are preparing readings ... If anyone needs to go out, he should put his book back in the cupboard, or, if he prefers to leave it in his place, he is to signal to the brother who is sitting next to him to keep an eye on it.[18]

This implies a book-store in the cloister such as monks also had, and the phrase *communis libraria* which occurs in Dominican legislation may have meant no more than that. In 1308 it was ruled that all books, by whatever means they were acquired, were to come to the *communis libraria* and to be sold only if they were duplicates or of no use. Books of no great value could be given to needy brethren either outright or for life. These principles were reaffirmed the following year, when reference was also made to books which had belonged to dead brothers.[19] That individual friars could have books in their possession suggests that they had somewhere to keep them, either in a chest under the bed or in a cell.

We get at least a stylized view of what these cells and their contents were like from the remarkable series of frescoes of Dominican worthies which was painted in 1352 by Tommaso da Modena in the chapter-house of the convent at Treviso in north-eastern Italy.[20] Saint, pope or cardinal, all are shown at work in their cells. This idea of portraying a scholar at work was not in itself innovatory; it derives from 'a Late Antique tradition of author portraits as the frontispieces of their books' which had shaped the representation of the Evangelists in Byzantine and Carolingian gospel books and subsequently also that of the Fathers of the Church, the quartet of Ambrose, Jerome, Augustine and Gregory, who are still to be seen in many medieval and Renaissance programmes of church decoration. Over a period of centuries there had been a gradual development of specialized equipment for reading and writing, which (it has been argued) accompanied a shift not only to silent reading but to silent writing, copying by eye rather than at dictation.[21] The Treviso frescoes might be said to sum up these developments.

In all the cells depicted most of the space is taken up by the all-purpose reading and writing desk, with a shelf on the adjacent wall which accommodates a book or two or sometimes other items. Several of the brethren are using the lower shelf of this unit as a lectern, propping an open book on it. The standard storage space for books appears, however, to be under the desk and no one has more than five or six in all. When Tommaso a few years later painted an imposing figure of St Jerome on a pier in the Dominican church itself, he permitted him a more impressive library of twenty-three volumes.[22] Books apart, pens, penknives and inkwells are naturally standard equipment, but they do not appear in every fresco, for Tommaso sometimes chooses to depict more novel items, most famously the earliest depiction of spectacles in European art, which are worn by the Cardinal Hugues de St-Cher.[23] This is not the only optical aid on view, for Cardinal Nicholas de Fréauville is using a reading-glass. Pierre de la Palud is opening a letter 'with the aid of scissors of a remarkably modern design' while next to him Agostino of Trau is ruling up his page with a straight-edge. In sum, this is 'as complete an account as any existing of the work of the scholars and scribes of the Middle Ages'.[24] The cells (including Jerome's) are screened by a drawn curtain behind the man at work. This seems to have been a way of according temporary privacy without permitting or requiring a door behind which the brother could retreat. A contemporary Master General, probably Simon de Langres (1352–66), instructed that the *velamina cellarum* were to be removed after compline.[25]

Little remains of the Dominican friaries of medieval England, but at Gloucester there are some remarkable vestiges of the arrangements made for students late in the thirteenth century. On the upper floor of the south range of the cloister there was an apartment with long sides subdivided into cubicles, each with its window and separated from its neighbour by a wall a little less than five inches thick.[26] The brother sat sideways on to the window and it may be that he was screened from distraction by a curtain, for at one end of one of the rows of cubicles there is a curved stone projection, which may have been designed to support a curtain rail.[27] Different interpretations of this apartment are possible. As it seems that there was a dormitory in the adjacent west range, it may have been entirely devoted to study, but alternatively it may have been a second dormitory, reserved for the students and *lectores*. If so, the beds must have stood in the central floor space, for the window-recesses could not have accommodated them. There was an eleven-foot-long space at the western end in which there were no cubicles and which might have been used for book storage.

We do not know what the Gloucester brethren called their study-cubicles, but it is possible to make an informed guess. The Close Rolls record that in 1258 Henry III directed the guardian of Salcey Forest to supply the Friars Preachers of Northampton with six stout oaks 'for the making of their studies' (*ad studia sua inde facienda*). In February 1261 the king's clerks of works at Westminster were instructed to give two thousand pounds of stone to the London Dominicans *ad studia sua perficienda* and in 1269 the *custos* of Shotover Forest was to provide seven oaks to the Preachers of Oxford for the same purpose.[28] We seem here to be in the presence of a linguistic innovation which has had enduring effects, certainly on English.

The word *studium* was much used in the medieval period in a variety of senses, only some of which had existed in classical Latin. It continued to mean effort, zeal or enthusiasm in general and also that special kind of effort which was invested in intellectual exercises. Rarely if ever, in classical Latin, did the word designate a place, but in the thirteenth century it became a standard term for a 'school' of higher learning as well as continuing to mean the process of study itself: what we call a 'university' came to be called a *studium generale*, an institution rather than a place, but obviously one possessing a geographical location. The Close Roll references can hardly be to the process of study, and it must be presumed that the friars, in their petitions to the king for assistance, had called the cubicles that they wished to build 'studies'. Two centuries later, in 1456, an indulgence granted by the archbishop of York referred to 'thirty-four cells and *studia*' in the Dominican convent there which had been destroyed by fire.[29] By this time the equivalent word was established not only in English but in other European vernaculars. Never however was *studium* used in this sense in Dominican legislation, where *cella* remained the term for a study-cubicle.

The friars understandably exerted a considerable attraction on bright young recruits to the religious life, but the monks were not left entirely to their own devices in responding to the challenge. The Fourth Lateran Council in 1215 imposed on the Benedictines (and also on the Augustinian canons) the requirement not only of holding provincial general chapters and instituting a system of visitation but of making systematic provision for study by sending selected brothers to the universities. At meetings held in 1277–9 the English Benedictines acknowledged that the amplification of the divine office beyond the requirements of the Rule (*prolixitas officii*) had been responsible for deterring the best young men from enlisting and therefore for the deterioration of monastic learning from its ancient glories. Abbots were enjoined to see that their charges were constantly occupied in study and the copying, correction and binding of books or other suitable manual work, and provision was made for sending students to Oxford.[30] These initiatives notwithstanding, the Dominicans launched a broadside against the monks at the Council of Vienne in 1311. Apart from criticisms of excessive drinking, 'worldly conversation' and so forth, they complained of the decay of 'the discipline of letters' as it had once existed among the monks; 'mental reading' no longer took place in the cloister as the Rule enjoined, rendered impossible by 'the excessive prolixity of the Office', an 'unprofitable occupation' (*infructuosa occupacio*) which repelled educated seculars.[31]

Even while the Benedictines endeavoured to come to terms with these demands, they tried to repair and preserve the fabric of the common life. The Cistercian Pope Benedict XII affirmed this strategy when he promulgated his Constitutions for the Black Monks in 1337, specifically directing that any 'cells' that had been erected within monastic dormitories should be removed, but adding that 'cells may be provided for students next to the dormitory, in which they may study but not sleep'.[32] The issue was not whether students or others should have working accommodation but whether they were to be permitted to withdraw from community and to sleep in private rooms. The Dominicans had set the pace in making special provision for scholarly work, but in the fourteenth and fifteenth centuries they and the monks together had to confront the tension between the expectations, legitimate and otherwise, of the recruits they wished to attract and the maintenance of the principles that distinguished life within the cloister from life outside it.[33]

The *Gesta abbatum* of St Albans Abbey provide evidence for the improvement of facilities for monk-students in the fourteenth century. The abbots were usually learned men. Of the scholar and Oxford Master of Arts Michael de Mentmore (1335-49) it was said:

> He was always so favourable to scholars that he made every effort to accommodate himself to them, especially to those whom he knew were most fervent and made most progress in learning; and he believed that scholars who were devoting all their energies to learning should lack for nothing in terms of physical comfort. Wherefore, for the peace and comfort of his students, he built studies at his own expense adjacent to the dormitory.

Mentmore also decided that morning mass was to be celebrated immediately after Prime and no longer after Terce, in order to safeguard the students' reading and the continuity of their work. He regarded his provision of studies adjacent to the dormitory as consistent with the requirements of Benedict XII's *Constitutions* and believed that 'they would study more effectively and quietly there than in the cloister'.[34] The abbots provided studies for themselves as well as for their monks. The long-serving Thomas de la Mare (1349–96) undertook some extensive rebuilding at the cell of Redburn, erecting a fine *domus* where the common latrine had been, in which he could have a 'secret study' for use whenever it pleased him. At St Albans itself, he endowed what the chronicler calls his 'study or library' with many books. Himself a fast but ugly writer, he also erected the *domus scriptoriae* at his own expense and under the direction of Thomas Walsingham this produced numerous books for 'the library of the convent and for his study'.[35]

By the mid-fifteenth century the *libraria* of St Albans was clearly much more than a book-cupboard. Abbot John Whethamstede congratulated himself that he had

> left to his successor a library which he had long had in mind and for the building of which he assembled a great deal of material. Almost immediately after his inauguration he put it into operation and in the second year of his rule he completed it, both roof and walls, and added the leading. It is said that he spent on the mere erection of this building (*domus*), leaving the glazing, ceiling-timbers and installation of desks out of account, more than one hundred and fifty pounds.

Such an apartment was clearly intended to be worked in and not just to store books. There is another reference to a library built by Whethamstede adjacent to a 'noble chamber' which he intended for the reception of the king; he also undertook repairs to 'the abbot's study and the chamber called "the Clock-chamber", with the garderobe and study underneath'.[36]

When Bishop Alnwick of Lincoln visited Thornton Priory, a house of Augustinian canons, in 1440, he encountered and acceded to an unusual request. John Syward, the novice-master, supported by others, told him that not all the brothers in the dormitory could go to sleep immediately on going to bed. They begged permission to create a space in the 'Routing house' (literally the 'snoring house') in which these unfortunates could study or pray, lest, as Syward said, 'lying awake on their beds they should be disturbed by evil spirits' or, as Alnwick more prosaically put it, they should disturb the others. It sounds as if no cells existed at Thornton, inside or outside the dormitory, and that the 'Routing house' was an adjoining apartment, perhaps an annex to which persistent snorers were consigned. This surely cannot have been a unique problem.[37]

For many monks and canons the cloister remained the regular location for study. At a visitation of Peterborough Abbey conducted by Alnwick in 1437 it was complained that 'Brother Thomas Maksey irreligiously wanders among the students in the cloister, chatting with them and obstructing their work'. At Dunstable in 1442 the prior stated that the young canons, who were supposed to sit in the cloister, at least after midday, intent on some 'honourable pursuit', in fact wandered around the monastery without permission; they 'are not accustomed to study, reading or contemplation, but to vanities'. At Bicester in 1445 the canons who daily studied in the cloister asked for permission to take some recreation.[38] It was appropriate therefore to adapt the cloister to the needs of students. Bishop Gray of Lincoln in 1432 instructed the Augustinians of St Neot's to instal *sedilia*, 'in English *carales*', in their cloister within a year, and to ensure that *contemplacio* in the cloister was observed by all at the proper times.[39] Some Augustinian houses had evidently had carrels two centuries previously, to judge by a passing reference in the proceedings of the General Chapter of the northern province held at Gisburn in 1232: no brother was to have a lock on a carrel or on a chest (*in carolla sive in cista*).[40]

Bishop Gray believed that the English word 'carrel' was current in 1432, but the first occurrence recorded in the *Oxford English Dictionary* is in a late sixteenth-century description of the arrangement of the north walk of the cloister at Durham:

> In the north syde of ye cloister from ye Corner over against ye Church Dour to ye corner over against the Dorter dour was all fynely glased from ye hight to ye sole within a little of ye grownd into ye cloyster garth, & in every wyndowe iij° pewes or carrells where every one of the old monks had his Carrell severall by him selfe, that when they had dyned they did resorte to that place of cloister, and there studyed upon there bookes, every one in his carrell all ye afternone unto evensong tyme, this was there exercise every daie: all there pewes or Carrells was all fynely waynscotted, and verie close all but ye forept wch had carved wourke that gave light in at yer carrell doures of wainscott: and in every Carrell was a deske to lye there bookes on; and ye carrells was no greater then from one stanchell of the wyndowe to another.[41]

Even the Latin word still seemed a neologism when Prior Selling of Canterbury (1479–95) glazed the south alley of the cloister and 'made befitting new *textus*, which we now call *carolos*'. [42]

These cubicles were inserted into a number of monastic cloisters, at Westminster, Evesham, Abingdon and elsewhere.[43] There are survivors at Chester but, by a happy coincidence, the best surviving specimens are to be seen in the south walk of the cloister of what is now Gloucester Cathedral, within a few hundred yards of the Dominican convent with its study-cubicles. The carrel represented a way of improving facilities for monastic students which did not infringe on the demands of community. For nuns there was, officially, no alternative to the cloister. They were not sent to the universities and intellectual expectations of them were usually limited. Abbot de la Mare's regulations for the nuns of Sopwell (significantly promulgated in French rather than Latin) laid it down that, after the morning mass, 'they should all sit in the cloister until Prime, concentrating solely on their psalter, prayers and other devotions or recalling the divine service'; the cloister was not improved by the construction of carrels.[44]

Meanwhile the study had penetrated the secular environment, although it was never the only place for reading. The literate often enjoyed their books in the bedchamber, or even in bed, as they still do. Chaucer describes himself at the beginning of *The Book of the Duchess* as reading in bed. Suffering from insomnia, he calls to his servant for a book so that he may 'rede and drive the night away'; he wakes at the end of the poem with the book still in his hand. Unlike the Emperor Augustus in a similar situation, he clearly expected to read for himself.[45] So too did Pope Eugenius IV in the next century; he kept books by his bed in case he should wake and called on his attendants only to bring him light and to take the book and the light away when he had read as much as he wished.[46] Two centuries earlier Gerald of Wales describes how he made Innocent III a present of some of his books, which he 'kept with him all together by his bed for a month', but we are not told whether he read them for himself (if he read them at all) or had them read aloud.[47]

None of these men was living under a religious rule, and to that extent they were free to adapt their ordinary living accommodation and routines to encompass their reading. One thirteenth-century scholar who did so fell victim to his own improvements. The ill-fated and short-lived Portuguese Pope John XXI had a *nova camera* built for him in the papal palace at Viterbo, but he died in May 1277 as a result of injuries received when the roof of this chamber, 'in which he used to sit alone at night studying', collapsed on him. The accounts of this incident refer to the apartment as either *camera* or *domus*.[48] Clearly rooms in private residences that were used principally or solely for the purposes of study long antedated the appearance of a special word for them.

The earliest recorded use of the English word 'study' occurs in 1303, a little under fifty years after Henry III's grant to the Dominicans of Northampton. In a popular manual for confessors written by a north-country cleric called Richard Brunne and splendidly entitled *Handlyng Synne*, it is said that Robert Grosseteste, bishop of Lincoln, loved to hear the music of the harp because it sharpened the wits, and so he arranged to have his personal harpist close at hand:

> Next hys chambre, besyde hys stody,
> Hys harpers chaumbre was fast therby.
> Many tymes, be nightys and dayys
> He had solace of notes and layys.[49]

That Grosseteste, a friend of the friars and a distinguished participant in the academic culture of his day, did in fact possess such an apartment, whatever he himself called it, seems far from unlikely.

This seems to be an isolated occurrence of 'study' in the early fourteenth century, but later both Chaucer and Langland use it.[50] In the B-Text of *Piers Plowman* Lady Mede tries to quote from the Book of Wisdom, 'He who gives gifts acquires honour', but Conscience hits back by likening her to a woman who once 'read a lesson' without turning the page to see how it finished:

> And so, madame, ferde ye – ye kouthe na moore finde
> Tho ye on Sapience looked, sittynge in youre studie.[51]

In the *Franklin's Tale* (line 1214), Chaucer describes the 'studie' of a magician, where he keeps his books and entertains prospective clients, and the Eagle in *The House of Fame* (line 633) informs the poet that Jove has taken pity upon him because he makes his head ache writing of love 'in thy studye'.[52]

Contemporaneously the word appeared in Italian. Petrarch preferred *bibliotheca*, which was doubtless congenial to him because it was used by Cicero. In a letter written in 1367 he recalled sitting 'alone in my library' (*in bibliotheca mea solus*) at Verona during the earthquake of January 1348, and in *De vita solitaria* he recalled the occasions on which Philippe de Cabassoles had 'crossed the threshold of my *bibliotheca*'.[53] In a fit of metaphor earlier in *De vita solitaria* he eulogized solitude as 'the library of the reader and the cell of the contemplative' (*bibliotheca legentium, cella meditantium*), thus paying homage to both the classical and the religious traditions.[54]

Within a few years of Petrarch's death, his friend and disciple the Florentine humanist and chancellor Coluccio Salutati was using a new alternative word for the scholarly sanctum. In a letter written in 1379 Salutati apologized for delay in answering a letter, which since he received it had 'remained hidden among the papers in my *studiolum*'; because he rarely had leisure for private study or writing at home, so it had remained until his masters (the Florentine priors) permitted him an unwonted day of leisure. In a single sentence Salutati employs the word *studium* in one of its established senses, (work or occupation) and the diminutive to signify a room.[55] In a letter written in the following year Lorenzo Ridolfi recalled sitting in Salutati's *studium*.[56]

The vernacular Italian *studio* appears only a little later. In the last years of the century, the Florentine notary Ser Lapo Mazzei, friend and correspondent of the Merchant of Prato, Francesco di Marco Datini, rejoiced in the peace and freedom he enjoyed in his *studio*, where he could be truly alone to mull over problems and where he experienced 'the happiness of the good hermits on the mountain'.[57] The glancing religious reference was appropriate, because it both recalled the ancestry of the *studio* and underlined the recommendation of withdrawal from the secular hurly-burly that Ser Lapo was trying to impress on the incorrigibly worldly Datini. At much the same time another Florentine, Giovanni Morelli, was exhorting his son to devote time to reading the classics in his *studio*.[58]

Private individuals in France too had their little bookish retreats. In 1375 a royal grant to Raoul des Presles, one of the scribes who provided Charles V with books, stated that he 'intended to build some spacious and secluded studies in which to put his books, of which he has several'.[59] Here the overlap of the term with *bibliotheca* seems clear. As for the king himself, Christine de Pizan exclaimed that 'there is no need to ask whether his fine study (*estude*) was well arranged, for he desired all his things to be fine and tidy, elegant and ordered, and it could not have been better'.[60] This reference appears to be to the Louvre, but Charles had *estudes* in other residences, notably at Vincennes, as did other great men such as the duke of Orléans somewhat later.[61] There was already a royal book collection, which in 1367–68 was newly installed in the tour de la Fauconnerie in the Louvre. The benches and desks were brought from the old library in the Palais Royal but were replaced when it was judged that they were worn out. It was originally intended that the library should occupy two floors of the tower, but a third proved necessary. The windows were barred by grilles to prevent birds and other pests from getting in.[62]

In May 1402 Jean Gerson completed his treatise against the *Roman de la Rose* 'sitting in his study'.[63] Gerson's hostility to the *Roman* was shared by Christine de Pizan, who, like Chaucer, belonged to the growing army of laypeople whose life revolved around books. *The Book of the City of Ladies* begins with her description of herself 'sitting in my study surrounded by many books of different kinds'.[64] Wearied by a day's work on weighty volumes, she seeks out something lighter and has just made her choice when her mother calls her down for supper. Returning the next day to what she soon discovers to be a rather objectionable work with a tiresome anti-feminist bias, she falls into a profound and melancholy meditation from which she is aroused by a beam of light which penetrates the study at a time of day when the sun could not. This proves to come from three glorious ladies who have managed to enter the room despite the fact that its doors and windows are all closed.

For literary purposes Christine's study here serves her like a religious cell, as a convenient location for a vision. Something very similar happens early in *Le chemin de longue etude*.[65] On 5 October 1400, in an unhappy mood, she desires solitude ('Voulentiers suis solitaire') in which to nurse her sorrows and she retires by herself 'en une estude petite', in which it was her frequent pleasure to read 'diverses aventures'. She leafs through a book or two but finds no solace and turns at last to *The Consolation of Philosophy* of Boethius. This was a significant choice: it was not only one of the most widely read books of the medieval period (Chaucer translated it) but depicted an intellectual who in an enforced and unhappy solitude received a consoling visitation from Lady Philosophy herself. It is noteworthy that Christine here uses the word *estude* in a double sense: rather like *cuisine*, it denotes both an activity and a room in which it is carried out. Some manuscripts of her writings contain miniatures depicting her at work. In one she is obviously seated in a room in an ordinary dwelling house, one wall of which has been opened up by the artist to reveal her within. The door of the room and the mullioned window with its shutters can be seen, and above her the roof with two dormer windows. She sits writing at a table covered with a green cloth, a small dog at her feet.[66]

Women depicted in such a setting are few and far between, but St Katherine of Alexandria keeps Christine company in both word and image. A few years after 1400, one of the artists of the *Belles Heures de Jean de Berry* included in his cycle of the life and death of St Katherine a unique miniature of the saint at work at her books.[67] Her seat is like a choir-stall with its curved canopy and her (invisible) book is on a lectern before her; not far away there is an elaborate two-tiered bookstand crowned with a figure of Moses. Behind her the space opens out into a chapel, on the altar of which stands another statue of Moses. Katherine is here visually assimilated to the august company of the learned men of the church. There is also a St Jerome cycle in the *Belles Heures*, which includes a miniature (fol. 187v) showing him in his study, working at a circular lectern in an ecclesiastical setting, complete with a lion, his constant if apocryphal companion. This way of representing Jerome, new in northern art, was of Italian origin; Tommaso da Modena had so depicted him at Treviso.

Jerome, as both hermit and scholar, was to become the Renaissance icon of the learned man and a frequent item in the decoration of the pious scholar's inner sanctum. He might be shown either as the breast-beating penitent in the 'desert' or as the Doctor of the Church in his own study, although his desert cave is sometimes given some of the appurtenances of a study. In either case he recalled to the spectator the purposes of learning, the justification of scholarship and its ultimate subordination to the requirements of salvation.[68] In her quasi-ecclesiastical setting in the *Belles Heures*, Katherine too recalls this model. The miniature implicitly underlines the theme of the Latin Life and its derivatives that Katherine's erudition, albeit striking in a woman, was firmly subordinated to her desire to serve Christ and achieve paradise.

According to the author of an English *Life* of Katherine composed around 1430, the saint's royal father, perceiving her intelligence, 'ordeyned hir a toure in his paleys wyth diverse studyes and chambres that she myght be at hir owne leyser in hir studye and noon to lette hire bot whanne hir liste'. Later, Our Lady tells the hermit Adrian that he will find Katherine 'allone in hir studie'. He 'entred yn at the dores that he saw open and passed from chambre to chambre tyle he came yn to hir secret study where no creature used to come bot her self allone'. Katherine herself refers to 'our privye studye'.[69] There was more to come in John Capgrave's version of the *Life*, written a decade or so later. Here Katherine's doting father seems to have provided her not just with one study in his palace but with several in a palace of her own:

> Hir stodyes there ful craftely were i-pyght,
> Wyth deskes and chayeris and moche other gere
> A-rayed on the best wyse, and glased ful bryght ...[70]

Capgrave's *Life*, and to a more limited but still significant extent that of his anonymous forerunner, show an author responding to the need to capture his audience's attention in a specific way. Both import into the story a large quantity of descriptive detail to enable the reader or hearer to locate the action in a recognizable milieu. We do not have to imagine that female intellectuals were numerous in the fifteenth century, but we may assume that Capgrave's audience, like Chaucer's, liked to be able to visualize characters in a well-defined setting and also that they knew what 'studies' were.[71] The word does not occur all that often in fourteenth- and fifteenth-century English sources, but it is frequent enough to indicate that it was current and intelligible. Numerous individuals, lay and ecclesiastical, must have possessed a room that they used as a study, and certainly possessed enough books to furnish it, even if they did not actually use the term. In itself it is only an indicator, although a very suggestive one, pointing not to the appearance of a new feature in domestic architecture but to an awareness of the uses to which an ordinary 'chamber' or closet might be put by the literate householder.

Wills and inventories suggest that before the early fifteenth century English ecclesiastics were more likely than laymen to possess studies, or at least to refer to them by that word.[72] The inventory of the goods of William Ledale, chaplain of York, taken in 1438, included the heading 'Studium cum Libris'; the furnishings included a 'writer's chair' (*cathedra scriptoris*).[73] For others, their chapel served as a bookstore, while William Kexby, precentor of York, in 1410 refers to 'a chest for books' that stood in his chamber.[74] By the middle of the fifteenth century, the devout layman of middling rank was making his appearance among study-owners. John Dautre, lawyer of York, possessed several books of both secular and sacred character and in his will, dated 1459, referred to a chest which was to be found *in studio meo*. He had inherited a number of his books from his father, Thomas, another lawyer who had served the church of York. Thomas, whose will was made in 1437, owned a Petrarch, among other things, but makes no mention of a study.[75] Yet another member of this occupational group, William Westerdale, late registrar of the court of York and notary public, was feeling ill when he made his will in September 1474, 'sitting in his study in the morning'.[76] These were all Latin wills. John Dautre's equally devout contemporary, John Baret of Bury St Edmunds, made a lengthy and elaborate English will in 1463, from which it appears that he had a study in his principal town house, for 'a litle grene coffre for kerchys' which he was leaving to a niece was to be found standing in it.[77] Baret was a man with a great deal of business both worldly and ecclesiastical to transact and he possessed at least a few books. Perhaps he needed to wear spectacles; at all events he bequeathed 'a peyre spectaclys of sylvir and ovyr gilt' to the monk John Ixnyng.

To what extent did studies contain specialized furniture? Chaucer is our witness that by the later fourteenth century an Englishman had words for the desks and shelves he might put his books on. 'Desk' appears first in the *Franklin's Tale*. The brother of the lovesick Aurelius remembers how in his student days at Orleans he saw a book of 'magyk natureel' which a fellow-student 'hadde prively upon his desk ylaft' (line 1128). The Latin word *discus* meant a table, for example a high table in a refectory, and later often denoted a reading-desk or lectern (as it may do here). In *The Miller's Tale*, the mischievous Oxford student Nicholas has a room to himself, the fourteenth-century equivalent of the modern student's bedsitter, in a carpenter's house. 'Allone, withouten any compaignye', he fits it out to his liking (lines 3203–15). He has a clothes press covered with a rough cloth on which he keeps his psaltery; this he plays at night 'So swetely that all the chambre rong'. More important for present purposes, he also has

> His Almageste, and bookes grete and smale,
> His astrelabe, longynge for his art,
> His augrym stones layen faire apart,
> On shelves couched at his beddes hed.

Possibly another Oxford student, the threadbare Clerk, who bought books with all the money he could lay hands on and paid more attention to study than to anything else, also had shelves in his lodgings,

> For hym was levere have at his beddes heed
> Twenty bookes, clad in blak or reed,
> Of Aristotle and his philosophie,
> Than robes riche, or fithele, or gay sautrie.[78]

Nicholas took a broader view of life. Even if he was some kind of clerk, his celibacy, like Petrarch's, was elastic. He and his room, like the author who described them, were signs of the fourteenth-century times; and had he been so minded (or had he been a more serious scholar) he might have referred to it as his 'study'.

Launched on its vernacular career in the fourteenth century, 'study' is still in common use in English, whereas the French *étude* has proved less enduring; *Larousse* regards it as archaic in the sense of what is now called a *cabinet du travail*. The brief heyday of *estude* was in fact a medieval moment, for the word *cabinet*, named 'after the piece of furniture in which precious objects or private papers were kept', took over from it in the course of the sixteenth century.[79] In fifteenth- and sixteenth-century Italy the *studiolo* became the perfection of the educated person's inner sanctum, equipped with purpose-built furniture and fittings for scholarly use or exquisitely decorated to gratify the taste of the connoisseur.[80] The study was also, however, the preserve of the merchant.

In Leon Battista Alberti's *Libri della famiglia*, written in dialogue form between 1432 and 1434, one of the protagonists, Giannozzo, tells how, within a few days of their marriage, when his wife was beginning to feel homesick, he took her by the hand and showed her the whole house, taking her at last into his *camera*. Here (having first locked the door) he showed her the valuables, hangings, clothes, jewels and other precious things, which he stored there. These things were to be kept safe and not exposed to everyone's view, but he thought it inappropriate that they should be concealed from his wife. There were, however, limits to his confidence:

> Then and always it was my pleasure just to keep the books and papers, mine and those of my ancestors, close so that my wife should not only not read them but not even see them. I always kept papers, not in my pockets, but locked away and kept in order in my study almost like sacred or religious objects. I never permitted my wife to enter this place, either with me or alone, and I also instructed her, if she ever came across a paper of mine, to give it to me at once.[81]

A wife was supposed to be competent to oversee the management of a household, but her writ did not run into every corner. She obtained all the privacy she needed from her usual domestic seclusion, for she could have no business that demanded confidentiality, nor was her intellectual culture likely to require the provision of a study; similar assumptions seem to have been made about nuns.

As a consequence, women were in a small minority among the possessors of studies. Christine de Pizan was one, but she was also a widow with a mother to keep house for her. Another exception was Isotta Nogarola of Verona, who in 1441, at the age of twenty-three, retired to a 'book-lined cell' to pursue sacred studies. A woodcut, published in 1497, shows her, like Christine, at her reading-desk, surrounded by her books. That her sanctum is described not as a study but as a 'cell' may reveal a need to represent, or understand, her withdrawal from the world as religious in character; yet the pursuit of scholarship distinguished the life she led in her room from the lives led in earlier times by Umiliana de' Cerchi or Catherine of Siena in theirs.[82] Isotta did not escape misunderstanding and indeed calumny. Things may have been a little easier for women who were married to men of the highest rank. Among those who in the later fifteenth century proved able to use their resources to create spaces for reading and writing were Ippolita Sforza, the wife of

Alfonso, duke of Calabria, Eleanora of Aragon, duchess of Ferrara, and her daughter Isabella d'Este. It has been suggested that Ippolita, who set about creating a *studio* for herself in the Castel Capuano at Naples on her marriage in 1465, may have been inspired by the example of her own father, the *condottiere* made good Francesco Sforza. He in his turn may have modelled his study on the *studietto* that had been made for Piero de' Medici in the Medici palace at Florence. Another learned lady with a study was Aloysia Gonzaga Castiglione, the mother of Baldassare, the author of *Il libro del cortigiano*.[83] The courtly discussions recorded by Castiglione supposedly took place in 1507 in the private apartments of another Gonzaga woman, Elisabetta, who had become duchess of Urbino. At bedtime, at the end of one of these conversations, Elisabetta retires into her 'most private room' (*nella stanza sua più segreta*).[84]

For a woman who possessed the necessary income, inclinations and determination there was scope to adapt such apartments to whatever purposes she desired. Her own tastes and education, which were likely to owe much to her family background, were obviously critical factors. At all social levels there was the possibility of active discouragement of female intellectual activity, but perhaps more insidious was an inability to conceive that it was possible. As in much more recent times, this would entail low expectations on the part not only of men but of women themselves and a ready acceptance of a clear-cut division of functions between the sexes.

11

Gardens

'The idea that cemeteries should be quiet and beautiful places is a recent one, stemming from the eighteenth-century Romantic movement.'[1] Hugh of Eversden, abbot of St Albans from 1309 to 1327, might have been surprised by this statement.

> The cemetery of the brothers, which had almost been made a wasteland by bushes and other noxious weeds and was much deteriorated, he had properly cleaned up, tidied and put into decent order. The place became so pleasing and delightful to all that seculars and regulars alike became more devout as a result of strolling around it and more disposed to pray for the souls of those whose bodies lay there. He also granted permission to all the brethren to visit this place at any suitable hour of the day for the purpose of prayer, but the rule of silence was not relaxed.[2]

It is not clear whether Abbot Hugh had the cemetery planted as a garden, but it seems probable. Thirteenth-century English ecclesiastical legislation laid it down that cemeteries and their contents were church property over which the laity had no rights, and this included the plants and trees that grew there. Archbishop John Pecham of Canterbury (1279–92) proclaimed that no lay person was to dispose of such plants, which were entirely in the power of the rectors of the churches or chapels concerned. If the rectors themselves without good cause 'tear up, damage or uproot trees growing in such cemeteries, which to no small degree adorn those cemeteries and the places near churches and chapels where they are planted', they were to be punished.[3] Pecham evidently thought of these plants as ornament.

At St Albans, the cemetery was a place for walking and meditation which it seems was open to *seculares*, perhaps visitors both lay and clerical. The openness of monastic gardens was sometimes a matter of concern. Monastic enclosures were large and complex spaces and gardens could be a weak point in the defences, too easily penetrated by outsiders or simply over-used by the religious themselves. The rules laid down by Abbot Thomas de la Mare of St Albans for the nuns of Sopwell included directions about the hours at which the doors to the gardens should be opened.[4] At Ramsey Abbey in 1432 Bishop Gray of Lincoln added the gardens to his list of places which women were not to be permitted to enter.[5] At Daventry there was a slightly different problem: the sacrist alleged in 1442 that the prior was given to *solivagacio*, which it is tempting to translate as 'mooching', both around the outlying monastic properties and *in ortis et gardinis*.[6]

The monastic cloister, the place of study and meditation, somewhat resembled the Roman peristyle garden with its surrounding arcaded walkways. It often had a green plot at its centre and a fountain at the centre of that, and was sometimes planted with cypresses or other trees. Hugues de Fouilloy declared that

> The green sward (*viriditas pratelli*) which is in the middle of the earthly cloister, refreshes the eyes of the monks and makes them more eager to read. It is the nature of the colour green that the sight of it helps the eyes.

The same was true of the green grass at the centre of the celestial cloister, which unlike its earthly counterpart was watered only by dew, not by floods of rain, and did not change in colour with the seasons.[7]

The cloister was thus amenable to metaphorical treatment, but some were true gardens. There is a story that William Rufus came with his entourage to Romsey Abbey and asked that he should be admitted in order (so he said) to pray (*orandi gratia*). His real motive was to inspect the Scottish princess Matilda, a descendant of the Saxon royal house and the future queen of his brother and successor Henry I, who was a boarder there. While 'the king went into our cloister as if to look at the roses and other flowering plants' the abbess, fearing his intentions, hastily veiled Matilda as if she were a professed nun.[8] We do not need to suppose that Rufus was a dedicated rose-fancier, but the nuns themselves and their better-intentioned visitors probably did indeed take pleasure in flowers that were probably cultivated chiefly for the decoration of the church.

The layout and contents of monastic gardens were not unfamiliar to those laymen who were likely to have gardens of their own, for such people were likely to be the kinsmen, neighbours and patrons of monks. This was as true of the patricians of early renaissance Florence as it was of the *seculares* who strolled contemplatively in the cemetery at St Albans. The intellectual circles which the early Medici gathered around them could as easily use the garden as a setting for philosophical reflection and discussion as monks could use it for prayer and meditation on the scriptures. Such laymen would also have been familiar with contemporary painting which invested the garden space with a variety of spiritual meanings: the garden of paradise, the Virgin in the *hortus conclusus* which signified her purity, the garden-plots of the hermits of the Thebaid which represented nature reclaimed from the wilds of sin.[9]

The understanding and appreciation of medieval gardening have been hampered by a number of difficulties. First and simplest is the fact that virtually no medieval gardens survive. Much effort and enthusiasm in recent times has gone into the reconstruction of medieval garden layouts, but these have had to be based on written sources of very varied kinds, archaeological research and artistic representations such as those just mentioned.[10] Also troublesome has been a narrow aestheticism which assumes that beauty, in gardens, as elsewhere, is most fully itself only when totally divorced from considerations of any other order. It is conventional to credit the monks of the west, especially in the early medieval period, with the preservation of something of the Roman horticultural heritage in the midst of a world which had little time for the peaceful pursuit of beauty, but monastic gardening tends to be damned with faint praise because it is tainted by utility: to cultivate plants with the refectory or infirmary in mind was mere kitchen gardening. Monks (and nuns) grew flowers with which to decorate their churches, but the disposition to accord spiritual significance to plants (for example to view the rose and the lily as symbols of the Virgin Mary) is vaguely felt to impair the pure appreciation of form, colour and scent which should be the sole authentic objective of horticulture. Such attitudes have not gone unchallenged, however, and recent ecological and environmental enthusiasms have dented them further. A sage bush covered with bluish-purple flowers and alive with bees is no less an object of beauty because a few of its leaves may end up in the stuffing. We have little reason to doubt that monks who grew herbs with their culinary and therapeutic properties in mind also delighted in their sight and smell; but testimony to that delight is often indirect.

The Latin poem known as *Hortulus* (*The Little Garden*) was written by Walafrid Strabo, who in 838 became abbot of Reichenau, where he had been educated before spending some time first at Fulda as a pupil of Rabanus Maurus and then at the imperial court of Louis the Pious at Aachen.[11] It includes descriptions of twenty-three plants, beginning with sage and ending with the rose. The prominence that Walafrid gives to sage is noteworthy, for this was not a plant either widely known or highly regarded in antiquity and his enthusiasm for it has been described as unprecedented.[12]

> Sage is placed first, resplendent,
> Sweet of smell, with mighty virtues and healthy to drink;
> It has been found useful for many human diseases,
> It has deserved to remain in perpetual green youth.
> But it sustains civil strife; for the savage progeny
> Of its flowers, unless removed, destroys the parent [stem]
> And enviously makes the old branches perish.

The splendour of the flowering bush and its aroma are evoked alongside its medicinal properties – evidently sage tea was already known – while its evergreen character seems to be regarded as a reward for its usefulness. Walafrid had also observed the plant's habit of producing new non-flowering shoots in profusion beneath the flowering stems, which is given an unexpected interpretation as a state of war within the plant.[13]

Walafrid also treats the rose symbolically, in a less political and more predictable manner. It is the 'flower of flowers', surpassing all 'in virtue and fragrance', but not devoid of utility, for the properties of the oil that is derived from it are well known.[14]

Earlier in the poem Walafrid had devoted a classicizing strophe to the lily; now he brings rose and lily together as the two flowers which throughout the centuries have signified the glory of the church, the blood of the martyrs and the purity of faith and virginity. This leads into a hymn to the Virgin, who is exhorted to 'gather roses in time of war and joyous lilies in peace'. The poet's undoubted enthusiasm for plants as such comes bundled with symbolism and moral significance. Even if Walafrid had seen, enjoyed and even cultivated real gardens, he was unlikely to limit himself to factual botanical or horticultural description when it was so clear to him and his contemporaries that plants and gardens (like all of creation) carried much more than surface meanings. That cultivated outdoor spaces were in fact used for rest and recreation emerges from his dedication to his former teacher, Grimaldus, with which the poem ends. Grimaldus is pictured seated in his garden under the apple trees, surrounded by his pupils, the children of the monastery, at play; from the peach trees, which cast a dappled shade, they bring him the white fruit 'with their tender downy skin'.

The orchard offered peace, shade, visual beauty, fragrance and fruit, and it was by no means unusual for it to double as a pleasure-garden. Two and a half centuries before Walafrid, the court poet Venantius Fortunatus had praised the garden of Queen Ultrogotha, the widow of the Merovingian Childebert I, who had himself created it. Here roses gave scent, vines with their soft leaves provided shade as well as grapes and the apples, sweet both to smell and taste, recalled the late king's virtues which were now receiving their heavenly reward.[15] Venantius himself had a garden – a 'poor garden', or so he said, for had there been lilies or roses in it he would have presented them to Radegund, former queen and future saint, who was the recipient of several of his poems. As it was, he could manage only violets, which he commended for their regal purple dye. In another verse epistle he imagined Radegund and her adoptive daughter Agnes decking the altar with spring flowers: the violet here vividly contrasts with the gold of saffron. Venantius evokes a chromatic riot:

> the colours compete even in flowers, and in a place of peace you would imagine a battle of plants. This delights with its glossy whiteness, that glows with ruddy beauty; this has a more delightful scent, that is a more exquisite crimson.

At the end the poet hopes that Radegund and Agnes may themselves 'breathe with the scent of eternal flowers'.[16] Venantius just begins to hint at the symbolic and metaphorical treatment of gardens and their produce which in later centuries became the predominant mode. Equally enduring was his delight in the juxtaposition of red and white.

The idea of enclosure seems to be present in the etymology of most of the terms which have been used for gardens, including the standard Latin word, *hortus*. A similar sense attaches to the vulgar Latin *curtilagium*, a courtyard, often used to describe a small cultivated area. The Germanic root which branched out to give 'Garten', 'garden' and 'jardin', and in English also produced 'yard' and 'garth' (later used to describe the green plot in the centre of a cloister), has this sense. The Dutch 'tuin' looks different, but enshrines the same basic meaning, of a defined, contained area, which lies behind the related English 'town'. Paradise once existed on earth as a garden, and this word, of ancient Persian origin, again means an enclosure. An enclosure simultaneously protects and excludes, an idea with innumerable special applications. The paradise garden excludes sin and mortality, the garden of the monk or the scholar excludes distraction and nourishes meditation, the secular garden excludes everything that is not wanted, from unpleasant sights and sounds to undesirable company. The wall or fence preserves the pleasurable features which one desires either to keep to oneself or to share with the chosen few. Because the garden is an enclosure it can be a place of peace.

The practical garden too was enclosed. Productive cultivation requires the exclusion of brute nature; so St Antony rebuked the beasts which ate his plants, thus creating a paradigm for later saints including Godric of Finchale. The creation of a garden or gardens at Finchale marked a crucial transition in Godric's life. There had been an earlier period during which he obsessively avoided human contact and lived with (if not actually like) the wild beasts, eating roots and leaves.[17] The 'productive garden' (*hortus copiosus*) he later makes at Finchale was strictly utilitarian. It began controversially because it was taken out of common land. Godric first cultivated grain (which neighbouring peasants tried vainly to destroy) and we are later told that there were 'a few fields enclosed within the boundaries of the garden'.[18] These were evidently sufficiently large to need a plough.

The entire area which Godric reclaimed from the wild is called his *hortus*. That it was divided into different areas, including a *pomerium* or orchard, is suggested by the experience of a boy who after Godric's death is taken on a visionary tour of the site by St John the Baptist.[19] There is no mention at all of flowering plants, but (apart from grain) there were apple-trees and vegetables, cultivated to sustain Godric's guests and servants. It is made very clear that this involved hard work. A diabolical visitor who appeared when Godric was taking a rest from digging reproached him with his inability to emulate the heroic labours of the Desert Fathers.[20] There is a lengthy description of his efforts to graft apple-trees and his running battle with invading deer. Such labour, Reginald hints, introduced the variety into the unlettered Godric's routine that study could not.[21] Later in life he tried to help the hired labour which had come in to plough his *agri* by uprooting the weeds in their path; wearying of doing this by hand, he set fire to the weeds and managed to set fire also to the enclosing hedge.[22]

This hedge and what it contains also have symbolic value. Apart from the resentful peasants, who were soon put to shame, two categories of outsider threatened the garden. Demons perched on the hedge and on the entrance to the garden in various unpleasant guises; one even appeared in the autumn and asked Godric for apples, in what sounds like an inverted reminiscence of the Fall.[23] The wild creatures, although destructive, were less malicious. A 'little hare' who came from the neighbouring wood from which Godric had reclaimed his *ager* was thought likely to prefer delicate cultivated leaves if he could get them. Godric reminded the deer who menaced his apple trees that these crops were being grown for man, not beast.[24] Man, who is capable of regeneration, creates a garden, but as far as Godric is concerned, it seems to be a place of labour rather than of recreation.

There is of course no impermeable boundary between the two. Around 1220 Gerald of Wales reported that the hermit monks of Grandmont had

> gardens enclosed within their walls or ditches, which they are accustomed to cultivate, not without profit, as much for pleasure as if in place of work, as for the produce they obtain both from sundry sowings of kitchen herbs, leeks and vegetables and from precious and fragrant herbs and spices which they carefully sow and plant.[25]

Gerald's somewhat convoluted Latin makes it difficult to decide whether the Grandmontines actually used gardening as recreation or whether the discovery that the necessary labour was enjoyable proved an additional incentive to undertake it. Nor is it entirely clear whether it was the processes of digging, weeding and planting that were found to be innately rewarding or whether the monks discovered that the produce of their gardens had both aesthetic and practical value.

Godric dug and planted for practical reasons; Reginald of Durham does little more than hint that his garden and its hedge might bear further meanings. Reginald himself may have been aware of the fully developed symbolic literary mode that is represented by, say, St Bernard's twenty-third sermon on the Song of Songs. Here the saint likens the historical sense of scripture to a garden:

> I think that the historic sense is not unfitly referred to the garden, because in the history are found men of many virtues, as it were fruitful trees in the garden of the Bridegroom and in the Paradise of God; and from their conduct and their actions you may take examples, as from a tree you gather fruit. Who can question that a good man is, as it were, a plant of God? ... History is, then, as it were, a garden, and it is threefold; for it contains the creation, the reconciliation and the reparation of heaven and earth. Creation, that is like the sowing or planting of a garden. Reconciliation is, as it were, the germination of that which is sown or planted. For at the due time the heavens have distilled dew from above, the clouds have poured down righteousness, the earth has opened and brought forth the Saviour by whom was brought about the reconciliation of heaven and earth ... Reparation, again, is to come to pass at the ending of the dispensation. For there shall be a new heaven and a new earth; the good shall be gathered from among the evil, to be set in safety in the storehouse of God as fruits from a garden. 'In that day', it is said, shall the branch of the Lord be beautiful and glorious and the fruit of the earth shall be excellent and comely [Isaiah 4.2]. In this garden of the historic sense, then, you have three periods included.[26]

It would not be clear from this whether or not Bernard had ever looked at a real garden, but he was not the only Cistercian to use horticultural metaphors. In a sermon on psalmody Guerric of Igny first plays on the similarity and dissimilarity of gardens and tombs. The garden is the monk's spiritual habitat:

> It is you then, if I am not mistaken, who dwell in gardens, you who meditate on the law of the Lord day and night and walk about in as many gardens as you read books, pick as many apples as you select fine thoughts.

Then it becomes the monk's own soul: 'for I think that the man who enters his garden becomes a garden himself, his soul is like a watered garden ...' The true gardener is Christ:

> You were mistaken, Mary, when you thought he was the gardener of that poor and tiny garden in which he was buried. He is the gardener of the whole world, he is the gardener of the Church, which he plants and waters here until its growth is completed ...[27]

Obviously the Bible shaped this disposition. It was full of gardens, from Eden through the Song of Songs to Gethsemane and the garden in which Mary Magdalen encountered the risen Saviour. Our first parents had inhabited the garden of paradise until they were expelled from it; the Virgin Mary, a second Eve who repaired the damage done by her predecessor, was herself an enclosed and uninvaded garden (because of her virginity) and was often depicted, in word and image, in the setting of such a garden. Sometimes she received word of the Annunciation against the background of a *hortus conclusus*; sometimes she sat in one with the Christ Child, saints and angels, enjoying music and a picnic. Eulogies of the Virgin as rose and lily may well seem to bear only the most formal, stereotypical relation to the writer's experience of real flowers in real gardens: the latter exist to furnish the image rather than to be admired in their own right. Of course there was a gulf between any earthly garden or landscape, however delightful, and the paradise which it could only dimly prefigure; but the garden remained the finest available image of that perfection, not least because it represented the triumph of order over disordered nature.

The symbolic or allegorical mode of treating gardens, and particularly the Marian image of the rose as virginity guarded and preserved within a garden, was mocked in the thirteenth century by a secular exercise in allegory, the immensely popular *Roman de la Rose*, where the rose is destined to be plucked and violated by the lover.[28] Sacred or secular, these symbolic or allegorical styles of treatment amount to an unfamiliar way of viewing or describing plants which may too easily lead us to conclude that our ways of enjoying gardens are totally different. The fact that a literary framework may be satirical, allegorical or both does not, however, mean that all the descriptive detail is invented. The *Roman* contains some vivid pictures of the pleasure-garden as it was known or imagined by the authors and their audience. When artists produced manuscript illustrations for this and other literary works with garden settings they depicted aristocratic gardens and their recreational uses, showing fountains, turf seats, methods of fencing and walling as well as of planting, and many other details. Like some of the depictions of the Virgin already mentioned they provide information on which modern garden reconstructions have drawn.

The majority of these illustrations come from the period after *c.*1400, but there is an increasing quantity of written evidence for gardens during the previous three centuries. Alongside the symbolic-allegorical mode there was a burgeoning tradition of useful horticultural information. A quasi-academic interest in the subject developed in the twelfth century. Hildegard of Bingen (d. 1179) and the Englishmen Alexander Neckham (b. 1157) and John of Garland, working in Paris around 1220, produced extensive plant lists. In two works, the treatise *De naturis rerum* and the poem *De laudibus divinae sapientiae*, Neckham listed a total of some 140 plants; John of Garland's list was ostensibly of plants to be found in his own garden, woods and orchard.[29] The encyclopedia of Bartholomew the Englishman, who died around 1260, also included a chapter on plants, and a missing chapter of his work has been identified as a probable source for the treatment of pleasure-gardens by the Dominican polymath Albert the Great. This in its turn was taken over in its entirety in the principal medieval treatise on horticulture, the early fourteenth-century *Ruralium commodum liber* of Pietro de' Crescenzi of Bologna.[30] The illustrated manuscripts of this work can be added to our list of visual sources for garden practice and design; calendars may be valuable for the same reasons. Inasmuch as it includes calendar pictures which show a wide variety of types of cultivated ground and enclosures, the *Très riches heures* of the Duc de Berry can be regarded as a particularly august example. Writing as and for the private householder at a similar time and place, the Ménagier de Paris represented the practical tradition, devoting space not only to recipes but to useful hints which mostly had to do with herbs and vegetables.[31]

We may reasonably infer from the relatively abundant evidence for the existence of gardens and for expenditure on them after about 1100 that pleasure was taken in them by people whose culture was not monastic or even clerical. It seems reasonable therefore to suppose that there must have been ways of appreciating gardens which did not depend on allegorical interpretation; but here as in other subject areas we are handicapped by the fact that relatively little was written down by individuals of lay culture and that writings which deal with secular life do not always include all the features we might find interesting. Lambert of Ardres, who has so much to say about the marvellous house that was built at Ardres late in the eleventh century, does not describe its gardens, but does relate how the spritely Countess Petronilla bathed in the fishpond, for pleasure rather than for hygienic reasons, before an appreciative audience of knights and attendants.[32] If indeed there was a garden overlooked by a wooden gallery at Richmond Castle c.1100, we have no direct written testimony to the effect.[33]

However, even those whose culture was unquestionably ecclesiastical sometimes betray what seems a largely aesthetic appreciation of natural beauty. Late in the eleventh century, there is not a word of allegory in St Bruno's eulogy of his Calabrian solitude.[34] He delights in the amplitude of the plain, the long sweep of the mountains, the verdant expanses of grass and flowering meadows, the prospect of the hills gently rising all around, the shady retired valleys, the abundance of streams and fountains: 'Nor are there lacking well-watered gardens and a useful abundance of different trees.' The *horti* were most probably vegetable gardens and the useful trees bore fruit or nuts, but Bruno seems to contemplate the amplitude of nature beyond the garden fence with real pleasure, acknowledging that there are more important things to think about, but feeling that the mind, when wearied by spiritual exercises, can find necessary recreation in such prospects.

A little later, the poem *De ornatu mundi* of Hildebert of Lavardin (d. 1133) trembles on the boundary between the symbolic and the aesthetic. Its starting point seems to be the delight the poet takes in a grove (*nemus*) ('This place, O Paradise, is your rival!'), but it culminates in a vision of the beauties of Paradise itself. The *nemus* represents the utmost of what Nature can achieve, but to judge by its profusion of trees and other plants, it is such as nature never produced unaided and equally certainly does not resemble any garden of Hildebert's time or any other. The point rather seems to be that the visible beauties of the earth, real enough in themselves, severally and collectively point to their perfection in Paradise.[35] Hildebert's contemporary Marbod bishop of Rennes (d. 1123), who became a monk at the end of his long life, strikes a more down to earth note in several poems: 'Lovely are the gardens with the half-blown rose'. In one poem, significantly dedicated to the pursuit of solitude, he betakes himself to his brother's woodland farm to get away from it all:

> Green turf amid silent trees and soft light airs
> And a spring of running water in the grass,
> They freshen a jaded mind, they give me back to myself,
> They make me abide in myself.[36]

Certainly by this time bishops as well as monasteries possessed gardens which were appreciated for aesthetic and personal as well as for practical reasons. In 1108 Archbishop Gerard of York, who had been slightly indisposed, 'was lying for a little while in a garden next to his house, so that he might enjoy the healthier air out of doors with its scents of sweet-smelling flowers'. Here, unexpectedly, he died. This sounds like a small enclosed garden in which the emphasis was on flowering plants. The medieval gardener had a restricted range of flowers at his disposal and his garden must often have been an essay in shades of green, picked out with spots or splashes of colour, as in the 'flowery mead', an expanse of grass speckled with flowers, much celebrated in literature. Modern gardeners can draw on sources worldwide for a dazzling variety of flowering plants (usually sternly confined to their beds or to containers) but often have limited room for trees, which in every sense bulk large in medieval garden descriptions. Like their medieval predecessors, they do however like to introduce water, which makes a multiple appeal to the senses and in the shape of a small pond or fountain is less demanding of space, but they are unlikely to use it to drive mills or to raise fish for consumption.

Hildebert, Marbod and many others testify to this delight in water and trees, which of course they also found in the classical poetic models on which they drew.[37] William of Malmesbury describes the setting of Thorney Abbey as 'a copy of Paradise, giving us with its beauty a picture in this life of the heavens themselves'. The land was almost entirely cultivated, but William says nothing about flowering plants, speaking only of trees, including apples, vines and smooth expanses of grass.[38] The same emphasis on trees is to be found at a similar period in descriptions of gardens planned by the bishops of Coutances, Le Mans and Auxerre. A particularly keen sense of the visual relationship between garden and dwelling was evidently at work at Le Mans, for here 'those leaning out of the hall windows to admire the beauty of the trees, and others in the garden looking at the fair show of the windows, could both delight in what they saw'.[39] Later in the twelfth century, Gerald of Wales remembered the remarkable fishpond (*vivarium egregium*) at the Welsh castle of Manorbier where he was brought up; it was distinguished for its depth as well as for its 'majesty', which was presumably derived from its sheer size. He remembered also the 'beautiful orchard' on the same side of the castle, which was hemmed in by woods on rocky slopes, abundant in hazel-trees.[40] Archaeology has recently established that, two centuries later, the immediate surroundings of Bodiam Castle in Sussex, as of other late medieval houses, were landscaped with aesthetic as well as utilitarian or defensive considerations in mind.[41]

More often than not, medieval gardens and grounds were simultaneously intended to serve different purposes, which, as already suggested, has probably been one obstacle to modern understanding of how they were appreciated by their owners and users. In London houses, it was common to set aside a small patch of ground for recreation as well as for raising poultry or growing herbs. The Grocers' Company took trouble with their sunlit garden, which even contained butts for archery practice and 'six water potts of tyn for byrds to drynke of'.[42] Rather earlier, William fitz Stephen noted the gardens of suburban London, 'planted with trees, spacious and fair, adjoining one another'.[43] The merchant Francesco di Marco Datini (d. 1410) owned twenty houses in Prato apart from his principal residence, almost all of which had a garden of some sort. Prato evidently exemplified a common medieval urban pattern, shared by neighbouring Florence, in that the space within its imposing walls was not totally built up; orchards and gardens abounded and for many of the city's occupants, including Datini's tenants, their little gardens were doubtless both useful and agreeable. Some had orange and apple trees, or vine pergolas. Datini himself chose to spend six hundred florins on a pleasure-garden for his own house, 32 *braccia* by 14, in which 'oranges, roses and violets and other lovely flowers' were planted.

Few of his fellow-citizens could have afforded such an extravagance, but he regretted it, saying that he would have been wiser to put the money into a farm (*podere*).[44]

Albert the Great recognized the existence of gardens which were 'of no great utility or fruitfulness but designed for pleasure' and 'mainly designed for the delight of two sense, viz. sight and smell'. Green and flowering plants apart, he insisted on the provision of seats 'so that men may sit down there to take their repose pleasurably when their senses need refreshment' and a fountain of water 'for its purity gives much pleasure'. In sum, 'It is then delight rather than fruit that is looked for in the pleasure garden'.[45] There is a certain kinship here with the monastic gardens (or indeed cemeteries) in which the monks, whether sick or well, were intended to find recreation. In an early thirteenth-century description of Clairvaux it is remarked that an orchard (*pomarium*) adjacent to the infirmary, planted with trees so as to resemble a grove, 'affords no slight consolation to the sick brethren, since it offers a spacious walk to the up and about and a pleasant resting-place for those who are hot'. This was distinct from the adjacent *hortus*, which was divided into beds irrigated by streams flowing between them.[46]

At a very similar date the sacrist of Bury bought a vineyard and enclosed it within a stone wall 'for the solace of the sick and those being bled'.[47] Probably towards the end of 1335, Alexander, prior of Winchester, sought to obtain the royal licence for the monks to build an arch or gallery over the city wall and street, connecting their close 'called Mirabel' with their *viridaria et deambulatoria* on the other side of the public way, 'in order that they may enjoy much needed recreation without passing along the highways'.[48] According to a sixteenth-century description of the former cathedral monastery at Durham, there was 'a garding and a bowlinge allie' attached to the 'Common House' (or warming-house) 'for the Novyces Sume tymes to recreat theme selves', under the eye of their master.[49]

Some monastic gardens acquired a special reputation. Gerald of Wales told how the prior of Llanthony was laughingly asked why in the world he desired to become bishop of St David's when he already enjoyed so many amenities in his house and grounds at Gloucester, including wild vines (*vineae feraces*), pleasure gardens and orchards.[50] These gardens evidently remained famous. A century later, the queen mother, Eleanor of Provence, was living at Gloucester Castle and approached the monks of Llanthony, whose grounds adjoined the castle's, for permission to bridge the castle ditch so that she and her *familia* might walk in the priory garden. Richard II made similar arrangements a century later still.[51]

As the bride of Henry III Eleanor of Provence had brought with her to England ideas (and possibly plants such as lavender and wallflower) from a more southerly clime, and she acquired a husband who was not averse to spending money on gardens as on other construction works. Henry was not, however, the first king of England to interest himself in such things: the records of royal expenditures from the twelfth century on reveal how much the kings spent on their parks and gardens, not only at principal residences such as Windsor, Clarendon or Winchester, but at miscellaneous manors and hunting-lodges scattered about the country.[52] Henry I is the first English king about whose horticultural activities we know anything. When he founded the Augustinian priory at Dunstable he reserved his houses and garden in the town for his own use and they remained in royal hands until John granted them to the canons in 1204.[53]

Henry had a zoo-park at Woodstock and it remained a favourite residence for his successors. In 1165–66 expenditure is recorded on the spring (*fons*), which in the thirteenth century was known as Everswell and some centuries later as 'Rosamund's well'. The association of the spot with Henry II's celebrated mistress is attested already in the thirteenth century by mentions of 'Rosamund's chamber', which stood near the spring. Everswell, lying somewhat apart from the main palace, came to be a separate retreat of which the water was a principal feature. In Henry III's reign there were chambers for the king and queen around it, a chapel and more than one garden. It has been suggested that the layout was intended to recall the romance of *Tristan et Iseut*, in which the lovers meet in an enclosed orchard or garden, from one end of which a spring first fills a marble pool and then feeds a stream which runs through Iseut's apartments.[54]

A great deal of work, on houses and gardens alike, was done for or by queens, who spent more time than their husbands did in domestic seclusion. Eleanor of Provence was a major beneficiary. Among much else she had a walled garden to walk in at Woodstock, and a reconstruction of her pleasure-garden is to be seen at Winchester. The king's directions for the making of her garden at Woodstock in 1250 are instructive:

> To make two good high walls around the garden of the queen so that no-one may be able to enter, with a becoming and pleasant herbary near the king's fish-pond in which the same queen may be able to amuse herself …

Such a garden, it has been remarked, 'could have served lyric or romance'.[55]

Between 1279 and 1281 a new garden, planted with vines, was made at Langley for Eleanor's daughter-in-law Eleanor of Castile. When Odiham Castle in Hampshire was restored for the benefit of Edward III's queen, Philippa of Hainault, in the 1330s, an enclosed garden was created in the park; its features included a garderobe screened by a hedge.[56] Among the works done at Sheen in 1445 in readiness for the accommodation of Henry VI's queen Margaret of Anjou was the enclosure of the garden by a brick wall, and a few years later extensive alterations were made at Greenwich on her behalf; there was a gallery overlooking the garden, which was hedged around and provided with an arbour for her to sit in.

Kings too naturally took their ease in their gardens when they had the chance. In winter Charles V of France tended to read (indoors) until the supper hour, but in summer, after vespers, 'he sometimes went into his garden and sometimes, if he was in his house at Saint Pol, the queen came to him there or his children were brought to him. There he talked to the women and inquired into the well-being of his children.'[57] In this garden of about twenty acres, much more extensive than was possible at the Louvre, the king's head gardener, Philippart Persant, provided 'trellised pavilions, a labyrinth, tunnel arbours, plantations of cherry-trees, and many kinds of ornamental plant'. In 1398 Charles VI had these gardens replanted at considerable expense. There were abundant vines, some of them ornamental, fruit (cherry, plum, pear and apple) and bay trees, white and red roses, lilies and iris.[58]

Garden terminology was not fixed or exact and, with the multiplication of pleasure-gardens and the development of the vernaculars that were spoken by their owners, words came into being to distinguish them from 'kitchen gardens'. These words in their turn often entered or influenced current Latin. *Hortus* (or *ortus*) remained the generic Latin word for a garden, but gradually came to be particularly associated with what we would now call kitchen gardens (an association preserved in modern Italian, where *orto* can also mean a botanical garden). In 1108 Archbishop Gerald of York died in his *viridarium*, and Marbod's *viridaria* were beautified by the early rose. This was a frequently used Latin term for a pleasure-garden, used a century later by Bartholomew the Englishman together with several related words, including *virgultum* and *viretum*; he explained that all denoted 'a green place'. *Gardinus* was formed from the French *jardin* or its variously spelled ancestors, while *viridarium* and its kin were cognate with the French *vergier*.

Although *jardin* and its variants are as old in French as the first half of the twelfth century, Chrétien de Troyes and Marie de France almost invariably use *vergier* to signify a pleasure-garden. The fact that in modern French this word has come to mean exclusively an orchard itself hints at the importance of trees in the medieval garden. In Marie's *lai Le rossignol*, the *vergier* in which the nightingale is snared is full of hazel-trees and chestnuts, while the central feature of the garden which is made for the convalescent heroine Fenice in Chrétien's *Cliges* is a graft (*une ente*), laden with leaves and blossom, whose branches are so trained that, descending from a vertical central stem, they almost touch the ground. Fenice takes her repose on the grass (*pree*) under this tree.[59] The English word for such a graft was 'imp'. In the middle English romance *Sir Orfeo*, written about 1300, the Eurydice figure attracts the unwelcome attentions of the King of the Fairies by sleeping on the 'grene' under such a tree one noontide, when she had gone with her maidens 'To play bi an orchard-side, / To se the floures sprede and spring'.[60]

Jardin had successfully colonized the Tuscan vernacular before 1300. In *Il fiore*, an adaptation of the *Roman de la Rose* which is now generally thought to have been written by the young Dante in the 1280s, *giardin(o)* is the invariable term.[61] 'Garden' was first recorded in English as early as the eleventh century, but when John Trevisa translated Bartholomew the Englishman late in the fourteenth century he opted for 'herber' as an equivalent for *viridarium*.[62] This derivative of the Latin *herbarium*, which did not always mean a herb-garden in the modern sense, was in common use by this date. The bereaved father in *Pearl* loses his daughter 'in on erbere' and returns there to experience a consoling vision of her.[63] 'Herber' and 'garden' were often used as synonyms: in *Piers Plowman* Charity grows 'in a gardyn that God made himselfe' and 'the herber that it inne groweth' is the heart.[64]

Chaucer also uses both words. In *Troylus and Criseide* (line 1705), he has Helen and Deiphebus descend into a 'herber grene' to read a letter and in *The Legend of Good Women* he pictures himself lying down 'in a litel herber that I have' on a bench of freshly cut turves. In the English version of the first 1670 lines of the *Roman de la Rose* (Fragment A) which is almost certainly his work, 'gardyn' is the usual equivalent of 'vergier' but is supplemented, for variety, not by 'herber' but by 'yard' (a sense current in modern American English):

> Ther is no place in paradys
> So good inne for to dwelle or be
> As in that gardyn, thoughte me.
> For there was many a brydd syngyng,
> Throughout the yerd al thryngyng ...[65]

In his writings as a whole 'garden' seems to be Chaucer's preferred term. It is used by the Wife of Bath in her *Prologue*, and it also denotes the most pleasurable of pleasure-gardens in *The Knight's Tale*, *The Merchant's Tale* (in which the unfortunate January is cuckolded in a pear tree) and *The Franklin's Tale*. Such gardens are clearly if implicitly distinguished from the fenced 'yard' which belongs to the poor widow of *The Nun's Priest's Tale*, with its bed of worts in which the fox lies in wait for Chantecleer.[66] What they have in common is the sense of enclosure. The 'yard' is enclosed for utilitarian reasons, the garden or herber not only to protect the plants but to obtain seclusion for its occupants. January's garden is closed by a wicket-gate to which he has (so he thinks) the only key. Even if a fairly large number of people gather in a garden, as Dorigen does with her friends in *The Franklin's Tale*, the sense is still conveyed that this is a private retreat for a select company of friends.

Within its wall or fence, the pleasure-garden has many of its purely physical attributes in common with the literary 'flowery mead', which is topographically rather ill-defined but sometimes sounds rather like a very well-appointed village green or recreation ground, complete with running water, flowers and trees. Chrétien's Lancelot comes upon a 'pree' where knights and damsels are all taking advantage of the beauty of the place; there is chess and draughts, dancing, singing and even wrestling (lines 1634–48). Earlier, he goes after mass to a window overlooking *la pree* and gazes pensively at it (lines 539–43). In the *Conte du Graal*, Gawain arrives at a palace whose five hundred windows are occupied by ladies viewing 'les pres et les vergiers floriz' outside (line 7161). In such passages, *pree* may well, like the Italian equivalent *prato*, signify a 'lawn', a meadow designed for pleasure rather than for pasture.

When the hero of *Yvain* arrives at the ominously named Castle of Pesme Aventure he discovers in the *vergier* 'a gentleman lying on a silk robe and before him a maiden who was reading a book of romance'. The maiden's mother too is listening to the reading (lines 5356–66). This passage evokes an aspect of the garden that is familiar to us: the 'outdoor room' into which activities and recreations which were otherwise pursued inside the house could be extended. These might include eating, reading, playing board games, making music and amorous dalliance. The reconstructed garden of Queen Eleanor next to the great hall of Winchester Castle is intended, in the very confined space available, to bring such a setting to life with its fountain, turf seat, beds of aromatic plants and tunnel vine arbour, in which it would be possible to stroll up and down as one might in a loggia or cloister-walk or in the long gallery of an Elizabethan house.[67] Convalescence too was a process which in both the monastic and the secular environments was understood to require peace and quiet, whether indoors or out, with the option of gentle exercise. Like Archbishop Gerald of York, but with happier results, Fenice in *Cliges* believed that lying in a garden would be of benefit to her health.

If reading, music or conversation could be transported into the open air, so too could prayer. Already in the tenth century Wenceslas of Bohemia prayed by night in his garden, and in the thirteenth Benevenuta Boiani of Cividale del Friuli wore a patch like a well-used path in the green grass where she knelt.[68] In the Middle English romance *Sir Cleges* the central character, who has fallen on hard times, goes out into his garden to pray after mass early on Christmas morning, only to find a cherry tree in fruit.[69] Agnes Paston in 1456 matter-of-factly related how her neighbour Sir John Heveningham had come home 'never merrier' after hearing three masses at church and told his wife that he would go into his garden to say a little devotion; then he had a stroke and died.[70]

Among the most celebrated of all medieval descriptions of the garden as a place of health, retreat and entertainment are Boccaccio's in the *Decameron*. The Black Death has struck Florence and ten fashionable young people, seven female and three male, decide to take refuge in the countryside. The first 'palace' in which they take up residence is well provided 'with little meadows (or lawns, *pratelli*) round about and marvellous gardens' in which, immediately, they take advantage of the opportunity to stroll, converse, weave garlands and sing of love. The first round of story-telling takes place in a *pratello* which affords shade from the ascending sun; were it not for the stories, they could be playing chess or other board games. The second day begins in the gardens, and they break their fast *al fresco* (or, as Boccaccio puts it, *per lo fresco*). In the evening they divert themselves for a time in a *giardinetto*, which we can fairly imagine as a very small garden enclosed by walls or hedges; like *pratello*, the word illustrates the Italian predilection for diminutives. After a hiatus in the story-telling on Friday and Saturday, both fast-days, the company moves on to another *palazzo* and it is here, at the beginning of the Third Day, that Boccaccio produces his *tour de force* of garden description.

First of all the friends take refreshment in a central courtyard, full of flowers and leaves in season (perhaps in containers), with a well in the centre and overlooked by a loggia. Such a courtyard recalls the monastic cloister. They then have a walled garden alongside the palace opened and enter to marvel at its varied beauties. The place is criss-crossed by broad straight paths, arched over by pergolas of vines in full flower. Overwhelmed by scent as if by all the spices of the orient, they do not lack for shade, as the paths are almost enclosed by vines and jasmine. In the middle is a lawn (*prato*) of the finest grass, so green as almost to be black, dappled with flowers and surrounded by cedars and orange trees which are still bearing either their flowers or their fruit, according to their age. The *prato* itself has a white marble fountain at its centre which jets water high into the air. An unexpectedly practical note is now struck; the water, descending, drains invisibly under the lawn, reappearing in ornamental channels beyond it and running away through all parts of the garden, only to be gathered together once more and, as it descends towards lower ground, to drive two mills, 'with the greatest power and no little profit to the lord'. The company, with no great originality, exclaim that 'if there could be Paradise on earth they knew no other form that it could be given than that of this garden'. Its character as a lost Eden is reinforced when they observe, as if for the first time, that it is also full not only of birds but of animals of the more harmless kinds, rabbits, hares and deer, which leap among them as they sit. After the story-telling they turn to singing, chess and chasing the animals, and supper is taken around the fountain. When darkness falls, lighted torches are set up on the grass and among the flowers so that the singing can continue.

The conduct of this little party is seemly, but many of the stories are not. At the end of the work Boccaccio reminds the reader who may feel inclined to reprove him that the stories were told, not among clerks or philosophers, 'but in gardens, in a place of relaxation' (*ne' giardini, in luogo di sollazzo*). We may wonder whether Albert the Great, who acknowledged that pleasure gardens were indeed for pleasure, would have accepted the excuse. We may also wonder how much descriptions so obviously literary tell us about the reality of contemporary gardens; but Boccaccio was not without experience of real gardens and furthermore of a real garden enthusiast. In the spring of 1350 he stayed for about a week with Petrarch in his house at Padua and later remembered how Petrarch had been busy copying ancient authors while he copied Petrarch's own writings. After the day's work

> When evening came we rose together from our labours and went into your little garden, which was beautiful with the leaves and flowers of early spring ... and we sat talking quietly and on worthy themes until day had passed into night.[71]

Petrarch occupies an important place in the cultural history of the garden.[72] Most medieval testimonies to the pleasure of gardens come from their owners, or observers of the owners, and not from the people who were doing the work; but, although he naturally had servants and assistants, Petrarch was an enthusiastic practitioner. There were two gardens at the house in Parma where he lived for some years after 1342 and also at the house at Vaucluse in Provence which he occupied at intervals between 1337 and the spring of 1352 when he finally turned his back on Avignon. The Paduan house where Boccaccio visited him in 1350 was presumably the one he occupied by right of holding a canonry in the cathedral. Between 1353 and 1361 he spent much of his time in Milan in a house without a garden, but he obtained permission to dig and plant in the gardens of the monastery of Sant' Ambrogio, making notes about what he did in his copy of the *De horticultura* of Palladius. This was not just ornamental planting: in September–October 1353 he planted spinach and beets there and in April 1357 some trees.[73]

From a modern perspective Petrarch's enthusiasm for gardens goes naturally with his love of 'solitude' and belief in the recreation of the spirit in the countryside and in the open air. He himself was as well aware of the difference, indeed the conflict, between raw nature and cultivation as Godric of Finchale could have been, but his objective was to create a scholar's retreat rather than a productive garden. In several of the Latin metrical epistles which he addressed to friends he refers to the struggle involved in creating the gardens on the stony soil of Vaucluse. Guglielmo da Verona had apparently worked with him to shift rocks to create a *campus* which remained pretty stony; now 'you can see a garden blooming with various flowers, nature yielding to labour'. This space lay between the River Sorgue and the lower slopes of a mountain which cast noonday shade and was haunted by numerous birds which delighted both eye and ear.[74]

In an epistle addressed to Giovanni da Colonna in 1346 Petrarch described himself as engaged in a battle with the nymphs who were resisting the introduction of their enemies the Muses into their domain. He had suffered various reverses (rock falls and floods), but at last 'we have built an enduring palace for the sacred Muses on the bank of the river'. The struggle for his 'little garden' was ongoing, as he reported in another epistle a year later: 'Nevertheless a little corner remains to me among the rocks; what was a temple of the nymphs is now mine and the Muses'; big enough, for my guests are few ...' In a third epistle he described with pleasure how a dog that Giovanni had given him accompanied and guarded him as he lay on the grassy bank, engaged on his usual tasks (presumably reading), or retreated into a place girded by rocks and water that was accessible only to the birds.[75] Wild nature could be seen and heard from the garden, but the garden itself was a reclaimed area, order brought out of chaos by human labour.

In this underlying sentiment there is a profound continuity linking Petrarch both to the preceding monastic tradition and to the Renaissance patrons and humanists who read him and developed the idea of the villa as an oasis of tranquillity apart from the city. Here it was possible not merely to grow one's own produce but (as a speaker in Alberti's book of household management pointed out) to enjoy pure air and views which encompassed leafy hills, green plains and clear streams and springs.[76] The Villa Medici, on the hillside at Fiesole overlooking Florence, was built or rebuilt between 1451 and 1457 by Giovanni, the second son of Cosimo de' Medici. It has been seen as epoch-making in the primacy it gave to the landscape setting, whereas earlier Medici properties had been intended primarily to serve economic purposes. This 'appreciation of a hilltop view for its own sake' is contrasted with the moral interpretation of the landscape which is supposedly expressed in Petrarch's letters.[77]

It is hard to see such a clearcut distinction. Like Alberti after him, Petrarch seems not so much to invest the landscape itself with moral qualities as to contrast the tranquillity and rationality of a life lived in such surroundings with the hubbub and bestiality of (say) the papal curia at Avignon. As we have seen, individuals much earlier seem to have been capable of admiring the view without undue moralization. That the garden might come to be furnished with antique statuary and the meditations and discussions that took place in it develop a correspondingly classicizing flavour is another matter. Petrarch himself recalled to Guglielmo da Verona how together in his garden they had summoned the Muses back from their long exile and compared the Greek and Latin poets.[78]

In 1352 Petrarch described the totality of the work that had been achieved at Vaucluse:

> I have here two little gardens which could not be more agreeable to my disposition; if I tried to describe them I would be a long time about it. To be brief, I don't think it would be easy to find a spot like it in the world ... I call it my transalpine Helicon. One of them is shady, suitable only for study and sacred to Apollo. The infant Sorgue is nearby and beyond are only rocks and precipices accessible only to birds and wild beasts. The other garden is close to the house, more cultivated in appearance and congenial to Bacchus; it is situated, marvellous to relate, in the middle of a beautiful swift stream, and close by, separated only by a short bridge at the far end of the house, there is an arch of living rock which now, in the hot weather, keeps the heat off. It is a place which invites study and I think of it as similar to that little courtyard where Cicero used to declaim, except that that did not have the Sorgue next to it. There I pass the noontide, the morning on the hills, the evening in the fields or by the spring in my wilder garden where, overcoming nature with art, I have made a place under the high rock and between the waters, confined but inspiring, where the mind, although at leisure, can rise to the loftiest concerns.[79]

Petrarch was free to choose whether to sit in seclusion or to walk abroad, and we know how he valued his freedom. There is scattered evidence elsewhere of men walking out in agreeable surroundings for pleasure and exercise. In his description of twelfth-century London, William fitz Stephen described how 'great multitudes of students from the schools and of the young men of the city' went out on summer evenings to the holy wells in the suburbs, such as Holywell and Clerkenwell, whose clear waters were obviously regarded as an attraction.[80] Giovanni Cavalcanti sauntered alone among the tombs in Florence,[81] and the October miniature of the *Très riches heures* shows men strolling and conversing on the banks of the Seine. In a letter written around 1480 Sir William Sandes told William Stonor that 'sumtyme as y walke in my recreacon' he had noticed some damage that had been done in Stonor's woods.[82] Such a diversion was (in principle) more readily available to laymen and secular clerks than to monks or women. One of the merits of the garden was that it provided persons who were supposed to preserve seclusion with an easily accessible place for the relaxation and exercise which were understood to be necessary to everyone.

For women of quality, gardens must have possessed a peculiar value. When a garden was laid out adjacent to a lady's chamber she could either look out upon or walk out into it without any breach of her seclusion. Few women, we may suppose, were expected to use their gardens as monks or secular intellectuals did, but in his fanciful picture of St Katherine of Alexandria John Capgrave brought all these elements together. The author of an earlier life of Katherine had said that she was left 'at her leisure' to study when she so wished.[83] Giving the word a fuller meaning, Capgrave dwells on the necessity of 'leisure', observing that nature loves variety: 'Somtyme men stodye, sumtyme thei daunce.' Katherine benefited from a change of masters and her palace provided her with a choice of environments in which to work, including her garden:

> The grete gardeyn was the most hir scoole;
> It was fer a-wey from every maner wyght,
> It was made and ordeyned at hir owne devyse.
> There wolde she lye somtyme, stody and wright;
> It was set ful of trees, and that in strong wyse;
> Ther wolde she sitte, there wolde she ryse,
> There was hir walking and alle hir disport –
> Solitary life to stodieres is confort.

Katherine had the only key to this garden and 'Whan she wente in she shet it ful fast'.[84]

For Petrarch, as for the imaginary Katherine, gardens and gardening were not a matter of display but an integral part of the way of life that he chose to adopt. For others, they were doubtless primarily attributes of status, amenities that marked one out as a prosperous householder. The Merchant of Prato, who regretted his expenditure on a pleasure garden, probably fell into this category. A mingled appreciation of their beauty and utility was probably the usual rule, while the metaphorical mode of reference to gardens and their contents was remarkably enduring in a low key. Early in the year 1480 Sir William Stonor was apparently planning a new herb-garden. In a letter written in January William Harleston, a Suffolk gentleman and an uncle of Stonor's late wife, wrote to him, cautioning him against over-expenditure and litigation:

> And, syr, of on thing at is tolde me, that ye do make a fayre newe Garden: in the wiche I pray you for my sake to sette too herbis, the wiche ben, Paciens, Tyme: And that theis to herbis be put in the potage that ye ete, so as ye may ete them daily.

Here the homely English names of two herbs enabled William to achieve a moralistic pun.[85]

In social reality, gardens were among the amenities which the moderately well-off now prized not only for their utility but for their adaptability to the varied purposes of private life. By the fifteenth century, the gardens of the nobility might increasingly be intended to impress but, at least in part, they remained places reserved for the delectation of the owner and his intimates. As space and wealth permitted, this might well mean the division of the garden (as of the house) into spaces which served different purposes, from the more public to the more private and indeed the more utilitarian, in the shape of the kitchen-garden. This diversification implied an increasing awareness of different viewpoints: the view of the garden from the house, of one part of the garden from another, and even of the wider landscape to be obtained from the garden. Such considerations, as we have seen, were not entirely absent from the minds of medieval garden-lovers, but much stronger, or at least more frequently expressed, was the appreciation of the garden as a secluded, even a hidden, place.[86]

12

Loss of Community

In the later fourteenth century William Langland complained that the lords of his day were abandoning charity in favour of 'gayness and gluttony'. They did not break bread with the beggar as Isaiah enjoined and did not hearken to Tobit's words on the obligation to give freely of their wealth. Some behaved like fiddlers or friars, seeking out feasts in other men's homes and avoiding their own. When at home they evaded their duty:

> Elenge is the halle, ech day in the wike,
> Ther the lord ne the lady liketh noght to sitte.
> Now hath ech riche a rule – to eten by hymselve
> In a pryvee parlour for povere mennes sake,
> Or in a chambre with a chymenee, and leve the chief halle
> That was maad for meles, men to eten inne,
> And al to spare to spille that spende shal another.

Presumably the lords in question claimed that they were trying to save money to spend on charity, but the real motive was to save for themselves – pointlessly, for their heirs would squander their inheritance.[1] It has been debated whether this oft-quoted passage should in fact be taken at face value;[2] but even if Langland was right that this was happening in the later fourteenth century, was it a new development?

In principle it had been possible as long as the great possessed private withdrawing rooms. In the middle of the thirteenth century, twenty-eight household regulations, modelled on the *statuta* composed by Robert Grosseteste, bishop of Lincoln, for his own household, were compiled for the recently widowed countess of Lincoln. The twenty-sixth advised: 'Make special efforts to eat as far as possible in the dining hall before your people, except for reason of sickness and fatigue, because you may be sure that from it great benefit and honour will come to you.'[3] The twenty-second lays down the order in which 'your freemen and guests' are to be seated around the hall. Loud noise is to be strictly forbidden and the countess is to be centrally seated at the high table so that she can both see all that goes on and be seen to be doing so. Rule 24 decrees that she is to keep a watch on the serving to ensure that there is no favouritism in the distribution of the food. She herself is to be adequately served so that she 'may courteously give from your dish to right and left to all at high table and to whom else it pleases you that they have of the same as you had in front of you'. Her presence in the hall is designed to ensure both order and sociability. Her contemporary Eleanor, sister to Henry III and wife to Simon de Montfort, earl of Leicester, is known to have been almost always present in the hall.[4]

The regulations end: 'Forbid dinners and suppers outside the hall in hiding-places and in chambers because much waste results from this and no honour to lord or lady.' Early in the fourteenth century the moralist Robert Brunne condemned 'rere sopers in pryvyte', late meals taken after the proper time and in private. These ministered to gluttony (Brunne's ostensible subject) because the perpetrators have already had enough to eat; they meant 'moche waste' and they also led to 'lechery'. There were two sorts of 'rere soper', one indulged in by the lords and ladies themselves, the second by the servants, who, having preserved a sober appearance all day in the presence of their masters, let themselves go when the latter went to bed. Brunne's French-language original condemns only the servants' suppers, recalling the advice to the Countess of Lincoln; his added condemnation of the lords seems to anticipate Langland.[5]

The presence of a great hall in a house, even a newly built one, does not tell us how it was actually used. In some households probably only particularly solemn or sacred occasions were marked by feasts in the hall. At Penshurst Place, built in the 1340s, Sir John Pulteney possessed an impressive hall with a central hearth, but there was nothing to stop him having a dining-table put up in his solar if he chose. Bodiam Castle, built a generation after Penshurst and not much later than Langland wrote, abounded in private apartments.[6] In the south range there was a hall of modest size (about 40 by 24 feet) with a handsome south-facing window adjacent to the dais. It has been suggested that this apartment was intended for the exclusive use of the family and its honoured guests. It had its own kitchen and buttery; another kitchen in the west range served another hall, not much smaller than the lord's, in which it is supposed the rest of the household dined, at some distance from the family party.

If this interpretation is correct, the Great Hall might almost be described as a large dining-room, possibly used for little else. Whether it contained a chimneyed fireplace is uncertain, for the courtyard wall in which it would probably have been placed is missing, but there was a large chamber with a chimney adjacent to it in the east range, which probably served as the principal reception or withdrawing room. Above this room was another, which boasted the largest fireplace in the castle outside the kitchens; this is now designated 'The Lord's Hall'. Both chambers had fine window-seats which would have afforded views out over the moat and landscaped grounds. The chapel was not adjacent to the Great Hall but stood at the northern end of this eastern range, with access from the private apartments. The layout makes it possible at least to imagine the clear social distinctions within the household. Functions that we suppose to have been concentrated in the Great Halls of an earlier epoch were distributed over a number of sizeable rooms distributed throughout the castle; the soldiers of the garrison would doss down not in the Great Hall, but more probably in a large chamber on the first floor over the hall where they dined.

At all times, the semi-public order of the great hall was distinctly graded. In *Piers Plowman*, Imaginatyf declares that he has enough to eat, although he does not receive as much honour as they that sit at the side tables or at the high table but sits like a beggar, 'boardless', on the floor. In another passage, the poet's *alter ego* Will is seated with Patience, Clergy and Conscience at a side table while a great doctor does himself rather well 'on the heighe deis'.[7] Halls of varying dimensions continued to be built in England into the sixteenth century, and a study of their measurements reveals a tendency for them to get longer and relatively narrower. This, it has been commented, may reflect a trend towards 'social separatism', which could be just as graphically demonstrated by a sharply differentiated seating arrangement within the same room as by the lord's withdrawal into a separate apartment.[8] A similar alteration in the proportions of halls has been noticed in Italian bishops' palaces at an earlier date.[9]

In the fifteenth century John Russell, who describes himself as having been 'uschere in chambur' and 'mershalle also in halle' to a 'prynce full royalle', that is, Henry V's brother Humphrey duke of Gloucester, gives detailed instructions for allocating the several ranks of society to their proper places in the hall. Pope, emperor, king, cardinal, royal prince, archbishop or duke ought not to be there at all: for them, 'private' dining was the rule. Systematically working downwards, Russell distinguishes five groupings which together embrace everyone from bishops and earls on the highest level to esquires on the lowest. For example, the mayor of London, a baron, a mitred abbot, the three chief justices and the Speaker of the House of Commons may fitly be placed 'in Chambur or halle' at a single table, two or three to a 'mess' (a serving dish or place setting) if they be agreeable. Among those entitled to sit at a squire's table are preachers, parsons, merchants and franklins. Each of these five Estates 'syngularly in halle shalle sit downe', so that none of them sees the others 'at mete tyme'.[10] Russell had moved in exalted circles. The existence of the great hall in the house of a great man might for Langland evoke images of community and hospitality, but Russell implies sharp discrimination of rank.

If there was a desire for privacy, and perhaps also for a greater degree of intimacy and comfort, at the table, it was certainly not confined to England. In 1388 Langland's contemporary Giovanni de' Mussi recorded for posterity his impressions of the condition of his city, Piacenza in northern Italy.[11] He located his description in an historical perspective, gleaning information about Italian customs in the thirteenth century from an earlier chronicler, Riccobaldo da Ferrara (d. 1297). He thus obtained the impression 'that in the year 1241, in the time of the Emperor Frederick II, people in Italy were uncouth in their habits and customs'. Giovanni also referred to what he believed to have been the state of things before

1320. He was clearly convinced that there had been a real recent change, a marked increase in affluence and display. In earlier times,

> at dinner a man and his wife ate from one dish. Wooden knives were used at table. There were one or two drinking cups to a household. Those who dined at night lit the tables with torches, held by a boy or a servant, for candles of tallow or wax were not used.

Recent changes had affected what was eaten and drunk as well as the setting. Giovanni is informative on matters of diet, commenting on the extensive use of spices, almonds, rice and sugar at upper-class tables in Piacenza, but special interest attaches to what he has to say about the domestic surroundings of this moneyed class:

> The men of Piacenza at the present time live splendidly and with style and polish, and they use in their houses finer and better utensils and fittings than they used to up to seventy years ago, that is before the year 1320, and they have finer dwellings than they had then. In these houses there are for the most part beautiful rooms and fireplaces, conduits, courtyards, wells, gardens and kitchen-gardens and solars; and there are several chimneys for fire and smoke in one house, where there used to be no chimney in these houses at that time, because then they used to make one fire in the middle of the house under the apex of the roof, and all the members of the household used to stand about that fire, and there they used to do the cooking. And I've seen it in my time in several houses. And they didn't have wells in those houses, or very few, and few solars and courtyards. And all the citizens of Piacenza have better wines than the men of old. The mode of eating of the greater part of the Piacentines is that the master of the household with his wife and children eats at the first table near the fireplace, or in a room with a fire, and the household eats after them elsewhere, by another fire, or, usually, in the kitchen.

Giovanni refers again to the new prevalence of fireplaces:

> And many have two fires, one in the fireplace and one in the kitchen, or in a chamber with a fireplace. And many people have fine sugar and honey confectionery in their homes. All of which costs a lot.

Like Langland, Giovanni regarded it as a contemporary trend for the master's family to eat by themselves in a private apartment that was now made more comfortable by a chimneyed fireplace; but whereas Langland seems to have believed that the retreat from the great hall was motivated by the desire to save money, Giovanni sees the withdrawal into a family dining-room as the by-product of a competition to display wealth. Their common focus on dining habits is noteworthy. It was neither surprising nor novel that the social elite should have private sleeping accommodation (or for that matter comfortable sitting-rooms), but the fact that they no longer dined in company with the entire household excited remark in these two very different societies.

Giovanni's tone seems less sharply critical than Langland's, perhaps because the urban patricians of Italy did not have the traditional, inherited duty which Langland believed that his 'lords' had to their neighbours and retainers and to the poor. There was some room for argument about the social obligations of the wealthy layman and the degree to which he should keep open house and share his life with his inferiors. Different questions were raised by those individuals who chose to live an informal version of the religious life while remaining in the world or at least on its margins. Some of these individuals eschewed matrimony, which was commonly seen as the social duty of the lay person. Were such persons disguising self-absorption as devotion to God and failing in their obligations to their fellow man?

Having displayed his unfitness for a business career, Pilingotto of Urbino settled into a quasi-eremitical life in his parents' home. One day when his father and mother 'were sitting eating at the table together with the entire household, this glorious servant of God began to consider that it was not enough for him to live for himself if Christ's poor were dying of hunger'. Calling to mind a certain poor man in the neighbourhood who was perishing of want and hunger, he acted on his newly felt charitable inclinations. Pilingotto thus remembered the cautionary words of Christ, reported by St Matthew: 'What you have done for the least ... you have done for me.'[12]

It is notable that Pilingotto's conscience was pricked at the dinner table where his parents sat with the whole household. Catherine of Siena, a greater saint, trod a similar moral path on the instructions of Christ Himself. For Raymond of Capua, ingeniously interpreting the words of the Bridegroom in the *Song of Songs*, 'Open to me, my sister, my love', she was called upon by Christ to open not her own door (which was already open to the Lord) but 'the door of other souls'. The process began, after her mystical marriage with Christ, with her reintegration into the community of the family. Christ would sometimes say to her, 'Go, it is dinner time, and the rest of the family are about to sit down at table; go and be with them, and then come back to me'.[13] Catherine bitterly lamented this command, but the Lord carried His point. His intention was to fit her for a more active life of service to her neighbour; so Catherine joined the family at table, and as Christ assisted her 'in the art of being on easy terms with people' she began to involve herself more in the life of the household, beginning with housework. The next phase was practical charity to the poor and to the sick. As Catherine enlarged the sphere of her activities in obedience to the divine command, so Christ rewarded her by coming to her not only 'privately as He had done at first, but in public too'.[14]

While Catherine was in Siena, her 'cell' remained the refuge to which she retreated to pour out ardent prayers for heavenly assistance or for mercy on the afflicted. For the friars of her adopted order, the private formation and discipline of the individual soul was intended to lead to apostolic activity in the service of souls, which in its turn drew strength and refreshment from periods of study and contemplation. In her role as counsellor to the brethren, as to the church at large, Catherine insisted upon the links which bound the individual friar in his cell to the community and to the world. Towards the end of the *Dialogue* she speaks in Christ's voice of the contrast between 'obedient' and 'disobedient' brothers. The obedient 'make a heaven of their cell and find their pleasure in speaking and keeping company with me'. At the same time, they 'want to be the first to enter choir and the last to leave' and are stricken by 'holy envy' if they perceive that another is more obedient than they.

Commensality is an important ingredient in this obedience. 'The obedient never eat elsewhere than in the refectory but are regular in their presence there and take pleasure in being at table with the poor.'[15] The disobedient, naturally, are the reverse:

> They avoid their cell as if it were poison. They fell into disobedience when they left the cell of self-knowledge; therefore they cannot stand their material cell. As for the refectory, they would no more appear there than with their enemies so long as they have anything to spend, but if they have nothing to spend, necessity brings them there.

It follows that they are hoarders of private property and slack both in public and in mental prayer.[16] Catherine had herself learned to balance the demands of the cell and the community, but it was a problem for all those who embraced the religious life. In an encyclical letter of 1233, very early in the order's history, Jordan of Saxony accused many Dominicans of being careless in their attention to their studies, rarely in their cells and lukewarm in their exercises.[17] One has here to allow for the perennial religious tendency to indulge in pessimistic rhetoric about declining fervour, but difficulty in mustering the concentration and self-discipline to make proper use of one's cell was doubtless a psychological reality.

At the General Chapter in 1315 it was stated that there were sometimes insufficient cells to go round and students found themselves either waiting a long time for a cell or forced to move from one to another, to the great detriment of their studies. The conventual authorities were directed to provide sufficient cells and to reserve some of the best or at least of middling quality for the use of students, ensuring that they were not occupied by others. If they were so occupied when students were absent, they were to be yielded up on their return. Cells were to be allocated to other brothers, and also to students, according to the length of time they had been in the convent.[18] On the one hand the principle that separate accommodation was allocated according to need and function was theoretically upheld; on the other, it is clear that there was considerable pressure to make a cell a universal prerogative. In 1326 the General Chapter rejected this demand, declaring it was 'strictly forbidden' for *camerae* to be conceded to the brethren in general (*passim*) unless they were 'distinguished brothers to whom they may not fittingly be denied'. Those who had them were not to eat in them unless they were sick.

The authorities continued to try to resist pressures which threatened the total decay of the common life of dormitory and even refectory. In 1331 superiors were urged to take steps to reduce the impact of grants of *camerae* on the 'uniformity' of the order's observance 'in the common dormitory', while in 1335 it was complained that the trend away from eating in the refectory was being led by the principal conventual officers. In 1340 superiors were urged to be sparing in their dispensations to *lectores* to absent themselves from refectory or choir, and in the following year there were laments about the 'disordering of religion' which followed on the possession of rooms outside the dormitory. The 1341 chapter also sought to compel attendance at what it termed the 'devout sequel to compline', when the brethren gathered together for prayer and the singing of the *Salve Regina*. This induced 'great remembrance of souls' and rendered the individual more disposed to 'the things that are God's', in devotion and study, by day and night.[19]

Gradually the ground shifted. After the middle of the century the Dominicans, like other religious orders, felt the impact of plague on their existing numbers and on recruitment, which may indirectly have made it more difficult not to give people what they wanted. Eating remained a pivotal issue. Officially there were four legitimate eating-places in a convent: the refectory, guesthouse, infirmary and the *recreatorium* where the brethren recovered from bleeding. The General Chapter tried repeatedly to outlaw eating in other places, the wholesale granting of *camerae* and exemptions from attendance at refectory and choir. In 1353 it forbade any brother, 'even if he be a master of theology', to have *more than one* 'cell or chamber in the convent where he normally resides'. In 1370 the possession of 'two habitations' in a convent was again prohibited and also the employment of servants at the convent's expense; here (as so often) the possession of a superior dignity (regent master in a *studium generale*, inquisitor or procurator of the order) permitted exceptions.[20]

The decisions of the General Chapter in 1359 include a reference to *camerae* outside the dormitory which had been provided by individual brethren at their own expense. Still it was supposed to be impermissible for a healthy friar to have such a room unless he held one of a number of high offices, had completed fifty years in the order or was otherwise judged by the provincial to be a *frater emeritus*. Things had moved on by 1376, when the General Chapter, ostensibly revoking all previous concessions of rooms outside the dormitory, not only made the usual exceptions for high-ranking officers but excepted grants 'made to those brothers who have built them at their own expense and cost'. The reasoning might well have been that a dead brother could not take his room with him and that therefore his investment, even if self-interested, in the long run represented a benefaction to the convent. In 1378 this provision was repeated almost word for word, with the additional directive that all who possessed *camerae* within the dormitory were within fifteen days to take steps to block up any exits by which they could get out of the dormitory when it was supposed to be closed for the night, on pain of deprivation of the cell itself and of any goods which the order might have conferred on them. On the same occasion a renewed attempt was made to enforce eating in the refectory at least two or three times a week: senior office-holders were exhorted to do so at least once.[21]

The issues were established, as was the trend of reality. When in 1413 the Master General drew up ordinances for a Galician house he found a total absence of provision for the common life: there was no infirmary, no clothes store and no library. Observing tartly that 'there are many rooms here for individual brothers', the Master earmarked the next two of these to fall vacant for communal purposes. He tried to enforce sleeping in the dormitory, to bar women from private rooms and the dormitory alike, and somewhat despairingly commanded that henceforth 'the merits of the brothers should be considered more than money in the concession of rooms'.[22] At the General Chapters of 1428 and 1456 there were further efforts to prohibit eating in private rooms. The 1428 chapter reaffirmed a principle which nobody would have denied but few, it seemed, acted upon: 'Since according to our Rule we are bound to live as one (*unanimes*) in the house, so it must be that we sit together at the table.'[23]

The problems of the Dominicans were, to a very great degree, the problems of the religious life in general in the later middle ages. Monk and nun, regular canon and friar were all supposed to lead some version of the common life. The basic principles had been laid down in a very different age and society. Reformers might be prompted or influenced by contemporary circumstances, but they were bound to aim at the refurbishment of the ancient model, if only because there was no way of imagining or introducing a totally new one. This in itself can arguably be seen as one of the principal problems of late medieval monasticism.

The Carthusians were exceptional in that they spent much of their time in genuine solitude. The order was not without its late medieval problems, but its reputation and the flurry of new foundations which took place in the decades just before and after 1400 suggest that a monastic institute which imposed a visibly complete solitude on its members carried conviction with patrons, recruits and the pious public alike. Several York testators in the fifteenth century left bequests to the 'enclosed monks' (*monachis inclusis*) of Mount Grace and Hull; the phrase might seem tautological, given that all monks were meant to be enclosed, but may also reflect the perception of a distinctive way of life.[24] The Carthusians did offer something distinctive to their recruits: 'What hardship silence imposed, this amount of space must have compensated any monk. Space to oneself was a very rare comfort in the middle ages.'[25] Other monks (and nuns), however, were helping themselves to private space, with or without the silence.

Perhaps too many people were trying to lead the religious life, but it was as big a problem that they were spread among too many houses. Many orders and individual convents suffered severe losses of personnel, especially after the plague years of the later fourteenth century, and there can be little question that it was difficult to maintain a meaningful common life in a small and impoverished house. If numbers were large, however, how could monks sleep in a single dormitory or dine in a single refectory if these apartments, sometimes now very old, required repairs for which there was no money? Monks and nuns, furthermore, were as reluctant as anybody to move far from their natal soil and the reports of monastic visitations in England not infrequently reveal the close contacts they still had with their relatives. Every religious community also had (and indeed needed) patrons and benefactors among the laity, who were hard to repel if they came visiting or wanted to deposit a boarder or paying guest on the convent. These had always been facts of the religious life; the exclusion of the laity from the cloister had rarely been perfect or complete. It remained true, however, that the quality of the monk's or nun's prayers, and thus his or her value to society, were believed to depend on a way of life that differed from that of the common man.

The Benedictines discovered, as the Dominicans had done, that making provision for study could bring problems in its train, but this was only one element in a process which over a period of centuries introduced privilege and differentiation into the cloister. The tendency is discernible also among nuns, who did not usually enjoy special facilities for learning. It gathered momentum in the fourteenth and fifteenth centuries, but it was not new or sudden. Just as lords and ladies were able, if they wished, to withdraw from the society of the great hall for centuries before Langland complained about it, so the possibility had existed for a long time, at least for senior monks and office-holders.[26] The fact that the monks were pioneers in the provision of domestic amenities, such as running water and drainage, further complicates the problem of deciding whether the impulse towards a greater degree of comfort and privacy originated within the cloister or outside it in the society inhabited by the parents, brothers, sisters and cousins of monks and nuns.[27]

If then there were external pressures on monasticism in the later middle ages they cooperated with solvents at work within, many of which were far from new. To what extent could, should or did the abbot share in the common life? There is an instructive exchange in a polemical dialogue on the respective claims of the Cistercian and Cluniac monks, written around 1155 by a German Cistercian (and former Cluniac), Idung of Prüfenung. The Cistercian speaker declares that every day Cluniac abbots

> teach violation of the Rule because they have their table in the refectory with the brethren, whereas according to the precepts of the Rule abbots should always eat in the guest house with guests and travellers.

The Cluniac's contention that it is 'a mark of great monastic demeanor for the abbot to dine in refectory with the brethren' might seem unimpeachable, but the point is not conceded: no abbot has the power to pass judgement on the sacred Rule and the Rule itself is justified, should justification be required, because it gives priority to the demands of hospitality. The Cistercian admits no excuses: the abbot cannot argue that he wants to avoid 'silly women' in the guest-house, for the answer to that is not to receive women in the monastic enclosure at all. He is inclined to suspect that the real reason for the Cluniac custom is to save money and at the same time improve the menu for the monks in the refectory. Thus the Rule itself was invoked to justify the abbot's detachment from the common table, which it was the sacred obligation of the rest of the community to share.[28]

In theory, the abbot was not exempted from the other requirements of the common life. Late in the thirteenth century English abbots and priors were urged to show themselves 'in the cloister to hear confessions and instruct the brethren by example, in choir for the divine office and in the refectory for the sake of fraternal consolation'.[29] After all, there might not always be guests. Specific responsibilities within the monastery always, however, tended to confer various privileges on the holder, including the possession of office-space which could potentially be treated as a private sanctum. The existence of 'chambers' which could be used as private retreats was a fact by the early thirteenth century. Reviewing contemporary religious life around the year 1220, Gerald of Wales declared that, by contrast with the Cluniacs, the Cistercians publicly denied 'fatted meats (*saginata*)' both to themselves and their guests, 'but in private, that is in their infirmaries and chambers ... they feed voraciously'on them. He tells of a priest who was a near neighbour and benefactor of a house near Hereford where he ate (poorly) one day. Wandering around the monastery after the meal, he came 'to a certain inner room' which he entered by the open door, only to find the abbot and a company of monks devouring fat meats, capons and ducks with all the trimmings and drinking good ale and mead out of silver cups; everything was of the best.[30]

Gerald's thrust here was primarily against Cistercian hypocrisy in matters of diet, but the story hints at other problems. The physical act of withdrawal from refectory or dormitory into private apartments carried with it the threat that factions might form among the community, that the abbot or other senior officers might show partiality by inviting some but not others to these private parties. There was another internal weak point. It had always been recognized that the sick monk required not only special accommodation but a more generous diet. Gerald accused the Cistercians of secret indulgence not only in their 'chambers' but in their infirmaries: 'not only when they are being bled or in bad health, but as often as it seems opportune ... they pretend they need bleeding or medication'. It would have been surprising if this idea had occurred only to Cistercians. It was also affirmed in the thirteenth century that the sick must be treated in the infirmary and not 'in separate rooms', although the abbot could at need invite them to his chamber where (it could be assumed) they would get better and more lavish treatment.[31] In 1343 the English Benedictines ruled that no sick monk should presume to have a special servant attending to his wants.[32]

The infirmary carried with it another threat: to silence. The general chapter of the English Augustinian canons which was held at St Frideswide's in Oxford in 1234 attempted to outlaw the practice of lingering in the infirmary to chat with the inmates, 'for lengthy sitting around or conversation in the infirmary or elsewhere is often a cause of contention and dissolution'. All those who were sleeping in the regular dormitory were to be present at the common meal and at compline and then go to sleep in an orderly fashion with the rest of the community; the sick who were for the time being 'lying in the infirmary' were similarly to prepare themselves for bed after the meal so that they too could proceed to say compline without delay.[33] In the course of time partitions, which were intended to give the sick greater peace and comfort, were introduced into many monastic infirmaries. In itself this was a recognition of need which paralleled the development of spaces for study. These were issues on which the Benedictine Rule had nothing specific to say. Unfortunately, the physical modification of the infirmary space seems to have encouraged its appropriation as a suite of private lodgings, complete with a kitchen which provided better food for the hale and hearty than for the infirm.

By the time that the Cistercian Pope Benedict XII issued his Constitutions for the Black Monks in 1337, he was evidently forced to assume a certain degree of disintegration. Having begun a chapter 'on eating and abstaining from flesh' by establishing what the meatless days of the year were, he declared, 'On those days on which the monks in the infirmary eat meat, let it be required that at least half of the monks remain in the refectory.' The same was to apply when the abbot or other principal officer of the convent invited certain monks to their lodgings or chambers. When a number of monks were eating flesh together in the infirmary, there was to be reading and the preservation of silence. The abbot and other officers were to be careful not to invite to their table any secular person whose presence was likely to lead to unfavourable comment on themselves or on the order. The pope also laid it down that all the monks, or at least the greater number of them, should sleep together in the same *domus*, as rule and tradition required, 'and not in separate chambers or cells'. There were numerous permissible exceptions, however: those who were permitted to rest in 'the chambers or cells of the infirmary' because of old age or bodily weakness and also those who were exempted 'for other reasonable cause according to the disposition of the abbot or other official' or because of the requirements of their own position.[34] The abbot's discretion, which was doubtless often both a necessary and a benign force, was also distinctly two-edged and abbots were inclined to be prickly in their insistence upon it.

This was demonstrated when Henry V convened an extraordinary meeting of the English Benedictines at Westminster in May 1421 to respond to charges of laxity that had been voiced by the Carthusian prior of Mount Grace, once himself a Benedictine. The prior's former co-religionists were meant to live a life which differed in significant respects from the one he had now chosen to embrace, but surely they should keep their own Rule. The tenth of 'the King's Articles' accordingly proposed that 'no monk should have a distinct or separate cell or chamber'. Part of the purpose of this was to prevent the introduction of women (even mothers and sisters) into such private quarters. It was also proposed that all monks should sleep in the dormitory.

To the ban on private rooms the Benedictines responded that the provincial constitutions permitted the allocation of individual rooms at the all-important discretion of the abbot. Even more to the present point

> It does not seem agreeable to reason that doctors after their studious exertions should not have private chambers appropriate to their rank, that scholars too, occupied about sermons, should not be in separate rooms and that officials should be deprived of separate or private rooms in which to keep the things necessary to them.

The abbots were prepared to accept the exclusion of women but, on the subject of sleeping in the dormitory, they wished exceptions to be made for monastic superiors and their chaplains, other officials and also *doctores*; they also insisted on their historic discretionary powers.[35] At Westminster by the fifteenth century, it has been calculated that about 66 per cent of the entire community were exempted from the everyday round of services, which were sustained by the remainder. Not all of the former group occupied private chambers, however, the number who did so being estimated at around 45 per cent of the total number of monks.[36]

When in 1339 Benedict XII turned his attention to the Augustinian canons he echoed many of his provisions for the Benedictines. He had conceded to the monks that cells might be provided for students adjacent to the dormitory, for study and not for sleeping. Now he ruled that the canons were henceforth not to create cells in their dormitories, and where they already existed they were to be opened up at the front so that the inhabitant was open to inspection from without.[37] In 1343 the English Benedictines, invoking the pope's Constitutions, added that the monks' beds were not to be concealed behind curtains (the Dominicans, as we have seen, addressed the same issue). Some twenty years later visitors were enjoined to enquire whether all monks were sleeping together in one *domus*, the young among the old, with a light continually burning, and whether there were cells or curtains to prevent the monks being seen by the guardians of the order or other passers-by.[38]

The answers to these questions may well have been dispiriting, for the problems were already well established among monks and canons alike. In the 1330s and 1340s Bishop Grandisson of Exeter found a great deal to criticize among the Augustinians of his diocese. The issues that he identified included many hardy perennials: private property, private rooms, private eating, and the failure of superiors to participate in the common life, to impose discipline and to manage their resources. The troubles of Launceston Priory occupied the bishop over a period of years from 1330, and in 1346 he addressed a comprehensive set of injunctions to the new prior, Thomas.[39] Thomas was to make every effort to be in the company of his fellow-canons whenever it was possible, in church by day and night, in chapter, in the cloister, the refectory and the dormitory, teaching them by example to live according to their profession. The canons were to 'live together in one house, and let there be among them one heart and one soul in God'; there was to be no private property and no separate rooms, with the inevitable exceptions for 'those who hold certain duties and offices according to your direction'. In particular the prior was to forbid the possession of cupboards or chests 'in which foodstuffs or beverages have been up to now on any pretext hidden'. The canons were also to be forbidden the distracting possession of horses, dogs, servants, individual herb gardens, dovecotes or anything else of the kind.

It might at first seem surprising that Grandisson was concerned with the concealment of edibles rather than of valuables, but a later passage sheds further light. Thomas was to see that none of the canons sent any food or drink to anyone outside the convent. A god-fearing member of the community, 'a zealot for the poor', was to be appointed almoner and was to be present, personally or by a fit deputy, every day in the refectory at both the midday and evening meals to collect all the leftovers, except any that were to be rehashed for the evening, and allocate them to the poor. One reason for preventing monks or canons from withdrawing into private dining was therefore the effort to guarantee that their surplus was channelled to the needy, an aspect of their duty to the wider community and closely allied to their duty of hospitality.

Communal eating was also quite simply seen as basic to the maintenance of the common life, as well as helping to avoid waste and expense. In 1340 Grandisson exhorted the prior of Frithelstock both to sleep with his canons in the dormitory and to eat with them *in communi refectorio*, and not to maintain a separate hall or refectory for himself or for guests, of whatever rank they might be. The canons were no longer to receive money for clothing or food but to rest content with 'one kitchen' and with what was administered to them according to their needs.[40] Separate rooms were clearly ineradicable, but Grandisson continued to proclaim the ideal, remarking after a visitation of Bodmin Priory in 1346 that 'separate chambers among religious are often productive of dissolution' and that he desired the canons to live in common (*conversari et vivere in communi*) 'so that each one of you may be a witness to the life of the next'.[41] In the same diocese, Bishop Brantyngham in 1373 instructed the monks of Tavistock to give up 'the chambers you have hitherto used'; at least two-thirds of the community were to eat together daily in the refectory.[42]

The visitations carried out between 1420 and 1449 by three bishops of Lincoln, Richard Flemyng, William Gray and William Alnwick, provide a representative anthology of *gravamina* which give insight into the shape that these and other problems had assumed, in one large English diocese, a century after Grandisson's laments and a century before the Dissolution. The bishops' remit included

Benedictine houses which did not enjoy exemption, the Augustinian canons and nuns of all orders including Cistercians. A visitation in itself provided an opportunity for backbiting and troublemaking, and predictably sometimes produced allegations of gross scandal. More interesting is what is revealed about the mundane and seemingly intractable difficulties that beset the attempt to lead a viable community life which retained its distinctiveness from 'the world'. There is evidence of both external intrusion and internal division, formally distinguishable but in practice often experienced simultaneously and inextricably. Incompetence in the management of conventual property and failure to provide or maintain adequate facilities might be regarded as issues of a somewhat different order, but they too had a bearing on the ability of the religious to lead the life that some of them at least felt that they should be leading.

There were numerous complaints that an abbot, prior or prioress did not sleep in the common dormitory or, worse, failed to come regularly to choir. That he or she should keep a separate table was taken for granted, and as we have seen had the warrant of the Benedictine Rule, but it could nonetheless create problems and divisions. One brother of St James Northampton alleged that the abbot was not impartial in his invitations to the table in his chamber or his hall: one individual would be asked two or three times, others often.[43] There is a hint of something similar in Bishop Flemyng's injunction to the abbess of Elstow that she 'should invite to eat with her those nuns whom she knows to be most in need of recreation'.[44] Another problem was that a superior might invite members of the community to his or her table, only for the latter to find themselves unwillingly exposed to the presence of secular guests; the subprioress of Nuncoton asked in 1440 that no nun should be compelled to accept such an invitation.[45]

The bishops seem not to have been unduly disturbed when they discovered the existence of three 'households', as the groupings which ate together were known. There was usually one in the regular refectory, one in the abbot's hall or chamber, and a third who were being bled and therefore were permitted meat. Less acceptable were the further multiplication of *familiae*, the intrusion of outsiders into the refectory and illicit drinking or supper-parties after compline, the religious equivalent of the 'privy suppers' Robert Brunne criticized. Bishop Flemyng complained of such gatherings 'in private rooms and other places within the priory' when he visited St Frideswide's at Oxford in January 1423.[46] His successor Gray (1431–36) similarly deplored *potaciones aut comesaciones* in several houses including Bardney, Canons Ashby, Dunstable and Eynsham, sometimes accompanied by games and late-night or even all-night parties.[47] Given that the monk or canon was supposed to go to bed promptly after compline, these goings-on infringed the rules about both eating and sleeping; at Bardney Gray specifically insisted that the brethren were to complete their business and return to the cloister to sleep 'in the dormitory and by no means in private rooms'.

St Neot's exemplified another problem, which Gray noted when he visited the priory some time after Michaelmas in 1432. He left instructions that until a fit place was provided for 'servants and other secular persons to eat in', and unless there were guests of some standing, the monks, together with the prior, were to use the hall adjacent to the prior's chamber as their refectory, preserving proper observance by singing grace both before and after the meal.[48] The problem had not been solved by the time Alnwick came to St Neot's in 1439. One brother then testified that

> there is no place serving as a refectory where the monks eating together can possibly observe religion; where they now eat was once ordained as the refectory but secular outsiders sit in it, and the monastery servants, at the times of the monks' meals.

There could be no reading at meals or 'contemplation in the cloister' because of the constant presence of layfolk, including women.[49]

This deponent seems to have felt that it was the intrusion of the outside world rather than the internal divisions of the community that threatened 'religion'. In c. 38 of the Rule, St Benedict required that there should unfailingly be reading during meals, heard in *summum silentium*. Mealtimes therefore were occasions not only for fellowship but for edification and the continuing discipline of the silence in which the monk single-mindedly concentrated on the things of the spirit. At Newnham Priory in 1442 Alnwick commanded that seculars, 'however respectable', servants and workmen were to be excluded from the refectory, for it was manifestly absurd that they should be present at a time and place when regulars listened to reading in silence. The refectory, he repeated, was 'a place in which regular observances must be observed'. Reversing Gray's earlier solution, he directed that the prior must arrange for servants and workmen to be fed either in a place specially appointed for the purpose or in his own hall; honoured guests, similarly, were to be entertained in either his hall or his chamber. At Kyme Priory in 1440 he added the subtle variation that the prior must exclude secular persons from the refectory and from his own hall when members of the community were dining in it, 'with the exception of your own table': the prior, that is to say, could entertain outsiders at the 'high table' in his hall but should not expect his canons to mix with them.[50]

At Ramsey Abbey in 1439 Bishop Alnwick discovered a great deal that was typical.[51] He commented on the prevalence of eating 'in several private and out of the way places (*in plerisque locis privatis et latebris*)' and sleeping 'not in the dormitory but apart in separate rooms'. The bishop was told by the prior, John Styneck, that 'religion' was greatly harmed by the 'plurality of eating places'; furthermore, the abbey's resources (*temporalia*) were wasted on foodstuffs. Another monk deposed that when he had received the tonsure there were only three *domicilia* in the monastery: the *camera abbatis*, the refectory and the *aula minucionum* (the misericord, the apartment where the monks were bled). He echoed the prior's opinion that the community was damaged both spiritually and materially by the multiplication of such *domicilia*.

In the course of his enquiries at Ramsey Alnwick made notes of what he was going to demand. One-third of the community was always to eat in the frater (that is, the refectory) under the direction of a 'president'; all were to go to the dormitory after compline, not emerging until seven o'clock the next morning. 'The due hours of contemplation were to be daily observed according to the Rule in the cloister', which was not currently happening; eating was to take place only in the abbot's hall or chamber, the refectory and the *aula minucionum*. The bishop accepted that the whole community would not eat together and required only that the situation that had obtained some years previously should be restored. Finally, the sick should have more delicate foods, not the beef, bacon and other indigestible salt meats that they complained of.

This repeated emphasis on feeding arrangements seems to reveal a guilty awareness that something fundamental to the religious life was being violated. Deponents were sometimes keen to give the impression that they were more or less keeping the rules, but contradicted one another on the details. At the nunnery of St Michael, Stamford, in 1440 the prioress testified that the community ate together in the refectory on fish days and otherwise in her 'common hall', except that the sub-prioress, Agnes Multone, ate in her own 'hall' together with Margaret Croyland and a novice, Margery Morwood. Dame Elizabeth Willoughby said that they ate in the frater on Wednesdays, Fridays and Saturdays (all fish days) but that they had been unable to do so lately because there were cracks in it. Another nun, however, said that frater was kept only in Advent and Lent. Agnes Multone testified that they all slept together in the dormitory except for the prioress, who kept her own chamber; she also said that the prioress had seven or eight children under twelve at board for their education. The most scandalous item in an otherwise pedestrian catalogue of infringements was that Agnes Butifer had eloped with a lute-player called Robert Abbot and was living in Newcastle upon Tyne.

Alnwick directed that the subprioress's miniature *familia* was to be disbanded; it appeared that that of the prioress consisted of only five people. He further insisted that frater was to be kept, with reading, on all Wednesdays, Fridays and Saturdays and throughout Lent and Advent. When he returned to Stamford in 1442 Elizabeth Willoughby claimed that he had dispensed her from lying in the dorter or eating in the frater because she was unwell, which he totally denied. He now got to know about secular persons other than the schoolchildren who had been dwelling in the precinct. One Richard Gray, while a lodger there with his wife, had begotten a child upon none other than Elizabeth Willoughby; he got a penitential pilgrimage for his trouble. By August 1445, another nun, Margaret Mortymere, had conceived and given birth, which had entailed her absence from choir for a fortnight.[52]

It is easy to focus on the scandals. It is as much to the point to note the mundane issues which lie behind them: the apparently very small size of the community, which still tended to resolve into little sub-groupings, and its openness to the outside world, whether in the form of the child-boarders or of the troublesome Richard Gray. Multiple small *familiae* seem to have been characteristic of nunneries. Dame Rose Waldegrave, abbess of Elstow, told Alnwick that there were five *familiae* in the house, consisting of herself and five nuns; the prioress plus two; the sub-prioress plus two; the sacristan plus three; and Margaret Aylesbury plus two. Here the boys taught by the nuns sometimes attended mass in the choir and made a noise.[53] When Alnwick visited Stixwould Priory, a Cistercian nunnery, in 1440, he discovered again five distinct households: two widows, with their serving-maids, lodged with the prioress, the cellaress had two female lodgers, and there were numerous children of both sexes lodging with various nuns.[54] At Nuncoton, also in 1440, the prioress said that there were too many serving women and that secular persons lay in the dormitory. For eating purposes the community followed the standard division between the *aula priorisse*, the regular refectory and the lower frater where the nuns who were being bled were served meat.[55] At Langley Priory the bishop was told that there were 'only' seven secular servants in the house, but Lady Audley lodged there with twelve dogs which followed her to church and interrupted the psalm-singing.[56]

Male communities were naturally not exempt from these intrusions and divisions or from grosser scandals. The most troublesome invaders were often layfolk who, either as lodgers or as servants of the community, managed to insinuate themselves into the precinct, like William Marmyone, the farmer of the monastic warren, who occupied a chamber within the cloister at Dorchester Abbey. When he was in occupation the gates of the cloister were left open, permitting free access to other outsiders. Marmyone may have been symptomatic but he was not Dorchester's only problem. Alnwick's 1441 visitation produced an unusually large crop of accusations of sexual irregularities. Thomas Tewkesbury had appropriated a room to himself to which there was a 'concourse' not only of women (notably one Margaret Heny who seems to have been effectively living in) but of the canons, who foregathered there after the midday meal and also after compline, to play chess and do 'other things which are dishonourable'.[57] When Alnwick paid a return visit in 1445 another source of trouble was brought to his notice, the presence of the former abbot John Clifton, who had a room in the abbey with many suspect exits and entrances, notably one which gave on to a garden on the north. Clifton had to purge himself of accusations concerning a woman called Margaret Tyler.[58]

This was not a unique instance. There were no retirement homes for superannuated or insane monks except the monasteries themselves, and it was commonplace for a retired abbot like Clifton to be assigned lodgings in the house he had once ruled. In 1420 Bishop Flemyng gave detailed instructions for the accommodation and amenities that John, lately prior of Daventry, was to enjoy in 'a certain chamber called the Oriel', which evidently overlooked the cloister. It was to be a gentlemanly retirement: the bishop gave consideration to the furniture, utensils, fuel, straw, bread, beer, meat and money allowance that John should have. He took the precaution of insisting that his lodging should be open only towards the cloister and not to the outside world; John was to introduce no woman, except his sister, and no secular folk. He continued to attend chapter, for he was enjoined not to reveal any of the convent's secrets.[59]

Whether the presence of a former abbot was invariably welcome or helpful to his successor may be open to doubt, particularly when he had been not simply retired but stripped of office. In 1353 William of Dryinghowe, the Cistercian abbot of Meaux in East Yorkshire, was deposed and assigned a chamber in the abbey, the food allowance of two monks, food for a servant and an annual pension of five marks for life. After an ugly series of disputes with his successor, John Rysley, who was himself deposed for financial irregularities, William was prevailed upon to drop the lawsuit he had initiated and to come back to the monastery on even more generous terms, which included emancipation from all monastic obligations. He might come and go with his servant as he pleased (as long as he came back at night), speak with any secular person within the monastic precinct and have the right to a horse from the abbot's stable for himself and another 'honourable person', should he wish to ride out; he was to rank second after the abbot in choir, chapter and elsewhere.[60] This was perhaps an extreme case, but it is hard to see how the life of the community can have benefited from these goings-on; Lady Audley's dogs can scarcely have been more troublesome.

A retired abbot or indeed a lay notable who could afford to pay for his or her keep might well lead a comfortable life within the precinct, but the treatment of the ordinary sick brother or sister might be a different matter. The two issues were not unconnected, for there are indications that the infirmary space was being allocated either to healthy monks or to outsiders. The connection was all but explicit, as far as Bishop Flemyng was concerned, when he visited St Frideswide's at Oxford in 1423. He directed that no secular person was henceforth to be accommodated in the infirmary and also that 'no canon should henceforth have a separate or individual chamber assigned to him in the infirmary, unless he is broken by such sickness, old age or infirmity'. A befitting *domus* was to be provided forthwith for *seculares* (whether sick layfolk who needed nursing or mere guests is not entirely clear).[61] One wonders how often houses were able to afford the building or repair works which visiting bishops judged necessary to their spiritual health.

In January of the previous year Flemyng had visited Huntingdon Priory where a not dissimilar situation may have obtained:

> Two of the best chambers in the infirmary, with fireplaces and latrines, shall be kept completely ready and decent for sick canons, and for the duration of their infirmity superior, tastier and more delicate foodstuffs shall be administered to them out of the common resources of the community by which they may best be strengthened, and also doctors and medicine, so that with God's assistance they may recover as quickly as possible.[62]

If only two chambers were to be reserved for the sick, what was being done with the rest? The bishop may have accepted that they would be allocated to whomsoever wanted them – and, perhaps, was prepared to pay for them – and wished to ensure that these two at least were kept on permanent standby. At Newnham Priory, Gray directed that 'sick canons shall have decent rooms in the infirmary for the duration of their sickness', earmarking the room that had belonged to James Townhale, which was not to be used for any other purpose. Furthermore, any canon who had to spend the night in the infirmary was to receive an allowance of a quart of beer 'and no more, unless his infirmity, in the judgement of the sub-prior, demands more'![63]

At Peterborough, in 1432, Gray insisted that rooms in the infirmary must be available for those who needed them and that the *custos infirmarie* should be 'more diligent and gentle' with the sick, seeing to the fires and their other needs. He tried to restrict eating to the refectory and the misericord (or 'Seyny'), outlawing it in 'ly Chymney' (the warming-house or *calefactorium*), for this led to the destruction of almsgiving, presumably because monks foregathered there to eat up the leftovers of other meals.[64] Nuns too were criticized for their treatment of the sick. The Cistercian prioress of Legbourne in 1440 was guilty of a neglectful attitude to them and of refusing to let them have 'decent rooms in the infirmary or other decent places in which they could recover better'.[65]

In many places, then, the infirmary was both a source of supplementary income and a tempting target for monks and nuns who were looking for comfortable retreats within the precinct. It seems to have been open to the invasion of lay outsiders. At Bardney in 1437–38 Alnwick found that there were a great many illicit *vigilia*, in the infirmary and in the guesthouse, where beer was consumed from the refectory.[66] The abbot told him that the monks in the infirmary did not eat together but individually and sent their leftovers out into the town, wherever they liked, to the total destruction of almsgiving. It was quite likely that the sub-cellarer Thomas Barton was at the bottom of all this, or so at least his fellows wanted the bishop to believe. He was never to be seen in the dormitory, sleeping either in a room in the infirmary which he clearly had at his permanent disposal (although according to one witness he was strong and healthy) or in his own *camera* next to the kitchen. One Graystoke and his wife, from the town of Bardney, allegedly had permanent access to Barton's chamber in the infirmary and spent all day there eating the monastery's food, over which as sub-cellarer he had control.

If the weaker brethren, at Bardney and elsewhere, were thus shouldered aside it clearly does not speak well for the internal solidarity of religious communities. If half of what was said about Thomas Barton was true (and there was a great deal more), he was a bad lot; but it is the general picture, here as elsewhere, that is of more significance. Many of these abbeys were ancient. In the course of centuries populations had grown around them, in relation to which they functioned not merely as landlords but as sources of miscellaneous employment opportunities for local people. Monks did not do their own cooking, washing or odd jobs and the 'servants' that many had, from the abbot downwards, were laymen. This meant the automatic and constant presence of layfolk in the cloister, and like the monks themselves they had friends and relations. This openness to the world manifested itself in all kinds of ways. At Daventry in 1442 women came into the kitchen and into the cloister to draw water from the conduit, dirtying the step of the *lavatorium* with their feet. Alnwick found also that on every Sunday and feast-day layfolk both male and female sat around in the refectory and infirmary, eating and drinking to the great detriment of the priory's resources.[67]

The traffic was two-way, for superiors were often urged, as they were at Daventry, to prevent the brothers from wandering off into the town. The fleshpots of Bedford were apparently deeply alluring to the canons of Caldwell Priory,[68] while proximity to Oxford was (perhaps) not good news for nuns. Godstow Abbey had persistent trouble with the students, who in 1432 boldly said that 'they could have every kind of solace with the nuns whenever they wanted' and were still helping themselves in 1445.[69] In many places, including Godstow, the bishops directed that exits and entrances should be secured, but it is clear that this was a partial and negative answer to such problems, which fundamentally had more to do with the life that the inmates consented to lead.

Only rarely do we get a glimpse of the expectations with which a monk or nun entered the cloister. In 1440 Thomas Barton, an Augustinian of Elsham Priory, complained to Bishop Alnwick that 'when he entered religion it was his intention to make progress in letters and in religion, and the prior promised him these things'. The promise had not been kept because there was no one in the convent who could teach him.[70] This was not the only occasion on which poor educational provision was brought to the bishops' attention; but it is easier to guess what Thomas may have meant by progress in letters than what he believed 'religion' to consist of and how the two were related. Facilities for study might include private study space, but it appears that religious who were doing little studying were finding other ways of obtaining rooms of their own. When in 1442 Isabella Benet and Agnes Halesley, nuns of Catesby, refused to obey Bishop Alnwick's injunctions, especially in the matter of giving up their rooms, on the grounds that they were not subject to him, they were not defending their right to studies.[71] What they thought the religious life meant or what communal obligations they recognized is unknowable.

It is a known hazard of lamenting lost community that it may involve on the one hand romanticizing and overstating what has been lost, on the other failing to recognize new forms of solidarity as they take shape. Tests are not easy either to devise or to apply. There are persuasive signs that, despite (or perhaps because of) the demographic disasters of the later fourteenth century, some people achieved a higher standard of living and even luxury, as Giovanni de' Mussi thought he perceived at Piacenza. Cultural balances were also slowly shifting: if the educated layman reached new heights with the humanists of early Renaissance Italy, the breed was not unknown elsewhere and men and women capable of reading devotional texts were clearly increasingly numerous outside the cloister. Latin literacy was restricted outside the ranks of the clergy, but it was not as universal within those ranks or in the cloister as we might suppose. To judge by the Lincoln visitations, nuns were often not expected to understand anything except their mother tongue, while the bishops occasionally enjoined monks to converse, when that was permitted, in Latin or French and not to lapse into English. There was a diminishing distance between many religious and the educated layman or laywoman.

All of these considerations affected the environment of late medieval monasticism and the ways in which religious interacted with the world outside their gates. Episcopal visitations suggest that the ideal of an enclosed contemplative community, which the bishops and indeed the monks themselves continued to uphold in theory, was not being realized. Community, in this particular sense, may have been decaying; but it had never been easy to obtain or to preserve. This did not necessarily mean either that the monasteries were unpopular or that they failed to play a valued part in the life of the surrounding society. The glimpses we get of Daventry suggest that it was functioning as a kind of social centre, and it would be unwise to ignore the fact that it was offering religious services: one notes the reference to the concourse of people on Sundays and feast-days. We may remember also, early in the fourteenth century, the picture of monks and *seculares* walking meditatively in the restored cemetery at St Albans.[72]

Around 1100 monastic reformers had set store by location, seeking to establish themselves in genuine 'solitudes'. They might have considered themselves vindicated had they known of the problems that proximity even to quite modest centres of population seemed to bring in its train three centuries later, but they would probably have had difficulty in grasping the ways in which the world had changed in that period. Who in 1400 desired solitude, in the sense of isolation from the world, as distinct from a tranquil decent life within the cloister, with a measure of privacy, a room of one's own or at least some comfortable retreat in which to converse, play chess or music with one's special friends, religious or secular?

There is a fine depiction of domestic luxury in the right-hand wing of a diptych, now in the Museum of Fine Arts at Antwerp. It shows Christian d'Hondt, the Cistercian abbot of Ter Duinen, venerating the Virgin and Child, who occupy the other panel. He kneels on a green carpet, with a small dog asleep on it beside him; his mitre is on a pink cushion by the *prie-dieu*, draped in green velvet, on which his rather large, finely bound prayer-book rests on another tasselled cushion. His crozier is propped up against the splendid carved stone fireplace, complete with a set of fire-irons, from which a glowing fire radiates. The fine but plain timber roof rests on stone corbels; there is a mullioned window high in the fireplace wall. A dresser beyond the fireplace groans beneath the weight of the flagons arrayed upon it. A diptych (presumably of devotional character) hangs above the bed, which is sumptuously furnished in deep blue fabric. Another pink cushion rests on a high-backed chair, below a shelf which bears a couple of books and a chest with gilt clasps.[73] Only the habit, perhaps, would have enabled Bernard of Clairvaux to recognize Abbot Christian as a Cistercian. Yet the painting, in and by itself, does not enable us to pass judgment on him as man or monk. It does measure a material change which is suggestive of the changed environment in which not only the religious life, but the lives of the upper classes of lay society, was being lived by the end of the fifteenth century.

13

Conclusion: Individual and Society

The development of the Christian religious life in and after the fourth century sanctified a rejection of ordinary social relationships which was unintelligible and unacceptable to some Roman observers. As the event showed, however, there was not total unanimity about how the seeker after God should live. Should it be in a community of the like-minded or in genuine solitude, insofar as that was practicable? There was no final answer, and the evolving forms of the monastic and eremitical lives reflect differing positions. The cenobitic model rested on a faith in communal norms and the necessity of discipline; it had eloquent and persuasive advocates. The eremitical life nonetheless retained its allure, in literature and in reality: the solitary's detachment from the world and his (or her) real freedom seemed greater than that of the monk or nun who was ensconced in a highly organized, sometimes architecturally elaborate and economically prosperous setting. It remained a practical drawback that genuine solitude was in fact difficult to achieve and potentially dangerous both physically and morally, because of the threat of slackness, self-indulgence – and demons.

During the long period of the dismantling of the structures of Roman civilization cenobitic monasticism acquired an additional value that its pioneers neither intended nor expected. For several centuries, it provided almost the only setting in which intellectual pursuits could flourish or in which any interest in them was likely to be found. When that ceased to be true, it meant that changes were at work in society as a whole which inevitably affected the religious life itself. The monastic reforms which began in the eleventh century and flowered in the twelfth were in part a reaction to these accelerating changes, which produced a more populous and gradually a more urbanized society. There was a variety of environments, for example royal courts and episcopal households with burgeoning bureaucracies, in which men (if not women) could employ intellectual skills; and that meant that they had first to be able to develop them. Court and city were not solitudes, and peace and quiet were hard to find in them, or so it certainly seemed to many of their inhabitants. A number of monastic reformers were refugees from the cathedral schools, by definition located in cities, but many bright young men were more interested in their secular employment prospects.

The need to read at some level of difficulty, to study texts for what you could get out of them and even to reflect upon them, was felt by increasing numbers of people. From the point of view not just of the monasteries as centres of learning, but of the church as a whole, it was bound to be a significant fact that so much of this education was not religious in character but might consist of anything from a smattering of grammar through the more developed skills of the notary to the fully blown professional study of law or medicine. The appearance of the friars early in the thirteenth century represented a convergence: they lived in the cities and their purpose was to bring the fruits of centuries of theological learning and meditation (much of it monastic in origin) to bear directly on the salvation of mankind. The friars resembled the prosperous townsmen to whom they addressed themselves in that they were signs of the progressive division of labour and multiplication of ways of living, and of making a living, in later medieval society. Their convents, adaptations of the monastic model, were designed to provide them with the degree of withdrawal from the hubbub that was necessary to the fulfilment of the task, but that withdrawal was only part of their lives.

What if the individual's problem was too much solitude? We have become extremely familiar with loneliness, in both life and literature, but it is harder to identify in medieval sources. This is not just because the physical and social isolation of the individual is more frequent now; it also has a great deal to do with different expectations and expressive conventions arising from different ways of living. In a society in which your occupation, your marriage and even your friends were as like as not chosen for you, the issue of whether or not you as an individual were personally happy or 'fulfilled' did not have quite the central importance we now give it. As important was your own adaptation to the demands of those around you. This did not mean indifference to individual well-being so much as a rather different set of assumptions about how it was to be achieved – assumptions which are still made by millions of people outside the confines of western society.

There were unquestionably outcasts and 'marginals' in medieval society, some of them accidental casualties, others to all intents and purposes created by society itself, yet others (lepers, perhaps) both. They did not necessarily live in isolation: Jews, for example, might be marginalized by the Christian majority but constituted their own communities with their own binding rules, while 'lepers' were forced into association. The individual was born a member of a group; if things changed he or she was likely to become a member of another group. A well-born child offered to a religious order made the change from noble household to cloister without any choice in the matter, but even one who did choose the religious life at a more advanced age was volunteering, in principle, to sacrifice such freedom of action as he or she had ever possessed. The belief in the Fall and the consequent corruption of the human will provided an ideological justification for the imposition of an authoritarian collective discipline on all men and women, inside and outside the cloister.

An individual's sense of being alone was often expressed in terms of the loss of his rightful place in society, his support system. The lordless, friendless man of the Anglo-

Saxon poem *The Wanderer* feels his isolation as a moral and social condition, but the enjoyment of what is he is missing has a location, in the 'mead-hall' where a 'gold-giver' should be extending his protection to him and he would find company. This comfortable environment is bitterly contrasted with the cold sea on which (literally or metaphorically) he finds himself. This lament is in fact only part of the poem, which ends in moralistic reflection on the transience of the hall and its 'uproar', as if the author was contemplating a ruined building. The author of the equally famous *The Ruin*, which is often supposed to be a rumination on the remains of the city of Bath, imagines the shattered buildings in their days of glory, but in rather unRoman terms:

Bright were the buildings, halls where springs ran,
High, horngabled, much throng-noise;
These many meadhalls men filled
With loud cheerfulness.

It was the setting of *Beowulf* that the Wanderer was missing and the author of *The Ruin* evoking.[1]

Many centuries later, Dante too evoked the desolation of exile. His sense of being a choice spirit set apart who, as he came to think, had taken a wrong turning when he entered politics in the 1290s was nurtured in what proved to be a lifelong absence from his native city. His milieu, between 1303 and his death, was that of the deracinated intellectual, a guest at seigneurial courts and frequenter of circles of *literati* in northern Italy. In Paradise his ancestor Cacciaguida tells him that he will have to learn how salt is another man's bread, how hard his stair.[2] The personal poignancy of the emotion is beyond doubt, but a large part is played in it by Dante's bitterly resentful awareness that he has lost his proper place in the world. Wanting to make his own terms with his society, confident that he was in the right, unwillingly forced to be a citizen of the world, he reinterpreted community obligations within a universalist framework. They became obligations to the whole of human society (as of course Christian belief anyway implied). The narrower framework within which the Florentine discharged his social and political duties had been taken from him.

How well Dante understood what those duties might be is illustrated by an exchange with Virgil, his guide through the nether world, near the beginning of *Inferno* xxix. Virgil remarks, critically, that Dante has been unusually attentive to the fomenters of discord whose punishments they have just witnessed. Dante has in fact seen the spirit of one of his own kin, Geri del Bello, a victim of violent death which is still unavenged; because Dante himself shared the responsibility for carrying out that vengeance the spirit had refused to speak with him, indeed, as Virgil noticed, he had pointed at Dante and made threatening gestures towards him.[3] This was the world of obligations imposed by blood-relationship which the philosopher-poet would have continued to inhabit had his exile not intervened.

Dante was also keenly sensitive to place as such, and attached some touching images to the figure of the pilgrim, the voluntary exile who has abandoned home and kin and fears that he will never see them again. In the opening lines of the eighth canto of *Purgatorio* he evokes the pang felt by mariners and 'those who have said goodbye to their dear friends' as evening comes on. In the fortieth chapter of the *Vita Nuova*, he recalls seeing a group of Rome-bound pilgrims in the centre of Florence and realizing with some difficulty that their preoccupied air meant not that they were thinking about the recently dead Beatrice but about their own friends far away.[4]

A woman's secure place in society might be endangered by the death of her husband. Christine de Pizan was widowed and suffered as a consequence, but she seems also to have felt her loss keenly and made lyrical use of her predicament, beginning twenty-four of twenty-five lines of one poem with the words 'Seulette sui'.[5] Loss and bereavement were not emotions articulated only by poets. A Cambridge man told an inquest in 1308 that he remembered a birth in 1284 because his wife had just died and he was 'almost mad with grief'.[6] We can scarcely doubt that the feeling of desolation that we call loneliness was an ingredient in this grief, no matter how many people he had about him. At about the same date Richard Brunne told a story, adapted from Gregory the Great's *Dialogues*, of two hermits, Eutycyus and Florens. Eutycyus becomes abbot of a neighbouring monastery and poor Florens

> woned a-lonë yn hys celle.
> Florens madë gretë mone
> For that he should dwel alone;
> And had grete sorowe, and was drery
> As many be the that lese gode cumpany.[7]

It is not implied that Florens was morally at risk, only that he was unhappy. His earnest prayers to God for consolation were rewarded by the companionship of a bear.

It was easy enough to understand that the loss of 'good company', be it a dead wife or husband, a fellow-hermit, or the friends left behind by a pilgrim, was cause for despondency, for it was assumed that everyone did indeed depend on the right kind of society. The loneliness that arises not from lack of company but from not having the right company must surely have played a part in monastic *accidie*. How many monks (and nuns) were ill-adjusted to community life and did not feel any compensating inner assurance of God's constant presence? Such an unfortunate, William of St-Thierry implied, was 'not a solitary but alone'.

Accepting that an individual truly desired to be alone was more difficult. There was a marked tendency to point out the disadvantages and delusions of genuine physical solitude. We can still recognize ourselves in an Egyptian monk's fit of temper with an intransigent water-pot, which taught him that solitude was no cure for his irritability. Seneca had already thought that a man had to establish his credentials before being permitted to keep himself to himself and his words were remembered by the learned;

they chimed in with ways of thinking and living which were widely shared. Petrarch claimed the right of withdrawal for himself but would not have dissented from the general principle.

Economic reality too was determining. Petrarch could speak slightingly of money-making activities and assure Philippe Cabassoles that great riches were not necessary to the tranquil life, precisely because his material needs were supplied by income from sinecures, ecclesiastical benefices that did not require his personal attention. Few had the resources to withdraw from the economic routines which assured them a meagre living or from the associated social and familial obligations. The possession of riches was usually equally dependent on maintaining one's inherited or acquired place in society; one was committed by rank and office to live in the midst of men and discharge duties which might include extensive hospitality. One way to evade the common lot was to join a religious community, but if this brought emancipation from the toils of office-holding, commerce or hard physical labour it did so at the price of submission to an intensive and lifelong communal discipline. The choice nevertheless was probably often experienced as liberation from a harsher servitude elsewhere. For the generality of people, the absence of any conceivable alternative to the way they and theirs lived and had always lived doubtless ensured that what we might regard as a grim and monotonous necessity was very considerably mitigated – if indeed it was so estimated at all.

It was for the benefit of men profitably embroiled in mundane affairs that Leon Battista Alberti, one of the most notable fifteenth-century heirs of Petrarch's pioneering humanism, wrote his dialogue *Della famiglia*. Alberti puts into the mouth of one of his speakers, Lionardo, a condemnation of secretiveness and unsociability, which education (that is, the education of boys, which was all that mattered) should be designed to extirpate. A father should carefully monitor the disposition of his children as manifested in their day to day behaviour. Lionardo based his view that the innate characteristics of the young would inevitably reveal themselves to such observation on a classical doctrine of the nature of man. Men 'are naturally gregarious, eager and willing to be with others, and happy to live among other men, while they avoid, dislike and fear solitude'. Furthermore

> Nature, that excellent arbiter of things, has not only decreed that men live openly in the midst of other men, but has imposed on them the necessity of disclosing to others every passion and feeling, in words or other ways, and she rarely allows anyone to keep thoughts or deeds secret from others.

On this assumption, a father would easily be able to discover the true nature of his children. Lionardo thought it a promising sign if the young disliked idleness and 'want to do what they see others do'. A certain biddability was good in a young boy. He should also be prompt in his replies 'and courageous and willing to appear among men without timidity and boorish elusiveness'.

These desirable qualities would not be nurtured if a (male) child was allowed to remain too long among women. The society to which Lionardo wanted children to be accustomed was one to which women did not fully belong. In this context 'solitude' was womanish:

> It will therefore be useful not to shelter them in one's room and lap as some mothers do, but to accustom them to be with people and respectful toward all. They must not be left alone or allowed to languish in womanly idleness and vegetate among women. Plato used to reproach his Dion for being solitary, saying that solitude is the companion of stubbornness. Cato, seeing a young man alone and idle, asked him what he was doing. The latter answered that he was conversing with himself. 'Take care', said Cato, 'that you do not converse with an evil man.' He was a most prudent man, for he knew how in young minds desires corruped by lust, wrath or evil thoughts are more powerful than reason. He knew that this young man, busy in answering and listening to himself, was more apt to listen to his desires and appetites than to honesty, and less likely to believe in continence and avoiding lust than in the pleasures and delights he desired. With idleness and solitude one becomes stubborn, strange and full of vices.[8]

Lionardo's citations are classical, but the spirit which animates the passage is in some respects not very distant from the attitude of monastic writers who warned against easy recourse to the eremitical life.

One of the passages he quotes would have been familiar to many such counsellors, as it was to Petrarch. The rebuke of the solitary young man, here attributed to Cato, is in fact attributed by Seneca, in his tenth Epistle, to Crates, a Stoic philosopher of the second century before Christ:

> Crates, so it is said ... saw a young man walking by himself and asked him what he was doing alone. 'I am talking with myself', he said. Crates replied, 'Beware, I beg you, and take care, for you are talking with a bad man'.

Seneca himself qualified the caution: he was prepared to permit his Lucilius to withdraw into himself, because he was already morally qualified to do so safely. In the 25th epistle, however, he restated the fundamental principle: 'solitude persuades us to every kind of evil ... everyone is better off in the company of somebody or other no matter who, than in his own company.' It was all very well to counsel withdrawal into the self if one was forced to be in a crowd, 'provided you are a good, tranquil and self-restrained man; otherwise, you had better withdraw into a crowd in order get away from your self. Alone, you are too close to a rascal.'

If on such issues Seneca was quoted or echoed by writers apparently so very different over a considerable period of time (for example Peter the Chanter late in the twelfth century), it was because he articulated in an authoritative, quotable form fundamental assumptions about the nature of man in relation to society which they shared with him, rather than because they needed him to tell them novel truths. The possibility, which Seneca admitted, that moral education might fit one for solitude, was paralleled by the belief (however reluctantly conceded) that the individual might be fitted for the eremitical life by an adequate monastic probation.

Alberti and his audience lived in a society in which there were solvents of the old order of things at work, if fairly slowly as yet. Even in the harsh conditions of medieval society, everyone had moments of leisure, some of them imposed by the seasons, the weather or indeed the time of day, some of them because the church insisted on the observation of holy days. The need for variety and recreation was recognized even within the monastery. If discipline was slack, monks might find they had time on their hands. In the secular world some people had more leisure than others, if they did not have to wring their subsistence from a stony soil, could avoid military entanglements and were not directly responsible for ruling anyone else. Leisure was still, for the most part, spent in the company of others, but there were holes and corners in the daily routine, and also increasingly in living accommodation, in which some individuals could exercise some choice, for good or ill, as to how they spent their time and even with whom.

Wealth held out the promise of comforts which one did not have to share with everybody. They included this more diversified living-space and an increased number of material possessions, among them books and objects of beauty. The extension of literacy opened the allurements of learning to people whose forefathers would never have dreamed of it, and an education acquired to fit one for the church or the law sometimes opened up, as it did for Petrarch, different and wider horizons – even if the Church still had to provide the necessary income. The religious life itself was not proof against the changes that were going on outside it. When the opportunities for both education and civilized comfort multiplied, at least in the upper ranks of lay society, what was the monastic response to be: to create new models of austerity for a few, to try to keep the old models in repair, or to acquiesce in the desire of monks and nuns to lead a pious but genteel existence, in touch with the world outside the cloister but enjoying a measure of privacy within it?

The significance of these changes can easily and understandably be overshadowed by the scale of later ones. An imaginary medieval observer of the modern western world would undoubtedly find the sheer numbers of people and the transformation of the material environment hard to comprehend. Were this observer to focus his attention on social developments, he might well be astounded by the spectacle of so many individuals in so populous a society not only earning their keep without apparent regard for the wishes of their kin but living apart from them, often indeed entirely alone, and yet not being regarded as particularly eccentric, still less as outcasts. That there are numerous women among them would be scarcely less surprising. Now the individual can both reject and be rejected with greater ease than in less 'open' societies. It is in a world so constituted that both privacy as we know it and new forms of involuntary solitude have come to birth.

Notes

Notes to Introduction

1 The quotations are from the preface to *Privacy: Studies in Social and Cultural History* (New York, 1984), pp. ix–xi.
2 *Solitude* (London, 1989), p. ix. The book was first published in 1988 as *The School of Genius*.
3 See A. Grant, *Reason and Society in the Middle Ages* (Oxford, 1978), especially (but not solely) pt 3, 'Reading and Writing'.
4 *Memoirs of My Life*, ed. Betty Radice (Harmondsworth, 1984), p. 157.
5 See in general the essays in J. Haseldine, ed., *Friendship in Medieval Europe* (Stroud, 1999); B. McGuire, *Friendship and Community: The Monastic Experience, 350–1250* (Kalamazoo, Michigan, 1988).
6 In his introduction to Ovid, *The Erotic Poems* (Harmondsworth, 1982), p. 417, Peter Green observes: 'In certain circumstances we value solitude highly, whereas Mediterranean man did – and does – both fear and detest it.'
7 D. Lewis-Williams, *The Mind in the Cave* (London, 2002), p. 103.
8 Below, p. 151.
9 Valerie Flint, 'Space and Discipline in Early Medieval Europe' in B.A. Hanawalt and M. Kobialka (eds.), *Medieval Practices of Space* (Minneapolis, 2000), p. 149, suggests that 'For the organized use of space in early medieval Europe, one movement would be very hard to equal: the monastic movement within the Western Christian Church.'
10 *Agricola*, 30.
11 *De amicitia*, xxiiii, 18. For a twelfth-century example of the juxtaposition of the positive *solitarius* and the negative *solus*, see below p. 71.
12 Chaucer uses 'solitude' once (in the early *Complaint of Mars*, line 65). In French, 'Solitude s'emploie en parlant de la situation d'une personne seule, de façon momentanée ou durable, qui vit seule (1393), emploi rare avant le XVIIe s.' (*Le Robert dictionnaire historique de la langue française*, ed. A. Rey, 2 vols, Paris 1992.) In the seventeenth century it reacquires its Latin sense. The 1393 reference is to the version of the story of Griselda given by the Ménagier de Paris. For an early fourteenth-century Tuscan use of *solitario*, see below p. 146. The French equivalent was already available and the adjective 'solitary' occurs in the *Knight's Tale*.
13 For example by the Marxist critic Raymond Williams: *Keywords* (London, 1976), pp. 203–4: 'Private, that is, in its positive senses, is a record of the legitimation of a bourgeois view of life.'
14 Almost everywhere there is an adjective ultimately derived from *privatus* and formations comparable to 'private life' are not uncommon: *Privatleben*, *vie privée*, *vita privata*. Single nouns formed from the same root are however almost unknown and the synonyms suggested in dictionaries frequently invoke the notions of separation,

isolation or secrecy and can be used to convey these meanings, as 'privacy' rarely is in English. An Italian legal textbook, recently glimpsed in a bookshop window, bears the suggestive title *Il codice di privacy*.

15 See the *Le Robert dictionnaire historique*.

Notes to Chapter 1: Withdrawing from the World

1 *De reditu suo libri duo*, ed. C. H. Keene (London, 1907), also contains a translation. There are several others, including one by H. Isbell, *The Last Poets of Imperial Rome* (Harmondsworth, 1971), pp. 221–41.

2 *De reditu*, lines 439–52. Bellerophon, the legendary Greek warrior who killed the Chimaera and rode the winged horse Pegasus, incurred the enmity of the gods and ended his days wandering in grief-stricken solitude. His story is told in the sixth book of the *Iliad*.

3 *De reditu*, lines 515–26.

4 Quoted by C. White, *Early Christian Lives* (London, 1998), p. xxix . For the Greek text see Julian, Epistle 89b, to the high priest Theodore, in *Oeuvres complètes*, ed. and trans. J. Bidez (Paris, 1924), i, pt 2, pp. 155–56.

5 For this exchange and for Ausonius' biography, see *The Works of Ausonius*, edited by R.P.H. Green (Oxford, 1991). Helen Waddell drew attention to the episode in *The Wandering Scholars* (London, 1927), pp. 31–42; translations of parts of Paulinus' replies to Ausonius are in her *Medieval Latin Lyrics* (Harmondsworth, 1952), pp. 44–45.

6 Ep. xxi, lines 69–72 (*Works of Ausonius*, p. 224): 'Tristis, egens, deserta colat tacitusque pererret/Alpini convexa iugi, ceu dicitur olim/Mentis inops coetus hominum et vestigia vitans/Avia perlustrasse vagus loca Bellerophontes.'

7 Translated by P.G. Walsh, *The Poems of St Paulinus of Nola* (New York, 1975); see also his translations of *The Letters of St Paulinus of Nola* (2 vols, New York, 1966–67).

8 Paulinus' reply to Ausonius' Epistles 21 and 22 is in *Works of Ausonius*, pp. 708–17.

9 There were pre-Christian precedents for withdrawal into a life of peace and contemplation: the Jewish Essenes and the Therapeutae of Alexandria, described in the first century by the Jew Philo, bore some resemblance to the monastic communities of later Christianity. See the translations of the treatises *Quod omnis probus liber sit*, *De vita contemplativa* and *Hypothetica* by C. D. Yonge in *The Works of Philo* (New York, 1997), pp. 689–70, 699–706, 745–46.

10 The translation here is by Michael Grant: Cicero, *Selected Works* (Harmondsworth, 1965), p. 159. The Loeb translation (by Walter Miller) is virtually identical. Grant gives a brief but useful summary of Cicero's after-fame, pp. 24–32.

11 'I might say with truth that I was never less alone than when by myself.' (*Memoirs*, ed. Radice, p. 112.)

12 *De officiis*, iii, 1. 1.

13 *Sancti Ambrosii Mediolanensis De officiis*, ed. M. Testard (*Corpus Christianorum series Latina*, 15 (Turnhout, 2000), iii, 1, pp. 153–55.

14 L.D. Reynolds, *The Medieval Tradition of Seneca's Letters* (London, 1965), pp. 81–124, provides an invaluable survey down to the twelfth century.

15 *Meditations*, iv, 3. Cf. x, 23: 'Let it be clear to you that the peace of green fields can always be yours, in this, that or any other spot; and that nothing is any different here from what it would be either up in the hills, or down by the sea or wherever you will.'

16 *Epistles*, lv, 8; vii, 8.
17 *De amicitia* c. 23; *De officiis* I, c. 44.
18 *Epistle* viii, 2.
19 Below, p. 152.
20 Translation by Peter Green in *Ovid: The Poems of Exile* (London, 1994), p. 176.
21 Letters, ii. 17: text and translation by B. Radice in the Loeb edition, i, pp. 132–43. There is a conjectural plan of Laurentinum in ii, pp. 554–55. Pliny's *cubicula* clearly included rooms used for relaxation rather than just for sleeping. In this they somewhat resemble the 'chamber' of medieval usage. When Pliny wishes to emphasize that a room is used as a bedchamber, he may insert a qualification: *cubiculum noctis et somni*, a chamber of 'night and sleep', or the self-explanatory *cubiculum dormitorium*.
22 *Letters*, v. 2, ibid., pp. 336–55.
23 S. Ellis, *Roman Housing* (London, 2000), pp. 20, 191.
24 J.W. Baldwin, *Masters, princes and merchants: the social views of Peter the Chanter and his circle* (2 vols, Princeton, 1970), i, pp. 13–16. The *Verbum abbreviatum* survives in more than ninety manuscripts.
25 *PL*, 206, cols 204–207.
26 *PL*, 206, col. 205: 'Hoc primum philosophia promittit, scilicet sensum communem, humanitatem, socialitatem et congregationem, a qua professione dissimilitudo nos separabit.'
27 See for example the observations of Humbert of Romans, and his citations of Gregory, in *On the Formation of Preachers* (iv, 19); translation in *Early Dominicans: Selected Writings*, ed. S. Tugwell (London, 1982), pp. 252–53.
28 There is much on these aspects of Gregory's writings in C. Straw, *Gregory the Great: Perfection in Imperfection* (Berkeley, 1988).
29 *AS*, Maii 1, pp. 317–18. For Catherine of Siena's version see below p. 125.

Notes to Chapter 2, Pioneers of Solitude

1 Philip Rousseau, *Pachomius: The Making of a Community in Fourth-Century Egypt* (2nd edn, Berkeley, 1999), pp. 12–13. Many of the sources for Pachomian monasticism are translated by A. Veilleux in *Pachomian Koinonia* (3 vols, Kalamazoo, Michigan, 1980–82). Marilyn Dunn, *The Emergence of Monasticism: from the Desert Fathers to the Early Middle Ages* (Oxford, 2000) offers a recent account of early monastic development. Derwas Chitty, *The Desert a City* (Oxford, 1966), is a classic account of the 'desert fathers'.
2 See the discussion by R.M. Price in his introduction to Theodoret of Cyrrhus, *A History of the Monks of Syria* (Kalamazoo, Michigan, 1985), pp. xxiii–xxvii.
3 *The Conferences,* trans. B. Ramsey (New York, 1997), xviii, pp. 638–39.
4 'Cenobitic' derives from *coenobium*, a Latinization of the Greek *koinobion*, 'common life'; 'hermit' and 'anchorite' from *eremos* (a deserted place) and *anachoresis* (withdrawal).
5 The *Life* was written for the benefit of western monks who knew about Antony and wanted to be able to study the model he provided. The translation used here is by R.C. Gregg, *The Life of St Anthony and the Letter to Marcellinus* (New York, 1980). A complementary picture emerges from the *Apophthegmata* or 'Sayings' of the desert monks which were recorded in a number of collections. Benedicta Ward has translated both *The Sayings of the Desert Fathers: the Alphabetical Collection* (Kalamazoo,

Michigan, 1975), and *The Desert Fathers: Sayings of the Early Christian Monks* (London, 2003). The latter is organized thematically, under headings such as 'Fortitude' and 'Obedience'. Some of the same anecdotes appear in both collections.

6 *Life*, pp. 75–76; *Sayings*, pp. 5, 8. Nitria, according to Athanasius, was a thirteen-day journey from Antony's mountain.

7 *Life*, p. 93; *Sayings*, p. 3.

8 This version is translated by White, *Early Christian Lives*, pp. 7–70.

9 Translated by Norman Russell as *The Lives of the Desert Fathers* (Kalamazoo, Michigan, and Oxford, 1981). Rufinus also freely translated the *Ecclesiastical History* of Eusebius of Caesarea.

10 *The Lausiac History*, trans. Robert T. Meyer (New York, 1964). The title derives from its dedication to Lausius, chamberlain to the Emperor Theodosius II.

11 *The Institutes*, trans. B. Ramsey (New York, 2000).

12 Jerome imported into the legend of St Antony of Egypt a venerable predecessor, Paul of Thebes, of whom otherwise we know nothing. Jerome's *Lives* of Paul, Hilarion and also the Syrian hermit Malchus are translated by White, *Early Christian Lives*.

13 For Benedicta Ward's translation see above, n. 5.

14 'Nihil in illo indecens solitudo, nihil asperum quotidiana cum hostibus bella contulerant' (*PL*, 73, col. 134); an alternative translation is in White, *Early Christian Lives*, pp. 18–19.

15 *Sayings*, p. 3.

16 Ibid., p. 10.

17 The story is told in *Sayings*, pp. 208–10, about 'an *abba* from Rome'; in *Desert Fathers* pp. 106–8, Arsenius is named. A similar story is in *Sayings*, pp. 16–17.

18 *Conferences*, xviii, pp. 640–41, 646–67.

19 *Sayings*, p. 19.

20 Ibid., p. 183.

21 Ibid., pp. 124–25.

22 *Lives*, pp. 50, 67.

23 *Lausiac History*, p. 138.

24 *Lives*, p. 101.

25 For brief accounts of the physical environment of early monasticism, with maps and plans, see W. Braunfels, *Monasteries of Western Europe: the Architecture of the Orders* (London, 1972), pp. 13–19; M. Thompson, *Cloister Abbot and Precinct* (Stroud, 2001), pp. 18–25.

26 *Lives*, p. 73.

27 *Lausiac History*, xxxii, p. 92; Rousseau, *Pachomius*, p. 79. Jerome's version of the *Rules* is translated by Veilleux, *Pachomian Koinonia*, ii, pp. 145–67.

28 *Sayings*, p. 227.

29 Ibid., pp. 148–9.

30 *Lausiac History*, vii, pp. 40–41; xiii, pp. 48–49.

31 *Lives*, pp. 105–6, 148–49.

32 *Sayings*, p. 8.

33 For a brief account, with further references, see L. Regnault, *The Day-to-Day Life of the Desert Fathers in Fourth-Century Egypt*, trans. É. Poirier (Petersham, Massachusetts, 1999), ch. 4.

34 *Desert Fathers*, p. 46.

35 *Lives*, p. 82.

36 Paphnutius, *Histories of the Monks of Upper Egypt and The Life of Onnophrius*, trans. T. Vivian (Kalamazoo, Michigan, 1993), pp. 119, 126.

37 *Lausiac History*, xxxv, p. 99.
38 Ibid., xviii, p. 61.
39 *Conferences*, xix, trans. Ramsey, p. 675.
40 *Lausiac History*, lv, p. 136.
41 Ibid., lxi, p. 143; *Poems of St Paulinus of Nola*, pp. 182, 386 n.12.
42 *Lives*, pp. 50, 102.
43 *Life*, p. 32. The reference, a frequent one, is to 2 Thessalonians 3:10.
44 *Sayings*, p. 197.
45 *History of the Monks of Syria*, p. 89.
46 *Sayings*, pp. 223–4. In another anecdote (ibid., pp. 120–21), this censorious attitude to labour is identified with Messalian or Euchite heretics who vaunted an ideal of perpetual prayer. For Martha and Mary as types of the active and contemplative lives, see Giles Constable, 'The Interpretation of Mary and Martha', in *Three Studies in Medieval Religious and Social Thought* (Cambridge, 1995), pp. 3–141.
47 *Lausiac History*, lxi, p. 143. Candida, an imitator of the elder Melania (ibid., lvii, p. 138), would 'spend the whole night at the mill toiling with her hands to bring her body into subjection'.
48 *Sayings*, p. 2.
49 *Early Christian Lives*, p. 124.
50 *Lausiac History*, viii, p.41; *Sayings*, p. 60.
51 *Sayings*, pp. 225–6.
52 *The Lives of Simeon Stylites*, trans. Robert Doran (Kalamazoo, Michigan, 1992); the *Life* of Daniel is in *Three Byzantine Saints*, trans. Elizabeth Dawes and N.H. Baynes (Oxford, 1948), pp. 1–84. For the social role of these saints see Peter Brown, 'The Rise and Function of the Holy Man in Late Antiquity', in *Society and the Holy in Late Antiquity* (London, 1982), pp. 103–52, originally *Journal of Roman Studies*, 61 (1971), pp. 80–101.
53 John Moschos, *The Spiritual Meadow*, trans. J. Wortley (Kalamazoo, Michigan, 1992), p. 107.
54 *History of the Monks of Syria*, p. 135.
55 *Life*, p. 69. Jerome has Antony guided to Paul's hermitage by a friendly Hippocentaur: *Early Christian Lives*, p. 78.
56 *Lives*, p. 68.
57 *Desert Fathers*, p. 182.
58 Ibid., p. 116.
59 *Sayings*, p. 181.
60 Ibid., pp. 150–51.
61 *History of the Monks of Upper Egypt*, pp. 156, 164–65.
62 *Sayings*, pp. 148, 110.
63 Ibid., p. 102. Joseph presided over a group of disciples which provided John Cassian with the setting for thirteen of his *Conferences*.
64 *Desert Fathers*, p. 136.
65 Ibid., pp. 113–14.
66 Ibid., pp. 82–83.
67 *Sayings*, p. 129.
68 Ibid., p. 3.
69 Ibid., pp. 89–90.
70 Ibid., p. 11.
71 Ibid., pp. 17–18.

72 Ibid., pp. 131, 140.
73 Ibid., pp. 15, 76.
74 Ibid., p. 107.
75 Ibid., pp. 213, 217–18.
76 *Desert Fathers*, p. 27. Another variant of this *dictum* is attributed to the same father (p. 160), and Abba Lucius made a similar statement (ibid., p. 96; *Sayings*, p. 122).
77 *Sayings*, p. 42.
78 Ibid., p. 130.
79 Ibid., p. 217.
80 *Conferences*, x, p. 353.
81 *Lausiac History*, xvii, p. 55.
82 Ibid., xxxv, pp. 98–103; *Lives*, pp. 52–62.
83 *Sayings*, p. 203.
84 Ibid, p. 103.
85 Ibid., p. 74.
86 Ibid., pp. 99–100.
87 Ibid., p. 210. Compare the anonymous saying 'Someone who hands over his soul in obedience to a spiritual guide has a greater reward than one who retires alone to a hermitage' (*Desert Fathers*, p. 147).
88 *Sayings*, pp. 181, 188.
89 Ibid., p. 145.
90 Paphnutius, *History of the Monks of Upper Egypt*, p. 152.
91 *Sayings*, p. 114.
92 *Desert Fathers*, p. 71.
93 *Sayings*, p. 122.
94 *Conferences*, xix, pp. 676–77.
95 *Sayings*, p. 231. In another version (*Desert Fathers*, p. 143) obedience is preferable to *chastity*.
96 *Sayings*, p. 234; *Desert Fathers*, p. 11.
97 *Desert Fathers*, p. 11.

Notes to Chapter 3: The Western Desert

1 Dunn, *Emergence of Monasticism*, esp. ch. 8. For a convenient outline of the history of western monasticism, with further references, see C.H. Lawrence, *Medieval Monasticism* (London, 1984); for pre-Cluniac monastic architecture, Braunfels, *Monasteries*, pp. 19–46.
2 *Lives*, p. 50.
3 'militans sub regula vel abbate': *The Rule of St Benedict*, trans. and ed. J. McCann (London, 1952), c. 1, p. 14; hereafter cited simply by chapter.
4 It is to be noted that Benedict here uses the word *cella* to designate a monastery. This was not uncommon usage in later centuries: houses that were dependent on other monasteries were often called 'cells' and it was the standard term for a Grandmontine house.
5 Translated by H. Costello and E. de Bhaldraithe as *The Life of Saint Benedict*, with commentary by A. de Vogüé (Petersham, Massachusetts, 1993). De Vogüé has edited the complete text: *Dialogorum libri IV de miraculis patrum italicorum* (3 vols, *Sources Chrétiennes*, 251, 260, 265). There is a translation by O. Zimmerman, *Saint*

Gregory the Great: Dialogues (New York, 1959). The authorship and date of the *Dialogi* have been disputed and the question of what we know of Benedict apart from his Rule remains open.

6 *The Life*, pp. 30–31 (iii, 5–9).

7 For example, *The Life*, pp. 43 (vii, 1), 65 (xi, 1), 174 (xxxvii, 3).

8 Ibid, p. 164 (xxxv, 2).

9 Ibid, p. 101 (xxii, 1).

10 Adomnán of Iona, *Life of St Columba*, translated with an introduction by Richard Sharpe (London, 1995). Sharpe points out (pp. 60–62, 74) that Adomnán's picture of Columba and his monastery may reflect the circumstances of his own period rather than of Columba's lifetime a century earlier. For a general discussion of 'the monastic enclosure' in early Christian Ireland see Lisa M. Bitel, *Isle of the Saints: Monastic Settlement and Christian Community in Early Ireland* (Cork, 1990), pp. 57–82. Both Sharpe and Bitel cite A. Macdonald, 'Aspects of the Monastery and Monastic Life in Adomnán's Life of Columba', *Peritia*, 3 (1984), pp. 271–302.

11 Adomnán, *Life*, i, 25 (p. 130), 35 (p. 138); iii, 15 (p. 216), 22 (p. 223), 23 (p. 228).

12 *Life*, iii, 21 (pp. 222–3), 23 (p. 228).

13 Bitel, *Isle of the Saints*, p. 78.

14 *Vitae Sanctorum Hiberniae*, ed. Charles Plummer, 2 vols (Oxford, 1910), ii, p. 9.

15 *Life*, iii, 8 (p. 211); 16 (pp. 217–18).

16 *Life*, i, 24, p. 130 ; Bitel, *Isle of the Saints*, pp 76–7. The refectory at St Cainnech's monastery of Aghaboe, mentioned by Adomnán (ii, 13, p. 164) was probably in the 'great house'.

17 Ibid., iii, 12, p. 214, and n. 37, pp. 365–6. The reference to 'chambers' is in the chapter-heading of iii, 19, p. 220.

18 *Vitae Sanctorum Hiberniae*, ii, p. 14.

19 Bitel, *Isle of the Saints*, pp. 75–76, with further references.

20 Ibid., pp. 77–78.

21 *Vitae Sanctorum Hiberniae*, ii, p. 237.

22 Ibid., p. 228; i, p. 214.

23 *Vitae Sanctorum Hiberniae*, i, p. 206.

24 Ibid., pp. 234–57.

25 Ibid., ii, pp. 26–27.

26 *Felix's Life of Saint Guthlac*, ed. and trans. B. Colgrave (Cambridge, 1956). Felix persistently uses the word *heremus* or *eremus*, which Colgrave translates as 'desert'.

27 Translated in Braunfels, *Monasteries*, p. 236; for conjectural plan and discussion, see pp. 28–29. Braunfels suggests that the *domus maior* 'can only have contained study-rooms for the monks'.

28 Thompson, *Cloister, Abbot and Precinct*, pp. 33–38; oddly there is no mention here of Fontenelle. For discussion of the St Gall Plan, see ibid., pp. 38–46, and Braunfels, *Monasteries*, ch. 3.

29 Extracts translated by Braunfels, *Monasteries*, pp. 237–38.

30 Dunn, *Emergence of Monasticism*, p. 41, comments that St Basil 'took the first steps in the systematizing of the practice of child oblation', but there was as yet no obligation for the child brought up in a community to join it permanently.

31 *Rule*, cc. 30, 37, 39, 45, 63, 70.

32 Lawrence, *Medieval Monasticism*, pp. 76–96, provides a brief account with further references.

33 *Regula Solitariorum*, *PL*, 103, cols. 575–664.

34 Ibid., c. 16, col. 594.
35 Ibid., c. 17, col. 595.
36 Ibid., c. 22, col. 603.
37 Ibid., c. 43, col. 634.
38 The *Vita* was written by John, abbot of St Arnulf at Metz, who himself became a monk in 933 and died about forty years later: *MGH Scriptores*, 4, pp. 335–77. Though informative, this *Life* is structurally somewhat confusing, as it contains a number of capsule biographies within John's.
39 *MGH Scriptores*, 4, pp. 354, 356.
40 Ibid., p. 362: 'cunctisque intrinsecus fratrum habitationibus intra quadriennium expletis, muro in modum castri forinsecus cuncta circumdare animum intendit'.
41 *Les Miracles de Saint Benoît*, ed. E. de Certain (Paris, 1858), ii, 9, pp. 110–12; vi, 8, pp. 229–30.
42 *Vita Romualdi*, ed. G. Tabacco *Fonti per la Storia dell' Italia*, 94 (Rome 1957), p. 14. This text was familiar to Petrarch, who commends hunting to the seeker of solitude and the countryside: below, p. 151. For Romuald, see G. Tabacco, 'Romualdo di Ravenna e gli inizi dell' eremitismo camaldolese' in *Spiritualità e cultura nel medioevo* (Naples, 1993), pp. 195–248 (reprinted from *L'eremitismo in occidente nei secoli XI e XII: atti della Seconda Settimana Internazionale di Studio*, Milan, 1965, pp. 73–119).
43 *Vita Romualdi*, p. 13.
44 This grant is printed by U. Pasqui, *Documenti per la Storia della Città di Arezzo nel Medio Evo* (3 vols, Florence 1899–1937) i, pp. 180–82.
45 This description, it has been suggested, is coloured by the later developments of the Camaldolese ideal with which Damian himself was familiar and for which he was in part responsible: Tabacco, 'Romualdo di Ravenna', p. 204.
46 John of Lodi, *Vita Beatri Petri Damiani* in *PL*, 144, col. 126. For a brief introduction to Damian's life and works, see P. McNulty, *St Peter Damian: Selected Writings on the Spiritual Life* (London, 1959).
47 Translation in McNulty, *St Peter Damian*, pp. 53, 74.
48 Ibid., pp. 112–13.
49 Ibid., p. 127.
50 Ibid., p. 115.

Notes to Chapter 4: Living in the World

1 For a summary of the history of chess in medieval Europe see R. Eales, *Chess: The History of a Game* (London, 1985), pp. 48–70; for quarrels about chess, pp. 54–55.
2 *Life of Charlemagne*, c. 24. There are many editions and translations: see for example *Charlemagne's Courtier the Complete Einhard*, ed. P. Dutton (Peterborough, Ontario, 1998), p. 32.
3 *Miracles de Saint Benoît*, ed. de Certain, iii, 13, pp. 158–59.
4 M. Miller, *The Bishop's Palace: Architecture and Authority in Medieval Italy* (Ithaca, New York, 2000).
5 *Die Chronik des Bischofs Thietmar von Merseburg*, ed. R. Holtzmann, *MGH Scriptores*, new series 9 (1955), 4, 47, p. 184: 'Solus ad mensam quasi semicirculus factam loco cateris eminenciori sedebat.' The Latin is a little odd, but I agree with D. Warner, *Ottonian Germany: The Chronicon of Thietmar of Merseburg* (Manchester,

2001), p. 185, in thinking that *quasi semicirculus* applies to the table and not to the emperor, viz. it does *not* mean that he was (semi-) encircled by the rest of the court.

6 Penelope Eames, *Medieval Furniture* (London, 1977), p. 180. She goes on to observe that works of art which naturally focus on the splendid and ceremonial 'have fostered the mistaken view that the distinctive seat or chair was a rare object in the Middle Ages, instead of *an object in general ownership whose use was subject to social restraints*.' The italics are the original author's.

7 H. Mayr-Harting, *Ottonian Book Illumination: An Historical Study* (2 vols, London, 1991), esp. i, ch. 4.

8 I have used *Beowulf: A Glossed Text*, ed. M. Alexander (rev. edn, London, 2000) and his modern English version (London, 1973).

9 *Erec et Enide*, ed. J.-M. Fritz (Paris, 1992), line 399.

10 In *The Victorian House* (London, 2003) Judith Flanders stresses the Victorian aspiration to reserve every room for particular purposes, with furniture to match; but practice did not always match aspiration, at least in middle-class homes, and it was not unknown for servants to sleep in the kitchen.

11 'Bedchamber' appears in English in the late fourteenth century, e.g. in the A text of *Piers Plowman*, v, 136. Cf. *Bettkammere* in Middle High German.

12 The derivation of this word from *sol*, 'sun', seems obvious, and is upheld by the Oxford English Dictionary, but there has been some dispute as to whether it is not in fact derived from *soller* or *soler*, 'beam', because such a room rested on beams.

13 Below, Chapter 10.

14 'Room' was first used to denote an apartment within a house only in the mid-fifteenth century. The *OED* classifies this as the eighth sense of the word: its primary meanings, like those of its German equivalent *Raum*, are connected with space, as in our still current phrases 'having plenty of room' or 'making room for oneself'.

15 *MGH Scriptores*, 4, p. 407.

16 Ibid., p. 591.

17 Ibid., p. 391.

18 Ibid., p. 411.

19 Ibid., p. 257.

20 Widukind, *Res gesta Saxonicae*, iii, 74, in *MGH Scriptores Rerum Germanicarum*; *MGH Scriptores*, 4, p. 290.

21 Ibid., p. 216.

22 Ibid., p. 218: 'quamvis interdum nisi sub secretiore cubiculi vel ipsius thalami silentio orandi locus concedi non posset ...'

23 *Handbook for William: A Carolingian Woman's Counsel for her Son*, trans. Carol Neel (Lincoln, Nebraska, 1991), ii, 3 (pp. 18–20); iv, 1 (p. 44); iv, 4 (p. 48); x, 1 (p. 95).

24 *MGH Scriptores*, 4, p. 494.

25 Ibid., p. 837.

26 *Miracles de Saint Benoît*, ed. de Certain, viii, 16, pp. 298–300. The story of Florentius is in Gregory's *Dialogues*, ii, 8, vi. The translations in both *The Life of Saint Benedict* (p. 54) and White, *Early Christian Lives* (p. 177) render *solarium* as 'terrace'.

27 *Lamberti Ardensis historia comitum Ghisnensium*, in *MGH Scriptores*, 24, pp. 550–642; translation by L. Shopkow, *The History of the Counts of Guines and Lords of Ardres* (Philadelphia, 2001).

28 *MGH Scriptores*, 24, p. 596. Shopkow (p. 111) translates 'chambers, rooms, many lodgings and many passageways'.

29 *MGH Scriptores*, 24, p. 624. The word translated here as 'storeroom' is *penus*, which has the classical meaning of the victuals or provisions stored rather than of the storeroom, and is also used to mean the sanctuary of a temple. I have used 'cubby-hole' for *diversorium*, a word with a variety of meanings including, sometimes, an inn or lodging-place, and also a by-way or a niche.
30 Ibid., c. 127, pp. 160–1.
31 Ibid., cc. 80–81, pp. 113–15.
32 *Lancelot ou le chevalier de la charrette*, ed. J.-C. Aubailly (Paris, 1991), lines 34–42.
33 *Le Chevalier au Lion*, ed. D.F. Hult (Paris, 1994), lines 42–51.
34 *Erec et Enide*, lines 357–59.
35 For occurrences in *Erec et Enide*, see lines 1089, 1135, 1173, 2623; *Lancelot*, line 3012.
36 *Chevalier au Lion*, lines 2042–43, 2056–58, 2072–73.
37 *Lancelot*, lines 973–97.
38 *Chevalier au Lion*, line 5562.
39 *Erec et Enide*, lines 1584, 3435.
40 Ibid., lines 5183–34, 4266–69.
41 *Chevalier au Lion*, lines 4686–87, 6488–89.
42 *Lancelot*, line 6657.
43 *Chevalier au Lion*, lines 6408–9.
44 *Tristan, with the surviving fragments of the Tristan of Thomas*, trans. A. T. Hatto (Harmondsworth, 1960), p. 241.
45 *Histoire de Saint Louis*, ed. N. de Wailly (Paris 1868), p. 153; translation by M.R.B. Shaw in Joinville & Villehardouin, *Chronicles of the Crusades* (Harmondsworth, 1963), p. 271.
46 *Lancelot*, lines 539–70.
47 *Histoire*, p. 217; *Chronicles of the Crusades*, p. 316.
48 *Histoire*, p. 218: 'Lors s'enclost en sa garderobe, entre li et moy sans plus, et me mist mes dous mains entres les seues, et commensa à plorer mout durement'; *Chronicles of the Crusades*, p. 317.
49 *The Life of Christina of Markyate, a Twelfth-Century Recluse*, ed. C. H. Talbot (Oxford, 1959), pp. 42–43, 50–53, 76–77.

Notes to Chapter 5: In Search of Lost Solitude

1 For Bruno's biography see the introduction to *Lettres des premiers Chartreux*, i (*Sources Chrétiennes*, 88, Paris 1962).
2 *Lettres des premiers Chartreux*, pp. 68–70. The editor likens the *schema* of the treatment of solitude to that of St John Chrysostom's *Expositio in Psalmum*, ix (p. 68, n. 1).
3 *The Life of Ailred of Rievaulx*, trans. and ed. F.M. Powicke (London, 1950), pp. 12–13. The two passages are likened by R.W. Southern in *Revue Bénédictine*, 51 (1939), p. 265.
4 *Coutumes de Chartreuse*, edited by a Carthusian (*Sources Chrétiennes* 313, 1984).
5 *Self and Society in Medieval France: The Memoirs of Abbot Guibert of Nogent*, edited by John F. Benton (New York, 1970), pp. 60–62.
6 Braunfels, *Monasteries*, p. 111. He summarizes the development of Carthusian architecture, with plans, pp. 111–24. See also G. Coppack and M. Aston, *Christ's Poor Men: the Carthusians in England* (Stroud, 2002).
7 *Coutumes de Chartreuse*, c. 28, p. 222.

8 *Les Meditations*, edited by a Carthusian (*Sources Chrétiennes* 308, 1983) p. 204.

9 *Lettres des premiers Chartreux*, i, pp. 142, 144. Guigo draws here on a number of earlier sources, including Sidonius Apollinaris.

10 *De quadripartito exercitio cellae*, chap. 36, *PL*, 173, cols. 880–86. Previously a Premonstratensian canon, Adam wrote the treatise at the request of the prior of Witham, the first English Charterhouse.

11 *De consideratione ad Eugenium Papam*, ed. J. Leclerq and H. Rochais in *S. Bernardi Opera*, iii (Rome, 1963), pp. 393–493; translation by J. D. Anderson and E.T. Kennan, *Five Books on Consideration: Advice to a Pope* (Kalamazoo, Michigan, 1976).

12 Text in *Sermones super Cantica Canticorum*, ed J. Leclerq, C. H. Talbot and H.M. Rochais (=*S. Bernardi Opera*, i–ii), 2 vols (Rome, 1957–58), 2, p. 26. The translation used here is by Samuel Eales, *Cantica Canticorum: Eighty-six Sermons on the Song of Solomon* (London, 1895), pp. 252–55.

13 For Guerric's biography, see the introduction to his *Sermons*, ed. J. Morson & H. Costello, 2 vols (*Sources Chrétiennes*, 166, 202, Paris, 1970–73), pp. 7–19. There is a translation by monks of Mount St Bernard Abbey, *Liturgical Sermons* (2 vols, Kalamazoo, Michigan, 1970–71). The story of Guerric's conversion and of the troubles at Tournai is told in *Vita Hugonis Abbatis Marchianensis auctore anonymo eius discipulo*, in E. Martène and E. Durand, *Thesaurus Novorum Anecdotorum* (5 vols, Paris, 1717) iii, col. 1712.

14 *Vita Hugonis*, col. 1723.

15 Guerric, *Sermons*, i, pp. 34–5. These translations are the present writer's.

16 *Sermons*, ii, pp. 128 (Second Sermon on the Annunciation), 352 (Fourth Sermon on John the Baptist).

17 *Sermons*, i, pp. 152–56.

18 Cf. C.W. Bynum, 'The Cistercian Concept of Community', in *Jesus as Mother: Studies in the Spirituality of the High Middle Ages* (Berkeley, California, 1982), pp. 59–81; also H. Leyser, *Hermits and the New Monasticism* (London, 1984), esp. pp. 12–20.

19 Walter Daniel, *Ailred*, p. 11.

20 *PL* 176, col. 174.

21 *Sermons*, i, pp. 224–26 (Fifth for the Nativity).

22 *Sermons*, ii, pp. 156–58 (Third for the Annunciation).

23 *Sermons*, i, pp. 374–76 (Fifth for the Purification).

24 *Sermons*, i, p. 286 (Third for Epiphany).

25 See in general on this subject J. Leclerq, *The Love of Learning and the Desire for God*, trans. C. Misrahi (London, 1978). For further reflections on monastic reading see below, pp. 136–37.

26 *Sermons*, ed. A. Hoste and G. Raciti, 3 vols (*Sources Chrétiennes* 130, 207, 339, Paris 1967–87), i, p. 274 (Sermon 14).

27 Among recent contributions to the abundant literature on Cistercian art, architecture and uses of space see T. N. Kinder, *Cistercian Europe: Architecture of Contemplation* (Grand Rapids, Michigan, 2002) and M. Cassidy-Welch, *Monastic Spaces and their Meanings: Thirteenth-Century English Cistercian Monasteries* (Turnhout, 2001).

28 This seems to have been about 1167–68; Isaac later returned to L'Etoile but not to his old rank as abbot, and died probably c.1174. It seems that his actions were in some respects illicit and that the community established on Ré had to be regularized *ex post facto* by the General Chapter. For Isaac's biography see the introduction to *Sermons*, i; also the introduction by B. McGinn to the translation of Sermons 1–23 by H.

McCaffery, *Sermons on the Christian Year*, i (Kalamazoo, Michigan, 1979) (no more have yet appeared).

29 It has been suggested (*Sermons* i, p. 22 n.2) that they include 9–15, for the four Sundays after Epiphany, while actual references to the exile seem to be made in numbers 14, 15, 18, 19, 21, 22, 24, 27, 29, 31 and 33 (ibid., p. 279 n. 1).

30 *Sermons*, i, p. 154 (no. 5).

31 Ibid., pp. 270–78. The translation is the present writer's.

32 See Constable, 'The Interpretation of Mary and Martha' (above, p. 227, n. 46) For an example of the positive evaluation of Martha's contribution, see above p. 20.

33 *Sermons* i, pp. 286–90.

34 *Sermons* ii, pp. 7–10. The phrase 'generis fere humani iacturam facientes' looks like a reminiscence of Ovid, *Metamorphoses*, line 246.

35 *Sermons* ii, p. 60 (Sermon 18).

36 *Sermons* iii, p. 190 (Sermon 50). For another excellent example of Isaac's exaltation of the common life, see Sermon 31 (ibid. ii, pp. 200–202).

37 *Life of Ailred*, pp. 39–41, 50, 59. For the *scriptoriolum* of Bernard's secretary Nicholas at Clairvaux see below, p. 158.

38 *Selected Works*, trans. H. Feiss (Kalamazoo, Michigan, 1987), pp. 131–41.

39 Alternatively, the word might here simply mean 'the basic local unit where one lived the religious life, a unit which took different forms in different orders': ibid., p. 16. *Cella* does sometimes signify a convent as a whole (above, p. 228, n. 4).

40 Ibid., p. 140.

41 *Lettre aux frères de Mont-Dieu*, ed. J. Déchanet (*Sources Chrétiennes* 223, 1975). There is an English translation by Theodore Berkeley, *The Golden Epistle* (Kalamazoo, Michigan, 1971), but the translations here are by the present writer except when otherwise stated.

42 *Lettre*, c. 105, pp. 226, 228. Here Déchanet detects sources in Seneca's *Letters* xliii, 3 and xxviii, 10.

43 *De claustro animae*, iii, in *PL*, 171, cols. 1085–1130.

44 *Lettre*, cc. 29–30, p. 168.

45 It is surprising that this citation eludes Déchanet, who is more interested in William's Senecan echoes, but it does not escape Berkeley (*Golden Epistle*, p. 19 n. 16, and cf. p. 4 n. 5), who suggests that William may have obtained it via St Ambrose and draws attention to parallel passages elsewhere in his writings. The fact that William makes no use here of Cicero's subsequent words, *nunquam minus otiosus quam cum parum occupatus*, as he might easily have done, might support that theory.

46 *Lettre*, c. 84, p. 208. Déchanet here cites Seneca, *Epistle* xv, 6.

47 *Lettre*, c. 94, p. 218. This part of the *Epistle* is described by Déchanet as 'une sorte de centon des lettres à Lucilius'; cf. his 'Seneca noster, des Lettres à Lucilius à La Lettre aux Frères du Mont-Dieu', *Mélanges de Ghellinck* (Gembloux, 1951), pp. 753–66.

48 *Lettre*, c. 145, p. 158.

49 *Lettre*, c. 288, p. 374; 289, p. 376.

50 *De quadripartito exercitio cellae*, *PL*, 173, c. 28, col. 850.

51 Ibid., c. 24, col. 841.

52 Ibid., c. 9, cols 815–16. The last phrase echoes a sentiment expressed by Seneca in his tenth Epistle to Lucilius: when he goes out among crowds, 'nunquam mores quod extuli refero'.

53 *Sermons*, ii, p. 310 (Sermon 38).

54 *Beati Richalmi Speciosae Vallis in Franconia Abbatis Ord. Cisterciensis Liber Revelationum de Insidiis et Versutiis Daemonum adversus Homines*, in B. Pez, *Anecdotorum Thesaurus Novissimus*, 6 vols (Augsburg, 1721–29), ii, cols 373–472.
55 *Self and Society*, p. 80.
56 *Caesarii Heisterbacencis Monachi Ordinis Cisterciensis Dialogus Miraculorum*, ed. J. Strange, 2 vols (Cologne, 1851), i, pp. 24–25 (1, 17).
57 *Dialogus*, i, pp. 90–91 (bk 2, 21, 22).
58 Ibid., pp. 127–29 (bk 3, 14).
59 *Dialogus*, ii, p. 98 (bk 8, 20), pp. 162–63 (bk 8, 96).
60 Ibid., pp. 283–84 (bk 11, 15).
61 Ibid., pp. 268–69 (bk 11, 2).

Notes to Chapter 6: In the Midst of People

1 *Dialogus Miraculorum*, i, p. 350 (vi, 46).
2 Ibid., p. 332 (v, 47).
3 Ibid., pp. 252–53 (iv, 87).
4 Ibid., pp. 207–8 (iv, 39).
5 Letter 118, translated by B. Scott-James, *The Letters of St Bernard of Clairvaux* (London, 1953), pp. 179–80.
6 Aelred of Rievaulx, *La Vie de Recluse*, ed. C. Dumont (*Sources Chrétiennes*, 76, Paris 1961), p. 44. The translations are the present author's.
7 Ibid.
8 Ibid., pp. 48–52.
9 Ibid., pp. 62–64.
10 Ibid., p. 66 and n. 1.
11 Ibid., pp. 116–28. Earlier (pp. 108–14) Aelred uses Martha and Mary to support his point that prayer is charity: active poor relief was not the concern of the enclosed religious, but prayer was charity.
12 See E. A. Jones, 'Christina of Markyate and *The Hermits and Anchorites of England*', in *Christina of Markyate: A Twelfth-Century Holy Woman*, ed. Samuel Fanous and Henrietta Leyser (London, 2005), pp. 229–53. Jones lists and maps recluses in Hertfordshire, Bedfordshire and Huntingdonshire. The allusion in his title is to the classic work of Rotha Mary Clay, *The Hermits and Anchorites of England* (London, 1914).
13 On Roger, see Talbot's introduction, *Life of Christina*, pp. 20–22.
14 Ibid., pp. 80–81, 86–87, 108–9, 110–13.
15 Ibid., pp. 11–12, 140–45, 154–55, 156–59, 182–83. Gregory was on at least one occasion permitted to stay for a time with his sister at Markyate and celebrate mass there. Christina also had a married sister and another brother, a citizen of Huntingdon.
16 Ibid., p. 92: 'in secretissimam amarissimamque cameram vix illi pre angustia sufficientem detrusa'.
17 Ibid., pp. 100–107.
18 Ibid., pp. 146–47. This was Alexander (1123–1148); his predecessor Robert Bloet had been Christina's inveterate enemy. While the principle that all recluses should have episcopal approval was old-established, the formal requirement of a licence does not seem in England to have preceded the thirteenth century: ibid., p. 17 and n. 5.

19 Ibid., pp. 160–61, 126–27. The phrase *quociens clausulam egrediebatur eremi*, apparently referring to Christina, occurs in a damaged portion of the text (pp. 140–41).

20 Ibid., p. 21. Roger and Siger shared a tomb in the monastery church in the thirteenth century, to which Henry III made benefactions; it survives in part.

21 Ibid., p. 12: 'even apart from Christina and her circle all the names of those connected with the hermit movement in England, like Godric and Wulfric, are Anglo-Saxon'. Roger called Christina (in English) his 'Sunday daughter' (pp. 106–7). Aelred of Rievaulx and his sister too were English. However, even if it is true that the relatively informal anchoritic life had quasi-nationalist associations, its exponents had little difficulty winning the favour of abbots and monks who were themselves 'Normans'.

22 *Wulfric of Haselbury*, ed. Dom Maurice Bell (*Somerset Record Society*, 47, 1933). The *Life*, written probably *c.* 1185–86, was dedicated first to Bartholomew bishop of Exeter, secondly to Baldwin archbishop of Canterbury. For John of Forde's sources, see pp. xx–xli. Glastonbury is described (p. 93) as half a day's journey from Haselbury.

23 *Wulfric*, pp. xx–xli.

24 Ibid., pp. 14–15.

25 Ibid., p. 16.

26 Ibid., pp. 30–31. See H. Mayr-Harting, 'Functions of a Twelfth-Century Recluse', *History*, 60 (1975), pp. 337–52.

27 *Wulfric*, pp. 51–2.

28 Ibid., pp. xxix–xxx.

29 Ibid., pp. 37–8.

30 Ibid., p. 58.

31 Ibid., p. 21.

32 Ibid., p. 110.

33 For modern English renderings of the principal works in this category, with introductions and further reference, see *Anchoritic Spirituality: Ancrene Wisse and Associated Works*, trans. A. Savage and N. Watson (New York, 1991). The translation in this volume is based on the text edited by J.R.R. Tolkien, *Ancrene Wisse, Ms. Corpus Christi College Cambridge 402* (EETS 249, 1962). There is another modern English version by Hugh White, *Ancrene Wisse: Guide for Anchoresses* (Harmondsworth, 1993).

34 The evidence for the authorship and audience of *Ancrene Wisse* is summarized in *Anchoritic Spirituality*, pp. 9–11, on the basis of the work of E. J. Dobson, *The Origins of Ancrene Wisse* (Oxford, 1976).

35 In the Corpus manuscript the phrase here translated 'loneliest place of all' is 'anlukest stude of alle'. 'Most solitary' would surely be preferable.

36 *Anchoritic Spirituality*, pp. 137, 153.

37 *Ancrene Wisse*, ed. Tolkien, p. 77. According to the OED these are among the very earliest appearances of 'privity' in English.

38 A. K. Warren, *Anchorites and their Patrons in Medieval England* (Berkeley, California, 1985), esp. pp. 114 ff.

39 Summarized in *Anchoritic Spirituality*, p. 348, n. 5.

40 There is a possible further alternative, that this window gave on to an interior courtyard (possibly used, among other things, for hygienic purposes); Bishop Gray's somewhat later licence for Beatrice Franke, noted below, mentions both a *domus* and a *clausura*. These may be synonyms, but alternatively may designate a dwelling and some kind of courtyard.

41 *Visitations*, pp. 113–15. Warren, *Anchorites*, pp. 66–67, suggests that this particular process was 'perfunctory', not because Beatrice was not suitable for enclosure, but rather because it was well known to all concerned that she was. The speed of the whole transaction suggests that it was a *fait accompli* already when Gray issued his commission on 3 January; the anchorhold had certainly been built and established by the time the abbot arrived at Winterton on the 21st, for Beatrice was there waiting for him.

42 A. Benvenuti Papi, *'In Castro Poenitentiae': santità e società femminile nell' Italia medievale* (Rome, 1990), pp. 272–73. The fourteenth-century altarpiece, of which a seventeenth-century drawing survives, provides the only near-contemporary evidence for Giulia's life; the predella was added in the fifteenth century.

43 Clay, *Hermits and Anchorites*, pp. 83, 214–15. The names of two of the anchorites of Chester-le-Street are known: John Wessington, who in 1383–4 received a quarterly allowance of ten shillings from the bishop of Durham, and John Blenkinsop, who was licensed c.1400.

44 *Yvain*, lines 2829–2884.

45 There are two versions of Rainieri's *Vita*. The earlier and shorter is edited by R. Grégoire, *San Ranieri di Pisa* (Pisa, 1990); the longer and later is in *AS*, Junii 5, pp. 421–65. See also C. Morris, 'San Ranieri of Pisa', *Journal of Ecclesiastical History* 45 (1994), pp. 588–99.

46 Grégoire, *San Ranieri*, pp. 108, 109.

47 Ibid., p. 127. For the hermits of the Holy Land see A. Jotischky, *The Perfection of Solitude: Hermits and Monks in the Crusader States* (Philadelphia, 1995); curiously he does not mention Ranieri.

48 Grégoire, *San Ranieri*, p. 132.

49 *Libellus de Vita et Miraculis S. Godrici Heremitae de Finchale auctore Reginaldo monacho Dunelmensi* (SS, 20, 1847), p. 31.

50 Ibid., pp. 67–68, 71.

51 Ibid., pp. 91–92.

52 Ibid., p. 140. Later a monk of Durham came regularly to the hermitage to celebrate mass on Sundays; ibid., pp. 195, 202.

53 Ibid., pp. 166–7.

54 Ibid., p. 269.

55 P. Grosjean, *Vitae S. Roberti Knaresburgensis* (*Analecta Bollandiana*, 57, 1939, pp. 365–400) published a fragmentary life from Harleian 3755, which is the earliest source, and another, fuller and later, from Egerton 3143. *The Metrical Life of St Robert of Knaresborough*, ed. Joyce Bazire (EETS 228, 1953) is devoted to the contents of the Egerton manuscript and includes: another edition of the longer life; a Latin verse life; and Middle English texts from the same manuscript, of which the chief is the *Metrical Life*, which was clearly derived from the Latin sources. It also includes the earlier Harleian life, omitting the prologue.

56 *Metrical Life*, pp. 114, 118–19.

57 This stock phrase is used also by Caesarius to describe the site of Cîteaux (*Dialogus Miraculorum*, i, p. 5).

58 *Metrical Life*, p. 42. *Skerre* means rock or cliff, and the *creves* is a hole or cave ('crevice').

59 Ibid., pp. 129–30.

60 Ibid., pp. 50–1, 132.

61 Ibid., pp. 52–55, 116–18. Grimbald Bridge is a very short distance from St Robert's Cave.

62 Ibid., p. 58.

63 For a description of the cave and its dimensions, see *Metrical Life*, pp. 21–22.

Notes to Chapter 7: In Chamber and in Hall

1 Margaret Wood described Old Soar in a leaflet written for the then Ministry of Works (1950; subsequently reprinted in 1975), and later made several references to it in *The English Mediaeval House* (London, 1965) (plan, p. 69). See also Nathaniel Lloyd, *A History of the English House* (London, 1934; reprinted 1985), in which fig. 58 (p. 180) shows the east end of the chapel in a much altered state, reversed by more recent restoration. For the chapel see below p. 129–30.

2 J. Munby and H. Summerson, *Stokesay Castle* (English Heritage, 2002). See also the references in E. Mercer, *English Architecture to 1900: the Shropshire experience* (Logaston, Herefordshire, 2003), especially pp. 96–98. Stokesay (like Old Soar) is an example of the ground-floor hall, which contrasts with the first-floor hall previously typical of castles and grander house: see Mercer's discussion, ibid., pp. 103–11, and his references to the literature.

3 There is an abundant literature on these basic components of domestic architecture: for example, M.W. Thompson, *The Medieval Hall: the basis of secular domestic life, 600–1600 AD* (London, 1995); J. Blair, 'Hall and Chamber: English Domestic Planning 1000–1250' in M. Jones & G. I. Meirion-Jones, *Manorial Domestic Buildings in England and Northern France* (London, 1991), pp. 1–21.

4 *The Piers Plowman Tradition*, ed. H. Barr (London, 1993), p. 138 (lines 38–39). Elsewhere in the poem a franklin's freehold is described as 'a faire hous with halles and chambres' (p. 171, line 945).

5 *The Romance of Guy of Warwick: the Second or Fifteenth Century Version*, ed. J. Zupitza, EETS, Extra Series 25–26 (1875–76), p. 77 (line 2674).

6 *Passus* v, line 218.

7 *The Romance of Guy of Warwick*, p. 5 (ll. 151–52).

8 D. Thackray, *Bodiam Castle* (The National Trust, 1991), with plans; Charles Coulson, 'Some Analysis of the Castle of Bodiam, East Sussex', in C. Harper-Bill and R. Harvey (ed.), *Medieval Knighthood IV: Papers from the Fifth Strawberry Hill Conference* (Woodbridge, 1992), pp. 51–108; Matthew Johnson, *Behind the Castle Gate: From Medieval to Renaissance* (London, 2002), pp. 19–33. There are also numerous references in Coulson, *Castles in Medieval Society: Fortresses in England, France and Ireland in the Central Middle Ages* (Oxford, 2003).

9 L. Dresbeck, 'The Chimney and Social Change in Medieval England', *Albion*, 3 (1971), pp. 21–32.

10 Later, when the host returns from hunting, he finds a fire burning there on the floor ('fire upon flet', lines 831–32).

11 In floor area, the solar at Old Soar was just over a third of the size of the adjacent hall, which measured 42 feet 9 inches by 33 feet 9 inches. The hall at Ightham measures 30 feet by 20 feet, at Penshurst 62 feet by 39 feet.

12 Now re-erected at the Weald and Downland Museum at Singleton, Sussex. It takes its name from fifteenth-century tenants, the Baileys.

13 A. Quiney, *Town Houses of Medieval Britain* (London, 2003), p. 197.

14 M. Thompson, 'The architectural context of Gainsborough Old Hall', in *Gainsborough Old Hall*, ed. P. Lindley (*Occasional Papers in Lincolnshire History and Archaeology*, 8, Lincoln, 1991), p. 17.

15 M. Girouard, *Life in the French Country House* (London, 2000), pp. 78–79: the English great hall is described as 'an invention of such genius that it has lasted at least 600 years and is still going strong – not in a country-house context, perhaps, but in

university colleges and legal inns of court.' Certainly the concept was more than 600 years old in 2000.

16 *Egil's Saga*, c. 60, in *The Sagas of Icelanders*, introduction by R. Kellogg (London, 2000), pp. 112–13. I have made extensive use of the translations contained in this volume, which first appeared in *The Complete Sagas of Icelanders*, ed. V. Hreinsson (5 vols, Reykjavik, 1997); another selection from this collection appears in *Sagas of Warrior Poets*, ed. Diana Whaley (Harmondsworth, 2002). There is another translation of *Egil's Saga* by H. Pálsson and P. Edwards (Harmondsworth, 1976).

17 *Njal's Saga*, trans. M. Magnusson and H. Pálsson (Harmondsworth, 1960), c. 77, p. 169.

18 For this plan see *Sagas of Icelanders*, pp. 733–35; also, and for Viking houses in general, J. Graham-Campbell, ed., *Cultural Atlas of the Viking World* (Oxford, 1994), pp. 62–3, 172–73, where it is suggested that the supposed 'latrine' at Stöng may have been a workshop in which wool was prepared using urine.

19 *Laxdaela Saga* cc. 46, 47, in *Sagas of Icelanders*, pp. 363, 365. There is another translation of this saga by M. Magnusson and H. Pálsson (Harmondsworth, 1969).

20 *Egil's Saga* cc. 43, 44, in *Sagas of Icelanders*, pp. 66–69.

21 *Egil's Saga*, c.11, ibid., pp. 20–21.

22 For the terminology of domestic building, see the glossary in *Sagas of Icelanders*, pp. 740–58, s.v. 'bed closet', 'cross bench', 'fire hall', 'hall', 'high seat', 'main room'.

23 *Eyrbyggja Saga*, trans. H. Pálsson and P. Edwards (revised edn, Harmondsworth, 1989), cc. 52, 54, pp. 135, 138–39.

24 Ibid., c. 54, pp. 1380–39.

25 *Egil's Saga*, c. 72, in *Sagas of Icelanders*, p. 141.

26 *Gisli's Saga*, c. 9, ibid., p. 509.

27 *Egil's Saga*, c. 32, ibid., p. 53.

28 *Njal's Saga*, c. 44, p. 114.

29 *Kormak's Saga*, c. 3, in *Sagas of Warrior-Poets*, pp. 7–10.

30 *Laxdaela Saga*, c. 7, in *Sagas of Icelanders*, pp. 281–82.

31 *Egil's Saga* , c. 79, in *Sagas of Icelanders*, pp. 150–51; c. 88, ibid., p. 181.

32 W. Rösener, *Peasants in the Middle Ages*, trans. A. Stützer (Urbana, Illinois, 1992), chapter 5, pp. 63–82, offers a brief summary, with further references, for central and northern Europe. For the influence of urban housing styles, see ibid., pp. 75–6.

33 For one overview of English peasant housing see J. Grenville, *Medieval Housing* (London, 1997), chap. 5, who reviews sharply divergent opinions on such issues as its permanence and quality, citing *inter alia* C. Dyer, 'English Peasant Buildings in the Later Middle Ages (1200–1500)', in his *Everyday Life in Medieval England* (London, 2000), pp. 133–65 (originally in *Medieval Archaeology*, 30 (1986), pp. 18–45). Mercer, *English Architecture*, chapter 8, discusses the timber houses of gentry and peasantry in one English county (Shropshire) and places them in a broader context.

34 R.K. Field, 'Worcestershire Peasant Buildings, Household Goods and Farming Equipment in the Later Middle Ages', *Medieval Archaeology*, 9 (1965), pp. 105–43. A *solarium* and stairs are mentioned in a three-bay house in 1474 (p. 127).

35 A two-roomed cottage from Hangleton in Sussex (which may give some idea of the widow's environment) and a three-bayed hall from Boarhunt in Hampshire can be seen at the Weald and Downland Museum.

36 Field, 'Worcestershire peasant buildings', pp. 128 (1482), 132 (1434) . Examples of *aula* and *camera* occur on p. 126. The word 'room' occasionally appears as an equivalent for 'bay' or for the Latin *spacium* or *intersticium* in the Worcestershire sources.

37 It has been calculated that a house which consisted of three bays, each of the standard length (15 feet), and which housed a family of five would have made some 90 square feet of living accommodation available to each family member, compared to 65 square feet *per capita* in late medieval Provence or less than 40 in rural India in the 1960s: Dyer, 'English Peasant Buildings', pp. 163–64.
38 Rösener, *Peasants*, pp. 79–80.
39 R. Stopani, *Medievali 'Case da Lavoratore' nella Campagna Fiorentina* (Florence, 1978), pp. 22–3.
40 M.S. Mazzi and S. Raveggi, *Gli uomini e le cose nella campagne fiorentine del quattrocento* (Florence, 1983), pp. 143–53; numerous inventories are printed in the documentary appendices.
41 Ibid., p. 148 and appendix 8, pp. 332–38.
42 Mazzi and Raveggi, *Gli uomini e le cose*, appendix 16, pp. 351–53.
43 *Cronica*, xi, 94, quoted by R. Stopani, *Medievali 'Case da Signore' nella Campagna Fiorentina* (Florence, 1981), p. 31, and by J. Ackerman, *The Villa: Form and Ideology of Country Houses* (London, 1990), p. 64.
44 Mazzi and Raveggi, *Gli uomini e le cose*, p. 149.
45 See the reprinted eighteenth-century translation *The Ten Books of Architecture: The 1755 Leoni Edition* (New York, 1986).
46 Ackerman, *The Villa*, p. 87, and, for the importance of Petrarch 'for the revival of the ideology of the villa', p. 64.
47 Below, pp. 149–50.
48 Richard Goldthwaite, *The Building of Renaissance Florence* (Baltimore, 1980), pp. 102–112. On the furnishings of the Italian house, see Peter Thornton, *The Italian Renaissance Interior, 1400–1600* (London, 1991).
49 Dale Kent, *Cosimo de' Medici and Florentine Renaissance* (New Haven, 2000), p. 243 (with plans). For another Florentine *palazzo*, see *Giovanni Rucellai ed il suo Zibaldone*, 2: *A Florentine Patrician and his Palace (Studies of the Warburg Institute*, 24 pt ii, 1981). For studies, see below, Chapter 10.
50 fitz Stephen's description has been several times translated, for example by H. E. Butler under the title *Norman London* (London, 1934; reprinted New York, 1990).
51 C. Kightly, *Barley Hall York* (York, 1999); Grenville, *Medieval Housing*, pp. 89, 91, 111; Quiney, *Town Houses*, pp. 204–205 (with plan).
52 Ibid., pp. 217–34. For the instructive late medieval development of the guest accommodation at Kirkstall Abbey (Leeds), see S. Wrathmell, *Kirkstall Abbey: the Guest House* (2nd edn, Wakefield, 1987).
53 For some examples, see Quiney, *Town Houses*, pp. 226–7, 229.
54 Ibid, pp. 201–2, and for late medieval inns in general, pp. 200–8.
55 C. Platt & R. Coleman-Smith, *Excavations in Medieval Southampton 1953–1969* (2 vols, Leicester, 1975), 1, p. 107; G. Coppack, *Medieval Merchant's House Southampton* (London, 1991); Quiney, *Town Houses*, pp. 248–9 (with plan).
56 A fragment of the hood by chance survived when the fireplace was destroyed in the nineteenth century and made this interpretation and reconstruction possible.
57 Latin text in L.F. Salzman, *Building in England down to 1540* (Oxford, 1967), pp. 417–18; translation in H.T. Riley, *Memorials of London* (London, 1868), p. 66. For London houses in general see J. Schofield, *Medieval London Houses* (New Haven, 1995).
58 Salzman, *Building in England*, pp. 418–19.
59 Ibid., p. 601; Quiney, *Town Houses*, pp. 253–54.

60 Ibid., p. 212; S. Knights, *Dragon Hall: A History* (Norwich, 1991).
61 Sylvia Thrupp, *The Merchant Class of Medieval London* (Ann Arbor, Michigan, 1962), pp. 130–42.
62 *The Paston Letters*, ed. James Gairdner (6 vols, London, 1904), iii, pp. 166–89. For a brief description of Caister, with a plan, see Johnson, *Behind the Castle Gate*, pp. 50–52.
63 The following observations are based on wills and inventories, dating from the mid-fourteenth century to the early sixteenth, collected by James Raine in the first four volumes of *Testamenta Eboracensia*, as follows: i (Surtees Society, 4, 1836); ii (ibid., 30, 1855); 3 (45, 1865); 4 (53, 1869). Inventories such as that of the possessions of the goldsmith John Colan in 1490 (*Testamenta* 4, pp. 56–60) have been used in the reconstruction of Barley Hall.
64 *Testamenta* i, p. 8.
65 *Testamenta* iv, p. 284. Collins had a very notable library, but perhaps more unexpectedly he had a hand-gun (a 'magonale') in the 'fourth chamber' of his house at York.
66 *Testamenta*, i, p. 102.
67 Ibid., p. 89.
68 Ibid., p. 167.
69 For example, William Halifax of Nottingham in 1454 and William Warde of York in 1496 (*Testamenta*, iv, p. 115).
70 Ibid., p. 36.
71 Ibid., p. 186.
72 *Testamenta* ii, pp. 96–105.
73 Ibid., p. 50: 'in quadam alta camera ad superiorem partem aulae'.
74 R. Goldthwaite, *Building of Renaissance Florence* p. 403, observes that many more examples appear in Flemish than in Florentine painting. For the importance of the decorative arts in the Florentine living-space, see pp. 400–407 generally; for the importance of this consumer market for art in the generation of Renaissance culture, Goldthwaite, *Wealth and the Demand for Art in Italy, 1300–1600* (Baltimore, 1993).
75 E. Clark, 'Some Aspects of Social Security in Medieval England', *Journal of Family History*, 7 (1982), pp. 307–20.
76 G. Homans, *English Villagers of the Thirteenth Century* (New York, 1975), pp. 144–45.
77 Field, 'Worcestershire Peasant Buildings', p. 126.
78 Homans, *English Villagers*, p. 145.
79 Clark, 'Some Aspects of Social Security', p. 311.
80 Ibid., p. 318.
81 D. Nicholas, *The Domestic Life of a Medieval City: Women, Children and the Family in Fourteenth-Century Ghent* (Lincoln, Nebraska, 1985), pp. 177–83.
82 D. Herlihy and C. Klapisch-Zuber, *Tuscans and their Families: A Study of the Florentine Catasto of 1427* (New Haven, 1985), p. 311.
83 Herlihy and Klapisch-Zuber, *Tuscans*, p. 292.
84 Ibid., p. 216. The proportions of these groups in the towns and smaller cities of Tuscany are closer to those in the countryside although somewhat smaller.
85 For unmarried women see the essays in Judith Bennett and Amy Froide, ed., *Singlewomen in the European Past, 1250–1800* (Philadelphia, 1999). There is a vast and growing literature on women in the medieval town, in which marital status is one of the key issues: for example, P.J.P. Goldberg, *Women, Work and Life Cycle in a*

Medieval Economy: Women in York and Yorkshire, c. 1300–1520 (Oxford, 1992); Barbara Hanawalt, ed., *Women and Work in Preindustrial Europe* (Bloomington, Indiana, 1986); Erika Uitz, *Women in the Medieval Town* (London, 1988); Martha Howell, *Women, Production and Patriarchy in Late Medieval Cities* (Chicago, 1986).

86 Sharon Farmer, '"It is Not Good that [Wo]man Should Be Alone: Elite Responses to Singlewomen in High Medieval Paris', in Bennett and Froide, *Singlewomen*, p. 86.

87 Nicholas, *Domestic Life*, p. 181.

88 See the many observations on this subject in Goldberg, *Women, Work and Life Cycle*.

89 *Testamenta*, iii, p. 201.

90 H.M. Smyser, 'The Domestic Background of *Troilus and Criseyde*', *Speculum*, 31 (1956), pp. 287–315. Chaucer obtained the core of his story from Boccaccio's *Filostrato*, but himself supplied most of the topographical detail.

91 I. Ragusa and R. B. Green, *Meditations on the Life of Christ; an Illustrated Manuscript of the Fourteenth Century* (Princeton, 1961), p. 84, ill. 74; pp. 101–2; cf. ills 87, 88 and 89 (pp. 100–1).

92 J. Nuechterlein, 'The domesticity of sacred space in the fifteenth-century Netherlands' in *Defining the Holy: Sacred Space in Medieval and Early Modern Europe*, ed. Andrew Spicer and Sarah Hamilton (Aldershot, 2005), p. 66. The painting is illustrated in F. Thürlemann, *Robert Campin* (London, 2002), pp. 74–75.

Notes to Chapter 8: Religion in the Home

1 *Dialogus Miraculorum*, ii, p. 192.

2 Ibid., pp. 191–92.

3 *Dialogus*, i, p. 251.

4 Ibid., i, p. 89.

5 W. Simons, *Cities of Ladies: Beguine Communities in the Medieval Low Countries, 1200–1565* (Philadelphia, 2001). Many of the surviving Flemish beguinages have been classified as World Heritage Sites: S. Van Aerschot and M. Heirman, *Vlaamse Begijnhoven Werelderfgoed* (Leuven, 2001).

6 Ibid., pp. 56, 77, 256.

7 *Le Ménagier de Paris*, ed. G. Brereton and J. Ferrier (Oxford, 1981), pp. 127, 130, 132, 135, 136; trans. Eileen Power, *The Goodman of Paris* (2nd edn, London, 1992), pp. 136, 138–40, 142–43.

8 B. McGuire, 'Late Medieval Care and Control of Women: Jean Gerson and his Sisters', *Revue d'Histoire Ecclésiastique*, 92 (1997), pp. 5–37. Gerson's criticism of beguines is quoted p. 8, n. 14.

9 Quoted by A. Vauchez, *Les laïcs au moyen âge* (Paris, 1987), p. 101. For late medieval sanctity in general and the place of lay saints within it, see Vauchez, *La sainteté en occident aux derniers siécles du moyen age* (Rome, 1981); English translation by J. Birrell, *Sainthood in the Later Middle Ages* (Cambridge, 1997).

10 Cf. the remarks of Jean Miniac in his introduction to his French translation of the *Vita*: Jacques de Vitry, *Vie de Marie d'Oignies* (Arles, 1997), p. 12. The Latin text is in *AS*, Junii 5, pp. 547–72.

11 On lay 'penitents' in the thirteenth-century Italian city, see A. Thompson, *Cities of God: the Religion of the Italian Communes, 1125–1325* (Philadelphia, 2005), chapter 2.

12 Translated by D. Webb, *Saints and Cities in Medieval Italy* (Manchester, 2006), pp. 97–140.
13 Ibid., p. 113.
14 *AS*, Octobris 13, pp. 152–53.
15 *Vita* in *AS*, Junii 1, pp. 148–55.
16 Webb, *Saints and Cities*, pp. 193–241.
17 Ibid., pp. 246–56.
18 Ibid., pp. 163–90.
19 Blessed Raymond of Capua, *The Life of St Catherine of Siena*, trans. G. Lamb (London, 1960). The Latin text is in *AS*, Aprilis 3, pp. 853–959.
20 Catherine's struggle for her 'cell' is narrated in *Life*, pp. 42–51.
21 *Life*, p. 51.
22 Ibid., p. 71.
23 Ibid., p. 101. For Catherine's embrace of social obligations see below pp. 197–98.
24 Ibid., pp. 96–97. Owners of books of hours may well have read them in a similar fashion: below, p. 141.
25 *AS*, Martii 3, p. 183.
26 *AS*, Maii 6, p. 390. For this image see H. B. Maginnis, 'Images, devotion and the Beata Umiliana de' Cerchi', in A. Ladis & S. Zuraw, ed., *Images of Holiness: art and devotion in Renaissance Italy* (Georgia, 2001), pp. 13–20. See also V. Schmidt, 'Painting and individual devotion in late medieval Italy: the case of Saint Catherine of Alexandria', ibid., pp. 21–36.
27 See B. McGuire, 'Late medieval care and control of women'.
28 Ibid., p. 21; *Jean Gerson: Early Works*, trans. B. McGuire (New York, 1998), pp. 156–57.
29 *Early Works*, p. 126.
30 Translated in *Early Works*, pp. 75–127.
31 Ibid., c. 3, p. 77.
32 Ibid., c. 18, pp. 90–91.
33 Ibid., c. 23, pp. 95–96.
34 Ibid., c. 24, pp. 96–97.
35 Ibid., c. 25, p. 98.
36 *Early Works*, p. 159.
37 C.A.J. Armstrong, 'The Piety of Cicely, Duchess of York: A Study in Late Medieval Culture', in *England, France and Burgundy in the Fifteenth Century* (London, 1983), pp. 141–43.
38 In the nineteenth century, in search of York wills, James Raine discovered and published 127 records of the formal veiling of widows in the dioceses of York and Carlisle between 1311 and 1520: *Testamenta*, iii , pp. 312–71; iv, pp. 337–40.
39 Thomas's and Joan's wills are in *Testamenta*, ii, pp. 163–64, 177–78; the record of Joan's veiling is ibid., iii, p. 332. Thomas had a private chapel, the contents of which he left to his eldest son John; he also made bequests of 6s 8d to 'each of five poor widows in my almshouse next to the chapel (*in elemosinario meo juxta capellam existenti*).'
40 Ibid., iii, p. 139.
41 Ibid., ii, pp. 232–33. This was most probably what is often called the parlour, a ground-floor chamber adjacent to the hall.
42 *Calendar of Entries in the Papal Registers*, ix, p. 365; S. Tymms (ed.), *Wills and Inventories from the Registers of the Commissary of Bury St Edmunds and the Archdeacon of Sudbury* (Camden 1st Series, 49, 1850), p. 22.

43 For Old Soar, see above p. 97. There is a general discussion and list of chapels in Wood, *English Mediaeval House*, pp. 227–46.
44 For a summary of the rules that Sutton applied, see *The Rolls and Registers of Bishop Oliver Sutton, 1280–1299*, ed. Rosalind Hill, iii (Lincoln Record Society, 48, 1954), pp. l–lii.
45 D. Kent, *Cosimo de' Medici*, pp. 305–28; R. Hatfield, 'Cosimo de' Medici and the Chapel of his Palace', in F. Ames-Lewis (ed.), *Cosimo 'il Vecchio' de' Medici, 1389–1464* (Oxford, 1992), pp. 221–44.
46 F.W. Kent, 'The Making of a Renaissance Patron', in *Giovanni Rucellai ed il suo Zibaldone*, 2, *A Florentine Patrician and his Palace*, pp. 57–60.
47 For general observations on the Florentine preference for 'public' religion, see R. Trexler, *Public Life in Renaissance Florence* (Ithaca, New York, 1991), p. 160; for Giovanni Morelli, pp. 174–85.
48 R. Wieck, *Painted Prayers: The Book of Hours in Medieval and Renaissance Art* (New York, 1997), p. 12.
49 G. Gibson, *The Theatre of Devotion* (Chicago, 1989), p. 10.
50 *The Ten Books of Architecture: The 1755 Leoni edition*, v, 17, p. 107.
51 D. Robb, 'The Iconography of the Annunciation in the Fourteenth and Fifteenth Centuries', *Art Bulletin*, 18 (1936), pp. 480–526. See also Nuechterlein, 'The Domesticity of Sacred Space', in *Defining the Holy*, ed. Spicer and Hamilton (above p. 242, n. 92).
52 For further observations on some of the subjects treated in this chapter, see D. Webb 'Domestic Space and Devotion in the Middle ages', in *Defining the Holy*, pp. 27–47.

Notes to Chapter 9: Men of Letters

1 'Plus ne prestray livre quoi qui aviengne': *Selected Poems*, ed. I.S. Laurie and D.M. Sinnreich-Levi (London, 2003), pp. 54–55.
2 For various aspects of what follows see P. Saenger, *Space between Words: the Origins of Silent Reading* (Stanford, California, 1997); M.T. Clanchy, *From Memory to Written Record*, (2nd edn, Oxford, 1993); the essays collected in M. A. and R. H. Rouse, *Authentic Witness: Approaches to Medieval Texts and Manuscripts* (Notre Dame, Illinois, 1991); S. Hindman, *Sealed in Parchment: rereadings of knighthood in the Illuminated Manuscripts of Chrétien de Troyes* (Chicago, 1994).
3 *Confessions*, trans. R. Pine-Coffin (Harmondsworth, 1961), vi. 3, p. 114. There is a remarkably similar description of Dr Thomas Arnold of Rugby reading 'with no attempt at seclusion, conversation going on around him', in A. P. Stanley, *Life and Correspondence of Thomas Arnold, D.D.* (London, 1844), p. 127; but Arnold was willing at any moment to break off and answer a question.
4 *The School of the Cloister*, xix, 3, in *Selected Works*, translated Feiss, p. 103.
5 *The Coucher Book of Selby*, i, ed. J. T. Fowler, Yorkshire Archaeological and Topographical Association, Record Series 10 (1891), p. 26.
6 *PL*, 171, col. 1074: 'Est tempus et locus loquendi et tacendi. Aperitur ostium in claustro hora constituta lectioni, in capitulo confessioni, in ecclesia orationi.'
7 Saenger, *Space between Words*, p. 263.
8 *Gesta Regum*, ed. W. Stubbs (2 vols, RS, 90), ii, p. 519.
9 *S. Anselmi Cantuariensis Archiepiscopi Opera Omnia*, ed. F.V. Schmidt (6 vols, Edinburgh, 1938–61), iii, p. 3; *The Prayers and Meditations of Saint Anselm*, trans. B. Ward (Harmondsworth, 1973), p. 89.

10 Ibid., p. 13: 'quaedam sunt, quae si intimo corde dicantur, cum vacat, plus tendunt ad accendendum amorem'.
11 *Epistola de Vita Contemplativa*, ed. E. Colledge and J. Walsh (*Sources Chretiennes*, 163, Paris, 1970), p. 84.
12 Ibid., pp. 108–12.
13 *The Didascalicon of Hugh of St Victor*, iii, 6, trans. J. Taylor (New York, 1991), p. 91. On Hugh and the meaning of reading, see I. Ilich, *In the Vineyard of the Text: a Commentary to Hugh's Didascalicon* (Chicago, 1993).
14 *The Metalogicon of John of Salisbury: A Twelfth-Century Defense of the Verbal and Logical Arts of the Trivium*, i, 24, trans. D. McGarry (Gloucester, Massachusetts, 1971) pp. 65–66.
15 *Didascalicon*, iii, 12, trans. Taylor, p. 94; John of Salisbury, *Policraticus sive de nugis curialium et vestigiis philosophorum libri VIII*, ed. C.C. J. Webb (2 vols, Oxford, 1909), ii, p. 145 (vii, 13).
16 *Policraticus*, p. 150.
17 Above, p. 73.
18 *De Rebus a se gestis*, III. 18, in *Opera*, i, p. 119: 'copiose litteratus erat et literaturam dilexit'.
19 *De jure et statu Menevensis ecclesiae*, in *Opera*, iii, pp. 165, 182; see Clanchy, *From Memory to Written Record*, p. 267.
20 *Opera*, iii, p. 180.
21 Richard of Bury, *Philobiblon*, ed. A. Altamura (Naples, 1954), xii, p. 114.
22 T. Wren and S. McKendrick, *Illuminating the Renaissance: The Triumph of Flemish Manuscript Painting in Europe* (London, 2003), p. 63, with references.
23 Thrupp, *Merchant Class of Medieval London*, p. 158.
24 Saenger, *Space between Words*, pp. 249–50; Guibert, *Self and Society*, pp. 87–88, 91.
25 *PL*, 156, col. 340.
26 *Philobiblon*, i, p. 79.
27 Ibid, xv, p. 120.
28 On literacy and heresy, see, among much else, P. Biller and A. Hudson, ed., *Heresy and Literacy, 1000–1350* (Cambridge, 1994); M. Aston, *Lollards and Reformers: Images and Literacy in Late Medieval Religion* (London, 1984); Anne Hudson, *Lollards and their Books* (London, 1985). Older but still valuable is M. Deanesley, *The Lollard Bible* (Cambridge, 1920).
29 Translation in Deanesley, *Lollard Bible*, p. 31.
30 Ibid., pp. 30–34, for the whole episode.
31 Ibid., p. 36.
32 Wieck, *Painted Prayers*, p. 10. A larger vernacular element intruded after c.1400 and the influence of the *devotio moderna* made Dutch-language Books of Hours popular in the northern Netherlands. On this subject in general see also Wieck, *The Book of Hours in Medieval Art and Life* (London, 1988) and J. Harthan, *Books of Hours* (London, 1977).
33 *The Goodman of Paris*, trans. Power, pp. 35–63.
34 D. Herlihy, *Opera Muliebria: Women and Work in Medieval Europe* (New York, 1990), pp. 55–61.
35 *Le Chevalier au Lion*, lines 1417–18.
36 *The Saxon Mirror: a Sachenspiegel of the Fourteenth Century*, trans. M. Dobozy (Philadelphia, 1999) p. 77. The use of the word *vrouw*, rather than *wib*, in this text may

indicate that it applied, or was expected to apply, only to upper-class women, but Dobozy observes that usage is not consistent enough for certainty.

37 There is a fine example in a window in All Saints' North Street, York.

38 *Convivio*, i. 9. The translation by C. Ryan slightly glosses Dante's highly elliptical Italian: *The Banquet* (Saratoga, 1989), p. 30.

39 *The Treasure of the City of Ladies*, trans. S. Lawson (London, 1985), i, 15, p. 68; iii, 5, p. 161; iii, 8, p. 168; iii, 12, p. 176.

40 I. Origo, *The Merchant of Prato* (London, 1963), pp. 213–14. For Catherine of Siena's illiteracy see above p. 126.

41 The quotations are from the translation by G.H. McWilliam (Harmondsworth, 1972), pp. 46–47, 829–32.

42 I. Origo, *The World of San Bernardino* (London, 1964), pp. 64–65.

43 Bernardino da Siena, *Prediche volgari sul Campo di Siena 1427*, xxx, ed. C. Delcorno (2 vols, Milan, 1989), ii, p. 862.

44 Deanesley, *Lollard Bible*, p. 45.

45 Above, p. 137.

46 Deanesley, *Lollard Bible*, p. 355.

47 *Seinte Katerine*, ed. E.J. Dobson and S. d'Ardenne (EETS Supplementary Series, 7, 1981), p. 148: 'Hanc pater / ab annis puerilibus studiis liberalibus / imbuendam tradiderat ...'

48 *The Life of St Catherine of Alexandria*, ed. C. Horstmann (EETS, 100, 1893).

49 Giovanni Villani, *Nuova cronica*, ed. G. Porta (3 vols, Florence, 1990), ii, p. 337 (Bk 10, c. 136).

50 *Cronica*, ed. G. Luzzatto (Turin, 1978), i, 20, p. 48: 'cortese e ardito ma sdegnoso e solitario e intento allo studio'. There is a translation by D. Bornstein, *Dino Compagni's Chronicle of Florence* (Philadelphia, 1986).

51 *Decameron*, trans. McWilliam, pp. 503–505 (sixth day, ninth story).

52 *Historia ecclesiastica*, in L. A. Muratori, *Rerum Italicarum Scriptores*, 11, col. 1178.

53 Translation by Barbara Reynolds (Harmondsworth, 1969).

54 *Convivio* iii. 9, 15: *The Banquet*, p. 105.

55 E. Rosen, 'The Invention of Eyeglasses', *Journal of the History of Medicine and Allied Sciences*, 11 (1956), pp. 13–14, 183–218. C. Frugoni, *Medioevo sul naso: occhiali, bottoni e altre invenzioni medievali* (Bari, 2001), pp. 3–27. For Petrarch's lament in the letter *Posteritati*, see *Prose*, ed. G. Martellotti et al. (Milan, 1955), p. 2.

56 For a convenient summary of Petrarch's biography see K. Foster, *Petrarch: Poet and Humanist* (Edinburgh, 1984), pp. 1–18.

57 *Prose*, p. 12.

58 Ibid., pp. 286–590.

59 The prior of Camaldoli, displeased to find that there was no mention of Romuald in early recensions of the treatise, in 1372 personally supplied Petrarch with a copy of Damian's *Vita*: ibid., p. 464, n. 2.

60 *De vita solitaria* (i, 1), p. 296.

61 Ibid. (ii. 14), p. 568.

62 Ibid. (ii, 15), pp. 584–6.

63 Ibid. (i, 6), p. 354.

64 Ibid. (ii, 15), p. 586.

65 Ibid. (ii, 13), pp. 550–52.

66 Ibid. (i, 6), pp. 356–58.

67 Ibid. (i, 3), p. 330. The quotation from Cicero is from *Tusculan Disputations* v, 36, 105; from Seneca, *Epistolae ad Lucilium*, lxxxii, 3. The same passage is quoted by Richard of Bury, *Philobiblon* xv, p. 121.
68 *De vita solitaria* (i, 4), pp. 336–8. The quotation is from Quintilian, *De institutione oratoris*, x, 3, 27–30. This work only became available to Petrarch in 1350.
69 Ibid. (i, 7), pp. 364–6.
70 *Tusculan Disputations*, v, 36.
71 *De vita solitaria*, ii, 12, p. 532.
72 Ibid. (i, 7), p. 370, quoting Seneca, *Epistolae* x and xxv.
73 *Epistolae familiares*, xxiv, 3, in *Prose*, p. 1024.
74 *De vita solitaria* (ii, 15), pp. 586–8.
75 Ibid., (i, 1), p. 300.
76 Ibid., (i, 3), pp. 322–4. The citation is of *De officiis* iii, 5, 25.
77 In ii, 10 (pp. 502–4) Petrarch refers to Mary Magdalen as the type of ascetic withdrawal, giving Martha her usual second-best due. The cave in which the Magdalen had supposedly lived her life of penitence was not far from the Charterhouse of Montrieux where Petrarch's brother Gerard lived, and he himself had visited it.
78 *Prose*, pp. 2–4.
79 *De vita solitaria* (ii, 15), p. 576.
80 Ibid. (ii, 15), pp. 578–80.

Notes to Chapter 10: Studies

1 *Familiares*, vii, 1.
2 Suetonius, *Augustus*, 72, 78. It is not entirely clear whether this couch was located in his *cubiculum* or in the private room aloft. In the Loeb edition J.C. Rolfe imports the word 'study' into his translation: 'a couch in his study'. Seneca too refers to the use of a bed or couch which could be used for study, observing (*Epistle* lxii, 2) that 'There are things which one can write in a carriage; some require a couch and leisure and seclusion.'
3 *Epistolae* xi, 27; cf. above p. 8.
4 *AS*, Novembris 3, p. 436. *Cubile* sometimes means a den or lair.
5 It has been suggested that *bibliotheca* here may mean nothing more or less than the Bible, seen as a collection of books from which the monk was to select one for his personal reading: McCann, *The Rule of St Benedict*, p. 208. On this interpretation, the monk was to take for his annual reading one of the volumes into which the Bible was divided. A good specimen of a book-cupboard can seen at the Augustinian priory of Lilleshall in Shropshire. For the development of libraries and book-storage, see H. Petroski, *The Book on the Bookshelf* (New York, 1999); K. S. Staikos, *The Great Libraries from Antiquity to the Renaissance*, trans. T. Cullen (Delaware and London, 2000).
6 *Herimanno Liber de restauratione S. Martini Tornacensis*, in *MGH Scriptores*, 14, p. 313.
7 Nicholas of Clairvaux, Epistle 35, *PL*, 196, cols. 1126–7. For an account of Nicholas, with full references, see *The Letters of Peter the Venerable*, ed. Giles Constable (2 vols, Cambridge, Massachusetts, 1967), ii, pp. 313–30.
8 '... haec mihi tradita est ad legendum, ad scribendam, ad dictandum, ad meditandum, ad orandum et adorandum Dominum majestatis...' Note that *dictare* is distinguished from *scribere*, the physical act of writing.

9 Braunfels, *Monasteries*, pp. 132–35.
10 Translated in M.-H. Vicaire, *Saint Dominic and his Times*, trans. K. Pond (London, 1964), p. 313.
11 Ibid., pp. 214–15, 497 n. 153: 'Edificatum est claustrum cellas habens ad studendum et dormiendum desuper satis aptas.'
12 *Lives of the Brethren of the Order of Preachers*, trans. P. Conway and ed. B. Jarrett (London, 1955), p. 20.
13 *Acta capitulorum generalium Ordinis Praedicatorum* 1, *ab anno 1220 usque ad annum 1303*, ed. B. M. Reichert (Rome, 1898), pp. 75, 208.
14 Ibid., p. 309.
15 Ibid., p. 233. In 1303 what was required of students in terms of attendance at choir and refectory was laid down in some detail: ibid., p. 374.
16 Ibid., pp. 252–3.
17 R. Creytens, 'L'instruction des novices à la fin du XVe siècle', *Archivum Fratrum Predicatorum*, 22 (1952), p. 217: 'Cancellas cellarum non obstruant vel obstacula ponant ut videri nequeant.'
18 See the 1228 Constitutions, c. 9, in *Early Dominicans: Selected Writings*, ed. S. Tugwell (London, 1982), p. 452.
19 *Acta capitulorum generalium*, ii, ed. Reichert (Rome, 1899), pp. 35, 39.
20 R. Gibbs, *Tomaso da Modena: Painting in Emilia and the March of Treviso, 1340–1380* (Cambridge, 1989), pp. 67–87. Gibbs suggests that the occasion was the Provincial Chapter which met at Treviso in August 1351.
21 Saenger, *Space between Words*, pp. 252–53.
22 Gibbs, *Tomaso da Modena*, pp. 77, 101–104.
23 This, as it happened, was anachronistic. Although spectacles were about half a century old at the time the frescoes were painted, Hugues had died in 1263, before their invention.
24 Gibbs, *Tomaso da Modena*, p. 86.
25 T. Kaeppeli, 'Fragment d'*Ordinationes* d'un Maître Général dominicain (*c.*1355–65)', *Archivum Fratrum Predicatorum*, 24 (1954), p. 288.
26 W.H. Knowles, 'Black Friars of Gloucester', *Transactions of the Bristol and Gloucestershire Archaeological Society*, 54 (1932), pp. 188–94. See p. 190 for the dimensions and a sketch reconstruction of one of these cubicles. See also W.A. Hinnebusch, *The Early English Friars Preachers* (Rome, 1951), pp. 169–80.
27 This is a possible inference from the presence of a feature in the masonry at the east end of the northern wall, a curved hollow in the upper edge of the projecting wall which may have been designed to hold a curtain rail. I am most grateful to Malcolm Watkins for pointing this out to me and for enabling me to see the Gloucester site, which was not at the time open to the public.
28 *Calendars of Close Rolls, 1256–1259*, p. 270; *1259–61*, p. 347; *1268–72*, p. 56. The stone, if not the timber, suggests the building of more than partitions: Hinnebusch, *History of the Dominican Order* (2 vols, New York, 1965–1973), i, p. 356.
29 Hinnebusch, *Dominican Order*, i, p. 358.
30 W.A. Pantin, ed., *Documents Illustrating the Activities of the General and Provincial Chapters of the English Black Monks 1215–1540* (3 vols, Camden Third Series, 45, 47, 54), i, pp. 64, 74–5.
31 Ibid., p. 173.
32 David Wilkins, *Concilia Magna Brittanicae et Hiberniae* (4 vols, London, 1737), ii, p. 609 (c. 37).

33 See below, chap. 12.
34 *Gesta abbatum* (3 vols, RS 28, iv), iv, pp. 302, 306.
35 Ibid, p. 399; iii, pp. 389, 392–3.
36 Ibid, ii, p. 423; *Annales Amundesham* (2 vols, RS 28, vi), i, pp. 258, 260. It is not clear whether these two references are to the same library. Whethamstede resigned in 1440 but was re-elected on the death of his successor in 1451.
37 *Visitations*, iii, pp. 376–77.
38 Ibid., p. 293; ii, pp. 83, 36.
39 *Visitations*, i, p. 110.
40 *Chapters of the Augustinian Canons*, ed. H. E. Salter (Canterbury and York Society, 29, 1922), p. 26.
41 Ibid., p. 262. This, according to the OED (s.v. 'carol'), is the earliest occurrence of the word in English.
42 *Rites of Durham: Being a Description or Brief Declaration of all the Ancient Monuments, Rites & Customs Belonging or Being Within the Monastical Church of Durham Before the Suppression. Written 1593* (SS 107, 1903), p. 83.
43 Knowles, 'Black Friars of Gloucester', p. 198.
44 *Gesta abbatum*, iii, p. 514. Cf. R. Gilchrist, *Gender and Material Culture: The Archaeology of Religious Women* (London, 1994) p. 95.
45 *The Book of the Duchess*, lines 44–49, 1324–29. Suetonius, *Augustus*, 78, describes how the emperor would send for 'readers or story-tellers' if he was unable to sleep.
46 Vespasiano degli Bisticci, *Vite degli uomini illustri del secolo XV*, ed. P. d'Ancona and E. Aeschlimann (Milan, 1951), p. 19.
47 *Opera*, i, p. 119.
48 According to the *Continuatio* of the Chronicle of Martinus Polonus, 'camera, in qua ad studendum solus de nocte sedebat, funditus corruit ...' (*MGH Scriptores*, 30, p. 711). The sources for the incident are listed by Horace Mann, *The Lives of the Popes in the Middle Ages*, xvi (London, 1932), pp. 54–5.
49 Robert of Brunne, *Handlyng Synne*, ed. F. J. Furnivall, EETS, 119, 123 (1901), p. 158. For the most part this is an English adaptation of the *Manuel des pechiez* by William of Wadington, but the passage in question is one of Brunne's additions to his original.
50 *Larousse* suggests that the word 'estude' occurs in an early thirteenth-century (1212) version of the *Life* of Gregory the Great by Angier, a religious of St Frideswide at Oxford: 'La Vie de Saint Grégoire le Grand, traduite du Latin par Frère Angier, religieux de Saint-Frideswide', ed. P. Mayer, *Romania*, 12 (1883), pp. 145–208. Describing the pope's last days, lines 2739–40 read 'Trestot l'estude entrelessa/E ses durs jors pleinst e plora': line 2739 is a translation of 'a studio expositionis omnino desisteret' and it seems likely that *studium* here signifies the activity of study.
51 *The Vision of Piers Plowman*, ed. A.V. Schmidt (London, 1995), lines 344–45, p. 52.
52 In these passages it seems indisputable that a room is meant; some other Chaucerian uses of the word are more ambiguous. Earlier in *The Franklin's Tale* (line 1207) it seems possible that it means ' a period of study'. In the G text of the Prologue to *The Legend of Good Women* (line 40) the poet hails the coming of spring and exclaims 'Farwel my stodye, as lastynge that sesoun!' The corrresponding line 39 of the F text, however, reads 'Farewel my bok and my devocioun!'
53 *Senilium rerum libri 6* (x, 2), in *Prose*, ed. Martellotti, p. 1122; *De vita solitaria*, ii, 14, ibid., p. 562.
54 Ibid., p. 468.

55 *Epistolario*, ed. F. Novati (4 vols, *Fonti per la Storia d'Italia* 15), i, p. 335: 'stetit interim illa latitans inter studioli mee cartulas, ut quia raro possum in habitationis mee diversorio privato vacare studio vel scripture'.

56 'Cum igitur die quodam optimo meo preceptore Colucyo in suo studio residerem ...': R. G. Witt, *Hercules at the Crossroads: The Life, Works and Thought of Coluccio Salutati* (Durham, North Carolina, 1983), p. 183 n. 12.

57 C. Guasti, ed., *Lettere di un notaio ad un mercante* (2 vols, Bologna, 1880), i, pp. 12, 87, 118.

58 *Ricordi*, ed. V. Branca (Florence, 1956) pp. 51–52.

59 J. Godefroy, *Dictionnaire de l'ancienne langue française*, 3 (Paris, 1884), p. 661: 'Comme maistre Raoul de Preselles a entention de faire aucunes estudes spacieuses et secretes pour mettres ses livres, don't il a pluseurs.'

60 *Le livre des fais et bonnes moeurs du sage roy Charles V*, ed. S. Solente (2 vols, Paris, 1936–40), I, p. 42; translation in *The Writings of Christine de Pizan*, ed. C.C. Willard (New York, 1994), p. 240.

61 Girouard, *French Country House*, pp. 55, 114.

62 L. Deslisle, *Recherches sur la librairie de Charles V* (2 vols, Paris, 1907), pp. 7–8. Building accounts related to the construction are printed pp. 367–68.

63 *Oeuvres complètes*, ed. M. Glorieux (10 vols, Paris 1960–73), vii, 1, p. 320: 'je me trouvay en mon estude a la vespree, l'an de grace mil quatre cens et deux ...'

64 Translation by R. Brown-Grant (London, 1999), p. 5.

65 Ed. A. Tarnowski (Paris, 2000), pp. 96–100.

66 British Library, Harley MS 4431. Another miniature of Christine in her study is illustrated by Girouard, *French Country House*, p. 112. She is shown at her writing-desk, attended by the three ladies, in a manuscript of *Le Livre de la Cité des Dames* in the Bibliotheque Nationale, MS 1177.

67 M. Meiss and E.H. Beatson, *Les Belles Heures de Jean duc de Berry* (London, 1974), fol. 15: the scene 'is unprecedented and may be unique'. The miniature is tentatively ascribed to Jean de Limbourg.

68 M. Meiss, 'Scholarship and Penitence in the Early Renaissance: The Image of St Jerome', *Pantheon*, 32 (1974), pp. 134–40, reprinted in *The Painter's Choice: Problems in the Interpretation of Renaissance Art* (New York, 1976) pp. 189–202. For Tommaso's frescoes see above, pp. 160–1.

69 *The Life and Martyrdom of Saint Katherine of Alexandria, Virgin and Martyr* (Roxburghe Club, 1884), pp. 8, 14, 16.

70 *Life of St Catherine*, p. 33.

71 It was still possible to give a much more limited account of Katherine, stressing her martyrdom and omitting all the extraneous detail, as Capgrave's disciple Osbern Bokenham did around 1447 for the benefit of the Suffolk ladies Katherine Howard and Katherine Denston. Bokenham specifically refers to the work of 'my spiritual father, Master John Capgrave' which however 'is rare and hard to acquire'. Here Katherine's education and her use of it are what they were in the Latin *Life* and its derivatives, notably the *Golden Legend*. There is a translation by S. Delany in *A Legend of Holy Women: A Translation of Osbern Bokenham's Legends of Holy Women* (Notre Dame, Indiana, 1992), pp. 125–40.

72 Examples to be found among the York wills collected by James Raine in the nineteenth century include: Thomas Farnylawe, chancellor of the church of York, 1378 (*Testamenta*, i, p. 102); John of Scarborough, rector of Tichmarsh

and notary public, 1395 (ibid., iii, p. 6); William Noion, canon of York and rector of Haddenham in Cambridgeshire, 1405 (ibid., p. 28).

73 *Testamenta*, iii, p. 94.
74 Ibid., p. 45.
75 *Testamenta*, ii, pp. 232, 61.
76 *Testamenta*, iii, p. 210.
77 Tymms, ed., *Wills & Inventories*, p. 33. For Baret and his family, see R.S. Gottfried, *Bury St Edmunds and the Urban Crisis, 1290–1539* (Princeton, 1982), pp. 153–59; for his tomb, G.G. Gibson, *The Theater of Devotion*, pp. 72–79.
78 *General Prologue*, lines 293–6.
79 Girouard, *French Country House*, p. 115.
80 D. Thornton, *The Scholar in his Study: Ownership and Experience in Renaissance Italy* (New Haven and London, 1997); W. Liebenwein, *Lo Studiolo: Die Enstehung eines Raumtypus und seine Entwicklung bis um 1600* (Berlin, 1977); F. Cardini, 'The Sacred Circle of Mantua', in S. Bertelli, ed., *Italian Renaissance Courts* (London, 1986), pp. 78–125.
81 L. B. Alberti, *I libri della famiglia*, ed. R. Romano and A. Tenenti (Turin, 1969), pp. 266–67. Giannozzo chose to call this room his *studio*, but another Italian businessman might have preferred the term *scrittoio*, for which there is no precise English equivalent: 'office', in its modern sense, comes closest.
82 Margaret L. King, *Women of the Renaissance* (Chicago, 1991), pp. 195–98. The woodcut is reproduced in Thornton, *Scholar in his Study*, p. 94, and Petroski, *The Book on the Bookshelf*, p. 102.
83 Thornton, *Scholar in his Study*, pp. 90–92.
84 *Il libro del cortigiano*, ed. E. Bonora (Milan, 1972), iii, 77, p. 282; G. Bull, *The Book of the Courtier* (Harmondsworth, 1967), p. 278, translates as 'inner room'.

Notes to Chapter 11: Gardens

1 N. Orme, 'The Dead Beneath Our Feet', *History Today*, 54, no. 2 (February 2004), p. 21.
2 *Gesta abbatum*, ii, pp. 125–36.
3 *Councils and Synods with Other Documents Relating to the English Church, ii, AD 1205–1313*, ed. F.M. Powicke and C.R. Cheney (2 vols, Oxford, 1964), ii, pp. 1123–24.
4 *Gesta abbatum*, ii, p. 515.
5 *Visitations*, i, p.104.
6 Ibid., iii, p. 62.
7 *De claustro animae*, iv, 34 (*PL* 171, col. 1172).
8 *Liber Herimanni de restauratione S. Martini Tornacensis*, *MGH Scriptores*, 14, p. 281. This was one version of the stories told, in order to prove that Matilda had never really been a nun, when her marriage with Henry was mooted. E.A. Freeman discusses this and also Eadmer's version, which does not mention Rufus or the garden, in *The Reign of William Rufus* (2 vols, Oxford, 1882), ii, pp. 32, 121, 127–28, 598–603. Alicia Amherst, *A History of Gardening in England* (London, 1895), p. 7, repeated the Rufus story, but gave the impression that Eadmer was the source. John Harvey repeats her revealingly imprecise reference to Eadmer and also misleadingly states that Rufus sought admission to the convent *in order* to see the flowers: *Mediaeval Gardens* (London, 1981), pp. 8, 148.

9 See the essays in C. Acidini Luchinat, ed., *Giardini Medicei: giardini di palazzo e di villa nella Firenze del Quattrocento* (Milan, 1996).

10 Guidance to the sources and older bibliography will be found in the following selection from the ample modern literature: Harvey, *Mediaeval Gardens*; T. McLean, *Medieval English Gardens* (London, 1981); S. Landsberg, *The Medieval Garden* (London [1996]). Landsberg is a leading practitioner of garden reconstruction, for which see also the splendidly illustrated M.-F. Valery, *Jardins du Moyen Age* (Tournai, 2001).

11 H.-D. Stoffler, *Der Hortulus des Walahfrid Strabo: aus dem Kräutergarten des Klosters Reichenau* (5th edn, Sigmaringen, 1997).

12 Ibid., pp. 46–47.

13 Ibid., p. 128. It has been suggested that he intended this as a reference to the conflict between Louis the Pious and his sons, which erupted after 829: Louis was the flowering shoot who was being crowded out by his progeny. Walafrid was a supporter of the emperor, who was behind his appointment as abbot of Reichenau in 838, but after the latter's death he had to flee the territories of Louis the German and was unable to function as abbot until Grimaldus (dedicatee of the *Hortulus*) effected a reconciliation in 842 (p. 10).

14 Ibid., pp. 148–51.

15 Translation in Venantius Fortunatus, *Personal and Political Poems*, trans. J. George (Liverpool, 1995), pp. 51–52. Venantius was something of an enthusiast for apples: in another letter he thanked Bishop Gregory of Tours for both fruit and grafts (p. 22).

16 Ibid., pp. 70–71.

17 *Libellus de vita et miraculis S. Godrici*, p. 71.

18 Ibid., p. 265: 'pauci agri … infra horti ipsius ambitum inclusi'.

19 Ibid., pp. 339–42.

20 Ibid., p. 107.

21 Ibid., pp. 95–97.

22 Ibid., pp. 265–66.

23 Ibid., p. 261.

24 Ibid., pp. 148–49.

25 Gerald, *Opera*, iv, p. 255: '… tantum hortis suis intra fossata sua seu muralia clausis, quos tam ad delectationem quasi loco laboris, quam ad fructum quoque, tam ex variis olerum et porrorum atque leguminum seminariis, quam ex herbis et speciebus odoriferis ac pretiosis diligenter insertis et plantatis eliciendum non inutiliter consueverunt.'

26 Translation by Eales, *Cantica Canticorum*, pp. 132–33.

27 *Liturgical Sermons*, ii, pp. 213–16.

28 Prose translation by C. Dahlberg, *The Romance of the Rose* (Hanover, New England, 1983).

29 Harvey, *Mediaeval Gardens*, pp. 66–67, 73.

30 *Petrus de Crescentiis, Ruralia Commoda: das Wissen des volkommen Landwirtschaft um 1300*, ed. W. E. Richter (4 vols, Heidelberg, 1995–2002). Harvey, *Mediaeval Gardens*, p. 6, gives a full translation of Albert's chapter on the planting of pleasure-gardens.

31 *The Goodman of Paris*, trans. Power, pp. 128–34.

32 *History of the Counts of Guines*, trans. Shopkow, p. 169.

33 Above, p. 56.

34 *Lettres des premiers Chartreux*, i, p. 68.

35 *PL*, 171, cols. 1235–38. Hildebert was first bishop of Le Mans and then archbishop of Tours.
36 Latin texts and translations in H. Waddell, *More Latin Lyrics from Virgil to Milton* (London, 1976), pp. 240–41, 250–51.
37 For this inherited literary tradition see D. Pearsall and E. Salter, *Landscapes and Seasons of the Medieval World* (London, 1973), especially Chapter 1.
38 William of Malmesbury, *The Deeds of the Bishops of England*, trans. D. Preest (Woodbridge, 2002), c. 118, p. 174; c. 186, p. 220.
39 Harvey, *Mediaeval Gardens*, pp. 8, 10.
40 *Opera*, vi, p. 92.
41 Johnson, *Behind the Castle Gate*, pp. 33–54.
42 Thrupp, *Merchant Class of Medieval London*, p. 136.
43 *Norman London*, p. 49.
44 I. Origo, *The Merchant of Prato*, pp. 58, 66.
45 Translation in Harvey, *Mediaeval Gardens*, p. 6.
46 Text and translation in Braunfels, *Monasteries*, p. 245.
47 *Memorials of St Edmund's Abbey*, ed. T. Arnold (3 vols, RS, 96), ii, p. 293.
48 *Cartulary of Winchester Cathedral*, ed. A. S. W. Goodman (Winchester, 1927), n. 275, p. 123. The royal permission was granted on 20 February 1336 (*Calendar of Patent Rolls, 1334–1338*, p. 224).
49 *Rites of Durham*, p. 88.
50 *Opera*, iii, pp. 342–43.
51 Harvey, *Mediaeval Gardens*, pp. 84–86, 10.
52 Harvey, *Mediaeval Gardens*, has numerous observations and references on this subject; see also the index to R.A. Brown, H.M. Colvin and A. J. Taylor, *The History of the King's Works: The Middle Ages* (2 vols, London, 1963).
53 *King's Works*, ii, p. 925.
54 Ibid., pp. 1013–16. The assignations in the orchard are described in Gottfried von Strassburg's version of the Tristan story, written around 1210 and based on the earlier version (*c.* 1160) by Thomas, which may have been written for the Angevin court and now exists only in fragments: see *Tristan*, trans. A. J. Hatto, pp. 231–35.
55 Pearsall and Salter, *Landscapes and Seasons*, p. 77.
56 *King's Works*, ii, pp. 1012, 971, 768, 1001, 949.
57 Christine de Pizan, *Le livre des fais et bonnes moeurs*, i, pp. 46–7.
58 Harvey, *Mediaeval Gardens*, pp. 92–93, citing (for Charles VI) H. Sauval, *Histoire et recherches des antiquités de la ville de Paris* (3 vols, Paris, 1724), ii, pp. 283–84.
59 *Lais de Marie de France*, ed. K. Warnke (Paris, 1990), pp. 212, 214 (lines 60, 97); *Cligès*, ed. C. Méla and O. Collet (Paris, 1994), p. 428 (lines 6320–30). Chrétien uses *jardin* once in his last unfinished work, *Le Conte du Graal*, ed. C. Méla (Paris, 1990), p. 468, line 6625.
60 *Middle English Romances*, ed. S. H.A. Shepherd (New York, 1995), p. 176.
61 J.F. Took, *Dante: Lyric Poet and Philosopher, An Introduction to the Minor Works* (Oxford, 1990), pp. 29–43.
62 Harvey, *Mediaeval Gardens*, p. 4. A 'herber' was not the 'arbour' it rather confusingly resembles, for the latter word derives from the Latin word for tree, *arbor*; the OED remarks on the complex relationship and contamination between the two words.
63 *Sir Gawain and the Green Knight, Pearl, Cleanness, Patience*, ed. J. Anderson (London, 1996), pp. 1, 2, 45 (lines 9, 38, 1171).
64 *The Vision of Piers Plowman* (B Text), xvi, 15, 17.

65 Ronald Sutherland, *The Romaunt of the Rose and Le Roman de la Rose: a parallel-text edition* (Oxford, 1967), p. 14. The anonymous English translator of Fragment B sometimes uses an exact equivalent of the French, 'verger' (p. 90).
66 Some idea of what the widow's yard might have been like is conveyed by the 'retired peasant's garden of the thirteenth century' that has been reconstructed to accompany the cottage from Hangleton (Sussex) at the Wealden & Downland Museum: Landsberg, *Medieval Garden*, pp. 116–18.
67 Landsberg, who directed this reconstruction, describes it in *Medieval Garden*, pp. 120–28.
68 *AS*, Octobris 13, p. 152.
69 *Sir Cleges*, lines 193–201, in A. Laskaya & E. Salisbury (ed.), *The Middle English Breton Lays* (Kalamazoo, Michigan, 1995).
70 *Paston Letters*, ed. Gairdner, ii, p. 286.
71 Quoted by E. H. Wilkins, *Life of Petrarch* (Chicago, 1961) p. 101, from which the biographical data here are also taken.
72 P. de Nolhac, 'Pétrarque et son jardin', *Giornale storico della letteratura italiana*, 9. i (1887), pp. 404–14.
73 De Nolhac, 'Pétrarque', prints these notices, pp. 410–14.
74 *Epistole metriche*, iii, 3, in *Rime, trionfi e poesie latine*, ed. F. Neri, G. Martellotti, E. Bianchi and N. Sapegno (Milan, 1951), p. 784.
75 The three *epistole metriche* to Giovanni da Colonna are iii.1, 4 and 5 in *Rime, trionfi e poesie latine*, pp. 766–82.
76 L. B. Alberti, *I libri della famiglia*, ed. R. Romano and A. Tenenti (Turin, 1969), p. 244.
77 J. S. Ackerman, *The Villa: Form and Ideology of Country Houses* (London, 1990), p. 78. For the Villa Medici and its builder, see G. Galletti, 'Una committenza medicea poca nota: Giovanni di Cosimo e il giardino di Villa Medici a Fiesole', in *Giardini Medicei*, pp. 61–84.
78 *Rime, trionfi e epistole metriche*, p. 786.
79 *Epistolae familiares*, xiii, 8.
80 *Norman London*, p. 50.
81 Above, p. 146.
82 *The Stonor Letters and Papers 1290–1483* (2 vols, Camden Third Series 29, 30), ii, p. 132.
83 *The Life and Martyrdom of Saint Katherine of Alexandria*, p. 8. 'Leisure', a loose equivalent for *otium* in certain of its senses, was first used in English by the same Richard Brunne who had credited Robert Grosseteste with a 'study' (above, pp. 165–66). This and other early uses tend to have the sense of the free time that enables something to be done.
84 *The Life of St Catherine*, p. 37. For Katherine's 'studies' see above pp. 169–69.
85 *Stonor Letters and Papers*, ii, p. 99.
86 A point emphasized by Pearsall and Salter; see *Landscapes and Seasons*, especially Chapter 4, 'The Enclosed Garden'.

Notes to Chapter 12: Loss of Community

1 Passus x, lines 80–102.
2 Grenville, *Medieval Housing*, p. 107.

3 French text with modern English version in D. Oschinsky, *Walter of Henley and Other Treatises on Estate Management and Accounting* (Oxford, 1971), pp. 388–407; there is a fifteenth-century English version in *Early English Meals and Manners*, ed. F.J. Furnivall (EETS, 32, 1868), pp. 215–18.
4 E.W. Labarge, *Mistress, Maids and Men: Baronial Life in the Thirteenth Century* (London, 2003) (first published in 1965 as *A Baronial Household of the Thirteenth Century*), pp. 120–21.
5 *Handlyng Synne*, ed. Furnivall, pp. 232–33. Brunne uses the word 'privite' quite frequently, almost invariably with the sense of 'in secret', but here it comes close to 'in private'.
6 For Bodiam, see above, p. 99.
7 Passus xii, lines 198–200; xiii, lines 36, 61.
8 Grenville, *Medieval Housing*, p. 109. Note her remark, 'Clearly there is a great deal of work left to do before we can be confident about the reflection of social mores in the use of even the main room of the manor, let alone the subsidiary spaces.' Mercer, *English Architecture to 1900*, p. 136, suggests that 'the changing relationship between those who worked on the land and those who exercised property rights over it' was important in the decline of the hall.
9 Miller, *Bishop's Palace*, pp. 170–81.
10 *John Russell's Book of Nurture*, in *Early English Meals and Manners*, ed. Furnivall, pp. 73–74. Russell's prescriptions are echoed in a more summary form in the *Boke of Kervynge* published by Wynkyn de Worde in 1513 (ibid., pp. 170–71).
11 L.A. Muratori, *Rerum Italicarum Scriptores*, 16, cols. 579–84.
12 *AS*, Junii 1, p. 151.
13 *Life of St Catherine*, trans. Lamb, pp. 105, 107. See K. Scott, '"This is why I have put you among your neighbours": St Bernard's and St Catherine's understanding of the love of God and neighbor', *Atti del Simposio Internazionale Cateriniano-Bernardiniano*, ed. D. Maffeo and P. Nardi (Siena, 1982), pp. 279–94.
14 *Life of Catherine*, p. 164.
15 *The Dialogue*, trans. S. Noffke (New York, 1980), pp. 344–45.
16 Ibid., p. 350.
17 *Early Dominicans: Selected Writings*, trans. S. Tugwell, (London, 1982), p. 123; *Litterae Encyclicae annis 1233 et 1234 datae*, ed. E. Montanari (Spoleto, 1993).
18 *Acta Capitulorum Generalium Ordinis Predicatorum, ii (1304–1378)*, ed. Reichert, p. 79.
19 *Acta*, ii, pp. 165, 209, 229, 260, 269.
20 Ibid., pp. 353, 415.
21 Ibid., pp. 386, 432–33, 443–45.
22 R. Creytens, 'Ordonnances du Maître General Jean de Puinoix OP pour le convent de Vivero en Galice (1413)', *Archivum Fratrum Predicatorum*, 29 (1959), pp. 148–52.
23 *Acta*, iii, pp. 203, 262.
24 For an example, see the 1435 will of Robert Russell, citizen and merchant of York: *Testamenta*, ii, p. 56.
25 Nikolaus Pevsner on Mount Grace: *Yorkshire: The North Riding* (Harmondsworth, 1966), p. 259.
26 'The gradual departure from community life began soon after the Conquest': M.D. Knowles, *The Religious Orders in England*, ii (Cambridge, 1955), p. 244.
27 Ibid., p. 360.

28 *Cistercians and Cluniacs: The Case for Cîteaux*, trans. J.F. O'Sullivan (Kalamazoo, Michigan, 1977), pp. 73–75.
29 Pantin, *Documents*, p. 65.
30 *Speculum Ecclesiae*, iii, 13, in *Opera*, iv, p. 211.
31 This ruling is included in a recension of the statutes of the diocese of Ely compiled before 1268, but is derived from a decretal of Innocent III, *Cum ad monasterium*: Powicke and Cheney, *Councils and Synods*, ii, 2, p. 523.
32 Pantin, *Documents*, ii, p. 49.
33 *Chapters*, ed. Salter, p. 5.
34 Wilkins, *Concilia*, ii, p. 609. There is a newer edition of the Constitutions for the Augustinians in *Chapters*, ed. Salter, pp. 214–67.
35 Pantin, *Documents*, ii, p. 120. There is another version of the objections, p. 123.
36 Barbarba Harvey, *Living and Dying in England 1100–1450: The Monastic Experience* (Oxford, 1993), p. 77.
37 Wilkins, *Concilia*, ii, p. 648.
38 Pantin, *Documents*, ii, pp. 47–8, 85.
39 *The Register of John de Grandisson bishop of Exeter (AD 1327–1369)*, ed. F.C. Hingeston-Randolph (3 vols, London, 1894), ii, pp. 1007–8. The 1330 broadside is in i, pp. 564–65. For the appointment of a commission to inquire into the state of the house, on 10 February 1337, see ii, p. 837, and for ordinances for its reform in 1342, pp. 955–56.
40 *Register*, 2, p. 925.
41 Ibid., p. 1013.
42 *The Register of Thomas de Brantyngham (A.D. 1370–94)* (2 vols, London, 1901–1906), i, p. 312.
43 *Visitations*, iii, p. 245.
44 *Visitations*, i, p. 50.
45 *Visitations*, iii, p. 249.
46 *Visitations* i, pp. 97–98.
47 Ibid., pp. 2, 30, 46, 56.
48 Ibid., p. 110.
49 *Visitations*, iii, pp. 321–22. St Neot's had other problems. The prior slept in his own chamber and did not come to matins; more unusually, the sub-prior was not altogether of sound mind, but was maintained in office, 'lest worse should befall him'.
50 Ibid., p. 237.
51 Ibid., pp. 303–12.
52 Ibid., pp. 348–55.
53 *Visitations*, ii, p. 89.
54 *Visitations*, iii, p. 357.
55 Ibid., p. 249.
56 Ibid., p. 175.
57 *Visitations*, ii, pp. 69–78.
58 Ibid., pp. 80–82.
59 *Visitations*, i, pp. 40–42.
60 This was not the end of the matter, for William became abbot again in 1367, only for the deposed John Rysley to lay information against him in the papal court and seek his own restoration. The two were in negotiation when William died in 1372: *Chronicon Abbatie de Melsa*, ed. E. A. Bond (3 vols, RS 42), iii, pp. 86–87, 115, 165–67.

61 *Visitations*, i, pp. 96–97.
62 Ibid., p. 75.
63 Ibid., p. 89.
64 Ibid., p. 102.
65 *Visitations*, ii, p. 186.
66 Ibid., p. 14.
67 Ibid., pp. 61–63.
68 *Visitations*, i, pp. 25, 26, 28.
69 Ibid., p. 67, iii, p. 114.
70 *Visitations*, iii, p. 87.
71 Ibid., p. 50.
72 Above, p. 173.
73 Reproduced (in black and white) in Nuechterlein, 'Domesticity of Sacred Space', in *Defining the Holy*, ed. Spicer and Hamilton, p. 51.

Notes to Chapter 13: Conclusion: Individual and Society

1 See the translations by M. Alexander in *The Earliest English Poems* (Harmondsworth, 1966), pp. 30–31, 70–73.
2 *Paradiso* xvii, 58–60: 'Tu proverai sí come sa di sale / lo pane altrui, e come è duro calle / lo scendere e 'l salir per l'altrui scale'.
3 *Inferno*, xxix, 1–36; see the commentary by Charles Singleton, *The Divine Comedy: Inferno* (Princeton, 1970), pp. 528–9 (n. 27). The murderer was one of the Sacchetti family, and the feud between the Alighieri and the Sacchetti was not resolved until 1342, when Dante's own half-brother Francesco appeared as guarantor of an act of reconciliation on behalf of himself and other family members who included Dante's sons Pietro and Jacopo.
4 For a brief treatment of Dante's pilgrim images, see D. Webb, 'Saints and Pilgrims in Dante's Italy', in *Dante and the Middle Ages*, ed. J. Barnes and C. Ó Cuilleanáin (Dublin, 1995), pp. 35–36.
5 *Ballades, Rondeaux and Virelais*, ed. K. Varty (Leicester, 1965), p. 7.
6 *Calendars of Inquisitions Post Mortem*, v, n. 67, p. 36.
7 *Handlyng Synne*, pp. 136–37.
8 *I libri della famiglia*, pp. 57–8. The translation is by Guido Guarino, *The Albertis of Florence: Leon Battista Alberti's Della Famiglia*, (Lewisburg, 1971), pp. 67–8. Plato's rebuke to Dion comes from Plutarch's *Life* of Dion, viii, 3, 52, iii–iv; the citation of Cato is mistaken, and is probably due to Alberti's recollection that in *De officiis*, i, 1–3, Cato is quoted in praise of the contemplative life attainable by a mature man.

Abbreviations

AS	*Acta Sanctorum*
CYS	Canterbury and York Society
EETS	Early English Text Society
MGH	*Monumenta Germaniae Historiae*
PL	*Patrologia Latina*, ed. J.P. Migne
RS	Rolls Series
SS	Surtees Society
Visitations	*Visitations of Religious Houses in the Diocese of Lincoln*, ed. A. Hamilton Thompson (3 vols, CYS 17, 24, 33, 1915–27)

Index